Through the Kaleidoscope

Critical Studies in Latin American and Iberian Cultures

Series Editors: James Dunkerley and John King

This major series – the first of its kind to appear in English – is designed to map the field of contemporary Latin American and Iberian cultures, which have enjoyed increasing popularity in Britain and the United States in recent years.

The series aims to broaden the scope of criticism of Latin American and Iberian cultures, which tend still to extol the virtues of a few established 'master' works, and to examine cultural production within the context of twentieth-century history. These clear, accessible studies are aimed at those who wish to know more about some of the most important and influential cultural works and movements of our time.

Other titles in the series

DRAWING THE LINE: ART AND CULTURAL IDENTITY IN CONTEMPORARY LATIN AMERICA by Oriana Baddeley and Valerie Fraser

PLOTTING WOMEN: GENDER AND REPRESENTATION IN MEXICO by Jean Franco

THE GATHERING OF VOICES: THE TWENTIETH-CENTURY POETRY OF LATIN AMERICA by Mike Gonzalez and David Treece

THE MOTORCYCLE DIARIES: A JOURNEY AROUND SOUTH AMERICA by Ernesto Che Guevara

MAGICAL REELS: A HISTORY OF CINEMA IN LATIN AMERICA by John King

JOURNEYS THROUGH THE LABYRINTH: LATIN AMERICAN FICTION IN THE TWENTIETH CENTURY by Gerald Martin

PASSION OF THE PEOPLE? FOOTBALL IN SOUTH AMERICA by Tony Mason

IN THE SHADOW OF THE STATE: INTELLECTUALS AND THE QUEST FOR NATIONAL IDENTITY IN TWENTIETH-CENTURY SPANISH AMERICA by Nicola Miller

MEMORY AND MODERNITY: POPULAR CULTURE IN LATIN AMERICA by William Rowe and Vivian Schelling

JORGE LUIS BORGES: A WRITER ON THE EDGE by Beatriz Sarlo

MISPLACED IDEAS: ESSAYS ON BRAZILIAN CULTURE by Roberto Schwarz

DESIRE UNLIMITED: THE CINEMA OF PEDRO ALMODÓVAR by Paul Julian Smith

VISION MACHINES: CINEMA, LITERATURE AND SEXUALITY IN SPAIN AND CUBA, 1983–1993 by Paul Julian Smith

Through the Kaleidoscope

The Experience of Modernity
in Latin America

◆

Edited and introduced by
VIVIAN SCHELLING

Translations by
LORRAINE LEU

VERSO
London • New York

First published by Verso 2000
© in the collection Verso 2000
© in individual contributions the contributors 2000
All rights reserved

The moral rights of the authors and the editors have been asserted

Verso
UK: 6 Meard Street, London W1V 3HR
US: 180 Varick Street, New York, NY 10014–4606

Verso is the imprint of New Left Books

ISBN 1–85984–749–8
ISBN 1–85984–262–3 (pbk)

British Library Cataloguing in Publication Data
A catalogue record for this book is available from the British Library

Library of Congress Cataloging-in-Publication Data
A catalog record for this book is available from the Library of Congress

Typeset by SetSystems Ltd, Saffron Walden, Essex
Printed by Biddles Ltd, Guildford and King's Lynn

Contents

Acknowledgements

An edited collection of essays has many phases, beginning with the request for contributions from authors, to editing their chapters and revising the translations of their work, to the final stage of bringing them all together into a coherent and aesthetically pleasing whole. Throughout much of this process my editor at Verso, Jane Hindle, was of invaluable help. I thank her for her intellectual and moral support, for her good ideas and advice, and for her patience and humanity. I am also indebted to James Dunkerley, who, as editor of the Latin American series at Verso, originally supported the publication of this volume. I am most grateful to him for his thorough reading and detailed comments on the first draft of the introductory chapter. I am also particularly grateful to my friend and colleague Mathias-Roehrig Assunção for his support, the always stimulating conversations on Latin America and his thoughtful and useful observations on different aspects of this project. Luiz Rebaza Soraluz gave me many further insights into the dynamics of modernity in Latin America and I thank him also for his constructive comments on the introductory chapter. I am grateful to Lorraine Leu, who translated the Spanish and Portuguese contributions, and to Charles Peyton, the copy editor, for their always valuable comments and feedback. I thank Evi Fishburn, John King, Ettore Cingano, David Treece, Polly Josefowitz, Maureen Larkin and Pippa Hockton for the support and advice which they gave me at different important moments of the realisation of this project. Finally, I thank my husband and dear companion Anthony Summers for being a constant interlocutor and support, ranging from valuable dialogues about the book, to childcare and assistance with recalcitrant printers.

Vivian Schelling

Introduction: Reflections on the Experience of Modernity in Latin America

Vivian Schelling

Few topics have received as much scholarly attention in the recent past as modernity: it has been extensively analysed by exponents of different theoretical currents and connected to a broad and bewildering diversity of issues and social phenomena.[1] It is surprising that in the abundant literature on the subject in Europe and the USA, particularly in the English-speaking world, there are relatively few studies that have examined the quality and texture of an 'other' experience of modernity, in the 'peripheral' regions of the world. Studies on social change in Latin America have tended to privilege politics and economics at the expense of the more multi-dimensional approach linking a variety of long-term economic, political and cultural processes which the concept of modernity offers. Moreover, discussions of modernity and post-modernity in Latin America itself seem to have been of a predominantly theoretical nature with little apparent emphasis on empirical interdisciplinary research.[2]

The purpose of this collection of essays, written especially for this volume, is to provide an analysis of specific, concrete expressions of precisely this 'other' experience of modernity, exploring its 'phenomenology' by focusing on it through an interdisciplinary, multi-perspectival lens. The aim is to present the reader with an analysis of the ways in which modernist aesthetics, the new temporality and modes of perception created by urban life, the development of radio, television and cinema, and religious and social movements, are not only connected to processes of economic, social and political modernisation, but are also significantly shaped by Latin America's colonial legacy, as well as by contemporary globalising forces. The picture that emerges then is of a modernity characterised by heterogeneity and tension between a vast array of disparate forces.

An additional motive underlying this endeavour relates to the perennial debates since the nineteenth century on the identity of Latin America and its aspiration to autonomy, independence and realisation of potential which underpin them. Thus the hope which informs it is that a greater understanding of the heterogeneous, multiple elements which have shaped the experience of modernity in Latin America will bring to the fore the ways in which it is an experience *sui generis*, with its own dynamic and possibilities, rather than a second-rate version of North Atlantic modernities which it has 'failed' to follow. Furthermore, for those seeking a critical platform from which to re-evaluate the claims, distortions, failures and utopian aspirations of the project of modernity in general, insight into the experience of an 'other', 'peripheral' modernity will be of considerable value.

In order to contextualise the dilemmas and vicissitudes of modernity in Latin America addressed in the book, this introduction will briefly examine some of the main current definitions of modernity, and subsequently present in broad brush strokes key historical moments of its emergence, first in Europe and subsequently in Latin America.

In the process of discussing these historical moments and the predicaments and debates that have arisen from them, I will also be making use of the three senses, outlined by Peter Osborne, in which the term modernity can be used, namely as a *historical category of periodisation*, an *incomplete project* or set of aspirations and as a *mode of experience*.[3]

These three senses map on to the historical moments which I highlight, providing a useful framework for understanding and distinguishing between different expressions of modernity. My aim in taking this approach is not to present a historical narrative with a claim to comprehensiveness or a high level of historical detail, but to provide a condensed synoptic backdrop which will illuminate the diverse themes and approaches to modernity in Latin America contained in this book.

If we distil from the copious literature on modernity some of the fundamental uses and meanings of the term, we see specific features emerging as central in the characterisation of 'modern' societies.[4]

At the level of the economy, modern societies are seen as governed by instrumental rationality, defined by criteria of efficiency and productivity. Once this rationality prevails, the limits placed on economic activity by religious-ethical values in pre-modern, 'traditional' societies are burst asunder and technological innovation, rapid social change and an orientation towards the future become institutionalised. Capital accumulation, industrialisation, the growth of cities, massive migrations and the emergence of new social classes accompany these processes of modernisation.

At the level of the polity, modernity is characterised by the fact that sovereignty and legitimacy reside in the secular nation-state, which increasingly replaces religion, the village or the region as a source of collective identification. The nation becomes the symbolic or 'imagined' community to which allegiances are transferred.[5]

At the level of culture, modernity is associated with the rise of a profane, rationalist culture in which explanations of the universe and human society in terms of a stable cosmic order give way to a scientific world-view which claims privileged access to truth. At the same time, literacy, telecommunications and the mass media bring the newly formed classes, ethnicities and nation-states into contact with each other often for the first time.

A further characteristic that distinguishes modern from pre-modern societies is the differentiation of the parts from the whole, so that the economy, polity and culture are separated into distinctive spheres, which apparently function autonomously.

None of these characteristics of modernity, however, conveys the cataclysmic effect such processes have had on social relations and human perceptions of the self and the universe, and which have given rise to a very distinctive experience of modernity. According to Marshall Berman, at the centre of this experience lies both paradox and tragedy. While the speed of change and innovation and the expansion of modernity across the globe open up apparently infinite possibilities of advancement, transformation and communication; they are also destructive of the bonds and continuities through which life previously acquired stability and coherence, thus simultaneously plunging human beings into intense experiences of fragmentation and uprootedness. In Berman's words: 'modernity pours us all into a maelstrom of perpetual disintegration and renewal, of struggle and contradiction, of ambiguity and anguish, a universe in which "all that is solid melts into air" '.[6]

As has been pointed out, it is not possible to periodise precisely, according to an assumed evolutionary logic, the actual emergence of modernity. The various aspects associated with it developed within different time-scales, unevenly and in different combinations, depending on the specific historical context.[7] Put another way, the unfolding of modernity cannot be conceived in terms of a 'linear process of prolongation and expansion', but needs to take account of the differential temporalities at work in the formation of modern society.[8]

Nevertheless, for heuristic reasons, three key moments in its evolution can be distinguished.

Historians generally connect the rise of modernity with the Renaissance and Reformation of the fifteenth and sixteenth centuries and with the discovery of the 'New World' of the Americas. However it is the period of the Enlightenment in the eighteenth century which is seen as crystallising different dimensions of modernity into a definite shape, what Habermas has referred to as the 'project of modernity'.[9] This process was founded on the Enlightenment belief that knowledge obtained through the exercise of critical reason and the scientific method would lead to greater control of nature as well as forms of social organisation grounded in the rational understanding of human nature and society. This would lead ultimately to human emancipation, not only from the power of external nature, but also from the dark side of internal nature which, in the view of Enlightenment thinkers, was manifested in superstition, religion and the arbitrary exercise of power. Two important concepts of reason are contained within the Enlightenment project: reason as instrumental rationality, and reason as critique, the exercise of which leads to insight and emancipation.

In an essay on 'Modernity's Consciousness of Time and its Need for Self Reassurance', Habermas further observes that the notion of 'modern times' emerged around the 1800s as an epochal term used to divide history into the present, the Middle Ages and Antiquity.[10] This was accompanied by a novel conception of history as a unified process, and of the present not as a mere sequential moment in time but as a radical break with the past (and a perpetual transcendence of itself towards the future). In an unprecedented way, the 'modern' thus became associated with specific metaphors of movement: revolution, progress, emancipation, development, crisis. Two further consequences follow from this new socio-cultural constellation which have significant implications for understanding the experience of modernity in Latin America. First is an 'exclusive valorisation of the historical present over the past'[11] and a concomitant derogatory attitude towards societies defined as pre-modern.[12] Second, in contrast to terms like the Middle Ages or Renaissance, modernity is not a value-neutral periodising category. Because it signifies a rejection of the past and a valorisation of change, modernity implicitly poses the challenge of being either for or against it.[13]

The second key moment in the development of European modernity occurred in the nineteenth and early twentieth centuries, when the processes of industrialisation and imperial expansion led to further and deeper interconnections in the world economy. It was during this period that modernity as a mode of experience, full of contradiction and complexity, became both more generalised and articulated.[14] The rise of the machine, urban growth, the development of communications and the expansion of advertising brought about major transformations in everyday life. Displacement, migration, the instability of identity and the loss of old certainties became common experiences. Simultaneously, optimistic faith in the new, in the spectacular achievements of technology and its potential to harness the world's resources to bring about material improvements, constituted the other pole of modernity as a mode of experience. In some ways, the new modes of mass communication, particularly film, articulated and embodied this dual experience of on the one hand, an exciting world of flux and change, light, speed and desire, and, on the other, anxiety and a sense of loss.

This early twentieth-century experience of modernity was however qualitatively different from the eighteenth-century Enlightenment model, partly because the processes of social and economic modernisation were further advanced, but partly also because by the early twentieth century, despite the belief in the power of technology to solve the human ills generated by material scarcity, faith in the ideal of progress and rationality had been seriously undermined. The work of Marx and subsequent socialist movements problematised the idea of progress by pointing to the inequalities, poverty and suffering which accompanied the process of capitalist accumulation and economic growth. Max Weber referred to modern society as an 'iron cage' and mourned the 'disenchantment of nature' brought about by the process of rationalisation. Freud spoke of the guilt, repression and discontent generated by civilisation and the threat of rebellion against its constrictions, which the destructiveness of the European war of 1914–18 seemed to vindicate.

In this climate of spiritual and social crisis, artistic activity, along with the new means of communication, became a privileged medium through which the new experience of modernity was explored. Modernism in art, architecture, literature and music and the proliferation of divergent movements – cubism, surrealism, futurism, dadaism, expressionism, the Bauhaus – experimenting with and advocating new aesthetic codes, constituted an attempt to reconstruct society both aesthetically and politically. This was manifested particularly in the rich interplay during the 1920s between aesthetics, popular culture and political commitment in many of the avant-garde movements of the early twentieth century.

With the expansion of corporate power and the idea of the welfare

state in post-1945 Europe, a limited, positivistic and technocratic interpretation of the Enlightenment ideals of progress through the applica-
tion of reason began to emerge. Modernism began to lose the
subversive and critical qualities which characterised the avant-garde of
the 1920s and '30s and became instead part of a depoliticised, official
canon. This constitutes the third key moment in the development of
modernity.[15]

In the form of academic 'modernisation theory', a narrow, evolutionary understanding of the 'transition to modernity' in Europe was
exported as a model to be followed by the 'developing world' in order
to overcome poverty and reach comparable standards of living.
Grounded in the economic theories of Rostow and the sociological
work of Eisenstadt and Lerner, 'modernisation theory' advocated the
transfer of Western technology and the dissemination of an 'entrepreneurial' spirit and a scientific-instrumental rationality in order to
unleash the forces promoting 'development'.[16] Implicit in this theory is
a conception of the project of modernity as one single state the
transition to which is governed by a universal pattern. The ensuing
policies designated as 'developmentalism', which were adopted by many
intellectual and political elites in the 'Third World', legitimated the
elimination of economic practices and cultural traditions, which were
regarded as obstacles in the modernisation process.

Thus confined within narrowly defined boundaries, Modernity, Reason and Progress would come under attack from several corners,
becoming in the process highly contested concepts and ideals. Existen-
tialism posited that anguish and a sense of the absurd were an integral
part of the human condition in a world devoid of any determinate
meaning, purpose or underlying rationality. In the *Myth of Sisyphus*
Camus would state 'The absurd arises from this confrontation between
the human search for meaning' and the 'irrational silence of the
world.'[17]

In the wake of decolonisation in the 1950s and '60s, the Pan-African
Movement affirmed the need to recover an African cultural legacy
which in its emphasis on spirituality and the sense of community was
the antithesis of the technified consciousness created by European
rationalism. The student movements and counter-cultures of the late
1960s, their experimentation with drug-induced altered states of mind
and alternative, 'utopian' ways of life – as part of a broader critique of
the Cold War and late capitalist, consumer society – vindicated other
rationalities in ways that harked back to Romanticism and Surrealism.
Feminism in turn echoed the critical stance of these movements. By
exploring the ways in which modern science and the Western philo-

sophical tradition associated reason with maleness and irrationality and nature with femaleness, feminist scholarship pointed to the connections between the cultural exclusion of women and the domination of nature.[18]

Post-structuralism further attacked the Enlightenment assumption that science, social theory and philosophy, so called meta-narratives, are capable of providing overarching accounts of reality, (which by virtue of their universality can bring general benefit to humankind). Instead, the writings of contemporary post-structuralist thinkers, in particular Edward Said, Michel Foucault and Jacques Derrida, explored the ways in which the production of knowledge was connected with the history of European colonialism and racism, with patriarchy and a masculine rationality or 'logos'. Consequently, post-structuralism indirectly created a space for other voices and hidden histories – those of non-white ethnicities, women and formerly colonised peoples for example – to be heard as legitimate, with a right to their different and alternative concepts of knowledge and rationality. On the other hand, philosophers like Habermas, in his work on the liberating possibilities of human dialogue without domination, continued to defend the Enlightenment faith in the use of critical reason as a means of universal emancipation from fear and oppression.[19]

Notwithstanding these profound and heated debates on modernity and reason within the spheres of culture and intellectual debate, it is economic neo-liberalism which since the 1980s has become the dominant paradigm informing the actions of governments in a majority of countries in both the North and the South. Here, in the practical arena of economic policy-making, and despite the controversy surrounding these issues, it is unfettered market forces which are hailed as the harbinger of progress.

Modernity in Latin America

Latin America is part of the global history underpinning these developments but it is a part which deserves its own analysis. In order to understand the formation of a specifically Latin American modernity, we must bear in mind the extent to which Latin American societies have been marked by their colonial legacy and by uneven processes of development – the combination and simultaneity of modern and pre-modern modes of production and ways of life. As Steven Stern has pointed out in his stimulating essay on the colonial legacy in Latin America, despite the transformations that have occurred since independence, colonial-like social and economic relations persist in contemporary contexts, although in reinvented form: 'Time and time again in Latin America phenomena apparently centuries old and "dead" somehow resurface and reassert themselves. Despite vast changes, the present seems not so much to replace the past as to superimpose itself on it, only partly altering it. Time as linear sequence and the related notion of time as progress seem questionable.'[20]

Of course, drawing this contrast between modernity in a 'peripheral' region and what might be termed the 'metropolitan' modernity of Europe does not mean that the development of European modernity was a more or less seamless and even .process. As Tom Nairn has pointed out, the expansion of capitalism within Europe was itself an uneven process manifested to some extent in the compensatory character of nationalist ideologies, in particular in Germany and Italy in the mid nineteenth century, where the experience was one of falling behind in the 'development race' relative to France and Britain.[21] In nations on the margins of Western Europe, such as Russia, where modernisation was experienced as arriving predominantly from without, this unevenness is expressed in the highly ambivalent attitude towards modernity, as evidenced in the ideological conflicts between Westernisers and Slavophiles, in a way that is not dissimilar to the oscillation between 'cosmopolitanism' and 'localism' or 'nativism' in Latin America.

Nevertheless, it is still possible, in my view, to argue that the nature of Latin America's insertion in the world order, first as a European colony and subsequently in the post-independence period – and in ways which linked the continent to the forces of modernity in a highly segmented way – created a particularly heterogeneous society and culture.[22] Thus, as the articles in this collection demonstrate, when we speak of Latin America's cultural heterogeneity, we are referring not only to the coexistence of indigenous, Western and African traditions, but also, as Brunner points out, to a 'segmented participation' in a 'global market of messages and symbols, a differential participation according to local codes of reception' resulting in 'something similar to what is proclaimed by certain representatives of post-modernism: a de-centering, a deconstruction of Western culture as it is represented in the manuals; of its rationalism, its secularism, its key institutions; of the cognitive habits and styles it supposedly imposes in a uniform way.'[23]

This predicament has been the core subject of much Latin American literature and of a wide range of sociological and literary studies on the subcontinent. It is perhaps best encapsulated in Octavio Paz's image of

Mexican culture as labyrinthine and Gabriel García Márquez's observations about the solitude of Latin America.[24] Emerging out of the
violence of conquest as a half-breed, mestizo culture, full of ambiguity,
split between a dominant Europe and a subordinate African and
indigenous world, Latin America belongs not quite anywhere, its search
for identity necessarily following a labyrinthine path. The consequences
of this predicament for the development of both the idea and social
reality of modernity have been extraordinarily complex.

Octavio Ianni refers to 'modern Brazil' as a 'kaleidoscope of many
epochs, ways of life, of being, working and thinking, marked above all
by the legacy of slavery.'[25] Néstor García Canclini in *Culturas hibridas*,
addresses the view that while Latin America is 'exuberant' in its cultural
modernity it is deficient in its socio-economic and political modernity.
It has its own unique history of modernist movements, modern social
theorists and culture industry, yet citizenship and democratic polities
have remained underdeveloped. However, instead of regarding this as
a sign that Latin American modernity is a second-rate version of
metropolitan modernity, he argues in favour of seeing Latin America
as a 'complex articulation of modernities and traditions', of 'multiple
logics of development'.[26]

What conclusions are to be drawn from this predicament? Perhaps,
as several chapters in this collection suggest, the sense of paradox and
tragedy referred to by Berman is even more intense in the case of Latin
America, where the experience of modernity is frequently accompanied
by a sense of doubt as to whether it is possible, viable or desirable.[27] To
unravel this paradoxical experience more effectively, we can make use
again of the 'key moments' of modernity outlined earlier – this time
with the focus clearly on Latin America.

In the first three hundred years of colonialism, the 'New World'
constructed as the 'other' fulfilled an important role in the development of the European idea of modernity. Native American society was
at times idealised as the embodiment of the 'noble savage' and the site
of a new social utopia, an alternative to the artifice and class divisions
of European civilisation; at other times, when European power was
threatened by indigenous difference and resistance, it was deprecated
as 'barbarian' and even 'cannibalist'.[28] Both notions were central to the
emergence of the Enlightenment conception that social development
followed a given evolutionary path, in this case from a 'savage' American stage to a 'civilised' European stage. This idea would later inform
the rise of social science and lay the foundations for the view, espoused
by modernisation theory as well as by positivist versions of Marxism,
that there was a single path of development towards modernity. More-

over, while in Europe new forms of freedom and social mobility were
emerging, in Latin America slavery and other forms of forced labour
constituted the dark side of European modernity.[29] As Robin Blackburn
in his work on the connections between slavery and modernity has
observed, the sugar, cotton and tobacco plantations in the New World,
with their division of labour and impersonal, functional logic, resembled the factory system which would emerge in Europe with the
Industrial Revolution.[30]

In the eighteenth and nineteenth centuries, during the first moment
in the evolution of modernity, Latin America's struggle for independence was informed by various traditions. The creole elites drew on
republican and liberal ideals of equality, freedom and justice. In order
to vindicate an independent national identity, creole nationalists also
appropriated the symbols and imagery of indigenous culture, as evidenced, for example, in the exaltation of the Toltec past or of the
Virgin of Guadalupe in Mexico. Following independence, however, due
to the fact that the creole elites looked towards France, Britain and the
USA as models of the nation and progress, the legacy of Hispanic and
Native American culture was largely rejected; it came to be seen as
'backward' and an obstacle to 'progress'. Negating both the colonial
and pre-colonial worlds, they forfeited the possibility of making use of
local indigenous traditions of reciprocity and solidarity in order to
construct models of democracy rooted in Latin America's own historical
experience.[31]

The republican constitutions which governed the new social order
were limited by the legal restrictions placed on the political participation of the population, linking the right to vote to ownership of
property and literacy, thus disenfranchising the majority of blacks,
Indians and mestizos. Moreover, the discrepancy between the republican constitutions and the social reality of Latin America was augmented
by an authoritarian political culture based on patronage and personal-
ism, and on the cultural cleavages between Indians, mestizos and whites.
In the last quarter of the nineteenth century, European capital flowed
into Argentina, Brazil and Mexico, modernising the export trade,
creating docks and railways and expanding the production of primary
products for export. What occurred, then, was the partial modernisation of infrastructure without the social modernisation implicit in, for
instance, the formation of a nation-state of citizens.

This uneasy fit between republicanism and modernity as a project or
set of aspirations and the social reality of Latin America is encapsulated
in two key nineteenth century works in which the sense of anguish
about the viability of modernity is conceived in terms of a struggle

between 'civilisation' and 'barbarism'. In Domingo Faustino Sarmiento's fictional account of the life of the gaucho *caudillo* Facundo Quiroga, 'barbarism' is embodied in what he sees as the individualism and brutality of the gaucho way of life, which he argues is an impediment to the development of republican and democratic values. In Euclides da Cunha's epic *Os Sertões* (The Backlands) the theme of conflict between civilisation and barbarism is represented in the epic depiction of the peasant rebellion of Canudos in the north-east of Brazil. Da Cunha recounts the way in which the republican army, determined to carry out the positivist motto of 'Order and Progress' emblazoned on the new flag of republican Brazil, using modern instruments of war, and dressed in European attire, fights a war of attrition against a population of impoverished peasants whose guerrilla tactics, messianic faith and knowledge of their environment enable them to defeat the republican army several times before eventually being destroyed themselves. Da Cunha's account is informed by nineteenth-century evolutionary theory and its assumption that peoples of mixed race, less amenable to the civilising process, tended to be left behind in the progress of 'civilisation'. Yet through his detailed, passionate and empathetic depiction of the resistance of the people of Canudos and his equally merciless condemnation of the cruelty and genocidal actions of the republican army, da Cunha's work subverts any simplistic division between barbarism and civilisation, bearing testimony to the manifold ways in which modernity will eliminate those who stand in the way of 'progress'.[32] Similarly, in Sarmiento's account of the life of Facundo Quiroga there is a latent fascination with the freedom of life in the pampas and the indomitable character of Facundo. In both works, then, the concern with fostering the advance of 'civilisation' in Latin America is shot through with ambiguity.

Beyond the sphere of literature, the juxtaposition of barbarism and civilisation reappears in different guises in the discourses through which the governing classes in Latin America contemplate their societies (albeit with less awareness of its problematic nature and ambiguous meanings). Based on social Darwinist and evolutionary notions dominant in nineteenth-century Europe – that the relative economic and technological backwardness of non-European societies was due to their non-white racial make-up – Latin American political and intellectual elites at the turn of the nineteenth century conceived of progress and civilisation as inextricably linked with the whitening – the cultural and biological de-indigenisation and de-Africanisation – of their societies.[33] And given that, since the colonial period, the indigenous and African had already been associated with the trait of irrationality attributed to women and children, the whitening process, and hence the discourse of modernity, also acquired specific gender connotations.

In the twentieth century, the process of capitalist expansion and industrialisation through import substitution, particularly in the larger economies of Mexico, Brazil and Argentina, brought about remarkable development of the forces of production, the explosive growth of cities and the emergence of labour movements. In claiming to represent the broader aspirations of 'the people' to citizenship and economic and social well being, rather than merely the demands of the labour unions, the labour movements press for emancipation and modernisation 'from below'.[34] At the same time, the growth of the mass media in the form of radio broadcasting, a music industry, the development of cinema and of television from the 1950s onwards, transformed the idea of modernity into a lived experience transmitted through new narratives, sounds and images.[35] Despite these transformations, however, the new social order which aspires to modernity does not sweep aside the 'semi-feudal' social relations of the colonial era. As several studies on the capitalist development of Latin America have pointed out, the middle strata, too weak to develop a revolutionary hegemonic political project, relied on compromise and seemingly incongruous class alliances to implement policies of social and economic modernisation. A clear example of this can be seen in the populist governments of Peron and Vargas of the 1930s and '40s, which were based on the power of the military, the support of the labour movement, and alliances with the landed classes as providers of primary exports and much needed foreign currency.[36]

The second key moment in the development of modernity in Latin America was marked by the blossoming of the artistic avant-garde in the early twentieth century. Here again, European influences combined with local elements in such a way as to produce new and specific configurations. While in Europe artistic modernism was linked to a profound crisis at the core of European civilisation, in Latin America the *selective* use of modernist aesthetics leads to the exploration and positive re-evaluation of its black and native American legacy. The Russian Revolution of 1917, and the availability of a new analysis of Latin America's predicament in terms of the expansion of European capitalism, challenged the former Darwinian and racist interpretations of its 'backwardness'. Furthermore, with the Mexican Revolution of 1910 the peasantry increased its profile as an agent in history. This was complemented by a new perception of the USA, already foreshadowed in the work of Rodó and Martí, as the 'colossus of the North' threatening Latin America with imperial domination rather than a possible version of its own future. Thus, for perhaps the first time, Latin America's complex relationship to modernity, and its labyrinthine character, comes into focus with a growing awareness of the rift between intellectuals and 'the people', the city and the country, popular and high culture and with the urgent need to forge an identity which does justice to its many legacies and voices.[37]

In the 1950s and '60s during the third key moment in the unfolding of modernity, Developmentalism as a model of economic progress, aimed at creating an integrated industrial structure focused on steel, energy, machinery, vehicles and capital goods, was implemented in several Latin American countries. Buttressed by the 'captivating social metaphors' of 'state-supported heavy industry as the route to autonomy and wealth' and 'the mystique of planning and technification', Developmentalism promised 'the leap into the future'.[38] Moreover, with the rapid economic growth brought about by the military governments of the 1970s and '80s and the establishment of significant culture industries, particularly in Brazil and Mexico, modernity ceased in many ways to be an unrealized aspiration and became instead part of the fabric of everyday life. It is important to note, however, that the notion and practice of modernity which tended to prevail in this process of social transformation was predominantly instrumental and uncritical. In the 1990s, with the growing integration of Latin America into global markets and the adoption of neo-liberal economic thinking as the dominant paradigm, this technocratic conception of modernity has become increasingly hegemonic.[39] On the other hand, new forms of local resistance to the process of globalisation and, at an ideological level, the post-modern critique or 'de-centring' of Western modernity and its claims to universality, create a space for other modernities to emerge in which emancipation from hunger and oppression go hand in hand with an affirmation of plurality, or dialogue between the 'traditions' and 'modernities' which constitute Latin America's heterogeneity.

Having examined some of the dynamics underlying the development of Latin American modernity in general, it is important to give brief consideration to the role of popular culture, or what could be termed 'the force of popular culture' in its development.

In Latin American societies the creation of unified nation-states has been a most complex process due to their uneven development, their social and cultural heterogeneity and the consequent difficulties faced by governing elites in carrying out a hegemonic political project.

Popular memory in Latin America has never been thoroughly secularised. This means that magic, myth and a strong sense of the sacred –
originating in the traditions of popular catholicism, indigenous cosmog-
ony and African religious ritual – continue to play an important role in
popular culture. At the same time, the relative lack of differentiation
and specialisation of the spheres of 'high' and 'mass' culture has meant
that both are marked by their links with popular memory. In this
context, the popular cultures of Latin America, both rural and urban,
are not simply forms of 'folklore' consigned to the past, or degraded
versions of high culture and the culture industry, but a force strongly
shaping the specificity of the experience of modernity in Latin America.

In the case of the development of *political* modernity, the importance
of popular culture was first recognised by the populist governments
and political parties of the 1930s and '50s. They used populist rhetoric
and gave official support to elements of popular culture (football,
popular music, the indigenous legacies of Peru and Mexico) in order
to develop an identification between the nation and 'the people'.

More recently, the indigenist movements in Mexico, the Andean
regions and Guatemala offer alternative notions of the nation and of
the social based on 'cosmocentric' rather than 'anthropocentric' interpretations of reality. In Andean culture, for instance, the cultivation of
land, the *chacra*, is seen as a 'conversation' with nature, a relationship
of mutual nurturing and reciprocity, rather than as an act of domination through instrumental reason. Life is conceived as a cyclical process
of regeneration in which present natural or human forms contain and
manifest earlier forms: there is consequently no erasure of any form of
life,[40] and the past becomes part of the present by 'entering into
dialogue with the dead, who are embodied in the living through
ritual'.[41] Linear notions of time as a rupture with a 'backward' past that
is left behind are thus put into question.

The growing presence of indigenist movements in international
human rights organisations and activities have furthermore given rise
to a new indigenous intelligentsia demanding constitutional change
and the enshrining of indigenous demands for territorial autonomy,
self-determination and legal recognition of cultural diversity. In claiming not only individual but also collective rights, as well as the recognition of territorial boundaries unique to indigenous people, these
movements directly challenge the post-Independence construction of
the nation without Indians.[42] Such developments have led to new hybrid
configurations of modernity in which the defence of ethnic identity
goes hand in hand with the use, as in the case of the Zapatistas in
Mexico, of electronic media and non-indigenous forms of knowledge.[43]

Gutierrez points out how the very emergence of the modern nation-state in Mexico facilitated the rise of non-manual and urban indigenous sectors – primary school teachers, journalists and civil servants – who contest the official and non-indigenous constructions of indigenous culture which accompanied the process of nation-building following the Revolution of 1910.[44]

Similarly, in response to the military governments in the region, a broad variety of urban social movements concerned with housing, popular education, land rights and citizenship emerged in the 1960s and '70s. In the context of rural-urban migration and the growing poverty generated by the debt crisis in the 1980s and '90s, they have stimulated the growth of urban popular cultures in which pre-modern practices and traditions of mutual assistance, solidarity and reciprocity are re-functionalised in the urban context.[45]

If we turn now to the influence of popular culture on *cultural* modernity, what stands out is the importance of radio, and above all television. These technologies, it is important to recall, emerged in *conjunction* with the processes of urbanisation and industrialisation rather than, as was the case in Europe, only after the Enlightenment and industrialisation, shaping the experience of modernity in Latin America. As Renato Ortiz and Carlos Monsiváis have pointed out, the media have played a major role both in the development of an internal market and the consolidation of a national identity.[46] In post-revolutionary Mexico for example, radio and cinema represent 'the people' as a nation by making use of and amalgamating elements from the cultures of different regions. In Brazil, the *telenovela* and the radio have been instrumental in creating the imagined community of the nation. While on the one hand this is an aspect of capitalist development, it can also be seen as marked by the force of popular culture in that these media draw on the popular genres of melodrama and oral narrative, creating in the words of Martin Barbero a 'secondary orality' such that 'majorities in our countries appropriate the principles of modernity without leaving behind them their oral culture or going through the book'.[47]

At the level of literature and art, as Angel Rama has demonstrated, the study and incorporation of elements of Latin America's popular cultures have enabled Latin American artists and writers to make critical and selective use of the hegemonic traditions of European and North American high cultures, carrying out acts of 'transculturation' in order to elaborate the parameters of a specifically Latin American cultural modernity.[48]

However, the place and role of popular culture in the formation of Latin American modernity seems now to be changing in significant ways. The 'disembedding' of social relations once anchored in a specific time and place – largely the result of contemporary globalising, trading, financial and productive processes – has led to a 'scattering', a 'deterritorialisation' of cultural forms and identities and their recombination in different contexts. Moreover, through the intervention of the transnational culture industries, identities and differences are increasingly being transformed into what Stuart Hall defines as a 'discourse of global consumerism ... a global currency into which all specific traditions and distinct identities can be translated'.[49] According to Jean Franco, this deterritorialisation and resulting hybridisation of cultures has led to what she defines as a 'crisis of the popular' in Latin America, in the sense that it is no longer very clear where the popular – conceived either as a distinctive cultural practice of the popular classes, or as a form of political and cultural resistance – is located.[50] As Ortiz and Canclini note in this book, one of the consequences of this has been that modernity is no longer conceived as linked to the nation and the popular cultures which were used as a source of symbols of national identity, while politics and civic life have acquired the characteristics of a spectacle mediated by the logic of consumerism and the electronic media.

In order to draw out the links between different chapters and the significance of their contributions, I have grouped them according to specific broad themes and the logic of the argument which has arisen as a result, thus cutting across the more linear and consecutive division contained in the contents list.

Modernity and 'the popular'

One of the major themes in the essays collected here is the important and varying relationship between modernity and 'the popular' in Latin America. As outlined briefly above, 'popular' here is conceived broadly and loosely as pertaining to the popular classes, to popular political practices, to rural and urban popular cultures, popular religion, and subordinate ethnicities, as well as to aspects of the culture industry.

Nicolau Sevcenko's essay is an analysis of the conflict between the peasant settlement in Canudos in the north-east of Brazil and the republican army, between 1893 and 1897, referred to earlier. According to Sevcenko, what took place in Canudos can be seen as a confrontation between the new technical-scientific transformations which characterised the late nineteenth century, and archaic manifestations of the sacred, constituting in its violence a 'bloody duel between technology and the epiphanic'.

His thesis is that the mystical catholicism and utopian communitarian spirit of the Canudos settlement was informed by a tradition which has its roots in the doctrines of a Cistercian monk, Joaquino di Fiori, whose preachings on the imminence of the Age of the Holy Spirit, characterised by justice, peace and fraternity, spread throughout southern Europe in the thirteenth century and subsequently to Brazil, becoming in the process a pervasive 'structural component of popular culture'. This millenarian tradition and its emphasis on direct contact with the sacred came into brutal conflict with modernity on several other occasions. It was repeated during the modernisation of Rio de Janeiro when the authorities, involved in the implementation of urban reform, instigated the ruthless expulsion of the poor from the city centre as well as the persecution of the rituals and practices of the local Afro-Brazilian population, leading to a popular uprising which was branded as 'another Canudos' in 'the bosom of the capital', which it was necessary to eliminate in order to make way for progress. And progress, as we saw earlier, was associated by the positivist state not only with a technocratic concept of rationality but also with the 'whitening' of the Brazilian 'race'.

However, other and more fruitful relations between the popular and modernity have also been historically possible. Da Cunha's own seminal critique of the way in which identification with Europe had rendered essential aspects of Brazilian society invisible, and his own faith in the 'democratic redemption' of Brazilian society, could be seen as originating in the same cultural sediment. Similarly, the rediscovery and validation of Brazilian popular culture by European modernists, such as Blaise Cendrars and Darius Milhaud in the 1920s, significantly influenced the course of Brazilian modernism while simultaneously contributing to the flowering of European modernism.

There are further parallels in this process of cross-fertilisation between 'the redeeming and revolutionary impulse of modern art' and the 'latent millenarianism of Brazilian culture' according to Sevcenko. It is apparent in the emergence of São Paulo as a centre of new critical thinking in the social sciences, in cinematic, artistic and theatrical innovation, and in the creation of Brasília – the 'Capital of Hope' – as the new capital of the country. Dependency theory, Cinema Novo, the creation of the Museum of Modern Art (MASP), the architecture of Niemeyer and Costa, and the writings of João Cabral do Melo Neto embody the aspiration to modernity in the form of a 'widespread desire for rebirth, emancipation and autonomy' which characterised the 1950s and '60s, 'fertilising the ground for a general surge of creative energy' throughout Brazilian society.

In his chapter on religious plurality and modernity in contemporary Brazil, José Jorge de Carvalho also considers the ways in which the presence of the sacred, in particular the so-called 'marginal' religions of Spiritism, *candomblé* and *umbanda*, has given shape to an experience of modernity which has not entailed the progressive secularisation assumed by theories of modernity and modernisation.

Instead of privileging catholicism as the hegemonic religion with which other Christian, esoteric, Afro-Brazilian and indigenous traditions have to contend and interact, de Carvalho highlights the way Spiritism is at the centre of an increasingly active and vociferous inter-religious dialogue. Aided by the contemporary transformation of religion into a mass mediated spectacle, this inter-religious dialogue has become a veritable 'querela dos espíritos' ('dispute of the spirits') leading in turn to a dizzying proliferation of 'fusions, syncretisms and hybridisations' between the multiple elements which make up Brazilian religiosity. This progressive dispute of the spirits, 'always changing and increasingly kaleidoscopic', has moreover transcended the confines of religious debate and invaded the broader public sphere. Thus de Carvalho affirms that what we are witnessing, contrary to the assumptions of Max Weber on the disenchantment of the world or of contemporary social scientists such as Anthony Giddens and Pierre Bourdieu on the decline of religion in modernity, is instead the '*enchantment* of the public sphere' (my emphasis).

José de Souza Martins presents us with a further and original perspective on the connections between uneven forms of development and the peculiar manifestations of an incomplete and ambiguous modernity. Collective responses to the innovations and upheavals introduced by modernity are expressed, not with systematic critique, as was the case in the nineteenth-century European context, but with laughter and mockery, and in the pervasive 'irrational and traditional' use which is made of the modern in rural areas and on the outskirts of the big cities by the popular classes, whose integration into modern life at the level of production, consumption, politics and culture remains partial.

How this mask-like and ambiguous character of modernity is expressed is presented by de Souza Martins in several ethnographic vignettes of everyday life: in the use made of Ray-Ban glasses, of English words and phrases as a 'sign of the new' rather than as new functional objects or technologies, for instance. In these examples – and herein lies one of the important contributions of his work – de Souza Martins sees a peculiar form of alienation, an alienation indicative of Latin

America's incomplete, ambiguous modernity, which is fundamentally different from the concept of alienation described by Marx.

Furthermore, instead of eliminating 'traditional' or non-modern ways of life, modernity paradoxically gives them a new lease of life. Multinational companies such as VW in the Amazon region of Pará make use of slave-labour, while the MST (Movimento Sem Terra), or Landless Movement – one of the main contemporary social movements in Brazil demanding agrarian reform – uses modern forms of farming and commerce on the plots which they have been granted by the state, in order to recreate forms of mutual assistance based on reciprocity rather than introducing a modern, contractual division of labour. In the same state of Pará, the Parakateje Indians share the computers and television sets which they are able to buy with the revenue from the sale of Pará nuts, according to the ethos and rituals of tribal tradition. These are clear examples of how modernity in Latin America appropriates, and in the process de-centres and deconstructs Western culture.

Renato Ortiz and Ruben Oliven provide us with critical, although less sceptical, analyses of the ways in which the formation of the nation in Brazil has been intertwined with the themes of modernity and the crucial role which popular culture has played in its evolution.

Oliven takes us on a journey in which he surveys the ways in which attitudes towards modernity in the last hundred years have shaped the process of nation-building and the formation of Brazilian national identity. As a force coming from without, modernity's appropriation assumes different shapes in different epochs. In the nineteenth and early twentieth centuries it arrived in the guise of the Europeanisation of the city of Rio de Janeiro and the changing lifestyle of the ruling classes, creating, as Sevcenko has demonstrated, a rift between the city and the countryside, and between the educated and popular classes. In the 1950s and '60s modernisation theory and Marxism offered different paths towards modernity. However, this influx of modernising forces from the outside has been met with suspicion and equally strong affirmations of the significance and value of the national and regional, and hence also with politically and culturally diverse appropriations of outside influence, depending on the specific historical moment. This is evidenced in the Indianist or nativist literary current of the nineteenth century, in the modernist exploration and vindication of popular cultures, and in the Regionalist Movement's emphasis in the 1930s on preserving regional cultures as invaluable sources of cultural identity and meaning. It is present also in Gilberto Freyre's assertion that Brazil's racial mixture or *mestiçagem* was the sign of a unique tropical civilisation which, rather than being an impediment to development, had found a particularly felicitous and progressive solution to the problems of 'racial' conflict which bedevilled other less mixed and hence less fortunate nations. Indeed, as Ortiz points out, after the 1930s various aspects of popular culture – football, samba and carnival – became symbols of national identity, albeit at the cost of forfeiting their more rebellious qualities.

This concern for both the national and the regional appears again in the populist era between 1945 and 1964 when rapid industrialisation went hand in hand with intense political and cultural mobilisation. Thus constant controversy and ambivalence have surrounded the discourse of modernity, raising issues which, as Oliven observes, recur throughout Brazilian history: 'unified state versus a federal state, nation versus region, national versus foreign, popular versus erudite, tradition versus modernity.'

However, as both he and Ortiz point out, a dominant tendency towards authoritarian modernisation imposed 'from above' has always characterised the project of modernity in Brazil. This was particularly the case during the period of right-wing military rule between 1964 and 1985 when modernity, understood as the creation of an urban–industrial society, ceased to be an aspiration and became an actuality as rapid industrialisation was pursued by successive military governments, one key aspect of which was the establishment of a national mass culture industry. Yet, simultaneously, the emancipatory element which was also always present in the modernising project was marginalised. Political repression and persecution, intellectual censorship and physical torture virtually eliminated those political and intellectual currents whose hope was that the creation of a modern nation would entail the radical democratisation of Brazilian society. The consequence of this, which would have important repercussions beyond the demise of the military government period in 1985, was the new role assumed by 'popular culture' – one of the central pillars in the epic of modernity.

The 'popular', according to Ortiz, is no longer primarily the culture produced by the popular classes or the project of popular liberation, but the products of the culture industry. Thus, traditional popular culture as a source to draw on for symbols of national identity has been replaced by others such as the *telenovela* or Formula 1, reflecting the country's new-found status as an urban-industrial society. Moreover, the marriage between the nation and modernity has come apart with the increasing integration of a global capitalist economy, giving way to a 'world modernity', such that it is now possible to be modern without being national. This prevalence of a new international popular culture connected primarily to the world of consumption has plunged Brazil into a different crisis of identity, with which it has yet to grapple. It is traversed by and suffers the impact of cultural and economic flows in which the boundaries separating the 'internal' (national-regional) and the 'external' (foreign) can no longer be clearly identified, exposing Brazilian society to new perils and challenges.

As Oliven points out, the possibilities in this new situation are manifested in the fact that Brazil not only imports foreign cars and lifestyles but is also itself an exporter of manufactured goods and cultural products, in particular of religious currents, music and television programmes, as well as of people, shown in the large numbers of Brazilians emigrating abroad. This is counterbalanced by the dangers bound up in the unhappy conjunction of extreme forms of injustice and inequality with technical–material progress. Thus, modernity as an emancipatory project remains unrealized, and given the undermining of the nation and the crisis of the popular, it remains unclear who the agent or agents of emancipation are.

A further twist in the labyrinth of Latin American modernity is revealed by Nelson Manrique's study on the history of the 'Indian question' in the Andean area. He highlights, in ways that run parallel to Sevcenko's analysis of the place of Canudos and Afro-Brazilian religion in the Brazilian project of modernisation, how the anti-indigenous racism established during the colony was reinforced by the post-colonial political and intellectual elites of Peru, and their identification not with their own people but with Spain, France and Britain. Thus the process of post-Independence nation-building became racialised and inseparable from the de-indigenisation of Peru. According to Manrique, this notion that a process of de-indigenisation was inevitable (and, if not, at least a precondition for the establishment of a modern society) has been the prevailing common sense view in Peru across a broad spectrum of ideological positions, ranging from the work of García Calderon in the nineteenth century to the work of one of the foremost indigenist writers of contemporary Peru, José Maria Arguedas.

This common view created a fertile sediment for the unquestioned promotion of developmentalist projects in the 1950s, in which the 'cultural ethnocide' of the indigenous population was seen as a prerequisite for the modernisation of Andean societies. And the racism implicit in this view continued despite the unprecedented degree of rural to urban migration, the decrease in the indigenous population as biological *mestizaje* continued apace, and the growth of cities at the expense of the countryside.

Only recently has this relationship between modernity and de-indigenisation been challenged by what Xavier Albó has defined as 'the return of the Indian' – the rise of significant Indianist movements, particularly in Bolivia, Peru and Ecuador, which refuse to see participation in the modern nation-state as dependent in any way on relinquishing their Indian identity. These movements demand not only land, credit and basic services but also recognition of their cultural identity and autonomous political organisation. Some of these demands have been met and in a development of particular significance for this book's discussion on the nature of Latin American modernity, the Indianist movements have legitimated the 'right to difference'. They have demonstrated that the Indian is not a 'residue of tradition' to be eliminated in the process of social and economic modernisation, but is essential in the construction of a democratic polity, *sui generis*, giving an indigenous content to the emancipatory aspirations of the modern project.

Cultural modernity

Gwen Kirkpatrick's essay is concerned with the avant-garde movements of the twentieth century. In it she explores the tensions between the different 'narratives' which characterise Latin American modernisms: narratives of 'globalizing modernity', of 'subalternity' and 'marginality'.

Like their European counterparts, modernist writers such as Ruben Darío in Nicaragua, Cesar Vallejo in Peru, Gabriela Mistral in Chile, Jorge Luis Borges in Argentina and Oswald and Mário de Andrade in Brazil broke with realism and academic classicism and engaged in bold formal experimentation with new aesthetic codes and themes. Underlying this 'universalist' impulse, however, was the sense that Latin American modernity existed in a 'constant state of belatedness' with respect to the European model, a 'failed copy of the paradigm' whose deficiencies had to be compensated through a process of cultural renewal and updating.

It was a feeling, argues Kirkpatrick, permeating the artistic and intellectual circles at the beginning of the twentieth century, that 'narratives of a global modernity' were cut across and transformed by countervailing tendencies or 'narratives of subalternity and marginality', giving shape to other 'valid modernities', the contours and potentialities of which we have been trying to explore. Writers such as José Enrique Rodó and José Martí had already called for the need for self-definition in the face of European cultural tradition. And, as we saw earlier, the European modernists' disenchantment with rationality and the ideology of progress, their exploration of non-European cultures, of myth, magic, dream, non-representational and oral cultures, had helped Latin American writers and artists to develop tools with which to elaborate elements of their own cultures, in particular the African and indigenous heritage disparaged by the nineteenth-century Euro-centric discourse of modernity. The Mexican Revolution in 1910, the expansion of education, urbanisation and demands for land reform, had led to the emergence of new social actors and voices: the middle and popular classes, indigenous groups and women. This meant that aesthetic experimentation was linked, as Kirkpatrick points out, with bringing into public consciousness not just 'repressed sexualities, but also repressed populations, symbolic systems and languages'. Thus, much more so than in the case of European modernisms, Latin American modernisms were intertwined with radical politics, and with a constant concern with issues of origins, imitation and transformation. As Kirkpatrick observes, 'the radical heterogeneity of cultural experi-ence, and even of languages in many regions, had formed a matrix with which "international" modernism, identified with the literature of Joyce, T.S. Eliot, Virginia Woolf, European dadaists, surrealists and futurists, was not forced to deal'.

In Brazil, as Beatriz Rezende points out in her essay, the Modernist Movement was so successful in establishing a new aesthetic language that, paradoxically, it became a 'canonised revolution', which margin-alised a whole literary tradition (known as 'art-deco' literature) and which, in its portrayal of urban life in Rio de Janeiro in the 1920s and '30s, provided valuable insights into aspects of the experience of modernity in what was then the capital of Brazil. But it is only now, as a result of the post-modern critique of the way in which the once revolutionary avant-garde movements have become part of the estab-lished official culture, that these exclusions are becoming apparent. In a similar way, the propositions of the Cannibalist Movement of the 1920s are being re-elaborated and re-evaluated.

The Cannibalist Manifesto declared that the path to cultural inde-pendence and creativity lay not in the colonial and futile habit of attempting to imitate foreign models, nor in the equally futile affirma-tion of a presumed pure national culture, but in a selective, critical, 'devouring' or transculturating assimilation of external influences. This model for thinking about Brazilian identity and its heterogeneity as a 'constant and partial assimilation of difference' is being refined and questioned by new theoretical advances in the study of race and gender and their advocacy of a 'politics of difference'. One intellectual figure whose work straddles modernism and post-modernism is the writer and poet Mário de Andrade. His work and life exemplify the tensions between universalist erudite aesthetic experimentalism and a passionate commitment to incorporating the plurality of traditions within Brazilian culture – African, indigenous and popular – into a notion of national culture.

Perhaps the most evolved expression of Mário de Andrade's deep understanding of the predicament of modernity in the Latin American context is his novel *Macunaíma*, subtitled 'rhapsody of a hero without a character'. This mytho-poetic tale of an indigenous trickster figure from the Amazon forest, whose odyssey to the city of São Paulo in search of a lost amulet given to him by his lover, Ci, the Empress of the Forest, gives imaginative form to the 'multiple temporalities and logics of development' which characterise Latin American modernity.

The text itself draws on several cultural traditions: high and popular, European, Brazilian, Indian and African. It stitches together legends, stories, chronicles from the colonial period, proverbs and popular expressions in a manner which is akin to both a modernist collage and Brazilian folk-art compositional patterns. It is a text with many centres, hence 'without character'. But the hero himself, Macunaíma, in his many metamorphoses as he journeys through Brazil, is also without a fixed or moral character. Eventually this leads to his downfall and defeat as he comes into contact with modern civilisation in the city of São Paulo. It is in this sense that Rezende, in her discussion of Mário de Andrade's contemporary relevance, concurs with him in defining Macunaíma as the 'hero of our people', and that de Souza Martins uses him to exemplify the ambiguities and hesitations of modernity in Brazil.

In her analysis of early cinema and television in Latin America, Ana Lopez ties together several of the issues raised by Ortiz on the relationship between the nation and modernity and by Kirkpatrick in her exploration of the intersections between the universalist and localist tendencies in Latin American modernism.

Like the appropriation of the European avant-gardes at the beginning of the twentieth century, Latin American cinema appeared initially not as a by-product of large-scale processes of domestic industrialisation and urbanisation, but as a foreign import. Images of the experience of modernity circulated within the sphere of culture without equivalent processes of socio-economic modernisation. Early cinematic works – described by López as 'spectacular experiments' based on an 'aesthetics of astonishment' – consisted in recording the marvels of modernity: railways, roads, telephones, long-distance journeys and the exciting new perceptual possibilities engendered by these novel forms of transport and mobility. In this way cinema created the desire to have access to modernity, the centre of which was elsewhere, but also, crucially, suggested the possibility of a home-grown version, accessible through locally available means, thus linking modernity firmly with the fate of the nation.

Seen as a medium capable of faithfully recording 'objective truth', cinema was also aligned with notions of progress contained in the hegemonic positivist ideology of early twentieth-century Latin American governments. Above all, however, early cinema created significant images and narratives of the nation, as in documentaries of historic figures such as Porfirio Diaz, Hernán Cortez, Hidalgo and Morelos, in chronicles of everyday life in the city and countryside, and in films on foundational Latin American myths such as the struggle for independence in Argentina and the Mexican Revolution. Cinema thus played a key role in the construction of an imagined national community.

In subsequent decades, however, with the development of other media, it is television in particular which has, as both Lopez and Ortiz point out, become the vehicle through which the collective national imagination has been shaped. Simultaneously and paradoxically it has also become the means through which the products of the Latin American culture industry, in particular the *telenovela*, have transformed the local into a marketable commodity with a global reach, only to be supplanted in its hegemony by the new electronic media and their unpredictable and often subversive uses.

Contemporary challenges to modernity

The tragic end of Macunaíma's encounter with modernity, and his failure to understand and direct the forces which motivate him, resonates with the melancholy tone of some of the authors as they contemplate the ambiguous results of several decades of economic and social modernisation. This modernisation is characterised by overall advances in certain indicators of development, such as health and education and growth in GNP, but above all by massive inequities between social classes and regions, by political violence, corruption and perplexity regarding the future of Latin America.

For Néstor García Canclini, the Latin American project of modernity involved four key processes: emancipation, democratisation, cultural renewal and economic expansion. In each of these spheres, however, there have been worrying signs of regression. While in the 1960s, state educational investment was leading to the growth of a secular and critical culture, neo-liberal structural adjustment policies adopted in the 1980s have led, in his view, to a dramatic fall in investment in education, a decline of critical reason and a rise in 'religious and ethnic fundamentalisms' prone to authoritarian manipulation.

The decline in political participation, due both to the legacy of the military regimes of the 1970s and '80s and the privatisation of the public sphere by 'videopolitics' (the culture industries and their commercialised aesthetic), has led to the transformation of serious public debate into grotesque spectacle, undermining citizenship and cultural creativity. In the area of economic expansion, Latin American economies are increasingly characterised – and destabilised – by financial speculation, international financial crises and growing unemployment. Thus, higher levels of education, citizenship and political participation, social mobility and prosperity – Canclini's 'set of aspirations' underlying the modernising project – are all currently in a state of jeopardy.

Neo-liberal globalisation brings about new hybrid formations between the heterogeneous elements of Latin American societies, between 'the local and the global', the 'traditional and the hypermodern'. However, because these hybridisations are taking place in a context of new and growing forms of social exclusion and injustice, they are leading to the very real disintegration of the social fabric of Latin American societies, revealing again the unholy alliances which are possible between modernity and barbarism. These distortions of the project of modernity, Canclini emphasises, can only be overcome if the 'narratives of the ethnic, national and regional cultures neglected by globalization' are taken into account, and if the 'free circulation of citizens and the equitable appropriation of goods and messages' is privileged over the unregulated circulation of capital and commodities.

Beatriz Sarlo's essay on Buenos Aires unveils for the reader the various layerings, or in her words *pentimentos*, which made up the city as it rose like a beacon of modernity from the surrounding plains, the *pampas*, in various phases from the 1890s to the present. She describes how the old Hispanic creole city was metamorphosed with the arrival of electricity, the speed of new modes of transport and the massive influx of 'strangers' – immigrants from the countryside and abroad – creating a babelic cacophony of languages, including Yiddish, Italian and Polish. Anarchism, socialism, the development of radio broadcasting and a popular press, the spread of football and tango as national passions, the rise of populist politics in the form of Peronism: all attest to the importance of the popular classes as one of the key new actors on the stage of the modern city.

Sarlo demonstrates how 'these many superimpositions of material and symbolic networks' which made up the city were both captured and modified as the 'urban imagination projected images of the city'.

In the imaginations of Martinez Estrada, Borges, Roberto Arlt, the poet Oliviero Gerondo and the painter Xul Solar, the momentous changes provoked by modernity – or, to return to Berman's formulation, the simultaneous possibilities in advancement towards the new and the perils of destroying the old – are transfigured. New temporalities, subjectivities, sensibilities and textures, all of which form part of the experience of modernity in the city, are conveyed in images of excited anticipation about the future and nostalgic mourning for what is past.

In a recent work by the writer Sergio Chejfec, however, contemporary modernity acquires a new and almost exclusively sinister face: in 'El aire', Chejfec presents a nightmarish vision of Buenos Aires as a city which has fallen prey to a process of bizarre decay, ruin and slumification, becoming a wasteland and gradually returning to its original wild *pampas* state. According to Sarlo, this is a fictionalised vision of the present and real calamitous degeneration of Buenos Aires with its originally utopian character as 'the great city of the South'. For Sarlo, the convincing power of the almost fantastic imagery of Chefjec's work lies in its connection to social reality, in other words to the ways in which Buenos Aires is being deprived of 'the memory of its cultural characteristics' by the social and economic processes discussed and denounced in Canclini's text. In the exodus to the suburbs by the middle sectors, grown rich thanks to neo-liberal economic policies; in the post-modern transformation of select sites of the inner city into tourist theme parks; and in the invasion of other parts of the centre by the growing multitude of the unemployed and poor, we witness 'the other side of the enthusiasm, nostalgia, criticism and optimism' which inspired Buenos Aires' first modernity.

The image we have before us, then, is of a Latin America beset by new and often problematic currents: on the one hand, disillusionment and frustration with only partially realized promises of justice, equality and cohesion; on the other hand, a sense of anticipation at the possibilities opened up by economic and cultural globalisation: new markets, products and sources of income, new forms of cultural creativity and 'transculturation' and new transnational movements such as those formed by trans-American indigenist and Afro-American groupings. And yet late modernity, in this very framework of neo-liberal globalisation, is marked by ever greater internal inequalities within Latin America and an international balance of power which still favours Western Europe and above all North America.[51]. In this context it is all the more necessary to keep alive, as Sevcenko says, the cultural sources, the heterogeneous rationalities and legacies in Latin America, which proclaim a world of 'peace, fraternity and justice'. For the contemporary challenge, as he points out, is 'still that of redeeming the sacrifice of Canudos' – its women, men and children, dispersed among the landless in the backlands, the homeless in the cities and the legions of street-children – and the many parallel sacrifices which in Latin America have been made in the name of modernity.

Postscript

This volume was designed originally to include parallel chapters from Hispanic America and Brazil relating to a given topic on the experience of modernity in Latin America. The main purpose of this parallel structure was to counter the tendency, at least within the field of Latin American studies in the English-speaking world, to consider Hispanic America and Brazil separately. However, for reasons independent of the will of the editors, it was not possible to adhere strictly to this structure and the result is both a more thematic approach and a relatively greater emphasis on Brazil.

Notes

1 In addition to the theoretical debates on post-modernity, analyses of modernity such as *The Black Atlantic* by Paul Gilroy (1993) and *Modernity and the Holocaust* by Zygmunt Bauman (1989) have connected it to such disparate phenomena as the Atlantic slave trade and Nazi Germany, to gender issues as well as to a broad array of contemporary cultural practices in the fields of literature, the arts and media.

2 See in this respect Yudice (1989). Illuminating examples of the study of modernity in Latin America are Sarlo (1988), Sevcenko (1992) and Canclini (1990).

3 See Osborne (1992).

4 See the series of four books *Understanding Modern Societies* (1992) edited by Hall et al., *The Condition of Postmodernity* (1989) by Harvey and *Toward a Rational Society* (1971) by Habermas.

5 Anderson, *Imagined Communities* (1983).

6 Berman (1982), p. 15.

7 See Anderson (1984) and Hall (1992) for a discussion of the time-scales of different aspects of modernity, and Harvey (1989) for an illuminating periodisation of modernity.

8 Anderson (1984), p. 103.

9 See Habermas (1972).

10 Habermas, 'Modernity's Consciousness of Time and its Need for Self

Reassurance' in a collection of his essays *The Philosophical Discourse of Modernity* (1990).

11 Osborne (1992), p. 73.

12 See Habermas: 'Modernity's specific orientation towards the future only takes shape to the extent that the process of social modernisation tears apart and mobilizes the old European experiential space of the peasant-artisan lifeworld, devaluing its capacity to guide expectations.' *Der Philosophische Diskurs der Moderne* (1986), p. 22 (my translation).

13 See Felski (1995), p. 13.

14 O'Shea (1996a).

15 See Harvey (1989), p. 37.

16 See Rostow (1960), Eisenstadt (1973), Lerner (1964) and Germani (1973).

17 Camus (1955), p. 45.

18 See Felski (1995) and Lloyd (1984).

19 See Habermas (1981).

20 Stern (1999).

21 See Nairn (1974).

22 It is possible to argue that in comparison to India and Africa, which were also European colonies, heterogeneity is a more fundamentally constitutive feature of Latin America because the process of colonisation led to a greater destructuration of indigenous societies, so that the societies which emerged after the process of conquest and colonisation were heterogenous in their very constitution. In India and Africa, colonialism had a profound effect on the local culture, and social and economic structures created parallel forms of uneven development. However, the autochthonous element, perhaps particularly in India, was not affected in such a fundamental way, so that there is greater continuity of the social formation.

23 Brunner (1992), p. 104.

24 See Paz (1971) and Márquez (1987).

25 See Ianni (1992).

26 See Canclini (1990), p. 23.

27 According to Brunner, in the long history of debates about Latin America's relationship to modernity two broad positions can be outlined. Thus, some sectors of the Latin American intelligentsia have adopted a stance which Brunner, using García Márquez's depiction of the village of Macondo in *One Hundred Years of Solitude,* defines as 'macondismo'. This position entails a rejection of the calvinist, instrumental and Faustian rationality underlying European and North American societies, and recognition of the rise of a new rationality in Latin America out of its magical-realist sediment. Alternatively, Latin America is judged pessimistically in terms of its deficiencies – the absence of the Reformation, the Enlightenment, the French Revolution – in relation to the European path to modernity. For Brunner, neither the idealisation of magical-realism nor its negative comparison with Europe is valid. See Brunner (1992).

28 See Hall (1992b) for a discussion of the ways in which discourses about Europe and America during the sixteenth and seventeenth centuries influenced the development of social science. See also Quijano (1991) on the

relationship between the discovery of America and the development of the
European notion of modernity as liberation from domination.

29 See Stein (1970) for a discussion of the links between modernity in Europe
    and the colonisation of Latin America.
30 See Blackburn (1997).
31 See Quijano (1991).
32 See Levine (1992).
33 See Skidmore (1990), Knight (1990), Stepan (1991).
34 See Roxborough (1994).
35 See Barbero (1987).
36 See Coniff (1981) and Weffort (1978).
37 See Franco (1970), especially chapters 3 and 4.
38 See Sikkink (1991).
39 See Gwynne and Kay (1999).
40 See Apfel-Marglin and PRATEC (1998), p. 102–103.
41 See Harris (1995).
42 R. Stavenhagen, 'Pluricultural and Multiethnic: Evaluating the Implications
    for State and Society in Mesoamerica and the Andes' and D. Yashar,
    'Democracy, Indigenous Movements and the Post-Liberal Challenge in
    Latin America', papers given at the Institute of Latin American Studies,
    London, 30 March 2000.
43 See Varese (1991).
44 See Gutierrez (1998).
45 See Quijano (1991), Rowe and Schelling (1991) and Schelling (1999) for
    an analysis of the culture of rural migrants on the outskirts of Latin
    American cities.
46 See Ortiz (1988), and Monsiváis (1988).
47 Barbero (1996), p. 19.
48 See Rama (1982).
49 Hall (1992c), p. 303.
50 See Franco (1996).
51 See Gwynne and Kay (1999), p. 5, for data on the increasing asymmetries
    in the world economy between 1978 and 1995, specifically between the
    developed countries and the less developed countries. According to the
    authors, 'the per capita income enjoyed by inhabitants of the center
    countries of the world economy was virtually 5 times that of the highest
    income economies and 12 times that of the lowest income economies of
    Latin America ... by 1995 the ratios had increased to virtually 7 and 30,
    respectively.'

Bibliography

Anderson, B. (1983), *Imagined Communities: Reflections on the Origin and Spread of
   Nationalism*, London and New York, Verso.
Anderson, P. (1984), 'Modernity and Revolution', in *New Left Review* no. 144,
   March–April, pp. 96–114.

Apfel-Marglin, F. and PRATEC (eds.) (1998), *The Spirit of Regeneration*, London, Zed Books.

Barbero, J.M. (1987), *De los medios a los mediaciones*, Barcelona, Ed. Gustavo Gili.

Barbero, J.M. (1996), 'Communication and Modernity in Latin America', in C. Ferman (ed.), *The Postmodern in Latin American Cultural Narratives*, New York, Garland Publishing.

von Barloewen, C. (1995), *History and Modernity in Latin America*, Oxford, Berghahn Books.

Bauman, Z. (1989), *Modernity and the Holocaust*, Oxford, Polity Press.

Berman, M. (1982), *All That is Solid Melts into Air*, London, Verso.

Blackburn, R. (1997), *The Making of New World Slavery: from the Baroque to the Creole 1492–1800*, London, Verso.

Brunner, J.J. (1992), *America Latina: cultura y modernidad*, Mexico, Grijalbo.

Burbach, R. (1994), 'Roots of Post-Modern Rebellion in Chiapas' in *New Left Review* no. 205, May–June, pp. 113–125.

Camus, A. (1955), 'The Myth of Sisyphus and Other Essays', transl. J. O'Brien, New York.

Canclini, N.G. (1990), *Culturas híbridas*, Mexico, Grijalbo.

Colas, S. (1994), *Postmodernity in Latin America, the Argentine Paradigm*, Durham, NC, Duke University Press.

Coniff, M. (ed.) (1981), *Latin American Populism in Comparative Perspective*, Albuquerque, University of New Mexico Press.

da Cunha, E. (1944), *Rebellion in the Backlands*, Chicago, University of Chicago Press.

Eisenstadt, S.N. (1973), *Tradition, Change, Modernity*, New York, Wiley.

Escobar, T. (1988), 'Pos-Modernismo/Pre-Capitalismo', in *Casa de las Americas* no. 168, May–June, pp. 13–19.

Felski, R. (1995), *The Gender of Modernity*, Cambridge, Mass., Harvard University Press.

Follari, R.A. (n.d.), *Modernidad y posmodernidad: una optica desde America Latina*, Instituto de Estudios y Accion Social, Aique Grupo Editor, s.a.

Franco, J. (1970), *The Modern Culture of Latin America*, London, Penguin.

Franco, J. (1996), 'Globalization and the Crisis of the Popular', in T. Salman (ed.), *The Legacy of the Disinherited*, Amsterdam, CEDLA.

Germani, G. (1973), *Politica e sociedade numa epoca de transição*, São Paulo, Ed. Mestre Jou.

Giddens, A. (1990), *The Consequences of Modernity*, Cambridge, Polity Press.

Gilroy, P. (1993), *The Black Atlantic, Modernity and Double-Consciousness*, London and New York, Verso.

Gutierrez, N. (1998), 'What Indians Say about *Mestizos*: a critical view of a cultural archetype of Mexican nationalism', *Bulletin of Latin American Research*, vol. 17, no. 3, pp. 285–301.

Gwynne, R.N. & Kay, C. (1999), 'Latin America Transformed: Changing Paradigms, Debates and Alternatives', in R.N. Gwynne and C. Kay (eds.), *Latin America Transformed, Globalization and Modernity*, London, Arnold.

Habermas, J. (1971), *Toward a Rational Society*, London, Heinemann.

Habermas, J. (1972), *Knowledge and Human Interests*, London, Heinemann.

Habermas, J. (1981), *Theorie des kommunikativen Handelns*, Frankfurt, Suhrkamp.

Habermas, J. (1986), *Der philosophische Diskurs der Moderne*, Frankfurt, Suhrkamp.

Habermas, J. (1990), *The Philosophical Discourse of Modernity*, Cambridge, Polity Press.

Hall, S. (1992a), Introduction, in S. Hall and A. Gieben (eds.), *Formations of Modernity*, Cambridge, Polity Press.

Hall, S. (1992b), 'The West and the Rest: Discourse and Power' in *Formations of Modernity*, Cambridge, Polity Press.

Hall, S. (1992c), 'The Question of Cultural Identity' in *Modernity and its Futures*, Cambridge, Polity Press.

Harris, O. (1995), 'Knowing the Past' in R. Fardon (ed.), *Counterworks*, London, Routledge.

Harvey, D. (1989), *The Condition of Postmodernity*, Oxford, Basil Blackwell.

Horkheimer, M. and Adorno, T. (1969), *Dialektik der Aufklaerung*, Frankfurt, Fischer Verlag.

Ianni, O. (1992), *A ideia de Brasil moderno*, São Paulo, Brasiliense.

Jameson, F. (1984), 'Post-Modernism or the Cultural Logic of Late Capitalism', in *New Left Review* no. 146, July–August, pp. 53–93.

Knight, A. (1990), 'Racism, Revolution and *Indigenismo*: Mexico, 1910–1940, in R. Graham, (ed.), *The Idea of Race in Latin America, 1870–1940*, Austin, University of Texas Press.

Larrain, J. (1999), 'Modernity and Identity: Cultural Change in Latin America' in R. N. Gwynne & C. Kay (eds.), *Latin America Transformed: Globalization and Modernity*, London, Arnold.

Lerner, D. (1964), *The Passing of Traditional Society*, New York, Free Press.

Levine, D. (1992), *Vale of Tears: Revisiting the Canudos Massacre in Northeast Brazil*, Berkeley, University of California Press.

Lloyd, G. (1984), *The Man of Reason: 'Male' and 'Female' in Western Philosophy*, London, Methuen.

Márquez, G.G. (1987), 'The Solitude of Latin America' in B. McGuirk & R. Cardwell (eds.) *Gabriel Garcia Márquez: New Readings*, Cambridge, Cambridge University Press.

Monsiváis, C. (1988), in *Contratexto* no. 3, July.

Nairn, T. (1974), 'The Modern Janus', in *New Left Review*, August, pp. 3–29.

Ortiz, R. (1988), *A moderna tradição brasileira*, São Paulo, Brasiliense.

O'Shea, A. (1996a), 'English Subjects of Modernity' in M. Nava and A. O'Shea (eds.), *Modern Times*, London Routledge.

O'Shea, A. (1996b), 'What a Day for a Daydream' in M. Nava and A. O'Shea (eds.), *Modern Times*, London, Routledge.

Osborne, P. (1992), 'Modernity is a Qualitative not a Chronological Category', in *New Left Review* no. 192, March–April, pp. 65–82.

Paz, O. (1971), *The Labyrinth of Solitude*, New York, Grove Press.

Perez, A. J. (1995), *Modernismo, vanguardias, posmodernidad*, Buenos Aires, Ed. Corregidor.

Quijano, A. (1988), *Modernidad, identidad y utopia en America Latina*, Sociedad y Politica eds.

Quijano, A. (1991), 'Recovering Utopia' in *Report on the Americas*, vol. XXIV, no. 5, February, pp. 34–38.

Rama, A. (1982), *Transculturación narrativa en America Latina*, Mexico, Siglo XXl.

Rostow, W.W. (1960), *The Stages of Economic Growth: A Non-Communist Manifesto*, Cambridge, Cambridge University Press.

Rowe, W. & Schelling, V. (1991), *Memory and Modernity, Popular Culture in Latin America*, London, Verso.

Roxborough, I (1994), 'The Urban Working Class and Labour Movement in Latin America Since 1930', in *Cambridge History of Latin America*, vol. 6, part 2, pp. 307–379.

Sarlo, B. (1988), *Una modernidad periferica, 1920–1930*, Buenos Aires, Ed. Nueva Vision.

Sarmiento, D.F. (1845), *Civilización y barbarie. La vida de Juan Facundo Quiroga*, Santiago de Chile, n.p.

Schelling, V. (1999), '"The People's Radio" of Vila Nossa Senhora Aparecida: Alternative Communication and Cultures of Resistance in Brazil', in T. Skelton and T. Allen (eds.), *Culture and Global Change*, London, Routledge.

Sevcenko. N. (1992), *Orfeu extático na metrópole*, São Paulo, Companhia das Letras.

Sikkink, K. (1991), *Ideas and Institutions: Developmentalism in Brazil and Argentina*, Ithaca, Cornell University Press.

Skidmore, T.E. (1990), 'Racial Ideas and Social Policy in Brazil, 1870–1940' in T. Graham, (ed.), *The Idea of Race in Latin America*, Austin, University of Texas Press.

Stein, S. and Stein, B. (1970), *The Colonial Heritage of Latin America*, New York, Oxford University Press.

Stepan, N.L. (1991), *The Hour of Eugenics*, Ithaca, Cornell University Press.

Stern, S. (1999), 'The Tricks of Time: Colonial Legacies and Historical Sensibilities in Latin America', in J. Adelman (ed.), *Colonial Legacies*, London, Routledge.

Varese, S. (1991), 'Think Globally, Act Locally', in *Report on the Americas*, vol. XXV, no. 3, December, pp. 13–18.

Weffort, F. (1978), *O populismo na política brasileira*, Rio de Janeiro, Paz e Terra.

Yudice, G. (1989), 'Puede hablarse de posmodernidad en America Latina?' in *Revista de critica literaria latinoamericana*, no. 29, first semester, pp. 105–128.

Part I

Predicaments of a Peripheral Modernity

Contradictory Modernities and Globalisation in Latin America

Néstor García Canclini

Another debate on modernity? A scientist from the 'hard' sciences who took a look at the standard bibliographies for humanities and the social sciences would be surprised to find the periodic reappearance of diverse theories on the modern, each time associated with different problems and concepts. The creation of modern societies was a central preoccupation of the founders of the Latin American nations in the nineteenth century, who tried to model these projects on European paradigms. Later, the revolutions of the twentieth century – from the Mexican to the Cuban and Nicaraguan – posed the question of how to accelerate modernisation while developing a unique identity based on local traditions. The hard scientist would be further surprised that not even the development of the modern social sciences in the sixties enabled us to establish rigorous, unanimously agreed criteria for characterising what is understood by 'modernity'. At that time, empirical sociology equated the modern with industrialisation and urbanisation, and sought to contribute its insights to promoting the transition from the local and the traditional, from the 'backward', to an advanced stage of development defined as modern.

Post-modern thinking and neo-liberal policies called into question both the evolutionary approach underlying this way of conceiving history and the principle that societies would be modified through endogenous industrialisation and the greater autonomy of their economies and their political and cultural systems. Today, however, these critiques of the modern project generate less support, or are repeated with less conviction, than they were in the 1980s. In the United States,

Europe and Latin America post-modern thinking has lost momentum, while economic crises, as well as the failures of neo-liberal policies, render uncertain and problematic what was previously hailed as common sense.

Despite the appearance in recent years of several books and issues of journals dedicated to post-modern themes, the innovative impulse which characterised the post-modern approach ten or twenty years ago has been lost. In Latin American writing, of the books published in the nineties concerned with post-modernity, the three which could be considered most significant can be read as discussions of modernisation. I am thinking of *América Latina: cultura y modernidad*, by José Joaquín Brunner;[1] *Mundialização e cultura*, by Renato Ortiz;[2] and *Escenas de la vida posmoderna*, by Beatriz Sarlo.[3] Even when the word 'post-modern' appears in the titles and indexes of these and other books, it seems that the questions generated by so-called post-modernity, rather than constituting a specific current of thought and investigation, have contributed to challenging, reformulating and enriching the analysis of modernity.

The hard scientist we were imagining would continue to be disconcerted on discovering that the debates on modernity are now principally associated with globalisation and seem to have a different conception of what it means to be modern. Where do we place Latin America in this reformulation? Various pubications and many conferences in the last few years give a rather discouraging assessment.

In a recent symposium concerned with the international evaluation of Cultural Studies (Pittsburgh, April 1998), Ellen Spielman evoked the negative references made by various Europeans to Latin America. For example, in 1997 Ulrich Beck, perhaps the most important sociologist in Germany today (if we consider that Jürgen Habermas and Niklas Luhman are close to retirement), published the book *Was ist Globalisierung?*[4] While the axis of Habermas' work was the reconstruction of the unfinished project of modernity, Beck maintains that the rupture in the world order established by enlightened modernity has created the opportunity to establish a second modernity. This would involve leaving behind the orthodoxies of the first modernising movement and opening the way towards a new era in which the central question would be: How is social justice possible in the global era? If we do not resolve this, says Beck, the future of Europe is the Brazil of today. In other words he sees Brazil in apocalyptic terms. This is similar to British sociologist Anthony Giddens' statement in his last book, *Beyond Left and Right*: If Europe fails, what awaits it is Brazilianisation.[5]

In a volume published in 1996, *Cinéma européen et identités culturelles*, film-maker Wim Wenders contributes an essay in which he tries to convince Europeans that as the industries of war and arms become obsolete, so the industries of images and sound will replace them. 'The wars of the future,' claims Wenders, 'will be wars of images.' The vision of European unification cannot take root in the imagination and consciousness of future Europeans if they do not have access to European myths. And these unifying myths will be formed in the cinema of the future. Television and all of the new information technologies will continue to depend heavily on the popular attraction and imaginative power of the cinema. Don't think, Wenders adds, that the North Americans have permanently seized control of the cinema screens. They too 'need a multitude of multicultural images. The images, the stories cannot come from a monopoly . . . North Americans and North-American cinema need a European cinema, and an Asian cinema, and an African cinema . . . The door is still half-open.' And what happens if the door were to close forever? Wenders answers: 'Europe, expelled from its own images, would become a Third World continent'.[6]

What can Latin America – this part of the Third World whose most powerful country, Brazil, appears to Europeans as the incarnation of impending disaster – do in the face of such a state of affairs? I want to retain two aspects from these narratives of the future. The first is the relationship that these authors make between the crisis of modernity and the possibility of reformulating it in the future and the relation of both processes to the audiovisual industries. Second is the idea that the industrial production of culture involves not only industry and economics, but is also a question of culture; both aspects are interwoven. It seems to me that these two assertions are indicative of some of the principal differences which characterise investigations of modernity following post-modernity. They will also be useful in examining the actual contradictions of the modern project in Latin America under the rules of globalisation.

The disintegration of modern societies

I would like to conduct an exercise based on the analytical model which I elaborated in the book *Culturas híbridas*[7] a decade ago, confronting it with the facts of the current crisis of economic and cultural development in Latin America. If we begin from what could be called the theories of enlightened modernity, as conceived by Jürgen Habermas and Marshall Berman, or from the definitions of art and modern literature of Pierre Bourdieu, Howard S. Becker and Fredric Jameson, it is feasible, in spite of the differences between these authors, to understand modernity in terms of four processes: emancipation, renewal, democratisation and expansion.[8]

Emancipation

Emancipation can be said to have arrived in Latin American societies with the secularisation of the cultural sphere. Science, art and literature achieved an autonomy less extensive and integrated than in the metropolises, but notably greater than in Asia or Africa. From the nineteenth century political structures were liberalised and social life was rationalised. Positivism, as widespread in some Latin American countries as in Europe, promoted the humanities and the sciences, while university reform, initiated in Argentina, led to the creation of lay universities, organised with the democratic participation of the students, fifty years before the movements of 1968 achieved this in France, Germany and Italy.

The results of this process are encouraging if, for example, certain figures from 1950 are compared with those from the end of the 1980s. In the middle of the century

> 61 per cent of the population was rural; the level of illiteracy of those over fifteen years of age stood at almost 50 per cent and the figure for those in secondary education barely reached 7 per cent. The proportion of the population older than twenty-five with post-secondary education rises, in several countries, to 5–7 per cent, a figure comparable to that of Austria, Hungary and Italy.[9]

However, in the 1980s and '90s state investment in public education fell by half, owing to the same policies of structural adjustment responsible for taking the figure for those leaving primary school to over 50 per cent. The reduction of public investment in education and scientific and technological research has reinforced the gap between Latin American countries and the metropolises. As a consequence, religious, ethnic and political fundamentalism have increased, as if large sectors of our society would prefer to undo the secularity of modernity and rediscover sacred doctrines and 'infallible' charismatic authorities with which to entrust, not just their lives, but their destinies.

Renewal

Cultural renewal was achieved as ways of life and political organisation were secularised. Throughout the twentieth century there was rapid growth in middle and higher education, artistic and literary experimentation and, above all, in institutions of higher education. Eric Hobsbawm emphasised a few years ago that 'three of the most developed and educated countries – Germany, France and Great Britain – with a total population of 150 million, before the second World War did not have more than 150 thousand university students. In the 1980s, little Ecuador had more than double that'.[10]

But in the last two decades, in addition to cuts in the education budget, for the first time enrolment at many universities has also declined; some middle and lower sectors of society are abandoning the idea of higher education altogether as a means of social mobility. Many bookstores are closing and cinematic output is being reduced – books and films are two key areas of cultural modernisation, which in Argentina and Mexico were thriving industries between the 1940s and '60s. Several surviving publishers have been bought out by Spanish, Italian or American companies. Governments are increasingly less inclined to give financial support to culture, while closing down organisations which promote the creativity and diffusion of both fine and popular art. Private companies, which according to neo-liberal doctrine should take the economic initiative, are not accustomed to cultural patronage in Latin America. Moreover, the general recession and the difficulties of international competition are dissuading them from taking such action. Only transnational communication companies like Televisa and Globo are increasing their investment, and then only in the areas where it is most likely to be recouped (television, video and mass circulation magazines). As Jesús Martín Barbero wrote:

in the 'lost decade' of the eighties the only industry which developed in Latin America was communication. The number of television stations multiplied – from 205 in 1970 to more than 1,459 in 1988; Brazil and Mexico were equipped with their own satellites; radio and television created international links via satellite; data networks, satellite dishes and TV cables were installed; regional television channels were established. However, all of this growth was achieved by following the movement of the market, with hardly any intervention from the State. What's more, it undermined the purpose and the possibilities of State intervention, that is, by diminishing the public sphere and increasing monopolistic concentration.[11]

It is worth analysing how this process of privatisation, characterized by commercialized aesthetic, unaccompanied by risk, is related to the decline of the public sphere. For those companies, cultural innovation, artistic experimentation and critique are antagonistic to commercial profit.

Democratisation

In order to give support to the process of democratisation, political structures have gradually permitted greater citizen participation. This was done with many more interruptions and different procedures than imagined by classical liberalism. Democratisation initially took place, as anticipated by the French Revolution, with the expansion of education, the diffusion of art and science, and participation in political parties and trade unions. But in the second half of the twentieth century democratis-ation and the modernisation of political culture were promoted, above all, by the electronic media and by different youth, urban, feminist and human rights organisations. Some of these, such as the indigenous and ecological organisations, were very critical of modernisation.

This social fragmentation and electronic mediation are due in part to the fact that democratisation after the dictatorships of the 1970s and '80s revealed a rather discouraging landscape. We did not go from military authoritarianism and one-party régimes (of the Mexican type) to pluralist systems facilitating greater participation and the emergence of solutions to our chronic and dramatic social problems. In countries where the vote is voluntary more than half of the population abstains; where it is obligatory, 30 or 40 per cent of the electorate do not know for whom they will vote a week before the polls open. The public sphere is regarded with scepticism: there is increasingly less organis-ation through popular participation. Debt negotiation and structural adjustments, free trade agreements and privatisations are decided by negotiations between techno-bureaucrats and businessmen. The trade unions and social movements only find out what has occurred through the newspapers or on TV. (The Uruguayan plebiscite of 1992, in which the majority rejected privatisations, remains an exception.)

Video-politics converts the debates and exchanges of information, previously at the centre of the modern public sphere, into spectacles where action is replaced by acting. Engaging in discussion or reasoned negotiation gives way to farcical gossip and the sudden conversion of actors and celebrities into holders of government office.[12] 'If the media doesn't cover it, it's not politics', they say in many countries. Some sociologists see these changes as a post-modern reorganisation of the public sphere. The democratisation promoted by social movements which emerged outside political parties, and the forms of political solidarity created around media figures, are interpreted as an expression of 'the demand for social integration' or the 'desire for community', compensating for the disintegration produced by the neo-liberal economy.[13]

However, other analysts of Latin American society do not perceive this process as a reformulation of democracy. They find that the public sphere has suffered from the prevailing scepticism towards political parties and trade unions, the weakness of alternative social movements, corruption, the bureaucratisation of intermediary leaders and video-politics. Electoral democratisation and greater recognition of individual rights are stymied by the growth of inequality and the precarious living conditions of the majority. The result is the 'shredding' of the social fabric, the destruction of collective identities and the 'apathy of enormous social groups, especially in the popular sectors'. More than a desire for integration or community, such commentators see an 'erosion of the intermediary identities' which mediated 'between the dispersed sphere of the social and the neoliberal state': the middle and upper classes become part of the new economic policies by means of 'a possessive individualism centred on personalised consumerism'; the popular sectors, excluded or threatened with exclusion, fall back on the family and the culture of the youth gang, on a 'savage utilitarianism' and anomie.[14]

Expansion

Moves to achieve expansion have been the least successful aspect of Latin American modernity. If we understand expansion as the growth of knowledge and the appropriation of nature, of production and consumption, its impact has been fading since the urbanisation, industrialisation and developmentalist euphoria of the 1950s and '60s. Since then, Latin American participation in world commerce and technological innovation has contracted, while salaries and internal consumption have declined. The only things on the increase have been financial speculation, corruption, abandonment of education and urban insecurity.

However, the regression of the last decade has not been uniform. In the 1980s 5 per cent of the wealthiest sector of the population maintained or increased its income, while 75 per cent felt that its income was reduced. Some of those who have stopped manufacturing – generating unemployment and a fall in the standard of living of the majority – have turned to importing goods and speculation, earning more than if they were contributing to expanding gross national product. The growth in some countries' gross domestic product, which seemed to survive the depression of the 1980s, has evaporated in the context of international financial crises (Mexico, 1994; South-East Asia, 1996 to the present). The flight of capital from the region, the collapse of many banks, industries and businesses, and the increase of unemployment to an average of 21 per cent have accompanied outbreaks of unrest in many nations. Even in countries like Chile, where the economic revival was a little more prolonged, the opportunity to increase social or cultural expenditure in order to correct the setbacks of the past decades is not being taken.

What can globalisation change?

For many decades Latin American societies placed their faith in this modernising project. Not only did governments promote education, industrial development and democratising processes, but other factors too indicated the degree of social participation that was prevalent: parents sent their children to school en masse believing that it was a means of social mobility, while millions of Latin Americans moved from the country to the cities in the hope of improving their incomes and health to gain access to the goods and messages produced by modernity. Now they find that education is privatised or degenerating, while many industries are closing down, and the cities, replete with the unemployed, their budgets reduced, deteriorate while their insecurity increases.

Meanwhile, business people and governments attempt to convince the people that there is a new way to modernise, one that is encapsulated in the double formula of 'globalisation and regional integration'. What can be understood by this catch-phrase is a question which we will consider in the next few pages. But the first point to observe is the gap between what the economic or political elites preach and what these societies think and experience.

In April 1998 the second Summit of the Americas took place in Santiago de Chile, in which the United States – in alliance with various Latin American governments – promoted the creation of an Area of Free Trade of the Americas. It promised that this opening-up and integration of national economies would favour import and export activity, and improve the position of the continent in terms of global competition.

However, analysis of 17,500 interviews, conducted by the Latinobarómetro Corporation in November and December of 1997, and covering seventeen of the region's countries, shows that their citizens do not share this optimism. The results of this study, delivered to the governments at the Summit, indicated that just 23 per cent believed that their country was progressing, and that in almost all of the nations such a belief had diminished with respect to 1996. The institutions which the interviewees considered most powerful (government, large companies, the military, banks, political parties) were those which they trusted the least. The crisis of governability, devaluations, and the rises in unemployment and poverty were some of the factors that led a growing number to doubt democracy and desire a harder line to be taken. The percentage of people believing this was lower in countries which had just emerged from military dictatorships (Argentina, Chile, Brazil), but significantly high in others with processes of incipient democracy, among them Paraguay and Mexico. Over the space of a year the proportion of those in favour of 'authoritarian' solutions rose from 26 per cent to 42 per cent in Paraguay, and from 23 per cent to 31 per cent in Mexico. With the exceptions of Costa Rica and Uruguay, where belief in the political system remained strong, in the rest of Latin America 65 per cent are 'not very, or not at all satisfied' with the practice of democracy.[15]

As the same survey reveals, the increase in authoritarianism in political culture is associated with citizens' conviction that their governments possess increasingly less power. From 1996 to 1997 the percentage of those who believed that the government was the most powerful agent declined from 60 per cent to 48 per cent. The conviction is becoming more pronounced that decisions which determine the future are increasingly being made by transnational companies, and to a large extent by the military.

What can be expected from this weakening of national governments and the globalised rearticulation of power and wealth? What does this process imply for culture, and in particular for its most dynamic and influential area – communications? Globalisation, which exacerbates international competition and undermines endogenous cultural production, favours the expansion of companies with the capacity to homogenise and deal with sectoral and regional diversities in a particular way: It destroys or weakens inefficient producers, and presents peripheral cultures with the choice of remaining fixed within their local traditions, or exporting themselves in a stylised, folkloristic form amenable to the demands of transnational communications companies.

The concentration of innovation in scientific research, information and entertainment in the United States, Europe and Japan accentuates the distance between those areas and the rachitic and out-of-date production of peripheral nations. With respect to Europe, for instance, the disparity is increasing: Latin America, with 9 per cent or the planet's population, provides 0.8 per cent of its export of cultural goods, while the European Union, with 7 per cent of the world's population, exports 37.5 per cent and imports 43.6 per cent of all commercialised cultural goods.[16]

The contrast is accentuated by the recent expansion of American terrestrial and cable television transnational corporations in Latin America and other regions. The most powerful Latin American businesses, and those which have several years' experience in audiovisual export (in Argentina, Brazil, Colombia, Chile, Mexico and Venezuela), have managed to negotiate unequal exchanges with CNN, MTV, TVE and other transnational groups, which at least facilitate a certain recognition of Latin American products on the transnational circuit. Not just soap operas, but records, music videos, rock, folk and other musical styles find niches outside their home country.

What political, cultural and aesthetic transformations are generated by these new modes of exchange? With regard to the first aspect, global restructuring sits uncomfortably with the role of social mediators, informers and political actors – a role played by the mass media from the 1980s, in the context of the vacuum of representation created in many countries by military dictatorship and the deterioration of the party-political system. In the nineties, the press, radio to a lesser extent, and television almost not at all, played a part in the restructuring of the social fabric to compensate for the collapse brought about by neo-liberal policies. However, the commercial and clientelistic logic of the media meant their response was merely reactive, dependent on the potential of the news to be transformed into spectacle, and on its weekly obsolescence.

But in the context of the breakdown of regimes like those of Menem in Argentina and the PRI in Mexico, the media have partially fulfilled the functions of investigation and communication, at times much more effectively than parliaments. In the face of human rights violations (the assassination of politicians, social militants and journalists) and natural catastrophes (earthquakes, hurricanes), the media reveal a capacity for prompt communication and ad hoc social organisation. But the ephemeral dynamic of media information, and the political parties' and social movements' inability to be a real part of the media, have made it difficult to construct medium- or long-term socio-political agendas which address structural questions and are capable of bringing together the traditional spheres of politics, the media and social movements. Several studies conducted in Latin American radio and television phone-ins, or other audience-participation programmes, demonstrate that their contribution to transparency and social democratisation is too insignificant; the way the stations select and edit opinions converts demands, complaints and so on into a homogenous discourse which reproduces the social order and the commonplaces of political culture.[17]

The themes of globalisation and regional integration, particularly in their structural aspects, have a low profile in the most influential audiovisual media, only emerging in a superficial form when, for example, a financial crisis, or a presidential visit to Chile to participate in the Summit of the Americas, generates polemical debate. Studies on the role of the written and visual media in promoting inter-cultural knowledge[18] show the scant significance they place on processes of economic, political and cultural integration; their pages or screens with international information tend to affirm nationalism and stereotypes of other countries, and rarely facilitate a reasoned understanding of difference. (I am aware that the necessary brevity of these reflections cannot take into account the complex, although not very diversified, relationships of the media with globalisation, which begins to occupy a prominent place in political agendas and the study of modernity at the beginning of the twenty-first century.)

The double agenda of the globalisers

From this perspective, it is a complex but necessary task to identify the processes that deconstruct and reconstruct globalisation in modernity. We should distinguish the integrationist and communicative agenda of globalisation from its segregationist and dispersing agenda. The most frequent narrative on globalisation tells of the expansion of post-industrial capital and mass communications as a process of unification and/or articulation of productive companies, financial systems, regimes of information and entertainment. Wall Street, the Bundesbank, Micro-soft, Hollywood, CNN and MTV are some of the key characters of this narrative. Although not simple allies, they share the tendency to transcend the national contexts in which they emerged and to compete as organising agents of a world system.

At the same time, this world unification of the material and symbolic markets is, as Lawrence Grossberg calls it, a 'stratifying machine', which operates not so much to erase differences but to reorder them to produce new frontiers, less tied to territories than to the unequal distribution of markets.[19] I would add that globalisation – or rather the global strategies of corporations and many States – comprises both segregating and dispersing mechanisms: their policies of 'labour flexibility' produce disaffiliation from trade unions, promote informal markets connected by networks of corruption and lumpenisation, audiovisual cultures opposed to a lettered culture. The tyranny of ratings in the broadcasting media divides culture into serious and light, sharpens the oppositions between nationalisms, and selects the most folkloric and spectacular elements. All this is to the detriment of what could potentially be communicated to those who live in different countries, elaborating their differences on the basis of reasoned information. Just as it unifies vast layers of transnationalised consumers, neo-liberal globalisation creates impoverished workers who see without being able to consume, temporary migrants who oscillate between one culture and another, people without documents and with restricted rights, consumers and television viewers confined within their domestic lives – all without the capacity to respond to hegemonic policies in a collective way.

The integrationist and communicative agenda is asserted in particular by hegemonic actors. Sociological and anthropological theories of globalisation have only recently begun to reveal that, from the point of view of civil society, globalisation produces what Sergio Zermeño calls a 'shattering of the social': the destruction of the entrepreneurial class and of the proletariat who contributed to import substitution industrialisation, of the middle sectors of public workers, of the spaces which mediated between social actors and the State (trade unions, political parties, popular movements).[20]

An open modernity

Instead of affirming that modernity is an era that has been superseded by post-modernity, as was believed in the 1980s, or that modernity is an unfinished project, as argued by Habermas, it should be thought of as an open and uncertain movement. Globalisation does not imply the end of history, as Francis Fukuyama claims;[21] nor the end of geography, as proposed by Paul Virilio[22] and the Internet ideologues of a world without centre or borders. The history of globalisation has hardly begun. Its aim of general interactivity is thwarted not just by the 'backwardness' of semi-integrated cultures – peasants, indigenous people, the unemployed, young people who do not succeed in entering higher education or the labour market – but also by the new frontiers and the segmentation of networks and publics invented by those who claim to place the world in a state of 'telepresence'. Historical and local differences persist not so much because globalising powers are still insufficient, but because their way of reproducing and expanding themselves requires that the centre not be everywhere, that there be differences between the global circulation of goods and the unequal distribution of the political capacity to use them. In addition the logic of inequality prompts those excluded from work, commerce and unified consumption to revitalise artisanal products, to persist with strikes which are ignored or repressed. Just like the compulsive interruption of a film by commercial advertising every few minutes, the story of globalisation is interrupted by the incorporation of local demands which either remain unmet or feel compelled to respond to the maniacal call to compete. Post-modern discourses are accustomed to celebrating this fragmentation, but in a world which the monopolies seek to encompass in totalitarian fashion, it is worth asking how local dissidence and subaltern protests can be articulated in order to modify the neo-liberal order which excludes them.

In other cases, the excluded integrate themselves into the global networks of drug-smuggling and crime, relying on national bureaucracies and structures of 'pre-modern' power. The fact that the globalised trade in arms and drugs conducted electronically is approaching 100 per cent of global electronic commerce (approximately a billion dollars per annum) suggests in what way the administrators of the interconnected world and of the perpetual present need to co-exist with the different temporalities of Algerian and Serbo-Croat fundamentalisms, with the apparatuses of ex-communist national states and the neo-liberal Latin American populisms which maintain cordial links with them.

Like the electronic money which passes between corrupt laundering operations and the formal economy, from local economies to trans-national companies, so global communications traffic with local and archaic cultures: some traditional crafts and music end up as part of the ecological, new age imaginary and as world music. Just as, according to Manuel Castells, 'the global criminal economy is an advanced capitalist form'[23] (because of its commercial logic, the conditions of investment and its financial activities), the assassinations in which the breakdown of national policies culminate (for example in Colombia and Mexico) destabilise the order of global exchange. At the same time, opportunely filmed, they renew every week the televisual imagination. Never were the aesthetic strategies of the transnational communications companies, whose visual discourse condemns these events but also celebrates them through incessant transmission, so close to the marginalised and lumpen popular cultures that accompany these processes: more than 500 *corridos* dedicated to narrating the adventures of drug dealers and not yet incorporated into television are transmitted by radio on the Mexican frontier and disseminated on pirated and legal cassettes, constituting one of the most frequently played types of music heard in a bus or taxi. Many media and advanced technology corporations share with the sectors excluded from the formal economy that hegemonic culture according to which identity and power are based on merciless competition, the transformation of cruelty into spectacle, family accumulation of money, traditional codes of honour and loyalty, religious and rural traditions, together with electronic ostentation and frivolous cosmopolitanism.

A methodological warning: so many interconnections and complicities between the local and the global, the traditional and the hyper-modern, the popular and the super-informed cannot be interpreted as a harmonious Machiavellian world plan. If one seeks examples of hybridisation that do not reconcile the diverse, one has only to remember the number of intercultural fusions which explode every day in the big cities: the co-existence of migrants from different countries can either lead to us becoming multicultural gourmets, or alternatively aggravate social prejudice. The acceleration of exchanges and the greater proximity of the distant increase the information we have about others, but rarely does this create greater understanding of their differences, which often become unbearable: xenophobia and racism also grow with globalisation. While some networks can be used in a 'benign' way – like the Internet, which started out as a military system – there are more networks designated for ferocious competition and the surveillance of dissidents or transgressors. However, competition and surveillance also function in a fragmented fashion. They do not result in a world government, because economic globalisation has assumed that it can advance more rapidly without States or transnational public powers – in short, without political globalisation.

This repositioning of the progress and interpretation of modernity under the rules of globalisation shows that the difference in meanings which 'the modern' has acquired has had to do with economic–political disputes and not just with epistemological questions. While it is important to construct a coherent paradigm which articulates modernity and globalisation, it is also necessary to analyse the destructive or benign effects of global narratives with the greatest rigour that the social sciences and the humanities can muster. We need cultural, political and media programmes with a different vision of social and cultural integration, which take into account the narratives of ethnic, national and regional cultures ignored by globalisation. The supranational integrations which have been negotiated and approved too hastily (NAFTA, MERCOSUR) only facilitate the free circulation of capital and goods, and do little or nothing to enable citizens to travel freely or to appropriate goods and messages in a more egalitarian way. These are, it seems to me, some of the principal scientific and political challenges with which we are crossing from one century to another.

Notes

1 José Joaquín Brunner, *América Latina: cultura y modernidad*, México, Grijalbo, 1992.
2 Renato Ortiz, *Mundialização e cultura*, São Paulo, Brasiliense, 1994.
3 Beatriz Sarlo, *Escenas de la vida posmoderna: Intelectuales, arte y videocultura en la Argentina*, Buenos Aires, Ariel, 1994.
4 Ulrich Beck, *Que es la globalizacion? Falacias del globalismo, respuestas a la globalizacion*, Barcelona, Paidos, 1998.
5 Anthony Giddens, *La tercera vía. La renovación de la social-democracia*, Madrid, Taurus, 1999.
6 Wim Wenders, 'Cinq malentendus autour du cinéma européen', in *Cinéma européen et identités culturelles*, Revue de l'Université de Bruxelles, 1995, 1–4, March 1996.
7 Néstor García Canclini, *Culturas híbridas: estrategias para entrar y salir de la modernidad*, México, Grijalbo, 1990. *Hybrid Cultures. Stategies for Entering and Leaving Modernity*, Minneapolis, University of Minnesota Press, 1995.
8 Here I expand, with new data, the analysis conducted in the article 'Una modernidad que atrasa', *Journal of Latin American Anthropology*, vol. 1, no. 1 (1995), Arlington, VA, pp. 2–19.
9 José Joaquín Brunner, *Tradicionalismo y modernidad en la cultura latinoamericana*, Santiago de Chile, FLACSO, 1990, p. 11.
10 Eric J. Hobsbawm, 'Crisis de la ideología, la cultura y la civilización', in *Coloquio de invierno, I: La situación mundial y la democracia*, México, CNCA, 1992, p. 50.
11 Jesús Martín Barbero, 'Comunicación e imaginarios de la integración', in *Taller de Comunicación*, Cali, 1995, p. 2.
12 This is not exclusive to politics. It also occurs in the media trivialisation of academic and intellectual debates, which have to do with the relationship between cosmopolitanism and emancipation. I cannot deal with this matter here, but an article by Richard Rorty deals with the polemic between Anglo-Saxon and French philosophers; see 'Cosmopolitanism without emancipation: a response to Lyotard', in Scott Lash and Jonathan Friedman, *Modernity and Identity*, Oxford and Cambridge, Blackwell, 1992.
13 Norbert Lechner, 'La búsqueda de la comunidad perdida: los retos de la

democracia en América Latina', *Sociológica*, year 7, no. 19 (May–August 1992), Mexico, UAm-Azcapotzalco.

14 See the articles by Eugenio Tironi, 'Para una sociología de la decadencia', *Proposiciones 12*, Santiago de Chile, Sur Ediciones, 1992; and Sergio Zermeño, 'Desidentidad y desorden: México en la economía global y el libre comercio', *Revista Mexicana de Sociología*, no. 3, (July–September 1991).

15 Javier Moreno, 'Los latinoamericanos temen que su crisis sea eterna', *El País*, 18 April 1998, p. 4.

16 Manuel Antonio Garretón, 'Políticas, financiamiento e industrias culturales en América Latina y el Caribe', document of the 3rd meeting of the World Commission for Culture and Development, UNESCO, San José, Costa Rica, 22–26 February 1994.

17 Miguel Angel Aguilar Díaz, 'Espacio público y prensa urbana en la ciudad de México'; Angele Giglia & Rosalía Winocur, 'La participación en la radio: entre inquietudes ciudadanas y estrategias mediáticas', in *Perfiles Latinoamericanos*, year 5, no. 9 (December 1996), FLACSO, Mexico.

18 Hugo Achugar and Francisco Bustamante, 'MERCOSUR, intercambio cultural y perfiles de un imaginario'; Anibal Ford, Stella Martini and Nora Mazzotti, 'Construcciones de la información el la prensa argentina sobre el tratado del MERCOSUR', in Néstor García Canclini (ed.), *Culturas en Globalización*, Caracas, Nueva Sociedad–CNCA-CLACSO, 1996.

19 Lawrence Grossberg, 'Cultural Studies, Modern Logics, and Theories of Globalisation', in Angela McRobbie (ed.), *Back to Reality: Social Experience and Cultural Studies*, Manchester University Press, 1997.

20 Sergio Zermeño, [ref. to follow]

21 Francis Fukuyama, 'The End of History', in *The National Interest*, no. 16, (Summer 1989).

22 Paul Virilio, 'Un mundo sobre-expuesto', *Le Monde Diplomatique*, August 1997.

23 Manuel Castells, 'Crimen Global', in *El País*, 21 February 1997. See the same author's, *La era de la información: Economia, Sociedad y Cultura*, vols. 1 & 2, Madrid, Alianza Editorial, 1997.

Translated by Lorraine Leu

2

Brazil: The Modern in the Tropics

Ruben George Oliven

And how tedious it has become to be modern
Now I will be eternal.

Eterno (Carlos Drummond de Andrade, 1955)

The monument is very modern
It said nothing about the style of my suit
To hell with everything else . . .

Tropicália (Caetano Veloso, 1968)

I

The theme of modernity is a constant in Brazil and has preoccupied our intellectuals at various times over the years. It is a question of knowing where we stand in relation to the 'advanced world', first Europe and later the United States. In Brazil modernity is frequently seen as something which comes from outside, and which should be admired or adopted, or, on the contrary, viewed with caution by both the elites and the people. Importation implies intellectuals going to countries of the centre to seek out current ideas and models there; equally, it implies propagating these ideas in the new soil of Brazilian society. Modernity is also frequently confused with the idea of contemporaneity, in the sense that adopting everything that is in vogue in advanced countries is seen as being modern.

The way in which Brazilian intellectuals have considered these questions has varied. Thus at certain times Brazilian culture has been greatly devalued by the elites, who have regarded European culture (or more recently North American culture) as the model of modernity to be attained. In a reaction to this, certain manifestations of Brazilian culture have at other times become highly prized, with the exaltation of symbols such as Macunaíma, the Brazilian hero who has no character and is born lazy, from the eponymous Modernist novel (Mario de Andrade 1993), as well as carnival, samba and football (Oliven 1986).

II

In 1808 the Portuguese royal family, fleeing the Napoleonic advance, transferred to Brazil, which turned from a colony into the seat of the monarchy and viceroyalty. The thirteen years when the court remained in Rio de Janeiro were of great political and economic importance and were followed by the declaration of Brazil's independence in 1822. The opening of Brazilian ports to external trade brought a flood of foreign traders and travellers into the country. Several of them left very interesting descriptions of life and customs in Brazil during the nine-teenth century. A great many of these descriptions are focused on Rio de Janeiro, where the royal family lived, and which therefore became a cosmopolitan city where the better-off tried to behave in ways they presumed to be European. In Rio in particular, the cultural diffusion of an eminently urban, bourgeois lifestyle began to develop among the upper classes. There was less evidence of this in other cities, where life was quite simple in comparison with the capital (Pereira de Queiroz 1973).

The refined tastes of Rio de Janeiro's upper classes were observed by George Gardner, the British superindent of the Royal Botanical Gardens of Ceylon, who travelled in Brazil from 1836 to 1841: 'The great desire of the inhabitants seems to be to give an European air to the city. This has already been accomplished to a great extent, partly from the influx of Europeans themselves, and partly by those Brazili-ans who have visited Europe either for their education or otherwise.' (Gardner 1942: 5). But one should not generalise about the rest of the country based on what was happening in Rio de Janeiro . The 'modernisation' which the visitors were observing was in fact limited not only to the then capital of Brazil, but also to its upper class with which they had closest contact. Pereira de Queiroz formulated the hypothesis that the spread of a bourgeois lifestyle in Brazil began roughly in 1820, long before the country began to be industrialised. This new way of life differentiated the population not just economi-cally but even more so culturally, since the upper strata of society adopted the refinements and pretensions of intellectual life as a symbol of distinction. From this period on, life in the wealthier cities began to be very different at all social levels compared to that in the countryside (Pereira de Queiroz 1973: 210).

The opposite process occurs when intellectuals and elites value what is considered most authentically Brazilian. This tendency appeared as early as the second half of the nineteenth century in the writings of representatives of the Indianist school of literature and reached its peak in the novels of José de Alencar, with the celebration of Brazil's cultural roots in the Indian and in rural life, etc. Even so, the way of treating the issue was imported, appealing to European romanticism. The portrayal was that of the 'noble savage', when in fact Brazil's indigenous population had long been suffering the deleterious consequences of contact with white people. We see here an apparent discrepancy between reality and representation.

III

There is a widespread sense in Brazil that ideas and cultural practices which are appropriated from outside are somehow 'out of place', in particular with regard to political ideas. Brazil was one of the last countries to abolish slavery; it finally did so in 1888, in response to pressure from Britain. Although the Brazilian economy was for three centuries based on the exploitation of slave labour, part of the political elite at the time adhered to the liberal ideas created in and applied to Europe. Schwarz (1977) has argued that such a liberal ideology was 'out of place' in Imperial Brazil: what prevailed there was not the idea of human rights, but rather the oppression of slaves and paternalistic favour towards whites who did not own land.

This 'ideas out of place' thesis is not entirely sustainable, however. Logically, slavery was not incompatible with economic liberalism, since for the Brazilian elites slaves were commodities to be used and exchanged like any others.

Strictly speaking, nothing is ever 'in place' – everything leaves one place and enters another, where it is adapted to the interests of different groups and changing circumstances. Cultural borrowing is a constant in any culture (Burke 1997). As historians and anthropologists have shown, the cultural dynamic implies a process of de-territorialisation and re-territorialisation: ideas and practices which originate in one space end up migrating to others. There they find a very different atmosphere from that in which they originated, but they end up being adapted to the new context and so 'enter a new place'. One of the creative aspects of the Brazilian cultural dynamic is precisely the capacity to direct what comes from outside, re-elaborate it and give it its own characteristics, transforming it into something different and new (Oliven 1984).

There are several key moments in this process in Brazil. First, the military and politicians who proclaimed the Republic in 1889 were strongly imbued with positivist ideology. In spite of having been created in France, positivism had much more success in Brazil than in its country of origin. Even today there exists in Brazil what is called positivist architecture, referring to the buildings which were commissioned by those in power during the Old Republic (1889–1930), and positivist temples in cities like Rio de Janeiro and Porto Alegre. The Brazilian flag has as its motto the phrase 'Order and Progress', demonstrating the centrality of Auguste Comte in the country's symbolism (Carvalho 1990).

From the point of view of Brazil's elites, positivism was an ideology which foreshadowed modernity and justified the authoritarian means of attaining it. It was positivist soldiers who first considered what to do about the indigenous people. Thus, Marshal Rondon, whose life was dedicated to the indigenous cause, urged that they be resected and not eliminated, even though eventually they needed, in his view, to be integrated into civilisation. Positivism was a way not just for Brazil to modernise itself in relation to Europe, but for Indians to 'civilise' themselves in relation to Brazil. It was all conceived in terms of stages in an evolutionist linear approach that conformed to positivism's emphasis on progress.

The tendency of intellectuals to contemplate Brazil and discuss the viability of a civilisation in the tropics originates from the period of the Old Republic. There were two perceived obstacles to this civilising project: race and climate. Intellectuals like Silvio Romero, Euclides da Cunha, Nina Rodrigues, Oliveira Vianna and Arthur Ramos, concerned to explain Brazilian society through the interaction of race and the geographic environment, were profoundly pessimistic and prejudiced with regard to the Brazilian, who was characterised as apathetic and indolent. Our intellectual life was seen as infected with a subjective and morbid lyricism and as philosophically and scientifically impoverished. The only solution envisaged was the whitening of the population through the arrival of European immigrants.

It was only in the 1930s, as a result of the influence of Gilberto Freyre's work, that a new racial vision of Brazil was created in which the country was seen as a tropical civilisation with unique characteristics, such as *mestiçagem* (racial mixture) and the construction of a racial democracy. In Freyre's vision racial mixture is not a problem but an advantage in relation to other nations. The ideology of 'racial democracy' is so strong in Brazil that it permeates aspects of sociological thinking and Brazilian 'common-sense' (Ortiz 1985).

IV

In 1922 Brazil celebrated 100 years of independence from Portugal. In that year the Communist Party of Brazil was created. Strictly speaking this was Brazil's first national party, as until that period political parties were regionally based. It was in the same year that the first lieutenants' revolt occurred. The lieutenants were young officials of the national army who, having become acquainted with different parts of Brazil, felt a diffuse *malaise* in relation to the conduct of politics by the elites and began to develop authoritarian projects for governing the people.

It was also in 1922 that the Week of Modern Art took place in São Paulo. This event was led by young intellectuals from the elite of São Paulo, a city which was beginning to emerge as a future metropolis. With all its complexity and ideological differentiation, the Modernist movement which developed with the Week of 1922 represents a watershed. On the one hand, it signified the re-contemporisation of Brazil with regard to cultural and artistic movements occurring abroad; on the other, it entailed a search for national roots, emphasising what was thought to be most culturally authentic in Brazil.

One of the movement's contributions was to pose the question of the artistic–cultural contemporisation of an underdeveloped country while at the same time addressing the problem of nationhood. Thus in the second phase of Modernism (1924 onwards), the attack on the past was replaced by the emphasis on the elaboration of a national culture, with a rediscovery of Brazil by Brazilians. In spite of a certain bias towards São Paulo, the Modernists rejected regionalism, as they believed that it was only through nationalism that the universal could be reached. Thus, 'for the modernists, access to the universal was facilitated by the affirmation of Brazilianness' (Moraes 1978: 105). This is clear in a letter from Mário de Andrade, one of the principal exponents of Modernism, to Sérgio Millet:

> The immediate problem. The problem of being something. And one can only be, by being national. We have the current, national, moralising, human problem of Brazilianising Brazil. The immediate problem, modernism,

observe well, because today only national art is valued . . . And we will only be
universal when our Brazilian factor can share in a universal richness. (Quoted
in Moraes 1978: 52)

A letter that Mário de Andrade wrote in 1924 to the poet Carlos
Drummond de Andrade points in the same direction: 'We will only be
civilised in relation to well-established civilisations the day we create the
ideal, a Brazilian orientation. Then we will pass from imitation to a
phase of creation. And then we will be universal, because we are
national.' (Mário de Andrade 1983a). In accordance with this position,
Mário de Andrade became a self-proclaimed 'apprentice tourist', pur-
suing intensive research and travel, with a view to studying the elements
which made up Brazilian culture (Mário de Andrade 1983b).

In 1928 Oswald de Andrade, one of the exponents of the Modernist
Week, launched the Anthropophagist Manifesto. The text began by
affirming that 'only Anthropophagy unites us. Socially. Economically.
Philosophically'. (Oswald de Andrade 1978: 13). At the end the author
dated the manifesto as composed in the Year 374 of the Devouring of
Bishop Sardinha, a reference to the catholic Portuguese cleric who was
shipwrecked off the coast of Brazil and eaten by Indians in 1554.

What was being proposed in the Anthropophagist Manifesto was a
Brazilian modernity, characterised by knowing how to ingest and cre-
atively digest what comes from outside. Moreover, what Oswald de
Andrade argued was that Brazilians had been dedicating themselves to
this practice since the beginning of their history, in a joyful and
intuitive way: 'Before the Portuguese discovered Brazil, Brazil had
discovered happiness.' 'Mirth is the acid test' (Oswald de Andrade
1978: 18).

According to Moraes,

The anthropophagic instinct, on the one hand, destroys by devouring
elements of imported culture; on the other hand, it assures their survival in
our reality, through a process of transformation/absorption of certain
foreign elements. Or in other words: before the colonising process, there
was in the country a culture in which anthropophagy was practiced, and
which reacted, always anthropophagically but in varying levels, to the contact
of new diverse elements brought by Europeans. It is this anthropophagic
instinct which must now be valorised by the cultural project defended by
Oswald de Andrade. It is characterised by a tenacious defense of intuition
and by the capacity to synthesise within itself the prominent traits of
nationality which guarantees the unity of the nation (Moraes 1978: 144).

V

It is significant that, while the Modernist movement of 1922 emerged in São Paulo, a city which was already emerging as a future industrial metropolis, Gilberto Freyre's 1926 Regionalist Manifesto would be launched in Recife, at the time the most developed capital in the north-east. The 1926 movement was in a certain sense the inverse of that of 1922. It did not contemporise Brazilian culture in relation to the outside world; on the contrary, it sought to preserve not just tradition in general, but specifically that of an economically backward region.

Basically, the Regionalist Manifesto developed two interlinked themes: the defence of the region as a unit of national organisation and the preservation of the regional and traditional values of Brazil in general and of the north-east in particular. The Manifesto – which fifty years later Freyre would call 'regionalist, traditionalist and modernist in its own way' – defends the popular, which should be protected from 'bad cosmopolitanism and false modernity' (Freyre 1976: 80).

The need to reorganise Brazil – the first central theme of the Manifesto and a constant concern of intellectuals at the end of the nineteenth century and the beginning of the twentieth – was seen as resulting from the fact that since attaining nationhood, Brazil had suffered the harmful consequences of adopting foreign models, which had been imposed without taking into consideration the country's peculiarities, including its physical and social diversity. The formulation of an alternative system of organisation for Brazil was based on rejecting such incompatible models. The discussion of the suitability of importing foreign models and ideas was a recurring theme among Brazil's intellectuals, and the Manifesto of 1926 also dealt with this by analysing the question of tradition.

In calling for the need for inter-regional articulation, Freyre touched on an important and topical problem: namely, how to allow regional differences to exist within a national unity, in a country with Brazil's continental dimensions. What Freyre affirmed was that the only way of being national in Brazil was first to be regional. In a way, the Modernists arrived at a similar conclusion in the second phase of modernism, when they realised that the only way to be universal was first to be national.

Yet Freyre's argument was, in a way, the opposite of the Modernists', as it was not based on the need for cultural modernisation through external influence, but rather on the criticism of the evils of progress and the importation of foreign customs and values.

The preservation of the regional and traditional values of Brazil in general, and of the north-east in particular, was the second great theme of the Regionalist Manifesto. Freyre criticised the elites' habit of imitating customs which they considered modern, a tendency already signalled by Pereira de Queiroz (1973) with respect to the city of Rio de Janeiro following the arrival of the Portuguese royal family, as we have seen.

It is significant that on making an intransigent defence of the values of the north-east and the need to preserve them, Freyre highlighted things considered backward and/or symbols of poverty. For instance, he included a eulogy to the *mocambos* (shacks) as an example of the north-east's contribution to Brazilian culture, which he conceived as a form of human shelter adapted to tropical nature and as an economic solution to the problem of poor housing: 'maximum usage by man in a regional nature, represented by wood, straw, lianas, grass, easily available to the poor.' (Freyre 1976: 59). He also defended narrow streets and criticised the tendency, already apparent, to build wide avenues, and the mania for changing regional street names and the names of old places to celebrate the great and good of the day, or to politically insignificant dates. Another aspect defended by Freyre was north-eastern cuisine. After affirming that the tradition of north-eastern cooking was under threat and that tinned sweets and conserves were the order of the day, Freyre prophesied that 'a cuisine in crisis means a whole civilisation is in danger: the danger of losing its character' (Freyre 1976: 72).

On appointing himself the bastion for the defence of the popular, the author of the Manifesto constructed an opposition which, in the final analysis, can be summarised as: popular and regional equals traditional (good); cosmopolitan equals modernism (bad). His position was very close to that of the Romantics, who were concerned with popular culture in Europe in the nineteenth century, and for whom the authenticity contained in manifestations of the popular constituted the essence of the national (Ortiz 1992).

At least two readings of the Regionalist Manifesto are possible. The first would regard it as a document elaborated by an intellectual representing a rural, peripheral aristocracy and seeing the social order undergoing transformations which undermined the traditional norms of domination. His reaction was traditionalist, similar to the aristocratic reaction to the changes brought about by urbanisation and industrialisation and expressed in the criticism of the loss of community values and cultural purity that supposedly existed in the past.

A second reading, however, would highlight, behind the conservative orientation of the Manifesto, themes still current in Brazil today. It is precisely in the fusion of a conservative perspective with the raising of questions still unresolved in Brazil that the originality of the Regionalist Manifesto resides. It contains a series of recurring questions in our history: unitary state versus federation, nation versus region, unity versus diversity, national versus foreign, popular versus erudite, tradition versus modernity.

Brazil continues to discuss the formulation of models to organise the nation and that debate inevitably ends up as a discussion of what is national (and therefore authentic for some, but backward for others) and what is foreign (and therefore spurious for some, but modern for others). In other words, the country continues to ponder the question of national identity. This question re-emerges and is reformulated in new and different contexts.

VI

For a long time Brazil's population was predominantly rural. This led several intellectuals to believe that the country had an 'agrarian vocation'. Writing at the beginning of the twentieth century, Oliveira Vianna maintained that:

> Since the beginning of our history, we have been a people of farmers and herdsmen ... Urbanism is an extremely modern condition of our social evolution. Our whole history is the history of an agricultural people, it is the history of a society of farmhands and herders. It is in the countryside that our race and the intimate strengths of our civilisation were formed. The dynamism of our history in the colonial period comes from the countryside. The admirable stability of our society in the imperial period has its origins in the countryside. (Oliveira Vianna 1933: 49)

The extent to which some politicians still believed in the 'agrarian vocation' of Brazil in the first decades of the twentieth century is clear from the following affirmation made by Júlio Prestes, Getúlio Vargas' adversary in the presidential elections which ended by providing the pretext for the Revolution of 1930:

> [T]he *fazendeiro* [landowner] is the type that represents our nationality and the *fazenda* [landed estate] is still the Brazilian home par excellence, where labour is married to the sweetness of life and the honesty of customs completes the happy scene.... Brazil rests on this social nucleus expressed by fazendas. (quoted in Pereira 1965: 88–89)

If we compare this bucolic reverie with that of Getúlio Vargas in a 1943 speech in Volta Redonda, where the first Brazilian state ironworks was constructed, it is clear that there had occurred – at least at the level of discourse – a shift from an agrarian ideology to a more industrial one:

> The basic problem of our economy will soon be altered. The country that was semi-colonial, agrarian, importer of manufactured goods, exporter of raw materials, will be able to assume the responsibilities of an autonomous industrial life, providing its defence and equipment needs. The solution can be delayed no longer. Even the most hardened pro-agrarian conservatives understand that it is not possible to depend on the importation of machines and tools, when a hoe, that indispensable and primitive agrarian instrument, costs the labourer 30 *cruzeiros*, or, based on the average salary, a week's work. (Ianni 1971: 63)

The changes suggested in this speech, however, have deeper roots, which can be traced to the Old Republic (1889–1930). In that period, Brazil underwent important transformations which had broader repercussions in the New Republic (1930 onwards). To put it briefly, these transformations were: the creation of an industry of substitution in consumer goods; the growth of cities which were capitals of regional markets; the crisis of coffee; the crisis of the system based on political alliances of agrarian oligarchies (the 'politics of the governors'); and the outbreak of social and military revolts in the twenties which culminated in the Revolt of 1930.

It was during this period that a more centralised State apparatus was created and power increasingly shifted from the regional sphere to the national. For example, the State abolished inter-state taxes and began to intervene more in the economy, facilitating the use of part of the surplus wealth created by the agrarian oligarchies to initiate the process of industrialisation, while simultaneously maintaining the privileges of these oligarchies in an altered form. On the social level, the State regulated relations between capital and labour, creating labour legislation and a Ministry of Labour. It also created the Ministry of Education, to whom a fundamental role in the creation of nationhood would fall, to be achieved through the standardisation of the educational system. This included the introduction of national elements to the school curriculum and the cultural weakening of ethnic minorities (Schwartzman, Bomeny & Costa 1984).

From this period onwards it was necessary to rethink the country, which was undergoing a process of political and economic consolidation and which was to endure the consequences of the 1929 crisis and the Second World War. Nationalism gained impetus and the state was consolidated. In fact, it was the State which took upon itself the task of nation-building. This tendency was greatly accentuated during the dictatorship of the 'Estado Novo' (New State) (1937–45), when elected governors were replaced by administrators, and regional states' militia lost their power – measures which increased political and administrative centralisation. On the level of culture and ideology, the prohibition of teaching in foreign languages, the introduction of the educational discipline of Morality and Civics, the creation of the Department of Press and Propaganda (whose responsibility, apart from censorship, was the exaltation of the virtues of work) helped to create a model of nationhood centralised by the State.

In fact, the changes that occurred between 1930 and 1945 were profound. Therefore, when at the end of the Second World War the Estado Novo ended and a National Constituent Assembly was elected with the task of drawing up a new model of political and administrative organisation, Brazil was already a different country. Brazilians were beginning to lose their agrarian vocation; manufactured goods already accounted for 20 per cent of gross domestic product. The construction of highways and the abolition of the autonomy of individual states helped to unify the national internal market as well as diminishing the power of the local oligarchies. Migration from country to city increased and created new protagonists on the political scene: the urban masses who would serve as social agents under populism.

VII

The problematic of the national versus the foreign has been a constant feature of political life in Brazil. Thus in the post-war period, and specifically in the period from 1946 to 1964, the national question was resumed with intense debates pursued, for example, by the ISEB (Higher Institute for Brazilian Studies) and the CPCs (Popular Cultural Centres). In this period, among the accusations directed at Brazilian intellectuals were their colonised condition and their contribution to the creation of an alien culture, resulting from a situation of dependence. Hence the need for a vanguard to help produce an authentic national culture for the people, a category both vague and all-embracing.

The themes of progress and modernity were also burning issues during this period. It was a question of overcoming the condition of underdevelopment, a battle in which industry was a key element. Import substitution industries emerged, this time in durable goods, thus generating an even greater dependency in relation to foreign capital. This period also saw the creation of organs such as SUDENE (Superintendency of the Development of the North-East), whose explicit goal was to reduce regional inequalities, of which the north-east was considered the most significant example.

The inauguration of the new capital of Brasília in 1960, which would stimulate a westward march and consequently territorial integration, aroused heated debates revolving around its huge construction costs and the audacity of its architecture, which was considered extremely modern and advanced.

From 1964, with the seizure of power by the military, increasing political, economic and administrative centralisation of power was achieved by a number of means: the integration of the national market; the development of road, telephone and mass communications networks; the concentration of taxes at a federal level; the control of each individual state's military forces by the army; and intervention into states' politics. All of these processes diminished the power of the states substantially, so that if we compare the state presidents of the First Republic with the indirectly elected governors after 1964, we see that the latter usually were no more than agents of the President of the Republic, somewhat like the administrators of the New State, while the former enjoyed considerable autonomy.

The new regime took the accumulation of capital to higher levels, in association with foreign capital. There was new import substitution, so that today almost all consumer goods are produced within the country, and several of them, (including cultural) goods, are also exported. Brazil has undergone a process of uneven and combined development, creating extreme misery alongside elements of technical progress and modernity. From economic, political and cultural points of view, a new configuration has emerged.

Today, approximately 80 per cent of Brazil's population is urban, the majority of manufactured products consumed in the country are produced within its borders and the majority of its urban workforce are employed in the tertiary (service) sector. The country possesses a solid transport network and an efficient communications system, and the technical level of mass communications networks is comparable to that of the most developed countries. Brazil has nuclear power stations and offshore oil, carries out heart transplants, and has more than one hundred universities, several of them conducting post-graduate teaching.

In this context it is significant that the creators of Tropicalism, the artistic movement which emerged in 1968, were artists from the north-east, a region which continued to remain on the periphery. Tropicalism demonstrated, on a symbolic level, that Brazil's situation had changed significantly. Led by the Bahian composers Caetano Veloso and Gilberto Gil, Tropicalism proposed on the one hand an aesthetic and ideological rupture with the past, and on the other the resumption of themes raised by the Modernist Movement of 1922. Aesthetically, the rupture occurred through the introduction of instruments like the electric guitar and by the creation of dissonant rhythms; ideologically, the rupture was effected through the promotion of television as a means of expression, and by the fact that the Tropicalists sang of a Brazil in which there were planes in the air and barefoot children on the ground. In other words, this was a music which realised that the modern was increasingly articulated with the 'backward'.

The continuity of Tropicalism depended on its link with the Modernist Movement and the themes it stimulated – mainly those of the creator of the Anthropophagist Manifesto, Oswald de Andrade, whom Caetano Veloso admired greatly (Veloso 1997). This admiration resulted from the fact that Oswald de Andrade had thought of Brazil in an open way as a nation capable of digesting different, apparently contradictory influences.

During this period the debate about the national and the regional continued but was posed in new terms. Again the State claimed for itself the role of creator and bastion of national identity, responsible simultaneously for promoting progress and for keeping the memory of the nation alive. The State's initiation of a sweeping denationalisation programme was not viewed as contradictory, as the two issues were not seen to be connected. In this context, it is significant that it was the huge multinational companies like Shell and Xerox who began to invoke Brazilian folklore in their advertisements.

VIII

With the struggle for re-democratisation of the country and the process of political opening, which marked the end of the military cycle (1985), old questions began to resurface. Therefore, in spite of – or perhaps because of – growing centralisation, contrary tendencies can be observed, which are manifested in the emphasis on the need for a true federalism, the proclamation of the advantages of administrative decentralisation, the clamour for tax reform to increase the resources of the states and municipalities, and the affirmation of different regional identities (Oliven 1996). Such affirmations can be seen as a way of highlighting cultural differences and as a reaction to an attempt at cultural homogenisation. This rediscovery of difference – and the contemporary relevance of the question of federation in a period in which the country was fairly integrated from a political, economic and cultural point of view – suggests that in Brazil the national is first filtered through the regional.

It is precisely with the process of political liberalisation that culture began to gain more visibility in Brazil. New questions began to surface and popular movements began to be organised. Several of these movements are concerned more with issues often considered local and less important (although still fundamental) than with the great traditional themes.

What is evident in Brazil, after its re-democratisation, is an intense process of constituting new political actors and constructing new social identities. These include age (represented, for example, by youth as a social category), gender identity (such as the feminist and gay rights movements), religious identities (the growth of so-called popular religions), regional identities (the rebirth of regional cultures) and ethnic identities (represented by the black movements and the increasing organisation of indigenous communities).

The black movements focus discussion on the fact that in Brazil, a country which projects the image of a racial democracy, blacks are always in an inferior position with regard to income, employment, education, health and life expectancy. These groups also stress the importance of the fact that Brazil is a country with an impressive African presence, as well as the striking contribution of the black population to the cultural formation of Brazil, particularly in the areas of religion, music, dance, carnival, soccer and cuisine.

The indigenous movements, in turn, point to an alternative model of society to the extent that they assert a more integrated relationship with nature. Indigenous societies, where myth and magic are central elements, suggest that there are ways of thinking about the world other than with technical rationality.

IX

The advent of globalisation has strongly diversified Brazil's interaction with the rest of the world. Exchanges between different countries are unequal and depend on their positions in the world economic–political system. There are products – principally cultural – which are exported throughout the world on a growing scale. Among these are fast-food and televisual and musical products, manufactured by multinational corporations like MTV and CNN; in the same way, Hollywood cinema continues in its position of world hegemony. This has led some commentators to view Brazil as increasingly affected by cultural imperialism (Carvalho 1996–97). The situation, however, is more complex.

While for a long time people migrated to Brazil from elsewhere and the country imported manufactured goods and products of the culture industry, things have now changed. There are currently one and a half million Brazilians living abroad, the majority in the United States, Europe and Japan. With globalisation Brazil, traditionally a country that received immigrants, has begun to reverse the flow.

The exodus is not restricted to human migration, but is also evident in the export of material and cultural goods. For centuries, Brazil was an exporter of agricultural products and an importer of manufactured goods. Today the country exports a variety of manufactured goods, including aeroplanes. Consequently the idea of Brazil's 'rural vocation' has proved unsustainable. Brazil is currently an urban and industrialised country, whose goods compete on the world market.

Another area in which Brazil has begun to export is that of 'cultural goods'. Whereas in the past the country was seen as constantly importing ideas and modes of expression from the more developed world, today the situation has changed. Brazil continues, for example, to receive outside influences in the sphere of cinema and music, but for some time it has also been an exporter of culture, in the terms, for example, of religion, music and soap operas.

Religion is one of the areas where this has occured in a remarkable way. The penetration of Afro-Brazilian religions into Uruguay and Argentina is impressive, for these are countries which generally see themselves as European, and with little African influence. Equally, it is worth pointing out that the Universal Church of the Kingdom of God, a Pentecostal religion established in Brazil in 1977, has churches in more than forty other countries, including North America and members of the European Union, mobilising millions of faithful and large sums of money (Oro 1996).

With respect to music – apart from that which Brazil has always exported since the time of Carmen Miranda and, later, Bossa Nova – there are today Brazilian groups who compose songs in English and are successful in the United States and Europe. For instance, in order to seek out their roots, the members of the Brazilian band Sepultura went to a Xavante village in Mato Grosso. At the beginning of 1996 they launched an album called *Roots*, which in just fifteen days became one of the biggest-selling albums in Europe, surpassing Michael Jackson and

Madonna in Britain, and selling more than 500,000 copies in February
and March that year.

Globo, the largest Brazilian television network, has for some time
been producing the majority of the programmes it shows in Brazil. It
also exports its soap operas and series to countries like Portugal, France
and China, helping to make it a mass-media multinational.

During the populist phase of Brazil's history (1945–64), what came
from outside was often seen as impure, and therefore dangerous. Thus,
Coca-Cola and Hollywood films were often cited as examples of North-
American cultural imperialism, while samba and Cinema Novo (made
with 'an idea in the head and a camera in the hand', in the words of
the film-maker Glauber Rocha) were seen as examples of what was most
authentically national. Today the situation is more complex: the Coca-
Cola logo is on the shirts of our leading football teams and the English
rock-star Sting, sponsored by the same soft-drink company, professes to
defend the Indians of Brazil. The film *A Grande Arte* (1991), in spite of
being directed by a Brazilian and filmed in Brazil, has English dialogue.
Films like *O Quatrilho* (1995) and *O Que É Isto Companheiro* (1996) star
Rede Globo actors and compete for Oscars, their producers hiring
professional lobbyists to help them win awards.

X

One of the central aspects of the project of modernity was always that
of human emancipation. This meant that if technical modernity did
not engender social well-being and the achievement of full citizenship,
it lost its meaning. Now, however, Brazil is characterised by a shocking
contrast between a growing technological modernity and the failure to
bring about the social transformations which would give the majority of
the population access to the benefits of material progress.

In Brazil labour – particularly manual labour – is held in low esteem.
In Portuguese one word for 'to work' is 'mourejar', branding it as
something that should be left to the Moors; in Brazil a racist expression
refers to hard work as 'black man's work', a direct reference to slavery.
Even after the abolition of slavery and the introduction of waged labour
in factories, labour was still not valued, because the social order
continued to be extremely excluding. The construction of citizenship
in Brazil is an issue which has still to be fully addressed; there are still
widespread social and political relationships that show strong traces of
the colonial era and the legacy of slavery.

Brazil today is a society of immense social and economic inequality and, according to World Bank figures, has the worst income distribution in the world, with a monthly minimum wage of approximately US$100. Unlike other countries which underwent processes of urbanisation and industrialisation, Brazil's agrarian structure never altered, so there remain enormous, frequently unproductive landholdings. It is a country that underwent conservative modernisation, where the traditional combines with the modern, change articulates with continuity, and progress coexists with extreme poverty.

The concern in Brazil today is not to achieve technological modernity, for this has already been achieved to a large extent. The concern now is of a different order – namely, to decide which direction the country should follow. A key issue is: what should be done with the progress and wealth which have been generated? Will income and land continue to be concentrated in the hands of the few, or is there some way of redistributing them? In the age of globalisation this question has become more urgent, as neo-liberal policies introduced in several countries, including Brazil, have exacerbated unemployment and social exclusion.

XI

Modernisation is generally associated with the gradual replacement of the rich social networks of traditional societies by individualism. Brazil has followed a somewhat different path. Juridically speaking, we can bracket Brazil with other nations that have adopted individualist and liberal ideas, as is evident in the large number of relevant laws and regulations which exist in the country. But this is also a country in which personal relationships continue to be extremely important (Da Matta 1991); as a result a bureaucratic, formal and individualistic organisation of social life is combined with a personalised and informal way of resolving problems which modernity itself presents on a daily basis. This can mean that just as personal relations are used to maintain privilege and demarcate social frontiers, they can also be used to counterbalance excessive bureaucracy and formal social practices.

This raises the question of how Brazil will reconcile the characteristics associated with modernity with its particular ways of life. As in other Latin American countries, Brazilian intellectuals of different generations have been greatly concerned to discover whether in their countries the characteristics of rationality associated with modernity would be practicable, or if they would take a less rational and more emotional and personal route. Thus our choice of Brazilian heroes oscillates between the Duke of Caxias – patron of the Brazilian Army and symbol of extreme seriousness – and Macunaíma – the hero who has no character and is born lazy. The difficulty has always lain in reconciling the demands of modernity with Brazil's peculiar characteristics.

Such challenges indicate the syncretic character of Brazilian modernity. Just as there is a certain degree of *mestiçagem* of the population which is sometimes denied (when the 'whitening' of Brazil is being highlighted) and at other times exalted (when the 'dark-skinned' character of Brazil is asserted), Brazilian culture is a hybrid construction realised through a variety of creative appropriations. It is possible that the peculiarity of Brazilian society lies precisely in its capacity to take on those aspects of modernity that are of interest to it and to transform them into something suited to its own needs, in which the modern interacts with the traditional, the rational with the emotional and the formal with the personal.

Bibliography

Andrade, Mário de (1983a), *A Lição do Amigo. Cartas a Carlos Drummond de Andrade*, Rio de Janeiro, José Olympio.

Andrade, Mário de (1983b), *O Turista Aprendiz*. São Paulo, Duas Cidades.

Andrade, Mário (1993), *Macunaíma: o herói sem nenhum caráter*. Belo Horizonte, Villarica (first edition: 1928).

Andrade, Oswald de, 'Manifesto Antropófago', in *Do Pau-Brasil à Antropofagia e as Utopias*, Rio de Janeiro, Civilização Brasileira, 1978.

Burke, Peter, 'Inevitáveis empréstimos culturais'. *Folha de São Paulo*, 27 June 1997, caderno 5, p. 3.

Carvalho, José Jorge de (1996–97), 'Imperialismo Cultural Hoje: uma questão silenciada', *Revista USP*, no. 32, São Paulo.

Carvalho, José Murilo de (1990), *A Formação das Almas: O Imaginário de República no Brasil*, São Paulo, Companhia das Letras.

Da Matta, Roberto (1991), *Carnivals, Rogues and Hoeroes: An Interpretation of the Brazilian Dilemma*, Notre Dame, University of Notre Dame Press.

Freyre, Gilberto (1976), *Manifesto Regionalista*, Recife, Instituto Joaquim Nabuco de Pesquisas Sociais.

Gardner, George (1973), *Travels in the Interior of Brazil, principally through the northern provinces and the gold and diamond districts, during the years 1836–1841*, Boston, Milford House Inc.

Ianni, Octávio (1971), *Estado e Planejamento Econômico no Brasil (1930–1970)*, Rio de Janeiro, Civilização Brasileira.

Moraes, Eduardo Jardim de (1978), *A Brasilidade Modernista: Sua Dimensão Filosófica*, Rio de Janeiro.

Oliveira Vianna, Francisco José de (1933), *Evolução do Povo Brasileiro*, São Paulo, Editora Nacional.

Oliven, Ruben George (1984), 'The Production and Consumption of Culture in Brazil', *Latin American Perspectives*, vol. 11, no. 1, Riverside, California, USA.

Oliven, Ruben George (1986), 'State and Culture in Brazil', *Studies in Latin American Popular Culture*, vol. 5, Las Cruces, USA.

Oliven, Ruben George (1994), *Tradition Matters: Modern Gaúcho Identity in Brazil*, New York, Columbia University Press.

Oro, Ari Pedro (1996), 'Fronteiras Religiosas em Movimento no Cono-Sul', *Revista de Antropologia*, vol. 39, no. 1.

Ortiz, Renato (1985), *Cultura Brasileira e Identidade Nacional*, São Paulo, Brasiliense.

Ortiz, Renato (1992), *Cultura Popular: Românticos e Folcloristas*, São Paulo, Olho d'Água.

Pereira, Luiz (1965), *Trabalho e Desenvolvimento no Brasil*, São Paulo, DIFEL.

Pereira De Queiroz, Maria Isaura de (1973), 'Do Rural e do Urbano no Brasil', in Tamás Szmrecsányi and Oriowaldo Queda (eds.), *Vida Rural e Mudança Social no Brasil*, São Paulo, Editora Nacional.

Schwartzman, Simon, Bomeny, Helena Maria Bousquet and Costa, Vanda Maria Ribeiro (1984), *Tempos de Capanema*, Rio de Janeiro, Paz e Terra.

Schwarz, Roberto (1977), *Ao Vencedor as Batatas*, São Paulo, Duas Cidades.

Veloso, Caetano (1997), *Verdade Tropical*. São Paulo, Companhia das Letras.

Translated by Lorraine Leu

Part II

Modernity in the City

3

Peregrinations, Visions and the City: From Canudos to Brasília, the Backlands become the City and the City becomes the Backlands

Nicolau Sevcenko

There is an extremely revealing passage in the famous story *A Hora e a Vez de Augusto Matraga* (*The Hour and the Time of Augusto Matraga*), by the writer Guimarães Rosa. In it the title character, after a long period spent working voluntarily for a black peasant couple who had saved his life, suddenly decides to abandon the precarious small farm in which they live. Without any justification for his decision, he announces to his companions: 'Farewell, my friends, I can remain here no longer, as my time will soon come, and I must meet it elsewhere! . . . When the heart commands, we must obey! . . . And if I never return, everything that was mine will be yours.' He accepts a donkey which his hosts offer him, seats himself on the saddle and allows the animal to take whatever direction it wants, heading aimlessly into the backlands. To sing, alone, was not a sin. The roads sang . . . He wandered in the region of the rubber tappers, who gave him a place to sleep in their huts with roofs and walls of munity palm. He returned to the riverbank where the riverbank dwellers fed him manioc mush with pepper and fish. Then, he went off again.

At a certain moment in this aimless wandering, in the middle of the scrub-land of the backlands, Augusto Matraga comes across a blind man who has adopted the same practice. In search of his birthplace, he had roped himself to an old goat and allowed the animal to drift at random along the pathways, following it wherever it chose to roam. When the donkey sets off again, separating the two wanderers, Matraga just has time to shout in the direction of the blind man and the goat: 'I'm game for anything . . . How good it is to wander at will, bound to no one and at peace with God! . . .'[1]

What the extract above reveals is the itinerant, unstable and fluid order which characterises the most extensive and profound dimensions of Brazilian society. One of the first authors to perceive and study this systematically was Euclides da Cunha. In his attempt to understand the peculiar nature of backlands society, by means of research into the tragedy of the peasant rebellion in Canudos, he realised how superficial were the analyses which conflated the history of Brazil with that of the narrow coastal strips where the Portuguese colonists had settled with their sugar-cane plantations, their *entrepôt* cities, their military forts and fleets guaranteeing permanent contact with Europe, their true source of identity. His master work is not called *Os Sertões* (*Rebellion in the Backlands*) by accident. He insisted that a fundamentally different approach was necessary in order to understand the specific social formation of Brazil. In an article published in the newspaper *O Estado de São Paulo* in March 1902, he revealed his central concern, aimed as much at rethinking the practice of historiography as at a definition of the country's future direction: '(I had in mind) the political idea of the defense of the territory and the aim of incorporating the vigorous core of the backlands into our fragile lives, lacking autonomy and focused on the Atlantic . . . Let us look to the backlands.'[2]

It was the historian Sérgio Buarque de Holanda, however, who took the intellectual agenda of Euclides da Cunha furthest. In his first book, the classic *Raízes do Brasil* of 1936, he takes up the same theme of the need for a change in perspective to correct the distorted view of history created by a colonial perspective. 'Bringing from distant countries our ways of life, our institutions, our ideas, taking pride in maintaining them all in often unfavourable and hostile environments, we are still today strangers in our own land.'[3] In his later studies, *Monções* (Monsoons) of 1945 and *Caminhos e Fronteiras* (Paths and Borders) of 1957, he describes in rich and minute detail the lack of fixity and itinerant quality of backlands societies, their obstinate resistance to attempts by landowners and their representatives to impose (either formally via the colonial authorities or via threats and chicanery) a sedentary and subordinate way of life.

These works clashed with the dominant interpretations, which insisted on reducing Brazilian society to the simplistic polarity of land-owners of European origin on the one hand and slaves, indigenous peoples and (especially) blacks, on the other. They demonstrate the existence of a whole gamut of free people: acculturated Indians, poor whites and emancipated slaves, but, particularly, different ethnic combinations involving people from each one of these three groups. Living on the edges of the large landholdings, these men and women formed a free peasantry, each in a minimal unit of production, the small farm, around which they maintained a small clearing for planting corn, manioc and other foodstuffs, and reared small animals. Their specific skills and the assistance they could provide with tasks involving movement over wide areas, like woodcutting, canoeing, muleteering, and cattle droving, turned them into a workforce much sought after by the landowners, who were unable to rely on their own slaves for such tasks.[4]

This situation created a very tense relationship between the peasants and land-owners, who were interested in securing the labour of the free peasants at the lowest possible cost, if necessary by using their personal militias, or troops under the colonial authorities' control. This situation provoked a distinct, standard response from these free men and women. It was evident to them that their powers of negotiation were proportional to their exposure and vulnerability to the pressures exerted by the land-holders and officials. However, the greater their capacity for movement, to search out the most distant, virgin territories, the better their ability to negotiate favourably with the landowners was, by threatening to leave the fixed orbit of their authority.

The basic strategy which enabled this freedom of movement was the capacity to live with a minimum of material resources, all derived from nature: mud huts with palm-leaf roofs, straw mats, fibre nets, clay pots, objects made of wood, bone, leather and stone – objects and practices absorbed from the nomadic cultures of indigenous and African peoples. In addition, they relied on rigorous rituals of hospitality, charity and mutual help which strengthened community ties, deeply embedded in the mystical beliefs typical of popular Brazilian Catholicism. Faced with a threat of any kind, all they had to do was give away or burn everything and leave. There was nothing to lose, nothing important was left behind and there were always extensive areas of untouched fertile land available elsewhere. Additionally, they could always count on the fraternal support of other small farmers or communities that they encountered. Mobility was the most direct expression and sense of autonomy. In Augusto Matraga's words: 'It's all the same to me! Wherever the donkey takes me, we'll go, because we're going with God! . . .'.[5]

In addition to the routes of the mule caravans or the gullies and trails of the extensive backlands of the interior, there was always the alternative of the network of rivers which cut across the whole Brazilian territory, crossing the most dense and impenetrable areas of the tropical forest, 'the vast fluvial route which, with brief intervals, embraces almost all of Brazil, from the Tietê to Amazônia . . .'.[6] The country's climate is distinguished by two basic periods, the rainy season, when the rains are intense around summer, followed by the dry season around winter. This created a constant pattern, with the population of the backlands tending to move on in simple boats, modelled on indigenous canoes, taking advantage of the quickening of the currents during the rainy season – the so-called monsoons – settling afterwards on virgin land to begin their planting, when the waters receded in the dry period. In this situation, the boat itself became a home for long periods of people's lives, when they became an integral part of the continuously oscillating flux of the rivers, the swamps and marshes, surrounded by an intensely green landscape completely invaded by water.

The highest institutional authority, the Portuguese Crown, legitimated this errant activity. In its attempt to maintain control over this territory of continental dimensions, and taking into account its small population, the Portuguese government encouraged from the outset any practice which entailed the effective occupation of the colony. For this reason the royal government reserved the right, from the start, to revoke concessions if, within a determined period, there was no occupation of land through settlement.

The land itself, abundant as it was, was worth nothing – value was conferred on it by labour, earning the Crown dividends and guaranteeing the protection of territory. Thus, wherever someone, even without a document or previous title, resolved to settle and work, either on their own account or using slave labour, the authorities recognised this as legitimate possession. Accordingly, the small lots occupied by the farmers constituted, ipso facto, a spontaneous form of settlement recognised and guaranteed by Portuguese law. If they tended to move, in order to escape exploitation by landowners or because they were attracted by virgin land, this did not alter the fact that wherever they settled and worked, they created a situation of indisputable juridical legitimacy.

This situation changed abruptly from the middle of the nineteenth century. Faced with pressures to abolish slavery, domestically and from Britain, Brazilian landowners, through their representatives in the

Imperial Parliament, established a new law in 1850 linking ownership of land to a formal written title dependent on juridical recognition. The main underlying idea was to create a rural proletariat, expelling the farmers from their lands and so forcing them to offer themselves as cheap, abundant waged labour.[7] This new situation increased social tensions, which were already intense, to explosive levels; but this was not an isolated event. In fact, from the second half of the nineteenth century onwards a new and complex constellation emerged, shaking the very foundations of Brazilian social and economic life, bringing into conflict complex technical–scientific transformations and archaic manifestations of the sacred – a bloody duel between technology and the epiphanic. On different levels, this confrontation remained central in the history of contemporary Brazil and even today it manifests itself in the most unexpected forms and representations.

This new constellation began to take shape around 1870, when the Scientific–Technological Revolution, a phenonmenon of global significance representing a major quantitative and qualitative leap in comparison to the first phase of industrialisation almost a century earlier – was being consolidated. This first moment in the rise of an industrialised economy, centred on Britain and focused on the production of manufactured fabrics, was based on three basic factors; iron, coal and steam engines, leading to the emergence of the first productive units: factories.

However, the scale and nature of the Scientific–Technological Revolution, sometimes defined as a second 'industrial revolution' of industrialisation, was incomparably greater. It was based on the use of new scientific discoveries in the process of industrial production. These enabled the production of steel and gave rise to chemical industries, power stations and techniques for the extraction and refinement of petroleum, creating productive units and industrial complexes, involving hundreds, or even thousands of workers, technicians and engineers. The new sources of energy, derived from petroleum and electricity, promoted the development of new kinds of equipment, machines and means of transport and communication, which rapidly and extensively transformed the whole landscape, apparatus and practices of production on a global scale.[8]

These transformations occurred in a concentrated fashion in the countries of Northern Europe, then spread to the United States and soon after to Japan and Russia, unleashing among them an aggressive competition to guarantee consumer markets for their products, as well as suppliers of raw materials for their factories. It was this expansionist stimulus which led these nations to appropriate and carve up between themselves wide areas of the African and Asian continents, or to struggle for control of areas of Latin America. Moreover, in order to instil in them the way of life, practices of production and patterns of consumption appropriate to the new scientific–technological economy, it was necessary to go beyond mere territorial occupation or control and transform the way of life of traditional, local societies.

It was these attempts to change societies, their cultures and secular practices, which unleashed a series of revolts, uprisings and regional wars against the European, American, Russian and Japanese invaders between the second half of the nineteenth century and the beginning of the twentieth. These insurrections proliferated all over the world and were usually suppressed by means of widespread massacres, guaranteed by the inconquerable technical superiority of European armaments – in particular the new repeating firearms, artillery and howitzers, chemical explosives and incendiary weapons. These conflagrations formed a continuous sequence, including: the Indian Insurrection (1857–58), the Tai-Ping Rebellion in China (1850–66), the American Civil War (1861–65), the Meiji Restoration in Japan (1868), the Algerian Insurrection (1871), the Religious Reform of Al Afgahani in Afghanistan (1871–79), the Egyptian National Movement (1879–1882). In Latin America, this process was concentrated in particular around the economic and strategic axis represented by the River Plate and its network of rivers. Britain supported the military alliance between the Brazilian empire, Uruguay and Argentina against Paraguayan–Guarani resistance, under the leadership of Solano López (1864–70).[9]

The Paraguayan War created a debt crisis which destabilised the Brazilian Empire. It was in the context of this process of institutional destabilisation that the Republican Party was founded (1870), proposing the abolition of the monarchy, and that a new elite of young intellectuals, artists, politicians and members of the military emerged – the so-called 'generation of '70' – committed to a programme of modernisation of the 'ossified' structures of Empire, in accordance with the scientific and technical guidelines emanating from Europe. Their sources of inspiration were the current scientistic modes of thought: Spencer's social Darwinism, German monism and Auguste Comte's positivism. Their main source of economic and political support was derived from the recent wealth generated by the expansion of coffee cultivation in the south-east of the country, as a result of the growing demand for stimulants in societies where the pace of life and rhythm of work were growing increasingly fast and intense. The wealthy São Paulo coffee growers aimed to have a federalist system established within the Republic, assuring them control not just over their own profits, but also over the conditions for using their economic power to decide the country's destiny.

With the benefit of heavy British investment, the São Paulo coffee growers could increase their production by multiplying their plantations, modernise their agricultural techniques and improve the quality of coffee, in addition to constructing the most extensive and intricate railway network on Brazilian territory. Thanks to these circumstances, they had no difficulty establishing alliances with the political leaders and intellectuals committed to the federalist ideal, and through them organised a coup against the monarchy. On 15 November 1889 the head of the Brazilian Army, General Deodoro da Fonseca, proclaimed the Federal Republic of Brazil, declared the monarchy extinct and installed himself as first President of the new Federal District of Rio de Janeiro. Shortly afterwards he would be replaced by Marechal Floriano Peixoto, the leader of the more radical young positivists, seeking to promote the modernisation of the country 'at any cost'.

The rise of this technocratic and scientifically oriented elite would define the path taken by Brazilian society in the 20th century. Eager to initiate the process of industrialisation without further delay, they eliminated the barriers to the free penetration of European and American capital, introduced a stock exchange and multiplied offices for the issue of currency, resulting in a speculative race for shares in the most extraordinary and insecure investment projects. This rapidly degenerated into the most scandalous process of financial corruption in the history of the country. The immediate effect of this process was to ruin the most prominent capitalists – the economic elite during the period of the monarchy – facilitating the rise of a new group of arrivistes, made wealthy by the speculative dealings of the first years of the new régime. Paradoxically this class of wealthy people of dubious morality would become, together with the coffee growers of the southeast, the principal source of economic support of the scientific and technocratic elite schooled in a rigid positivist rationalism.[10]

The effects of this new political articulation on Brazilian society and culture as a whole is illustrated by the most traumatic episode of the start of the Republican period: the Canudos Revolt (1893–97). The Republican authorities only heard of the existence of the settlement of Canudos in the backlands of the state of Bahia in 1893, till the first year of the revolt, for until then it had not appeared on any official maps. The officials in Rio de Janeiro received complaints about a group of religious fanatics from the Bahian authorities. The group was led

by an individual called Antônio Vicente Mendes Maciel, who by preaching
subversive doctrines was doing great damage to religion and the State,
distracting the people from their obligations and dragging them along
behind him, attempting to convince them that he was the Holy Spirit, rising
up against the established authorities, whom he does not obey and encour-
ages others to disobey.[11]

Initially a police force was sent out to subdue the rebels, but it
was destroyed before arriving at the settlement. Immediately, two
army detachments were dispatched, only to be defeated by the
rebels. Finally, a heavily armed military expedition was sent out from
Rio de Janeiro itself, with heavy artillery and modern equipment,
commanded by the immediate aide to Marechal Floriano: Colonel
Moreira César, an obstinate positivist, notorious for the sanguinary
style with which he suppressed rebel groups. To general dismay, not
only was the expedition totally crushed, but Colonel Moreira César
was felled by enemy fire. There was widespread panic. The only way
of making sense of the catastrophe was by projecting onto the rebels
the image of monarchist conspirators, maintained, organised and
heavily armed from abroad by expatriate leaders of the Imperial
regime and determined to destroy the new order. Complete annihi-
lation was therefore a question of life or death for the young
Republic.

   In this spirit the fourth expedition was dispatched, composed of two
complete divisions of the army, leaving Rio de Janeiro with the most
concentrated destructive power gathered since the Paraguayan War.
After numerous skirmishes, in which they ran serious risk of being
destroyed before arriving at the settlement, the troops finally succeeded
in surrounding it, submitting it to the most intense siege, under close
fire of repeating firearms and artillery. As those taken prisoner by the
soldiers had their throats cut immediately, the survivors resisted to the
end. Unable to impose a military victory, the officials decided to pour
barrels of kerosene on the wood and straw huts, burning the rebels
alive and reducing Canudos to ashes. The final assault took place
against a single trench, in which an old man, two younger men and a
child fought to the death.

   On this last expedition, the young positivist writer with a military
background, Euclides da Cunha, participated as war correspondent and
wrote a book about the episode, today still considered a key text,
essential for an understanding of the tensions which characterise
Brazilian culture. The work is the aforementioned *Os Sertões* published
in Rio de Janeiro in 1902. In it Euclides narrates how he went to the
battle site piously believing that Canudos was in fact a monarchist

stronghold, financed from abroad and determined to overthrow the Republican government; it was only on arriving there that he discovered to his surprise that the rebels were only poor rural workers, with no formal education and profoundly religious, trying to defend themselves against the abuses of the authorities and local bosses with weapons they had seized from their own persecutors.

Drawn from rural migrant populations from different parts of the north-eastern backlands, expelled from the small areas of land they had settled due to the intensification of commercial farming and the increasing demand for labour, these workers had settled in Canudos under the charismatic influence of the mystical figure Maciel, whom they called the Counsellor. From the remains of an abandoned and deserted farm on the margins of the Vaza-Barris river, in less than a decade, Canudos became the second city of Bahia in terms of population, and stood as a model of social organisation, hard work, community collaboration and prosperity.[12] The feeling of spiritual elevation, collective solidarity and capacity for achievement of its inhabitants, under the religious inspiration of the Counsellor, was so strong that it gave them the strength and courage to react against all the traditional forms of exploitation to which people of humble origin were subjected in the Brazilian backlands. This was their crime and for this they were condemned.

Euclides also explained how they were able to defeat a military force in every way far outmatching their meagre resources. The problem lay in the characteristics of the Brazilian Army itself. Its officials were trained in French, by Belgian instructors, using Belgian manuals and tactics appropriate to the territories of the Netherlands. None of them had the slightest notion of typical conditions in the Brazilian backlands. Their red uniforms offered easy targets for the backlanders, their cannons sank in the sandy soil, and their woollen clothes were a recipe for certain dehydration under the desert sun. Euclides demonstrated that successive expeditions were defeated above all by their total ignorance of the land, people, customs and Brazilian popular culture. The officials were consummate representatives of the social, political and economic elite of the coastal cities: forever turned towards and identifying with the Old Continent, on the other side of the Atlantic.

Because of all this the writer considered the Canudos War a crime against the Brazilian people and made his book an indictment, appealing to the new generation of intellectuals and artists to turn from the coast to the backlands, from identification with European culture to a discovery of Brazilian culture. But he was himself unable to evaluate just how much his training as an engineer, steeped in the rigour of new scientific beliefs, made it difficult for him to understand this culture. Euclides tended to consider the Counsellor, if not a charlatan, at least as a being whose confused mind remained imprisoned within a medieval obscurity of superstition and credulity: a creature whose archaic thinking interrupted the linear and inexorable flow of 'order and progress', the positivist maxim which the young soldiers had emblazoned on the national flag itself. Instead of cannons and soldiers, it was books and school-teachers that the government should have sent to the backlands.

Considered more closely, the case of the Counsellor contains surprising revelations. In the first place, there is the fact that Brazilian popular catholicism is a religion of visions. The devout bring with them the conviction that at special moments or in special circumstances, they live epiphanic experiences, establishing direct and sensory contact with manifestations of the sacred. The origin of this tradition goes back to quite specific historical roots. Influenced by the teachings of the Cistercian monks and the Knights Templar (later banned by the papacy), the royal house of Portugal created a ceremony at the end of the thirteenth century which would be popularised to promote the dissemination of their ideas – the Feast of the Divine Holy Spirit. This feast ritualised the advent of a new time, in which all people would be equal, goods redistributed and prisoners freed. Under strong pressure from the pope, the Feast was prohibited in Portugal, but its practitioners took it to the islands of the Atlantic and, in a more direct and exalted form, to the remote territory of Brazil. From colonial times, therefore, the symbols of the Divine Holy Spirit became the mainstay of Brazilian popular catholicism, which retained a latent millenarianism. Thus, the belief in social redemption through epiphany became one of the main axes of the history of Brazil.[13]

From this perspective, what is striking is the paradoxical similarity between the liberal belief of the intellectual Euclides da Cunha in the democratic redemption of Brazilian society through the imminent and inevitable advent of the Positivist State, and the conviction of the people of Canudos that they were living through the eve of the kingdom of peace and fraternal justice, guaranteed by the coming of the Holy Spirit. It is obviously not accidental that both the positivist intellectual and the devout of the Holy Spirit shared the same epiphanical expectations, if we take into account that both were anchored in the same deep cultural sub-stratum. More surprising, in fact, was the attitude of the political and economic elites who, opposed to the writer's dream as well as to the hopes of the backlanders, saw both as obstacles to the modernisation of the country via the authoritarian implantation of European or North American models.

Other similar situations followed, confirming the constancy of this impasse and exemplified in the transformations experienced by the capital of the Republic. At the beginning of the twentieth century Rio de Janeiro had a population of a little less than a million inhabitants. Of these the majority were former slaves, freedmen of the city or recent arrivals from other areas following the abolition of slavery (1888) and in search of opportunities to earn a living linked to activities of the capital's port. This extremely poor population was concentrated in large, run-down old houses dating from the beginning of the nine-teenth century, located around the port in the city centre. Whole families lived in rented, overcrowded cubicles, with no infrastructure and in the most precarious and degrading conditions. For the auth-orities they represented a permanent threat to order and public health.

These large black and *mestiço* (mixed) populations preserved, as was to be expected, elements of their original religion and culture, such as links of a communal nature, survival strategies, and connections to their symbolic roots, as well as many other distinctive characteristics of their groups of origin. Despite the different areas and communities from which they had been kidnapped in Africa, their religious beliefs had elements in common, including traditions of enchantment, pos-session and direct contact with the sacred. Hence the different ways in which they were amalgamated with elements of Brazilian popular catholicism, giving rise to derivative forms such as *umbanda* and *candom-blé*. One of this community's most distinctive characteristics, however, was the central role attributed to drums and percussion instruments, and to exuberant and intricately choreographed dances as means of access to the epiphanic experience. Viewed as attacks on order and morality – in fact as witchcraft – such instruments, music, dances and rituals were prohibited, their practitioners imprisoned, and all of their instruments and ritual objects seized by the police.[14]

Another practice peculiar to the black community in Rio de Janeiro was *capoeira*, a form of martial art transmitted through the generations and taught to *mestiços*, whites and anyone who cared to learn it. Although it involved rhythmical and gestural elements of African origin, *capoeira*'s complex technique of personal defence was developed entirely in Brazil. As with everything involving rhythm for the black population, their sources of inspiration were sacred. Rhythm is the central principle of this practice, refined to the level of artistic excellence by its masters. As a form of fighting it is paradoxical: the objective is not to attack one's adversary, but on the contrary, never to allow oneself to be struck. The secret of the art is rhythmic control of the combatant's *ginga* (swing) – the ability to sway with the body and to jump, always in an unpredictable way, so that the opponent – firmly placed in a position of attack and looking for a fixed target, a vulnerable point to attack – succeeds only in striking empty space. The *capoeirista* thus defeats his enemy by humiliation. Hence the public nature of this art in which the *capoeirista* transforms his performance into a spectacle for the general delight of the audience. There were innumerable schools of this art in Rio de Janeiro, all with their famous masters and hierarchy of disciples. It was Marechal Floriano Peixoto himself, seeking to impose a monopoly on the use of force as an exclusive privilege of public authority, who declared the end of these institutions and the categorical prohibition of the practice of *capoeira*, even sanctioning the physical removal of those who dared to resist the measure.[15]

But the restriction or rigid control of the beliefs, rituals and practices of the black community and their allies was not enough for the authorities. Equally serious from their point of view were the threats to public health posed by the dense co-habitation of these people, in precarious sanitary conditions in the central areas of the city. Rio de Janeiro was the principal commercial port of the country and the third most important on the American continent, after New York and Buenos Aires. More than this, as capital of the Republic it was the showcase of the country. With its pressing needs for capital, technicians and immigrant labour, the city itself was supposed to be an attraction to foreigners. However, it was subject to a series of epidemics (the most serious threats were smallpox and yellow fever) which devastated its population and were even more destructive of foreigners who did not possess the antibodies developed over a long period of time by the local population. Because of this the city had, since the nineteenth century, the undesirable reputation as a 'foreigners' graveyard', a notoriety completely incompatible with its imperative need to act as a pole of attraction.

Apart from this problem, there was the question of the port. The port installations of Rio de Janeiro were obsolete, making the growing volume of commercial transactions impossible. The old quays were not very deep and did not allow large and modern transatlantic vessels to reach it directly, making it necessary to transport goods by a lengthy and laborious system of transfer in smaller vessels. In addition, even once they had arrived on terra firma the goods still had to cross the city, destined for railway lines which sent them to other points of the country. This was not a little complicated in a city whose transport infrastructure was still largely colonial, made up of narrow, tortuous lanes, where the trucks would inevitably carry out complex manoeuvres of retreat every time they encountered vehicles drawn by animals, as there was not enough room for both in the narrow spaces of the many alleyways.

The authorities conceived a three-pronged plan to confront all of these problems, comprising the simultaneous modernisation of the port, the sanitation of the city and urban reform. A team of technicians was nominated by President Rodrigues Alves: the engineer Lauro Müller for the reform of the port; the sanitation doctor Oswaldo Cruz for sanitation; and the engineer and urban planner Pereira Passos, who had worked on the reform of Paris under Baron Haussmann, for the remodelling of the city. The three were given unlimited powers to execute their tasks, making them immune to any judicial action, creating a situation of triple dictatorship in the city of Rio de Janeiro. As was expected, they all turned on the rambling old houses of the centre in which the majority of the poor lived, because they restricted access to the port, created an unhygienic environment and impeded the free flow of goods and people essential in a modern city. The demolition of the residences of the central area was initiated, to the approval of the quality press, who dubbed it the 'Regeneration'. For those affected by this intervention it was out-and-out tyranny, as no plans for compensation or re-housing of its victims were made. All they could do was gather their families and the scarce goods they possessed and disappear. With no other alternative, the evicted masses collected the wood from discarded boxes at the port and used it to begin constructing crude shacks on the steep sides of the hills which sur-rounded the city, covering them with tin plate from folded kerosene tins. This was the origin of the *favelas*.[16]

In addition to the *favelas* the crowds of homeless accumulated in slum tenements and cheap hotels, the *freges*, in which familes rented mats on the ground, lined up one alongside the other in sub-human conditions. As these alternatives still carried sanitation risks, the Health Ministry turned against them. Unleashing a massive campaign to eradi-cate smallpox, battalions of health visitors were employed who, accom-panied by police forces, invaded houses on the pretext of vaccinating the residents. But if signs of health risks were detected, which were inevitable in those conditions, they were authorised to order the house, tenement, *frege* or shack to be evacuated, eventually condemning it to compulsory demolition with no right to compensation. This was the last

straw for the poor, homeless and humiliated population. In a spontaneous surge, masses of hitherto cowed citizens turned against the
squadrons of health visitors and the police force, heading for the centre
of the city where the urban reform work was being carried out. On
arriving there they entrenched themselves in the open ditches and,
appropriating all the tools and construction materials as weapons, set
about confronting the reinforcements sent by the police. The rebellion
became known as the 1904 Revolt of the Vaccine, and is one of the
least understood episodes of Brazil's recent history. From the authorities' point of view, people revolted because in their ignorance they
were afraid of and were unable to understand the process of vaccination
against disease. From this perspective, it was an irrational uprising of
simple people with backward minds, incapable of comprehending the
course of progress. Because of this it was treated as a kind of Canudos
in the heart of the capital, which it was necessary to eliminate to save
the Republic.[17]

As the police were unable to subdue the rebels, whose ranks were
increasingly swelled by the rest of the population terrorised by the
draconian system of the triple reform, the National Guard was called
in. It was useless; the resistance only increased. Firemen were then
called into action, but the situation remained uncontrollable. The
President personally assumed control of suppressing the rebels, sum-
moning army troops into action. The insurrection continued. The navy
was then deployed, equally unsuccessfully, and auxiliary troops were
summoned from the bordering states of Minas Gerais and São Paulo.
Only then, with all of these concentrated forces and after ten days, was
the movement defeated. Then the repression began. Orders were given
by the chief of police that anyone found in the city who could give no
proof of address or fixed employment should be detained. As the
reform had created an immense housing deficit and as the population
lived on odd jobs in an unstable labour market, this decree affected
almost all of the poor. Those detained were taken to the Ilha das
Cobras, where, after being brutally beaten, they were put in the holds
of steamers, which left immediately for Amazônia. There they were
released in the middle of the forest, without any guidance, resources or
medical help and left to disappear into the jungle.

The Regeneration was completed at the end of 1904. It was marked
by the inauguration of the Avenida Central, the axis of the new
urbanisation project, conceived as a concourse of façades surrounding
the city with an architectural art-nouveau décor, in ivory and crystal,
combined with the elegant lamps of modern electric illumination and
the lights from the windows of the fine shops filled with imported

goods. Lifestyle magazines and the society pages of the quality press incited the affluent members of the population to parade their fashions on the great catwalk of the Avenida, the young men in the smart rigour of English suits and the women showing off the latest extravagances in fabrics, cuts and French hats. The cosmopolitan atmosphere which descended on the renovated city was such that, on the eve of the First World War, people whose paths crossed on the great boulevard no longer greeted each other in the Brazilian way, but repeated to each other 'Vive la France'. Correspondingly, people who were unable to dress decently – which is to say, formally – had their access to the central area of the city prohibited. In addition to this, the traditional popular feasts and customs in the vicinity, attracting people from the outskirts of the city, were repressed and even carnival was no longer celebrated with *entrudos, blocos,* masks, sambas and popular *maxixes,* but with carriage processions, flower battles and well-behaved pierrots and columbines, typical of the Venetian carnival.

The elites' indifference to the cultural traditions of the country and its peoples was noted and criticised by the great writers of the period: Euclides da Cunha, as we have seen, a *mestiço* of indigenous descent; Machado de Assis and Lima Barreto, both mulattos; and Cruz de Souza, who was black. Machado de Assis, one of the best Brazilian writers of all time, attacked with refined irony the gap which the institution of slavery had created between the owning classes and the immense population of the destitute, composed predominantly of blacks, *mestiços* and poor immigrants. Lima Barreto was a master of social criticism and denounced the brutal and arbitrary manner in which the dominant classes maintained the hierarchy and the system of discrimination which marginalised the majority of the Brazilian population. Cruz de Souza, a poet of sublime and inspired lyricism, sought to put into words in his verses the depth of pain, suffering and humiliation which constituted the daily life of the popular classes.

Changes to this tide of cosmopolitanism would come only after the Great War. It happened in various ways. One of the most interesting was the visit to Brazil of the acclaimed French poet Paul Claudel and the young composer Darius Milhaud, who fell in love with Rio de Janeiro – not with the scenery of the Avenida Central and the boulevards of the modernised city, which resembled an urban European setting, but with the popular culture of the outskirts and the *favelas* on the hillsides. Milhaud made contact with several popular musicians and through them developed his research on the rhythmic languages of the

Brazilian tradition. From here he went to the United States, where he made contact with black jazz musicians. From his apprenticeship during this period a work resulted which had enormous impact on the post-war European scene, a symphony called *The Ox on the Roof.*

The title was considered bizarre, in surrealist taste and in line with the aesthetic sensibility of the time. In fact it was the name of a *maxixe* which had been a hit with the population on the outskirts of Rio de Janeiro, written by a local composer, Zé Boiadeiro, and with a humorous allusion to a husband betrayed by his wife. In any case, its success was such that the music gave rise to a circus ballet of the same name, the fruit of a partnership between Milhaud and Jean Cocteau. This ballet caused such a sensation in cultured circles that when Milhaud and Cocteau decided to open a night club in Montparnasse, where music and the scenic and visual production of artists involved with modern art were being promoted, the name which they hit upon for the dancing cabaret was *Le Boeuf sur le Toit.* The cabaret soon became the showcase par excellence of the post-war aesthetic revolution in Paris. Thus, paradoxically, when the young Brazilian elite went to Paris on their customary annual visit to breathe 'the superior airs of civilisation', they discovered, to their enormous surprise, that the latest trends in Paris were based on the despised culture of the marginalised population of their own country.[18]

Incongruous situations such as these led to currents of change. In the post-war period, the devaluation of European currencies placed the dollar in a highly favourable position, while exchanges with Europe intensified on an unprecedented scale. This allowed the young people of well-to-do Brazilian families to consume prestigious technological products directly from the Old Continent. This was the case with Paulo Prado. Son of one of the wealthiest men of the period – owner of the largest coffee plantations in São Paulo, in addition to being an entrepreneur linked to activities as diverse as railways, banks and import and export companies – it was customary for him to travel to Paris to acquire the latest in sports cars. This was how he came to meet the poet Blaise Cendrars, who, together with Apollinaire, had inaugurated Cubist poetry in 1913.

When Prado proposed that he come to São Paulo, Cendrars accepted immediately, excited on the one hand by the phenomenon of coffee cultivation and its prodigious concentration of profit, and on the other by a Brazilian culture with which he was already familar, thanks to Milhaud and the cabaret. Paulo Prado was an important figure in the world of Brazilian art, stimulating new generations of artists involved with the modern aesthetic. He was later to sponsor the Week of Modern

Art in São Paulo in 1922, bringing together artists from São Paulo and Rio de Janeiro in order to sow the seeds of cultural change. The arrival of Cendrars formed part of this same project and had major repercussions.

From the moment of his arrival, Blaise Cendrars declared himself completely overwhelmed by the city of São Paulo. It seemed to him that it represented the epitome of that typical phenomenon of modernity which attracted him so strongly: the megalopolis.[19] 'Nowhere have I been so amazed by the manifest greatness of our time and by the constant beauty of human action', he wrote.[20] Actually São Paulo was an extreme case. In the mid nineteenth century it was still little more than a very small village, distant, obscure and extremely poor, which the Jesuits had founded at the beginning of the colonisation period, in the mid sixteenth century, as a base for the conversion of the Indians of the backlands. Due to the permanent scarcity of economic resources, the Jesuit nucleus became a source of migration into the interior of the area. Young men systematically abandoned the village, trying their luck in the backlands, either capturing Indians to sell as slaves to plantation owners on the coast, or turning their hand to prospecting ores and precious stones, combined with modest plots of manioc and pig-rearing for domestic consumption.[21] Because of this, the village population was mainly composed of women and children, the great majority mestiças of Indian and white parentage, with some blacks and mulattas.[22]

It was in the second half of the nineteenth century that coffee, hitherto barely known and little consumed, suddenly became an object indispensable to the conditions of modern life. The rapid expansion of coffee consumption generated high profits for its producers. When the plantation owners of the Brazilian Empire realised that the Valley of Paraíba, between Rio de Janeiro and São Paulo, offered favourable conditions for the planting of coffee, production expanded rapidly. On São Paulo territory, however, they came across soil enriched with volcanic sediment and the rhythm of expansion became a boom in coffee cultivation. In the final quarter of the nineteenth century, until the end of the 1920s, the State of São Paulo controlled more than 70 per cent of the world market for coffee.[23]

Or rather, São Paulo produced this quantity, but the markets were actually controlled by British traders, who acted as intermediaries in the process of production, as well as in the transport and commercialisation of the product. Through control of the credit operations, they financed the planting and bought all of the crop at the very moment it was harvested, when the prices were lowest, retaining stocks and only releasing them for export little by little, in small quotas each time, in order to keep the sale prices on the international market as high as possible. For the British investors, therefore, the whole business was a gigantic speculative manipulation on a global scale.

It was because of this that São Paulo, an insignificant village until the mid nineteenth century, suddenly became a city with the dizzying pace of metropolitanisation.[24] Since the British needed an intermediary point between the coffee plantations in the interior of the state and the port of Santos on the coast, they chose São Paulo as a strategic hub of the export network. All the railways converged there, financed and constructed by the British, keeping the stocks of coffee in the city at the top of the mountain range and allowing only small amounts out at a time, destined for external markets. Thus most of the wealth generated by the coffee economy ended up concentrated in the São Paulo state capital, attracting legions of immigrants from all over Brazil, and from the four corners of the world, to what became known, in a reference to the colour of the coffee fields, as 'the green gold rush'. The vast resources accumulated by coffee-related commerce stimulated the growth of other commercial, industrial and financial investments, in particular real estate speculation, one of the most lucrative forms of investment in a city undergoing explosive growth.[25]

The Prefecture of the city during this initial period of metropolitanisation, from 1891 to 1911, was Councillor Antônio Prado, father of the cultural patron Paulo Prado. The ideal underlying his administration was to use this concentration of wealth to construct an urban society based on the Paris of the Second Empire. To this end he commissioned Buvard and Couchet, two engineer-architects who had rendered extensive services to the Paris city council and to the landscaping project of the Universal Fairs centred in the city of light. The result had major impact. Practically everything that remained in the old colonial village was cleared away and the whole physiognomy of the city was redesigned in order to transform it into a metropolis in the European style.

The two main hills in the central area of the city, previously separated by steep inclines, swamps and the Anhangabaú river, were united by two viaducts in the form of wide, solemn steel arches, imported whole from Germany. A canal was built on the Anhangabaú and on it an extremely elegant forested park was planted. A series of large public buildings was erected as civic reference points, among them the Historical Museum of Ipiranga, in neo-classical French architectural style, the Station of Light, modelled on Paddington and imported whole from England, and the imposing Municipal Theatre, based on the Paris Opera, an eclectic architectural composition inspired by the Italian neo-Renaissance. Moreover, the construction of a cathedral was envisaged for the future, based on the model of Cologne Cathedral in Germany. A whole dense ribbon of adjoining landscaped areas was created which, starting from the Aclimação and Ipiranga Parks on the fringes of the city, were linked to the Dom Pedro II Park, in English style, at the foot of the central hills, culminating in the impressive panorama of the landscape of the valley of Anhangabaú, with its lines of giant imperial palms.

It was to this city that the poet Blaise Cendrars came, developing an immediate and complete empathy with it. He arrived in 1924 for a short visit, but his enthusiasm was such that he would return almost every year throughout the twenties, always for long periods of time. Dispensing with guides or interpreters and understanding not a word of Portuguese, he used to walk the streets of the city, gathering impressions at random, registering them rapidly in crystalline, spontaneous verses, in accordance with the immediate impressions which the scenes and landscapes of the city provoked in him. According to the aesthetic defined in his last book, *Kodak*, the poet should reproduce the instantaneous shock of exterior reality on his senses, without giving time for consciousness or the imagination to dilute that fragmentary instant into symbolic representation. This is exemplified in his poem on São Paulo:

> I adore this city
> São Paulo is like my heart
> Here no tradition
> No prejudice
> Neither ancient nor modern
> What counts is only this furious appetite this absolute confidence this
>   optimism this audacity this work this effort this
>   speculation which makes ten houses spring up every hour
>   of all styles ridiculous grotesque beautiful large
>   small north south Egyptian Yankee Cubist
> With no concern but to follow statistics predict
>   the future the comfort the utility the surplus value and attract
>   enormous migration
> All the countries
> All the peoples
> I love this
> The two or three old Portuguese houses which remain are
>   blue glazed tiles.[26]

In Cendrars' eyes, São Paulo was a gigantic work of modern art, a social experiment on a colossal scale.

There were, however, less visible yet particularly distressing aspects of this tumultuous process of urbanisation. The explosive growth of the city maintained a chaotic pace, subjecting the population to unimaginable hardship and deprivation. It would be more appropriate to call it a process of swelling rather than growth. The most significant fact from the cultural point of view, however, was that these people came from all over the world, as well as all over Brazil. Under pressure from extreme poverty, this population of the destitute had lost family, community and territorial ties. In the new environment, these men and women barely spoke a common language, they were strangers to each other and to modern urban life, and thus desperately needed a new identity and new ties of solidarity. The authorities learnt how to exploit this cultural vulnerability and spiritual need, providing a new mythology with the city at its very core, presented as the place where 'modernity' – the magic word which promised a magic world – could finally be manifested, as the inevitable result of persistent faith in energy, speed, action and conquest.

The authorities were very concerned to offer encouraging slogans, replete with the image of a modern El Dorado: 'São Paulo is unstoppable'; 'São Paulo is the engine of Brazil'; 'São Paulo is the capital of progress'; 'São Paulo is a roller-coaster ride'. But a more appropriate metaphor for the city would be a game of Russian roulette, such were the risks and difficulties involved in living and working there: two thirds of the children born in São Paulo died before the age of two; there were no housing, health, employment or social welfare policies; the working day generally lasted sixteen hours. The police kept the population in a permanent state of terror and police stations were given sinister names by the public. The Cambuci station was called 'The Dungeon', Liberdade's was 'The Mortuary', in 7 de Abril Street it was known as 'The Fridge' and in São Caetano Street, 'The Cemetery'. With all of these contradictions, if São Paulo was a modernist work of art, it corresponded more appropriately to an extreme manifestation of the theatre of the absurd, in which the population represented characters who, ignorant of the script, clung desperately to the ongoing action.

Apart from his perambulations to immerse himself in the marvellous experience of the metamorphosis of São Paulo, which led him to identify the city as the contradictory quintessence of modernity, Cendrars developed a parallel project. Unaware of the local intellectuals' keen interest in debates on Parisian aesthetics, Cendrars, who had already travelled through North Africa, collecting the native myths assembled in the ballet composition *The Creation of the World*, entertained plans to learn about all possible dimensions of Brazilian popular culture. Initially the great poet's refusal to speak about European themes came as a shock to Brazilian artists. Subsequently, they bowed to his insistence and, sponsored by Prado, placed themselves at his disposal as guides to significant manifestations of traditional culture. So it was that an expedition was organised to visit Rio de Janeiro and thereafter the historic cities of Minas Gerais.

Rio de Janeiro already exercised an enormous fascination on Blaise Cendrars, but a magical moment, the street carnival, which convulsed and transfigured the whole city, was chosen. Like Claudel and Milhaud before him, from his arrival in the city he showed no interest in the central areas, feeling attracted to the popular outskirts and the world concentrated in the huts precariously huddled on the hillsides. It was the carnival of these people that Blaise wanted to witness, with their anarchic and euphoric *cordões*, pressing against each other – dozens, hundreds of them in the streets and squares of the popular areas, with their traditional instruments: indigenous rattles, African drums, Iberian guitars, European brass instruments and Brazilian whistles, all in a deafening and enticing syncopation. They dressed as kings and princes, Indians and African characters, donning angels' wings and devils' masks. In a frenzied and indefatigable rhythmical step, they danced in intricate choreographed group routines or sensual solo swings and exhibited their bodies like divine offerings and catalysts of the senses. In addition to the sounds, the dances, the singing and the costumes, there was also the play of eyes meeting, bodies and desires in contact, passions converging, dreams projected, souls uniting, against a back-drop of songs which inspired joy, as well as voicing the pain of a people stigmatised by the colour of their skin, by the curse of humble origins and contempt for native cultures.

After Rio de Janeiro came the turn of Minas Gerais. The old area of gold and diamond mining, explored and exhausted in the eighteenth century, had given way to an original *mestiço* society, dispersed over several small, urban nuclei, each still preserving a significant artistic and architectural legacy. The mining area, extending to the backlands of the south-east, maintained its distance from the cosmopolitan pressures of the coastal capitals, preserving the most typical characteristics of traditional culture. The São Paulo excursionists planned their visit to coincide with the great feasts of Holy Week, the most important cluster of holy dates in Brazilian popular catholicism.

The spirit of these festivities was represented entirely according to the forms, staging and emotional climate derived from a popular version of the Baroque. Their theatricality spread through the streets, transformed into large-scale tableaux in the open air, interrupted by the incessant movement of huge crowds undulating in successive processions, featuring a wide variety of spectacles: trains of followers carrying lighted candles; solemn retinues preceded by the priest in his sumptuous robes; large crucifixes of gold and silver, holy images with dramatic expressions; decorated, multicoloured biers, covered with intricate lace; pennants and standards of the brotherhoods; large candles and silver-plated candlesticks, the incense-burners releasing thick rolls of perfumed smoke, the beads and rosaries of the penitents; tributes of branches and flowers, the gift offerings, the *ex–votos* for miracles performed; collective choruses interrupted by cries, shouts of praise and exaltation from the devout in ecstasy; lines of penitents dragging heavy crosses on their backs, stones on their shoulders, pulling themselves along in the dust on their knees or chests; the sobs, the tears – all the euphoria and the pain glorified in a public spectacle of flashing metals, flickering flames, vivid colours, confusing sounds, contrasting odours, tortured postures and extreme emotions. This vertiginous climax of the senses, spiritual as well as sensory, was captured by black and mulatto artisans who carved in stone and moulded in precious metals the tensions of this society in which extreme wealth had as its correlate the most acute forms of torment and suffering. Aleijadinho in particular stands out, a master craftsman who made his congenital physical deformities a source of inspiration in order to reproduce in his sculptures moral perversions, disfigurations of the soul, the anguish of disability and the mystical fervour of the desire for justice.

Much more than on Cendrars himself, these visits had a powerful effect on the Brazilian artists and intellectuals who accompanied him and confessed their delight with popular traditions. They ended up dubbing these expeditions the 'rediscovery' of Brazil.[27] After 400 years of seeing the territory and its peoples from a Lusitanian and European perspective, the time had come to invert the gaze and assume the native point of view. Thus the projects which gave rise to Brazilian cultural nationalism were born – the Brazilwood Manifesto of 1924 and the Anthropophagist Manifesto of 1928. They gave impetus to the so-called Modernist Generation, composed among others of the writers Mário de Andrade and Oswald de Andrade, the poets Manuel Bandeira and Carlos Drummond de Andrade, the painters Anita Malfatti and Tarsila do Amaral, the sculptor Victor Brecheret and the composer Heitor Villa-Lobos. Here again Blaise Cendrars had a decisive role, acting as the link between these artists and the group of European Modernists to which he was directly connected. He would present Oswald de Andrade to Jean Cocteau, Tarsila do Amaral to Léger, Brecheret to Brancusi, Villa-Lobos to the Group of Six, thus aligning Brazilian artistic production with the boldest and most creative nucleus of European art.[28]

This exchange would bring about a genuine transformation at the level of aesthetic principles, while also promoting engagement with the native and popular elements of national culture. Owing, however, to the commitments of the Modernists to their sponsors, and to a régime based on the wealth of coffee cultivation, their aesthetic nationalism tended to maintain a generally optimistic and celebratory tone with regard to cultural traditions, honouring their more conservative aspects. Hence the tendency of a significant part of this generation towards folkloric and ethnographic studies, and the creation of institutions and schools aimed at preserving the characteristics of Brazilian popular culture considered most pure. The implicit correlative of this attitude was resentment at the irreversible decline of agricultural export activity, until then the dominant part of the economy and structure of Brazilian society. Thus, paradoxically, nationalist modernism became a vehicle of resistance to what were seen as the destabilising international processes of modernisation, which threatened both the purity of popular culture and the coherence of traditional society.[29]

The final collapse of the hegemony of the coffee oligarchy came as a direct result of the world economic crisis of 1929. The régime maintained by the plantation owners ceded to internal tensions, led by regions which had been kept on the margins of the federalist political system. The leader of the rebels, the Porto Alegre politician Getúlio Vargas, organised the opposition alliance and in 1930 troops marched on Rio de Janeiro, deposing the last 'Paulista' president and installing a new institutional order, controlled by the victors. The new régime proposed to govern not in favour of any particular economic, regional, social or ethnic sector, but in favour of the nation as a whole, united in the political body of a strong State with Getúlio Vargas at the helm. Brought to power in 1930, Getúlio's dictatorial régime would be overthrown only in 1945 after the defeat of Fascism in Europe.[30]

From a cultural point of view the committed nationalism of the Modernists was extremely convenient for the new régime, in the sense that it proposed a rediscovery or rebirth of a new Brazil, seen as a total synthesis of all its regions and people. Under the tutelage of a strong institutional apparatus, they would be protected from the threatening fluctuations of the international market, from internal social and regional tensions and from the contamination of tradition resulting from immigration or the destabilising forces of modernisation. Development would come, with its promise of prosperity and social mobility, but controlled and softened, with its fruits equally distributed by the State. To this end, while in power the régime would set up a whole network of mechanisms of censorship and propaganda, in order to prevent the emergence of alternative discourses and impose its unitary and totalising vision of the identity and destiny of Brazil. Drawing on effective methods implemented by European Fascist régimes, the new leaders would put to full use the new means of social communication – especially radio, cinema, the phonographic industry and the illustrated press – monopolising them for propaganda purposes. Thus a centralised cultural politics was articulated by means of which educational institutions, as well as the press and popular culture, were administered by representatives of the régime. The Vargas personality cult and glorification of the régime were equated with patriotic love of the country. The leader and the régime became the focus of theatrical review shows, as well as film, popular music and even carnival and samba school *marchinhas*.[31]

The São Paulo leaders, removed from political power, responded in 1934 with the creation of a centre of intellectual excellence, the University of São Paulo, destined to be the bastion of resistance to the régime. The new institution was founded by a delegation of the most prestigious intellectuals from the University of Paris' Sorbonne, including names like Fernand Braudel, Claude Lévi-Strauss, Roger Bastide and Pierre Monbeig. This centre would be associated with some of the most outstanding intellectuals and thinkers of Brazil, such as the historians Caio Prado and Sérgio Buarque de Hollanda, with a nucleus of social scientists who introduced critical, rigorous and scientific modes of analysis and research, transcending the optimism of the Modernists and challenging the conformist nationalism of the authoritarian régime.

The impulse behind these new forms of knowledge was to denounce the history of colonialism and slavery, exposing the oppressive weight of its persistence in contemporary Brazilian society, in the form of underdevelopment, extreme social inequity, the most dramatic violence, prejudice, discrimination, and the denial of rights and guarantees to wide sectors of the population, deprived of access to education, health, housing and dignified forms of subsistence. Among the social scientists and critics involved the following stand out: Florestan Fernandes, Antônio Cândido, Fernando Henrique Cardoso, Octávio Ianni and Milton Santos. It would be this generation, in collaboration with Spanish American intellectuals in the 1950s and '60s, who would develop the so-called Theory of Dependence, a crucial critical tool in international debates on decolonisation, underdevelopment, political emancipation, democratisation and economic growth in the Third World.

This intellectual opposition benefited from the liberalising post-war climate which, hostile to régimes of a Fascist kind, strengthened internal opposition to Vargas' government and favoured the restoration of democratic institutions in Brazil. The Vargas interregnum also brought about the development of primary industry and the implementation of a policy of import substitution, which the war and the consequent credit in the balance of payments had made possible.

The main beneficiary of this new economic configuration was the state of São Paulo and its capital city, thanks to its concentration of capital and infrastructure deriving from the large-scale cultivation of coffee.[32] The process of metropolitanisation of the city of São Paulo was impressive: with only 270,000 inhabitants at the beginning of the century, by around 1950 its population had reached 2,662,786, displaying an extraordinary rate of growth, even greater than in previous decades. This impressive demographic increase has been maintained, with São Paulo entering the twenty-first century with a projected population of more than twenty-three million, making it the third largest conurbation on earth. This population is augmented by the continuous, successive waves of immigration, foreign as well as national, giving rise to an extremely complex, rich and diverse cultural environment. The new social elite, composed mainly of entrepreneurs – many of foreign origin, in competition both with each other and with the old coffee growing elite – would convert the city into a cultural centre, providing it with an extensive network of cultural institutions focused on the formation of an intellectual and cultural elite, the promotion of contacts, the exchange of information and the dissemination of new ideas.

The main objective of these initiatives was to re-establish contact with the international scene interrupted and suppressed by Vargas' policies, bringing the country up to date with the latest artistic developments, with a view to overcoming the narrow limits of the official nationalism of the deposed régime. One of the new cultural patrons was the Italian businessman Francisco 'Ciccillo' Matarazzo. His initiatives, in association with the new generation of São Paulo intellectuals and others who migrated to the city because of the war, were impressive, constituting an authentic political project of cultural renewal. With a team of advisors composed of directors and technicians from the Guggenheim Museum in New York, he established the Museum of Modern Art of São Paulo, inaugurated with a large exhibition of abstract art, such visual language having been forbidden in Brazil during the dictatorship. In 1951 the first Biennial of Fine Art was held, an international exhibition which would be accompanied by two others, the Biennal of Architecture and the Biennal of Theatre, with the support of prestigious institutions such as New York's Museum of Modern Art (MoMA) and the Kokusai Bunka Shinkokai in Tokyo. Matarazzo's involvement was also significant in the creation of the Brazilian Comedy Theatre, principal centre for the revival of national theatre, and the Vera Cruz Cinematographic Company, equipped with studios, technicians and artists of European origin which would become a source of knowhow for the later development of Brazilian cinema. He would also play a decisive role in the organisation of the International Festival of Cinema, the Museum of Archaeology and Ethnology and the International Biennial of the Book. In 1954, as president of the Commission for the celebration of the Fourth Centenary of the founding of the city of São Paulo, he proposed the creation of a large public park, the Ibirapucra park, conceived as a focus of cultural activity for the city. For this task he commissioned Oscar Niemeyer, one of the most important architects of the twentieth century and a young disciple of Le Corbusier.

In the context of this process of redemocratisation, Brazilian artists concentrated their efforts on seeking a new synthesis capable of reconciling languages expressive of modernity with the specific characteristics of a society still strongly marked by the weight of its colonial past. The work of painters like Cândido Portinari, poets like João Cabral de Melo Neto, and novelists like Graciliano Ramos and Jorge Amado, was informed by this aim. A particularly significant example of how these thematic and formal investigations worked can be found in the short story *A Terceira Margem do Rio (The Third Bank of the River)*, by Guimarães Rosa. It tells the story of an anonymous backlander somewhere in the vast area of the *sertão* (backlands) between the north of Minas Gerais and Bahia, who one day decides without any explanation to his wife, children or anyone else to get into a boat, row into the middle of the river and remain there indefinitely, without going anywhere and without ever approaching either of the banks. The story has a dramatic dénouement when the oldest son is called to take the place of his father. At this moment, the son, who is the narrator of the story, hesitates and reflects with the reader on the significance of this act, of his father's invention of an impossible place, which does not exist, and asks if the reader would undertake to enter this place, becoming paralysed like the father in a permanent mobility, enclosed in the continuous flow of atemporality.

The story is disturbingly emblematic. Written at the beginning of the 1960s, it reflects the cultural climate of the time marked by a catalysing event, which mobilised the creative energies of the country: the foundation of its new capital, the planned city of Brasília. This represented the high point of the modernising policy of President Juscelino Kubitschek (1956–61). His objective was to overcome the obstacles of underdevelopment inherited from colonialism which made the country incapable of promoting a more equal distribution of income and opportunities, indispensable conditions for the establishment of a democratic, stable and prosperous society. The construction of the new capital was designed to act, first, as a stimulus to large-scale state investment, encouraging private investment, multiplying jobs and consolidating the internal market. Second, however, the project also had a profound symbolic significance.

Since its discovery in 1500, the territory of Brazil, with its exuberant flora and fauna and continental dimensions, had provoked fantastical notions in the Portuguese navigators, who identified it with the legendary island of Brazil, where Saint Anton was said to have found Paradise during one of his most audacious mystical journeys. This belief that the Forbidden Garden was somewhere on Brazilian soil persisted and spread during the colonial period, merging with indigenous myths referring to the existence of a great lake of emeralds, Vabapuçu, source of eternal life and harmony. Innumerable expeditions were mounted by the colonisers to find this mystical place. Towards the end of the nineteenth century the Italian mystic Don Giovanni Bosco had a vision of a sacred city, which would appear in the heart of South America and be the mainstay for the emergence of a new humanity, which would inherit the earth and should therefore prepare for the coming of the Holy Spirit. This complex mythical and religious tradition interacted with the latent millenarianism of Brazilian culture, shaping the expectations with which the project of the New Capital was received.

The urban planner Lúcio Costa, the architect Oscar Niemeyer and the landscape designer Burle Marx merged this legacy with the utopian content intrinsic to the revolutionary and redeeming impulse of modern art, transforming the Brasília project into an experience of social levelling, a democratic symbol and an expression of the historic commitment to a future of autonomy and development. The Capital of

Hope, as it was called, would be, at one and the same time, the origin of the 'cosmic race' as conceived by one of the influential figures behind the Mexican muralists, José Vasconcelos, and the centre which heralded the 'third way' – the society resulting from the emancipation of colonial peoples from their past, as well as from the imperialist pretensions of powers locked into the Cold War. Brasília would be the 'third bank', the bridge between an undesirable past and a still impalpable future, the materialisation of the impossible.

The widespread utopian desire for rebirth, emancipation and autonomy spread throughout Brazilian society, paving the way for a general surge of creative energy. The desire for the new penetrated all areas of culture. The World Cup victory of 1958, with the consecration of popular players such as Didi, Garrincha and Pelé, seemed to be the premonition of a manifest destiny. It was during this transition between the 1950s and '60s that the rhythmical experimentation of young musicians created the original and irresistible style of bossa nova. In 1960 the Conference of Brazilian Cinematographic Criticism triggered the theoretical debates which would give rise to Cinema Novo, a major influence on the cultural agendas of the so-called non-aligned countries. In the area of theatre, the Teatro de Arena, the Teatro Oficina and the Teatro de Rua appeared in quick succession, developing innovative techniques of production, interpretation and direction which would have broad repercussions for the theatrical languages of Latin America and the European underground theatre. The formal experiments of concrete poetry and the fine arts, focusing on art as object, were infused with the same spirit. The unfolding of this creative impulse brought forth even more extraordinary creations. One example of this was the highly complex synthesis of Tropicalism. Echoing the irreverent spirit of the student rebellions of 1968, it combined elements of international pop art, the rhythmical inventions of bossa nova, and the research into Brazilian popular culture, with avant-garde electro-acoustic experiments and televisual innovations. There seemed to be no limits to the propagation of the 'new spirit'.

However, the interruption came, complete and brutal, with the military coup of 1964 which culminated at the end of 1967 and the beginning of 1968 with the revoking of the constitution, the end of the autonomy of Congress and of individuals' civil rights; it was the victory of the Cold War over the spirit of the 'third bank'. A climate of censorship, intolerance, accusations, repression and terror enveloped the country. The militancy of the most radical elements came to prevail, within both military régime and its opponents, averse to any experimentalism or innovations not associated with the terms posed by the confrontation of political forces. The systematic information blockade which characterised this period particularly marked the generation growing up, creating a rift with the cultural experiences of the recent past, and giving rise to what the critic Antônio Cândido termed 'the generation of silence'. The rupture of this link in the chain of generations allowed one of the dominant tendencies in the international market to fully affirm itself – namely mass culture. This was exemplified especially by commercial television based on the American model, the entertainment industry and aggressive advertising techniques, promoting consumerism as the basic nexus between the individual and society.

The gradual return to a democratic institutional order, at the beginning of the 1980s, revealed a country that had changed significantly. The development projects of successive military governments were based on the establishment of major state infrastructure companies as well as quangos and agencies designed to provide regional economic incentives. This led to growing inflation and encouraged corruption, due to the lack of control over budgets and fiscal spending. The rigid control exercised over trade unions, obstacles to political participation, serious abuses of human rights and censorship led broad sectors of civil society into systematic opposition, forcing the return to the rule of law. The growth and diversification of the economy accelerated the flow of the rural population to the cities where, in search of new opportunities, they swelled the slum areas on the peripheries of the capitals. The consequent intense demand for opportunities to participate in the market, for access to services, housing, health and education, stimulated, on the one hand, all kinds of demagogic and populist practices by the institutional parties and, on the other, the open confrontation of popular organisations with the new civil authorities.

This new political arrangement fragmented the previously unified opposition bloc, giving rise to cultural policies linked to support from governments, political parties and organisations, who favoured groups of artists or types of artistic production which served particularly to widen their acceptance and support bases. On the other hand, the large communications groups developed during the military period, which controlled wide networks of different media, were able – due to their capacity to standardise tastes and set consumer habits – to impose their standards of production and commercialisation. Caught in this way between the opportunities offered by the new cultural policies and the possibilities presented by the large entertainment companies, the artistic community lost much of its spontaneity and its historically rooted capacity to generate transformative events.

Political liberalisation did, on the other hand, make possible the renewal of contacts with the international scene and the bringing up-to-date of the country's cultural agenda. In the context of a general process of globalisation, however, this cultural opening up also exposed the Brazilian media to an invasion of dominant and more successful items of international pop culture, saturating the public with conventional formulae, with a star system of established artists, and with internationally standardised sales strategies. Everything proliferated throughout the country in the prescribed way: rock, punk, reggae, funk, rap, Michael Jackson, Madonna, E.T., Garfield, Schwarzenegger, *The Phantom of the Opera, Star Trek: The Next Generation.* However, once the great 'devouring' of the 1980s had passed, in the following decade this mixture of influences began to produce new forms of cross-fertilisation with Brazilian artistic currents of older traditions, with surprising and promising results. This was the case with the musical experiments mixing the tonalities and conventions of São Paulo pop, the new forms of choreographic expression flourishing in Belo Horizonte, the rhythmical exploration of cultural roots in Salvador and Rio de Janeiro, the hybrid forms derived from reggae in São Luís, funk in Rio de Janeiro, rap in São Paulo, or the amazing fusion of *manguebeat* in Recife, among other currents.

Circumstances have changed rapidly. Rio de Janeiro's carnival is increasingly a tourist and televisual event and less a popular street festival. Popular catholicism and African traditions are under attack from the invasion and aggressive competition of pentecostalism, whose band of followers multiplies continuously in the peripheries of the large cities. The great football stars prefer to chase money and fame in Europe or Japan rather than savour the joy of the Brazilian game. Although the pace of change increases, something nevertheless seems stubbornly to persist.

This something can be felt, for example, in the tragedy which struck the idol of the racing circuits, Ayrton Senna. As a Formula 1 driver, associated with a jet-setting lifestyle, mixing with celebrities and the practitioners of other dangerous sports, he was a living symbol of modernity in its most overwhelming sense. Yet the immense public shock provoked by his death seems to indicate that there was something more to his image. Ayrton in the cockpit of his car, always speeding, shooting around the race-tracks of the world, untouchable, unbeatable, setting his sights further and further ahead, had something about him of the man of the third bank of the river. It was possible to see him through the eyes with which for centuries the men and women of Brazil have sought the mysterious peacock, the enchanted bull, the Uirapurú bird, the Vabapuçu Lake – all these magical sources which proclaim a world of peace, fraternity and justice.

They are only visions, but it was from visions that Canudos was made. And Brazil's great challenge is still that of redeeming the sacrifice of Canudos, of its women, men and children – wherever they are today, dispersed among the mass of wandering landless in the backlands, the homeless in the cities and the legions of streetchildren. A population in perpetual movement, citizens without citizenship, cities of nomads, creatures whose only certainty is vision as destiny. As the son of the oarsman in Guimarães Rosa's story proclaimed: 'Put me too in a wretched little canoe, in this water, which never stops, with its wide banks: and me, down-river, up-river, midstream – the river.'[33]

Notes

1 João Guimarães Rosa, 'A Hora e a Vez de Augusto Matraga', in *Sagarana*, 18th edn, Rio de Janeiro, José Olympio, 1976, pp. 358–62.

2 Euclides da Cunha, *Obra Completa*, Rio de Janeiro, Aguilar, 1966, Vol. I, pp. 497–504.

3 Sérgio Buarque de Hollanda, *Raízes do Brasil*, 5th edn, Rio de Janeiro, José Olympio, 1977, p. 3.

4 For a detailed analysis of sugar-cane plantation society, see Stuart Schwartz, *Segredos Internos: engenhos e escravos na sociedade colonial*, São Paulo, Cia das Letras, 1988.

5 João Guimarães Rosa, op. cit., p. 362.

6 Sérgio Buarque de Hollanda, *Monções*, 2nd edn., São Paulo, Alfa-Omega, 1986, p. xv.

7 On the Land Law of 1850 see José de Souza Martins, 'A vida privada nas áreas de expansão da sociedade brasileira' in Lilia Moritz Schwarz (ed.), *História da Vida Privada no Brasil*, Vol. 4, São Paulo, Cia das Letras, 1998.

8 Eric J. Hobsbawm, *The Age of Empire, 1875–1914*, London, Weidenfeld and Nicolson, 1987, pp. 34–55; also Eric J. Hobsbawm, *The Age of Extremes, 1914–1991*, London, Abacus, pp. 85–141.

9 On the colonial rebellions, including the conflicts in Rio de la Plata, see Eric J. Hobsbawm, *The Age of Empire, 1875–1914*, op. cit., pp. 56–83; on the effect of the war on the destabilisation of the Brazilian monarchy, see Raymundo Faoro, *A Pirâmide e o Trapézio*, São Paulo, Nacional, 1974, especially pp. 40–89, and also *História Econômica do Brasil*, the chapter entitled 'A República Burguesa', by Caio Prado Jr., 20th edn, São Paulo, Brasiliense, 1977, pp. 207–286. Euclides da Cunha was wholly aware of the way in which European imperialist expansion was manifested in the attempt

by the Brazilian elites to establish greater control over the territories and populations of the backlands with the support of foreign capital. When he formulated his counsel 'let us look to the backlands', it was in the sense of integrating these areas into the national economy, as well as providing the backlands population with the rights and benefits of citizenship, while simultaneously protecting them from the voracity of new forms of internal colonialism. 'Let us reduce the exclusive attachment to the coast. Let us not be entirely taken up with contemplating the phantasm of that questionable civilisation which, strangling Asia with the steel collar of the Trans-Siberian, and seizing Africa with the claws of soldiers' bayonets, also dilutes the ferocity of the Boxers and remains unmoved before the heroic agony of the Transvaal . . .' Euclides da Cunha, op cit, vol. 1, p. 504.

10 On the *Encilhamento*, the period of wild speculation in the early period of the Republic, see Nicolau Sevcenko, *Literatura como Missão: tensões sociais e criação cultural na Primeira República*, 4th edn, São Paulo, Brasiliense, 1995, pp. 25–41.

11 Ralph della Cava, 'Um confronto entre Juazeiro, Canudos e Contestado', in Boris Fausto (ed.), *História Geral da Civilização Brasileira*, São Paulo, Difel, 1975, vol. 9, pp. 58–71; esp. p. 60.

12 In a recent, highly original work, Maria Cristina Cortez Wissenbach repositions the history of Canudos in the context of the processes of internal migration typical of the rural population, seeing it as an authentic city, and not just a settlement, village, or town, as it is often referred to, including by Euclides himself, thus minimising its complex structure and significance. M. C. C. Wissenbach, 'Da Escravidão à Liberdade: dimensões de uma privacidade possível', in N. Sevcenko (ed.), *História da Vida Privada no Brasil*, vol. 3, São Paulo, Cia das Letras, 1998, pp. 49–130.

13 N. Sevcenko, entry for millenarianism, in *Encyclopaedia of Latin American Culture*, London, Routledge (to be published).

14 On the black community, their roots, traditions and historical circumstances at the turn of the century, see Roberto Moura, *Tia Ciata e a Pequena África no Rio de Janeiro*, 2nd edn, Rio de Janeiro, Secretaria Municipal de Cultura, DGDIC, DE, 1995.

15 N. Sevcenko, 'O Prelúdio Republicano: astúcias da ordem e ilusões do progresso', in *História da Vida Privada*, vol. 3, pp. 7–49.

16 On the Regeneration and its social effects, see N. Sevcenko, *Literatura Como Missão: tensões sociais e craição cultural na Primeira República*, pp. 25–41, 51–68 *et passim*.

17 N. Sevcenko, *A Revolta da Vacina, mentes insanas em corpos rebeldes*, São Paulo, Scipione, 1993.

18 On the context of Paris-São Paulo relations after the Great War and during the 1920s, see N. Sevcenko, *Orfeu Extático na Metrópole, São Paulo sociedade e cultura nos frementes anos 20*, São Paulo, Cia das Letras, 1998. Also Alexandre Eulálio, *A Aventura Brasileira de Blaise Cendrars*, São Paulo/Brasília, Quíron/ INL, 1989, pp. 51–4.

19 N. Sevcenko, 'São Paulo: the quintessential, uninhibited megalopolis as seen by Blaise Cendrars in the 1920s', in Theo Barker and Anthony Sutcliffe

(eds.), *Megalopolis: The Giant City in History*, London, Macmillan, 1993, pp. 175–193.

20 N. Sevcenko, *Orfeu Extático na Metrópole*, p. 289.

21 Sérgio Buarque de Hollanda, 'Caminhos do Extremo Oeste', in *O Extremo Oeste*, São Paulo, Brasiliense, Secretaria de Estado da Cultura, 1986, pp. 25–88, esp. p. 26.

22 Maria Odila Leite da Silva Dias, *Quotidiano e Poder em São Paulo no Século XIX*, São Paulo, Brasiliense, 1984. (English edition: *Powers and Everyday Life: the Lives of Working Women in Nineteenth Century Brazil*, Cambridge, Polity Press, 1995.)

23 Elias Thomé Saliba (ed. and Introduction), *As Idéias Econômicas de Cincinato Braga*, Brasília/Rio de Janeiro, Senado Federal/Fundação Casa de Rui Barbosa/MEC, 1983, see p. 34 for quantitative data.

24 N. Sevcenko, 'São Paulo: the quintessential uninhibited megalopolis as seen by Blaise Cendrars', pp. 175–93.

25 According to the first census, carried out in 1872, when the city was already experiencing the great coffee boom in São Paulo territory, its population was 19,347 inhabitants. A number which had risen to 64,934 by the following census in 1890. At the beginning of the 20th century, the city already had 270,000 inhabitants, according to the survey of 1908. This figure doubled in 1920, reaching 587,000 and had almost doubled again by 1934, to reach 1,000,120 inhabitants. This means that in the space of 62 years, from 1872 to 1934, São Paulo experienced a massive 5,689 per cent increase in population, or in other words, the city grew at the rate of 6.77 per cent each year. These figures, compared to those of other world metropolises, fully justify the patriotic refrain, 'São Paulo is the fastest growing city in the world!' N. Sevcenko, *Orfeu Extático na Metrópole*, pp. 108–9. Also 'São Paulo: the quintessential uninhibited megalopolis as seen by Blaise Cendrars', pp. 190–93, where these figures are compared with other international metropolises.

26 Blaise Cendrars, 'Feuilles de Route', in *Au Coeur du Monde, Poésies Complètes: 1924–1929*, Paris, Gallimard, 1985, pp. 63–4.

27 Aracy Amaral, *Blaise Cendrars no Brasil e os Modernistas*, São Paulo, Martins, 1970, pp. 39–79; A. Eulálio, *A Aventura Brasileira de Blaise Cendrars*, pp. 51–4.

28 Aracy Amaral, *Tarsila, sua obra e seu tempo*, São Paulo, Perspectiva/EDUSP, 1975, 2 vols, pp. 84–97.

29 N. Sevcenko, *Orfeu Extático na Metrópole*, pp. 223–307.

30 Raymundo Faoro, *Os Donos do Poder, formação do patronato político brasileiro*, 2nd edn, Porto Alegre/São Paulo, Globo/EDUSP, 1975, vol. 2, pp. 579–730.

31 N. Sevcenko, 'O Prelúdio Republicano . . .', pp. 37–8.

32 N. Sevcenko, 'São Paulo: un laboratorio cultural sin fronteras', in *Revista de Occidente*, Madrid, No. 174, (November 1995) pp. 7–36

33 João Guimarães Rosa, 'A Terceira Margem do Rio', in *Sagarana*, p. 37.

Translated by Lorraine Leu

4

The Modern City:
Buenos Aires, The Peripheral Metropolis

Beatriz Sarlo

Travellers in 1918

> Before leaving for Buenos Aires everybody in New York told me that the
> Plaza Hotel was the only hotel in Buenos Aires, and that of course I would
> make it my headquarters during my sojourn there. But my information had
> been given me by men, and neither they nor I expected to find that the
> Plaza did not take women unaccompanied by their husbands or supposed
> husbands. Not even sisters accompanied by their brothers, or wives whose
> husbands have to travel, or widows, are made welcome. Much less respect-
> able maiden ladies![1]

The traveller who penned these lines arrived in Buenos Aires in 1918.
She was Katherine Dreier, a liberal and educated North American (who
years later would write an essay on Marcel Duchamp), to whom both
the city and the condition of its women appeared to be the product of
an entrenched, conservative Hispanic tradition.

She remained unimpressed with the 'Paris of the South' of which
she had heard so much, for two reasons: on the one hand, the
monotony of its layout in an orthogonal grid; on the other, the absence
of a lively and mobile social life in the public sphere. More than Paris,
Buenos Aires reminded her of Brooklyn. Dreier was probably not too
far off the mark, because her perception of Buenos Aires was independent of the idea that its elite had of their city:

> One beautiful avenue, called the Avenida de Mayo, which stretches a little
> more than a mile ..., might easily recall a Parisian boulevard, with its

avenues of trees and its many cafés with small tables and chairs on the
sidewalk. But how unlike Paris in reality! Here one rarely sees a woman,
and, unlike Paris, only men frequent the cafés ... Buenos Aires was
constantly reminding me of Brooklyn. There was only a small section which
was interesting and amusing, and the rest was endless, endless vistas of
streets. Sometimes with good pavement, sometimes with bad, but just streets,
streets, streets.[2]

Also in 1918, a traveller already known in the aesthetic circles of
New York (and undoubtedly a friend of Miss Dreier), Marcel Duchamp,
arrived with the intention of settling for a while in Buenos Aires. He
knew no one and his visit remained a secret; he left no trace and passed
unobserved in Argentina. Bored with a city he considered to be more
like a village, Duchamp returned to the United States in 1919. In letters
written from Buenos Aires before his departure, he judged it severely
and unenthusiastically. To him it seemed a small and vulgar provincial
city, whose elite was unrefined and ignorant of contemporary art.[3] Miss
Dreier shared his impression of the aesthetic tastes of the elite, who
(according to her) chose to decorate their mansions with *pompier* art
and were entirely ignorant of modern architecture.

These judgements on Buenos Aires at the end of the second decade
of the twentieth century describe rather well a society which had faced
a highly accelerated process of economic modernisation, but which was
still characterised by its provincial customs and by the cultural traditionalism of its elites. However, it was the elites who had directed the
process of economic modernisation, including the immigration policies
which changed the socio-cultural profile of Argentina for good.

Neither Dreier nor Duchamp were in a position to capture what lay
behind and underneath that draughts-board of straight streets whose
rectangularity was undoubtedly particularly 'unpicturesque'. Those
straight streets, 'just streets', extending endlessly, are the grid of
modern Buenos Aires, the geometric structure which has allowed it to
grow with unusual speed, its suburbs multiplying in just a few decades.[4]
Under this grid are the drainpipes and the tunnels of the first underground system (which was inaugurated in 1913); and on the surface,
following the lines of the grid, the tram lines, electricity lines and
telephone cables. Naturally, this failed to impress the traveller from
New York, but it did form the basis of an urban modernisation which
only a few years later would support the processes of cultural modernity.

The subterranean and aerial network of services and transport, which
Dreier and Duchamp glanced at uninterestedly or failed to note, was
one of the most dynamic layers of the real city. The city always appears
as a *pentimento* or layering: on to a surface which originated in the past,

different interventions are superimposed; these obscure the signs of the past, although such signs persist as traces which etch lines of heterogeneous and often contradictory origin. The city is like a historical atlas, with transparent maps that reveal the relief of the land, the course of avenues and tunnels, the transport system, the divisions of the different neighbourhoods, the demographic profile, the net of wireless communication, the circuits of work, commerce and leisure. All these maps have varied during the decades and the city results from their concrete and conflictive superimposition, in which one or several logics, principles of rationality and impulses of disorder are apparent. These dense material and symbolic networks contain, define and limit our imagination. Captured by these networks, but modifying them at the same time, distorting their web, the urban imagination projects images of the city.

New sensibility and nostalgia

Buenos Aires was, first of all, a Hispanic-creole city, probably the most impoverished seat of the Spanish viceroyalty, established on absolutely flat land, completely lacking in the picturesque. From the last third of the nineteenth century, the local elites were imagining and constructing a colonial city based on a European model, which not only tried to imitate French architectural styles but also based its modernity on the implantation of new urban technologies: a system of sewers and drain-pipes, running water and lighting, rapid transport routes, large administrative buildings, schools and hospitals.

To this city under accelerated construction European immigrants looking for opportunities of economic advancement arrived, enriching the landscape of modernity with their cultural and linguistic variation. As in São Paulo and New York, in Buenos Aires a major demographic change occurred, accompanied by urban and social transformations. Little by little the city was erasing the characteristics of its past, drawing a new map on the colonial outline, imposing new architecture on the blocks where old creole buildings still endured.

In the period of emergence and consolidation of the modern city (which began around 1890, accelerated from 1900, and became tumultuous in the 1920s and 1930s), there were rapid and dramatic changes, which are also clearly visible at the level of culture. Beginning with new perceptions of time and space these changes generated new forms of subjectivity. Men and women born in the city at the end of the nineteenth century and the beginning of the twentieth, if they still lived there twenty years later, did so in a city radically different from that of their childhood. The impression of change was even greater when someone arrived in Buenos Aires after having spent years away.

Jorge Luis Borges, to take an example of an author born in 1899, travelled with his family to Europe in 1914 and spent his adolescence in Switzerland. When he returned in 1921 the Buenos Aires which he had known as a child had receded to the outskirts, visible only in the distant suburbs which bordered the plain. This is precisely what Borges writes about in his first book of poems, published in 1923:

> The streets of Buenos Aires
> have become my heart and soul
> not the brisk street
> encumbered by haste and drudgery
> but the sweet suburban street
> mellowed by trees and sunset
> and those further off
> strangers to the merciful rows of trees
> where austere little houses scarcely venture
> troubled by immortal distances
> to intrude on the limitless view
> made of the vast plains and vaster sky.[5]

This Hispanic-creole city of his childhood emerged like a trace on the historical map, a *pentimento* which revealed the nostalgic remains of the past persisting in the present. Shops, patios, dirt tracks, borders between the city and the pampas, are the elements of the poetic landscape of this first Borges, who searched for Buenos Aires in the 1920s, underneath or far from the transformations of modernity, the memory of a creole city which was disappearing:

> Here again the eventuality of the pampa on any horizon
> and the wasteland which falls into a ruin of weeds and wires
> and the shop as clean as the new moon yesterday evening
> is familiar like the memory of a street corner
> with those long walkways and the promise of a patio
> merciful and easy as an ave maria.[6]

Borges remembered a city which was ceasing to exist or receding to the outskirts because Buenos Aires was moving with an unrestrainable impulse. Between 1890 and 1930 the outline of the city, following the form of blocks 100 metres square, was imposed over the entire area of the city, even on land which had been previously unoccupied but which soon would cease to be. Some intellectuals complained that the topography of Buenos Aires had become excessively monotonous and blamed the squareness for the city's inability to appear picturesque. Writers like Borges, however, who interpreted the squareness from the perspective of the pampas, followed the straight streets, 'languidly submissive',[7] until they emptied onto the plain. Others, like Roberto Arlt, looked at the new city in terms of its overcrowding, its lack of light, its layer of grime, but also in terms of its skyscrapers and luminous billboards, taller and brighter than those which existed elsewhere in 1930. Visitors like Le Corbusier observed two things: on the one hand, the need for the city to establish a spatial and scenic dialogue with the River Plate; on the other, that the small houses of the suburbs, constructed by Italian artisans, with their pure, geometric forms, their simplicity due to the scarcity imposed by tight budgets, unwittingly reflected the ordered clarity of modern forms.[8]

The tumult of change: 1920 to 1930

Horse-drawn traffic always travelled incredibly quickly through the Latin American villages that were later transformed into cities. But the spread of electricity-powered transport changed for all time the perception of the city, as well as the point of view from which it was perceived: the city began to be seen both at great speed and from above.

The incorporation of new technologies changed transport, lighting and, therefore, both the material and symbolic ways of experiencing the city. It was no longer possible to perceive buildings with lights and shadows changing with the advance or retreat of natural light, barely affected by weak street lighting. The urban landscapes, illuminated by gas or electricity, would never be the same again. Literature abounds with images of buildings which rapidly 'file past' before the eyes of passengers on an electric tram, and their façades are different, since the play of size, chiaroscuro and space alters with the 'expressionistic' effects of speed and light.

This technical modernity places Buenos Aires in line with other Western capitals. Paris had never been the only European model for Buenos Aires, although it was French Beaux Arts architecture which set the tone for the great mansions of the elites constructed at the turn of the twentieth century. Various ideas of the city – among them that of New York, the American metropolis par excellence – supplied images for thinking about the city of the River Plate. Insofar as modernisation made headway within the sphere of culture, New York began to function as a powerful influence on the imagination.

In 1928, just ten years after the impressions registered by the travellers Dreier and Duchamp, the novelist and journalist Roberto Arlt chose New York and not Paris to find a comparison with a commercial arcade in the centre of Buenos Aires. This arcade, called Güemes Passage, would have been conceived in terms of the famous Parisian passages.[9] However, the mix of different cultures and the disorder bring to the foreground of the imagination an intensely capitalist New York:

> The terror of the electric light from morning until night floods in eternum the crypts, vaults and kiosks of glass . . . The buzz of the elevators, ascending, or rather sliding vertically . . . and that sea of well-dressed and mysterious people who pass from morning until night, and who knows if they might be thieving gentiles, plainclothes police, or theatre impresarios. There one breathes the atmosphere of New York; it is the Babel of Yankeeland transplanted onto creole soil and imposing the prestige of its self-service bars, its yellow shoes, its gramophones, its rainbow-coloured billboards and its girls on their way to the theatres to watch variety numbers in the basements and the top floors.[10]

This quote captures various characteristics of modernisation in progress: the tall buildings in the centre of the city which replace the two- or three-storey houses from the last half of the nineteenth century; the electric light which produces that typically modern phenomenon in which the daily cycle of nature is replaced by the continuity of artificial illumination; the self-service bars and vending machines which, first of all, were seen in films as icons announcing a future where daily needs are automated; long-distance means of communication and the technical reproduction of works of art and popular music; the social mix in which the inhabitants of the modern city have ceased to have personalised relationships (the theme which Walter Benjamin developed with regard to Paris in the nineteenth century but which, in fact, was fully realised only in the cities of the twentieth century, particularly in the North American metropolises).

Strangers in the city

The extraordinary demographic shifts and growth in urban populations between 1880 and 1940 destroyed a network of direct social relationships; the city began to be inhabited by 'strangers'. Tens of thousands of foreigners were included in expanding urban networks. In the first decades of the twentieth century in Buenos Aires, there were more foreigners than 'natives'. Then, from the 1930s onwards, thousands of people arrived from the interior of the country.

These recent arrivals, the immigrants, did not conform (nor did they anywhere else in Latin America) to the notion of 'desirable' foreigners held by the elite – those thought to consolidate civil society and the labour market. The elites had imagined immigrants of the blond Piedmontese type, who were labourers or had a good knowledge of land cultivation and who were from an already modernised area of Italy, or the artisans and peasants from some German colonies, who disembarked in the province of Buenos Aires. Instead those who came were the wretched of Europe and Asia Minor: peasants from tiny villages in the south and north of Italy; illiterate or anarchist artisans from Spain; Jews escaped from the Polish or Russian ghettos; Syrians or Arabs.

As early as 1910, an essayist, historian and major critic, Ricardo Rojas, diagnosed with alarm the presence of the foreigner in Buenos Aires. He criticised the notices in shop windows written in Yiddish, Polish and Italian; the Italian-based societies, which exhibited photographs of King Umberto and the Italian flag; the newspapers and patriotic celebrations of various communities; the Jews with their frock coats and skull caps occupying some of the areas of Buenos Aires and building their synagogues there.[11]

This ethnic mix changed the colours and languages of the city. Twenty years after the fearful warnings of Ricardo Rojas, this process had unleashed its full potential and profoundly reconfigured the symbolic sphere, as well as daily life. Once again, Roberto Arlt offers a description sensitive to these new characteristics:

> For the spectator with only an average sense of colour, this ghetto of Semitic and Syrian appearance is almost indescribable. So many luminous and diverse nuances make up the beauty of this Levantine watercolour... A street of men who speak a language drier and more harsh than the desert sand and who inhabit market stalls and shops which remain fresh in the summer like the cellars of a harem. Streets with fabric of a thousand colours; streets with musical and bewitching names: Alidalla, Hassatrian, Oulman, with windows shaded with material like a metallic weave, with extravagant flowers of silver and bronze ... Fabrics. Threads. Vegetable silks. Wools. And men with noses like deformed grapefruit, with ears like cabbage leaves, pointed lips, twisted jaws ... The words crackle and spark or are dragged out guttural, nasal and incomprehensible. At times these men play like boys, push each other by the shoulders, run into the middle of the street, shout like dogs and then once again recover the rhythm of their tranquility and continue conversing.[12]

Trade unionism and anarchism also arrived with the immigrants; the first political clientele of socialism were immigrants, whose organisers actually belonged to the university-educated middle class. The political ideologies, the forms of labour organisation, the strategies for struggle and mobilisation, through unions and strikes, gave the elites additional cause for alarm. The Babel of foreign languages, the change of daily customs and the appearance of intellectuals of immigrant origin (two very different phenomena, but related in the imagination) were experienced as a threat to the cultural unity of the nation.

This idea of a threat to national cultural unity became central to the debates of the time – debates on the European origins of the Argentinian racial mix and on whether the social pre-eminence of the Hispanic-creole elite should be preserved in the face of the immigrant racial disorder. What did it mean to be Argentinean? Who had the right to define the limits of this cultural field where everything was beginning to be mixed?

The language of the immigrants could be heard everywhere in Buenos Aires. The sons and daughters of the Hispanic-creole elite felt that linguistic 'authenticity' was being threatened. 'Our city is called Babel', wrote Borges.[13] And he re-read the tradition of gauchesque poetry from the nineteenth century, asking himself who would be the writer in the twentieth century who would find a contemporary inflexion for literary language, without yielding to *lunfardo* (slang spoken by inhabitants of Buenos Aires) or the picturesque, just as José Hernández and the gauchesque poets had found a sonority and River Plate rhythm for Spanish.

A friend of Borges, the painter Xul Solar,[14] faced with this same conflict of languages, proposed an imaginary solution with the invention of 'neocreole', a Panamerican language based on Latin roots and local expressions. Xul Solar also invented a type of Esperanto, the 'panlanguage', some of whose phrases he inscribed in his paintings or used as titles. Both inventions (which have strong elements of play and vanguardist challenge) can be interpreted as a symbolic response to the malaise provoked by the intermixture of languages as well as a stake in this very intermixture (from Latin to the American languages), provided that this combination was realised under the hegemony of the elite. Borges himself experienced a strong fascination for artificial languages all his life. Already in 1925 he was writing: 'No intellectual prohibition can prevent us from believing that beyond our language other, different ones can emerge which will have to correspond to it like algebra to arithmetic and non-Euclidean geometry to ancient mathematics.'[15] To the social turbulence of the immigrants' languages, Borges counterposed the order and clarity of intellectual invention.

Means of communication

The mass media are an indisposable part of the modern city. In the 1920s in Buenos Aires two newspapers were already being published which marked a truly revolutionary turn in the written media. These were *Crítica* (modelled on the big popular American newspapers) and *El Mundo* (the first tabloid). In both of these a new type of professional journalist was involved, as well as the majority of the writers of the vanguard. Borges collaborated on *Crítica*, where he briefly directed a cultural supplement, and Roberto Arlt on *El Mundo*.

Along with the technical modernisation introduced by the rotary printing press – the reproduction of photographs and the use of cables as a source of national and international news – came the creation of popular journalistic genres: the sports section, the entertainment section (revolving at first around the theatre, then around film), sections dedicated to women and, as the great discursive genre of the popular press, crime reports. These newspapers changed the language of journalism, incorporating the inflexions of spoken language, and above all they established a permanent bond with their readers, who felt that they represented their culture and interests.

Towards the end of the 1920s another great innovation in technological communication appeared: the first radio broadcasts. Radio radically reconfigured the cultural field; its hegemony announced that, from here onwards, until the arrival of what today we call post-modernity, it would be the long-distance means of communication which set the tone for popular cultures. The speed with which radio spread in Buenos Aires (and soon after in the whole of Argentina) caused new relationships to emerge between the elite and popular cultures. From then on, the culture industry was competing with institutions like schools in the formation of taste and the imposition of cultural themes.

Indeed, the new forms of knowledge could not help but compete with the traditional humanistic knowledge of the elites. It was technical knowledge that fired all the fantasies of the technical imagination; modernity and technology were inseparable. This is evident in the news coverage of the popular press, which follows day by day the inventions which mark the first half of the century. It is also a central topic in the novels of Roberto Arlt and the poetry of Oliverio Girondo and, in general, in the avant-garde work of the 1920s and 1930s. Many of Xul Solar's paintings, for instance, combine technological forms and stylisations of parts of the human body; strange creatures of science fiction move around operating invented machines which are a hybrid of the

aeroplane and submarine. They are poetic and technological representations, futuristic and fantastic. From technical knowledge, modernity
extracts objects and figurations which pose the possibility of a new
culture in which the predominance of literary culture is no longer
guaranteed.

Between 1940 and 1990

In these same decades, from 1920 and especially since 1930, two other
fundamental events occurred in modern popular culture: the spread of
football as a national sport, which was very quickly professionalised; and
the peak of the tango, which generated not just a repertoire of popular
songs, but also films and large-scale theatrical spectacles. All of this
points to new masses occupying urban space both physically and
symbolically.

The crowd appeared, and became an issue in pessimistic essays on
the city (as it was in European thinking on mass society). In 1940
Ezequiel Martínez Estrada discovered the threatening aspect of those
multitudes who 'overrun the city, frequently in trucks, waving their
banners and singing jubilant refrains which are still not quite songs.
They are shouts, attitudes which they voice and throw in the faces of
passers-by, blasts of the breath of their cave-dwelling ancestors.'[16] Buenos Aires, which considered itself a metropolis when it had not yet
reached that stage, sixty years ago showed the signs which intellectuals
had learnt to fear in modern societies: the masses occupy the city, the
city is the stage for the masses.

Both the city and the crowd prefigured what was to become Peronism in Argentinean political culture. With Peronism the city became
aggressively social. The plebeian phantoms of politics occupied the
space of the perceived and imagined city. The cycle of economic
modernisation had been fulfilled and given its profile to Buenos Aires.
The modern and peripheral city had been receiving migrants from the
provinces since 1930. With Peronism in power, those 'cabecitas negras'
(as Argentines of mestizo origin are called) became protagonists in the
1940s and '50s.

Although it provoked a worsening in the political, economic and
working conditions of the working classes, as far as Buenos Aires was
concerned, the fall of Peron in 1955 initiated processes which brought
about the definitive consolidation of the modern city. Thus, in the
1970s, one could say that modernity had fulfilled its promises and
demonstrated its injustices and conflicts. With a military dictatorship

installed in 1976, Buenos Aires witnessed a technocratic politics and authoritarian modernisation in the area of transport, with the construction of motorways which ran almost to the centre of the city, the eradication of shanty towns and the consolidation of social inequities. The technologisation of the city is a powerful tendency which continues up to the present; some areas of Buenos Aires have been practically rebuilt on the model of close-of-the-century urban interventions in the large metropolises.

However, in the cultural and aesthetic imagination the city is often seen as a landscape of decadence. This perspective is based, on the one hand, on the deterioration of the old city centre and many other areas, and, on the other, on the exodus of the affluent sectors of society to the suburbs on the periphery. I would like now to offer an extended analysis of the work of two writers whose visions of the city are inscribed precisely in this image of urban–cultural deterioration.

In his novel *El aire* (1992), Sergio Chejfec – born in 1956, a year after the fall of Peronism – engages with the work of the great essayist Ezequiel Martínez Estrada, a writer of Borges' age who himself wrote three works on the subject of modern Argentina. *El aire* examines the way in which modernity configured Buenos Aires and the changes which the post-modern shift brought to the city. In the novel, Buenos Aires is a place of deviation and digression. Yet it is not about a superficial post-modern gaze in a culturally post-modern urban space, but about itineraries in a city with a destroyed, failed and fissured modernity.

Right at the close of the twentieth century, Buenos Aires appears for the first time in fiction not as a city that is full, or overflowing, but as a city which is being emptied. Martínez Estrada, in *Radiografía de la pampa* (1933), had stated that Buenos Aires was an excrescence of soil from the surrounding plain, that even the skyscrapers were layers of that thick, moist earth. As it grew, using buildings as a mask, Buenos Aires concealed the pampas which were its origin and will be its destiny. Martínez Estrada saw Buenos Aires as subject to superimpositions, additions, metastases, the filling of empty spaces which are never completely filled:

> All along a block the different buildings speak different languages of time, the cataclysms which have shaken them . . . Next to single storey houses, those of two storeys; and between them wasteland and skyscrapers of twenty or thirty floors which emerge with the prevailing ambition of the time . . . A skyscraper in a block of ground floor buildings, near to lands which still retain original pasture, indicates the same ambition as well as its reverse – ruin: the fracture of a piece of ground on which everything is situated . . .

On top of the single storey buildings, which formed the previous city, it seems that another city was beginning to be constructed on other floors . . . In the beginning one built on the land; today the first floor is used as the land, and the single storey houses are already the wastelands of the houses of two or more storeys. Because of this Buenos Aires has the structure of the pampa; the plain on which, like the sand and the loess, another plain continually superimposes itself, followed by another.[17]

Sixty years later, Chejfec imagines a city marked by opposite events: the plain returns to reclaim its rights and the country enters the city, where the ruins of the buildings turn into demolition sites, the demolition sites into wasteland, the wasteland into countryside:

Those undefined wastelands represented a spontaneous interjection of the countryside into the city, thus seeming to render a sad tribute to its original state. It constituted pure regression: the city was depopulated, it ceased to be a city, and nothing was done with the empty ground that from one day to the next gangs of bulldozers cleared: instantly it became pampa again. . . . In a literal way, the pampa advanced on Buenos Aires. In this way, I had read somewhere, with the retreat of the city, space, which is a fundamental category for the survival of collective memory, was disappearing into thin air. And not just because the buildings returned to nature when they were demolished, but also because the actual memories of the individual inhabitants – whether original inhabitants or not – were unable to recognise the city.[18]

The city has become precarious precisely because that which defines it as a city, its compact quality, the product of a deliberate, cultural gesture, is threatened with erosion through decadence. If that happens, nature (which, according to Martínez Estrada, lays siege to the city) takes its revenge: Buenos Aires returns to the pampa. As in a cross-section, the layers of old and new are all simultaneously visible; the countryside penetrates what the city abandons, in a movement whose direction restores Buenos Aires to what it was: the plains, nature. This fictional vision takes real processes into account. The centre of Buenos Aires has lost the appeal it acquired in the process of modernity, and, like many other cities in the West, the middle classes tend to move to economically and socially homogenous suburbs.

Martínez Estrada judged a city defined by an ascendent modernity. Chejfec fictionalises the city at the end of the twentieth century, when migration has reconfigured the social topography and many ultra-urbanised areas of the centre are occupied by the poor and turning into slums. These spatial mutations, which modify the cultural configuration of the familiar space, also annul the possibilities of identification with the city: memory is lost because, confronted with the plains, the city is erasing its own past as an urban incursion into the plain.

In *El aire*, the futuristic hypothesis of 'slumification' does not draw on the images of the shanty towns which have surrounded Buenos Aires since the forties, to the south, part of the north and part of the west. On the contrary, Chejfec is concerned with the inner city. The shanty towns, instead of spreading to the limits of the city as before, now occupy the terraces and the roofs of its buildings, taken over by the poor as precarious dwellings; they grow, like the skyscrapers, in the centre and upwards:

> Now one could distinguish a precarious organisation, often trembling in the breeze, of light bulbs and little lamps. They were the shanty towns of flat-roofed shacks, provided with light by a cable which ran up alongside the outside of the buildings. Barroso observed the women working, indefatigable even at night, cleaning the terrace, preparing the meal, looking after the children and speaking from time to time with their husbands, who generally stared ahead with their eyes lost in the void, with an intimidating air, smoking, with one arm leaning on the corner of the table, precarious as well, and which before going to bed they would all lift on its side, to take into the house.[19]

The Others, the migrants from the interior or from other parts of Latin America, which the modern city was depositing on its outskirts, penetrate it, depositing on high the waste from its dwellings. The skies, previously populated only by the silhouettes of skyscrapers, become the vertical dimension of urban marginality. The neon lights, which in the modernist and modern imagination should illuminate the highest points of the city, become the precarious lamps of elevated slums.

The symbolic consequences of these processes are evident in two forms of loss. The first is a 'dissimulated linguistic confusion', alterations and anomalies in the lexical system, which apparently tends to Latin Americanise itself or to objectivise itself in the form of a more neutral Spanish (possibly the Spanish which circulates in the virtual linguistic geography of the mass media), forgetting the characteristics which were previously considered distinctively national. The second is the loss of the qualities which constituted one of the masculine myths of urban culture in Buenos Aires – football:

> On arriving at the edge of the ruined area he saw a mass of people playing football. The goals were stones, pillars or destroyed dividing walls; in the interior of what were once rooms, young boys developed their first skills in the art of controlling the ball . . . The teams stretched out to the horizon. However, to their recurring surprise, the majority played badly. The enthusiasts stopped in the middle of the field not knowing what to do while someone or other was running.[20]

Martínez Estrada had seen in the football crowds a threatening concentration of the masses, an amorphous body, ungovernable and not subject to the rules of reason or morality; he had foreseen in these passionate crowds what would come to be, a few years later, the Peronist multitude. In 1940 he wrote:

> The people of the metropolis have their deep and unrestrainable passions. One of them, the most typical and vehement, takes the external appearance of football. The sports stadiums, with a capacity of over one hundred thousand people, on festive days become temples to which devotees of a very old and complex cult flock. The manner adopted is simple: attend a football game with unrestrained passion . . . It is an act which concentrates a violent urge to fight, the war instinct, the admiration of skill, the need to shout and hurl abuse.[21]

In Chejfec's novel, the inverse movement is again produced: the football masses are formed of disorientated men, unable to distinguish themselves even in this way. In the deteriorated scene of the city, they are deteriorated multitudes.

These urban, material and cultural processes produce forgetting: 'The actual memories of the individual inhabitants – whether original inhabitants or not – were unable to recognise the city.'[22] In effect, not only has the city changed, but the city of the past does not form a part of the image of the city of the present: the historical map, the *pentimento*, has ceased to exist. That which generates the density of the urban imagination – an idea of the past and an idea of the future – is absent from the Buenos Aires of *El aire*.

In the 1930s and '40s, Martínez Estrada believed himself to be diagnosing a metropolitan excess. His concern was luxury and the mask of prosperity. In the nineties, Chejfec believed that he was perceiving a deterioration and a lack. Both, however, concur in the idea that the plains are a 'horizontal delirium' which has marked culture. The city forgets its identity, amends its speech with light contaminations of 'international' Spanish, while it recedes to what is also an impossible place because there is no escape from the materiality of the city.

Within the space of a century, literature drew its inspiration from the city, celebrating it, criticising it, superimposing on its concrete scenery the aesthetic scenery of the anticipation of the future or nostalgia for the past. In Argentina, the idea of the city has both a utopian and a prophetic character, because the project of Buenos Aires as a great city of the South was articulated towards the middle of the nineteenth century, when the actual city was still a village, a conglomerate of cardboard, wood and rubbish, with a few poor colonial buildings. Since then Buenos Aires has been presenting to both ideologues and writers a much more powerful image than its material evidence has merited. It has often been said that Argentinian intellectuals invariably admired European cities. However, together with evidence of this admiration, one can discern pride in what Buenos Aires was and promised to be. Today the city seems to have lost its qualities, not just in the dreaded anonymity of the crowd, but by virtue of the narrative hypothesis of a return to the plains from whence it arose. Several processes are apparent here. First is the exodus from the city to the suburbs by the economic elites and the sections of the middle classes who were able to adapt or prosper during the years of neo-liberal transformation. Second is the conversion of the city centre into tourist spaces (where large international hotels are built); areas transformed into museums (chosen for their picturesqueness and embellished after their original inhabitants are expelled); and completely rundown districts where travelling vendors proliferate – those excluded from the labour market and the homeless. The city receives large international injections of capital directed at the service sector, which uses the urban past as decoration; alongside these enterprising models of capitalism lie areas of profound squalor, untouched by urban technification or post-modern architecture. Some traditionally dynamic parts of Buenos Aires have become slums; here we find hotels for migrants, old peeling houses still undiscovered by some developer with an interest in rebuilding, second-rate urban services, a lack of safety. These processes are occurring in a city which is changing with a speed previously experienced only at the close of the nineteenth century, when the ideal of urban expansion and the extension of services to all prevailed. In the metaphor of a Buenos Aires invaded by Others and deprived of the memory of its cultural characteristics, today we can discern the other side of the enthusiasm, nostalgia, criticism and optimism which inspired its first modernity.

Notes

1 Katherine S. Dreier, *Five Months in the Argentine from a Woman's Point of View: 1918 to 1919*, New York, Fredric Fairchild Sherman, 1920, p. 13.
2 Ibid., p. 265.
3 See Rodrigo Aguiar, *Buenos Aires ready made (Marcel Duchamp en Argentina, 1918–1919)*, Buenos Aires, Ediciones del Pirata, 1996; and *Marcel Duchamp*, Milan, Bompiani, 1993 (catalogue of the 1993 Venice exhibition).
4 Adrián Gorelik shows definitively how the grid of square blocks was an instrument of urban modernisation and not a legacy of the colonial city. That sucession of 'streets, streets, streets' which Miss Dreier considered

tedious, was precisely the advance of modern Buenos Aires. See Adrián Gorelik, *La grilla y el parque: Espacio público y cultura urbana en Buenos Aires, 1887–1936*, Quilmes, Editorial de la Universidad de Quilmes, 1998.

5 Jorge Luis Borges, 'Las calles', in *Fervor de Buenos Aires*, Buenos Aires, 1923. Quoted by Jorge Luis Borges, *Poemas (1922–1943)*, Buenos Aires, Losada, 1943, p. 11.

6 Jorge Luis Borges, 'Calle con almacén rosado', in *Luna de enfrente*, Buenos Aires, 1925, p. 77.

7 Jorge Luis Borges, 'Caminata', in *Fervor de Buenos Aires*, p. 59.

8 Le Corbusier, whose ideas were extremely influential on urban thinking until the 1940s, visited Buenos Aires in 1929 to give a series of lectures. He proposed linking the city with the River Plate through the construction of a set of skyscrapers on the river. The lectures were compiled in the volume *Le Corbusier en Buenos Aires, 1929*, Buenos Aires, Sociedad Central de Arquitectos, 1979. On this theme, see J. F. Liernur and P. Pschepiurca, 'Precisiones sobre los proyectos de Le Corbusier en Argentina 1929/1949', *Summa*, Buenos Aires, Dec 1987.

9 However, the Parisian model did not completely lose its influence, precisely because it is an uncontemplated commonplace, an image of the ideology more than a way of thinking about the city. In 'El otro cielo', a story by Julio Cortázar published in *Todos los fuegos el fuego* (Buenos Aires, Sudamericana, 1966), the Güemes Passage is related to the Vivienne Gallery in Paris.

10 Roberto Arlt, 'Pasaje Güemes', published in the newspaper *El Mundo*, 7 September 1928, re-published in Roberto Arlt, *Aguafuertes porteñas: Buenos Aires, vida cotidiana* (compilation and prologue by Sylvia Saitta), Buenos Aires, Alianza, 1993, p. 6.

11 Ricardo Rojas, *La restauración nacionalista*, Buenos Aires, Imprenta de la Penitenciaría, 1910.

12 Roberto Arlt, 'Sirio libaneses en el centro', published in the newspaper *El Mundo*, 23 July 1933, re-published in Roberto Arlt, op. cit., pp. 89–90.

13 'Queja de todo criollo', *Inquisiciones*, 1st edition, 1925. New edition: Buenos Aires, Seix Barral, 1994, p. 145.

14 For more on Xul Solar see: M. H. Gradowczyk (ed), *Xul Solar: Collection of Art Works of the Museum*, Buenos Aires, Fundación Pan Klub-Museo Xul Solar, 1990; and C. Green (ed), *Xul Solar: The Architecture*, Courtauld Institute, 1994 (which includes an essay by John King, 'Xul Solar: Buenos Aires, Modernity and Utopia').

15 Jorge Luis Borges, 'Examen de metaforas', in *Inquisiciones*, p. 52.

16 Ezequiel Martínez Estrada, *La cabeza de Goliat*, Buenos Aires, 1940. I quote the new edition, Buenos Aires, Centro Editor de América Latina, 1966, p. 253.

17 Ezequiel Martínez Estrada, *Radiografía de la pampa* (ed Leo Pollmann), Madrid, Colección Archivos, 1991, pp. 149–150.

18 Sergio Chejfec, *El aire*, Buenos Aires, Alfaguara, 1992, pp. 163–164.

19 Ibid., p. 162.

20 Ibid., p. 123.

21 Ezequiel Martínez Estrada, *La cabeza de Goliat*, p. 249.

22 Sergio Chejfec, *El aire*, p. 164.

Translated by Lorraine Leu

Part III

Modernity in Popular Culture and the Avant-Garde

5

Popular Culture, Modernity and Nation

Renato Ortiz

The fundamental idea which characterises the debate on culture in Latin America, and in Brazil in particular, is that of 'lack', of 'absence'. One can list a number of ways in which this theme has been approached, but I think there is a constant which spans the twentieth century, a key idea which always takes us back to the same point: that of national identity.[1] Of course, as we will see, this identity receives diverse treatment throughout history, but the preoccupation with the question 'Who are we?' remains. Identity, nation, popular are terms which we will find running through all Latin American thought. To these are added the concepts of backwardness, development, modernity and modernisation. The theme of identity thus mobilises artists (the Modernists for example in the 1920s), politicians, the literati and intellectuals: it becomes an obsession.

But what does this absence mean? Identity always exists in relation to a referent. For Latin American societies it is Western Europe and the United States which represent modernity. Because of this, in order to respond to the question 'Who are we?' we need to consider a preliminary question: 'What are we not?' This 'lack' is precisely the gap between what we aspire to be and what we really are. As we shall see, the debate on culture is a reflection of just these tensions.

The turn of the century

The dilemma which confronted the Brazilian elite at the turn of the nineteenth century is captured in this extract from a chronicle by Olavo Bilac:

A few Sundays ago I saw a cart overcrowded with pilgrims from Penha pass along the main avenue: in that splendid, wide boulevard, on the polished asphalt, against the magnificent facade of the lofty buildings, against the coaches and carriages which swept by, the encounter with the old vehicle in which the drunken faithful were bellowing, gave me an impression of a monstrous anachronism: it was the resurrection of barbarity – it was the return of a savage age, like the spirit of another world, coming to disturb and bring shame upon the life of a civilized age. If only the disgraceful orgy were confined to the Penha festivities! But no! Once the entertainment was over, the crowd spilled over like a victorious torrent towards the centre of the city.[2]

Bilac's lively description unveils an ideology peculiar to the dominant sectors of society. In it the facades of the tall buildings, the imposing aspect of the coaches, contrast with the 'primitive' side of Brazilian society. However, the stirring quality of this account lies in the idea of 'resurrection', immediately contradicted by the sentence which follows: 'If only the disgraceful orgy were confined to the Penha festivities.' A wish certainly shared by the local elite. The problems of Brazil could not be dismissed as the return of an era which ideally should have been buried; on the contrary, it was the atavistic present which caused discomfort. Because of this Bilac's chronicle brings with it a sense of malaise with regard to this population of 'savages' which the oligarchy would have liked to see confined more securely behind its prescribed frontiers.[3] As in peripheral societies the *mestiço* multitude took over the whole city, so the centre of Rio de Janeiro is only a dream of modernity, a facade which brought it closer to the values of Western civilisation. Alongside lay malaria, poverty and a slave-owning past which had to be eradicated from memory by any means.

This contradiction between 'appearance' and 'essence', between being and not being is intrinsic to Brazilian society. When Nina Rodrigues published his *L'Animisme Fétichiste des Nègres de Bahia*, he opened the book with the following affirmation:

Only official science, with its dogmatic and superficial instruction, could still today persist in claiming that the population of Bahia is overall a monotheistic, Christian one. Such a claim suggests, on the part of those who make it, either a wilful negligence *in the calculation of two thirds of black Africans and those of mixed race* who form the great majority of the population, or that ingenuous ignorance which believes blindly in outward appearances which the most superficial examination renders illusory and deceptive.[4]

In other words, an insistence on perceiving a modern, Christian world when what exists is a traditional society permeated by beliefs with fetishistic origins – an inconsistent portrait carefully drawn by those seeking to cultivate a comforting image of themselves.

Nineteenth-century intellectuals had to confront the contradiction between an aspiration to civilisation and the material conditions that persistently denied it. When he wrote *O Guarani*, José de Alencar could not simply transplant European Romanticism to Brazilian soil.[5] Foreign writers sought out the Other through picturesque journeys, travelling far and wide to observe the bizarre traits of Indians and savages. More romantic than their Brazilian counterparts, they wished to prevent the disappearance of the last traces of a millenarian culture threatened by the development of an industrial society.[6] Alencar lived in a particular universe in which the Indian was simultaneously a source of inspiration and a social threat. Because of this *O Guarani*, the foundational novel of the myth of Brazilianness, has as its central theme the question: How does one introduce civilisation into the realm of nature? In order to do this, fiction had to distinguish between a good savage, idealised by the writer, and the reality of savagery, which existed as a fact of Brazilian society. Alencar had to deal with these two extremes, as it was impossible for him to articulate the literary text solely through the image of the good savage. The Brazilian experience, powerful and threatening, imposed a different set of questions from that encountered by European writers. *O Guarani*'s Indian hero ironically finds himself too close to his roots.

Sílvio Romero's tone is different. His study of popular traditions leads to a bitter conclusion:

> We are a people in the process of formation; therefore we do not have long and extensive national traditions. Blacks and Indians could furnish little, and with the Renaissance the Portuguese had to some extent already forgotten the traditions of the Middle Ages, when the hand of Fate hurled them onto our lands. Hence the fragmentary state of our popular literature.[7]

There wasn't very much to preserve; the wheel of history was pushing Brazilian society towards a still uncertain future. This dilemma, recurring among intellectuals, revealed a problem of identity. When they first succeeded in affirming the existence of a 'Brazilian people' – the mixture of white, indigenous and black races – this 'identity card' then immediately escaped from their grasp. Since the nation was the result of the mixing of superior and inferior races (according to the theories which flourished at the time), a problem arose: the constructed identity, fleeting and contradictory, exiled the majority of the population – Indians, blacks and mulattos – to the domain of 'ignorance' and 'barbarity'.

Manifestations of popular culture were marked by this wider context of negativity. They represented the dark side of society, to be resisted in the name of a modernity that did not yet exist. There are several examples reflecting this. The 1890 penal code criminalised the art of healing, magic and shamanism, at a time when medicine was seeking to consolidate its doctrine of scientific legitimacy. Popular beliefs were seen as a factor in mental illness and, along with alcoholism and syphilis, as contributing to insanity and undermining the social order. Contemporary psychiatrists held that '[a]mong the social ills which in our country are cited as influential contributory factors to insanity, is the crude spiritualism which develops in a land permeated by ignorance and superstition'.[8] As we know, for the scientists of the time there was not much distance between crime and madness, which meant that 'possession cults' were duly associated with criminality.

Obviously this discriminatory view affected the African heritage in particular. Considered inferior, it appeared incompatible with the notion of civilisation that was aspired to. We must not forget that theories of race related criminality to people's physical characteristics. Medicine and psychiatry thus became complementary disciplines. It was no accident that in Brazil the study of the black population emerged in the medical schools. Nina Rodrigues was certainly the chief exponent of this tradition, particularly in the 1930s, and we can detect his influence on commentators such as the doctor and psychiatrist Arthur Ramos, or Gonçalves Fernandes, a member of the Mental Health Service of Recife.[9]

Society's intolerance of black practices was further manifested in the persecution of *capoeira* and popular festivities. The history of this repression is particularly marked in relation to the *terreiros* (temples). Afro-Brazilian cults became police targets in practically every area of the country. Gonçalves Fernandes speaks of the presence of *Xangôs* in disguise in carnival *blocos*, thus escaping the vigilance of the Recife police. In certain regions, such as the city of Maceió, the extent of the persecution in 1912 prompted an attitude of retreat in the black population, which was reflected in the very structure of their religion. A new liturgical formula emerged, *xangô-rezado-baixo*, in which dance and music disappeared and ceremonies were comprised of whispered prayers.[10] Arthur Ramos also comments on police incursions into Bahian territory, and we know that the same occurred in Rio de Janeiro, São Paulo and Porto Alegre.

This negative attitude was not restricted to black culture, but applied more widely to the popular classes as a whole. In the city of Rio de Janeiro the spirit of the Belle Époque clashed with the 'ignorance' and

the 'backwardness' of traditional pastimes, hence the restriction of the
Judas festivities, the *bumba-meu-boi* and the Penha celebrations.[11] The
case of carnival is a significant one. The press at the end of the
nineteenth century made a clear distinction between a 'large' and a
'small' carnival. The latter denomination included different popular
forms (*entrudo, ranchos, zés-pereira*), as the former was reserved for
denoting the more civilised form of celebrating the reign of the *Rei
Momo* (Buffoon King). Of urban origin, this carnival, inspired by the
European traditions of harlequins and columbines, was expressed in
the parades and processions organised by the carnival societies. The
attitude of the authorities to these two types of carnivals was markedly
different. In São Paulo, studies show that between 1876 and 1889 the
authorities' main concern was to repress the old forms of amusement.
The *entrudo*, which has now disappeared from Brazilian tradition, was
particularly affected. The treatment given to the Venetian-type carnival
was altogether different. As a newspaper of the time made clear, 'this
carnival symbolises the empire of light invading the empire of darkness
– civilisation over ignorance'.[12] The press even saw in this European
form of revelry a didactic element which could be used to educate the
populace:

> The carnival, bringing the people together, teaching them elegant manners
> and language, the conventions of courtesy, awakening in them the desire to
> learn about the characters it revives, will go on from year to year developing
> and taking advantage of all the circumstances which can contribute to its
> triumph.[13]

However, the theme of barbarity reappeared, and faced with the
persistence of popular forms of expression the press lamented, 'how
delightful would the joy of carnival be if only one could get rid of that
external trait of revelry from the African backlands'.[14]

1930 to 1964

This negative attitude to popular culture did change, however. The
urban–industrial society which emerged after the Revolution of 1930
succeeded in integrating some hitherto excluded sectors of the Brazilian population. Florestan Fernandes comments that 'the tragedy for
the black population between 1890 and 1930 was a result of their
incapacity to adjust to an urban lifestyle'.[15] By the '30s they were
seeking to take advantage of the openings which were appearing in
the social structure, although this process was full of obstacles and

contradictions. Various cultural manifestations with a popular character sought to occupy the new spaces within this class-bound society. This was the moment when carnival, football and *umbanda* ceased to be expressions restricted to defined social groups and became integrated into the context of society as a whole. Football was professionalised, ceasing to be the pastime of an elite in private clubs; the samba schools took the carnival to the streets, dethroning the old *corsos* (processions); *umbanda* was institutionalised as it sought to legitimise itself as a religion distinct from catholicism.

The case of *umbanda's terreiros* is an interesting one. Originating in the Afro-Brazilian cults and from Kardecism, they were marked by the stigma which surrounded descendants of slaves. Perceived as evidence of 'barbarity', of an uncivilised past, the *terreiros* were subject to social discrimination. However, in spite of this initial rejection, *umbanda* succeeded in adjusting to society's dominant norms. In 1939 the Federação Espírita de Umbanda ('Spiritualist Federation of Umbanda') was created in Rio de Janeiro and in 1941 the first Umbanda Congress was held, which sought to study and codify the rituals of the religion. The movement expanded, reaching a considerable sector of the urban middle classes.

There were other spaces which the popular classes sought to penetrate. The advent of radio, which became commercial in 1935, also opened up an opportunity for inclusion to those who traditionally possessed a certain 'ludic cultural capital'. The studio programmes functioned as virtual talent-spotting shows, revealing new singers and composers to the public. Samba, initially an ethnic musical form, took on radio, thus to an extent promoting the sector of society which had drawn the attention of the new mass media.[16]

One should not imagine that this opening up to popular forms of expression has been free and democratic. On the contrary, it is selective. For example, the code of *umbanda* priests states, 'It is forbidden to place at urban crossings items of so-called witchcraft containing bottles or other materials which disrupt traffic and endanger children, in addition to bringing shame on cults of African origin.' Another *terreiro* declares that 'the head of the centre or *terreiro* will not permit the conducting of ceremonies external to the cult, or which may be considered an affront to morality and decency, and cause public disturbance'. There are many examples of how the *umbanda* religion, in order to integrate into Brazilian society, had to assume certain values such as 'morality', 'self-restraint', 'decency', and 'public order'. Only in this way, by distancing itself from what are considered its impure origins, does a 'suspect' religious form succeed in adapting. The *umbanda* worshippers applied themselves so fully to this task of 'whitening' their rituals that the blood rituals, traditional in *candomblé*, tended to disappear.[17] They sought at all costs to erase the indelible mark of the past.

An analogous movement occurred with popular music. In the 1930s samba, as the saying went at the time, 'wore black tie', that is, it was musically reworked, with its features better adapted for an urban public. The music which sung of *malandragem* was now seen as an incentive to indolence and laziness, precisely at the time when the New State was promoting a work ethic compatible with the process of industrialisation occurring in Brazil. Hence the direct intervention of the State in censoring songs and replacing them with others that extolled the virtues of work and toil.[18] There was therefore an external and internal selection (made by composers), distinguishing between 'good' and 'bad' in popular forms of expression. However, in spite of this disciplining movement (in Foucauldian terms), or rather, on account of it, a set of practices previously excluded from society acquired a positive connotation.

The discussion on identity thus took a new direction in this period, social reality demanded new concepts. If at the start of the twentieth century the myth of the three races still contained a certain ambiguity – the mestiço was an inferior hybrid – by now it had been recast. Gilberto Freyre could define the Brazilian as a cross between black, indigenous and European cultures, positing racial mixture as an ideal constituent of national identity.[19] Being Brazilian no longer signified being 'indolent' or 'idle'; it now acquired a positive connotation. In this context the State played a crucial role in the rehabilitation of popular forms of expression. Samba, football and carnival were promoted to symbols of Brazilianness. The efforts of the State to Brazilianize certain (but not all) forms of popular expression were significant. Traditionally available cultural elements were reworked and gained new meanings. Evidently the State reaped the rewards of its integrating action, although while conferring a symbolic citizenship on all, in practice it denied the majority of the population real political citizenship. Swing and musicality became national symbols, and could even be exported in the form of the exoticism of Carmen Miranda, hotly contested football championships and the sensuality of the samba schools.

It is worth remembering that in the process of the construction of national identity the State relied only on certain elements of traditional popular culture: dance, music, festivities. It was as if, from a wider cast of popular forms, some were singled out and given special meaning.

One fact, however, stands out. In the Brazil of the 1930s and 1940s there was no 'mass' culture which could compete with the legitimacy of traditional popular culture. At this time, in spite of the advent of radio and the press, one still cannot speak of the presence of 'culture industries', and there was no system for the nation-wide dissemination of cultural goods. Even television, which began broadcasting in 1950, faced substantial obstacles to its development. The advertisements of the time clearly portray this contradiction between the idea and the reality of 'mass communication'. They demanded,

> Do you or don't you want television? To make television a reality in Brazil, a consortium of radio broadcasters and journalists (*Diários Associados*) have invested millions of *cruzeiros*. Now it's your turn. What will be your contribution towards sustaining such a great enterprise? The progress of our country and this marvel of electronic science depend on your support. Applause and glowing praise are not enough. You effectively give your support when you buy a television.[20]

The triumphalist discourse announcing the arrival of television in Brazil did not obscure the difficulties of this endeavour. Thus potential consumers had to be sensitised by a pedagogical discourse appealing to their patriotic sentiments, while the quality of the product was secondary. This indicates the precariousness of the communication system of the time, with a consumer market still far short of mass proportions.

After 1964

The transformations which took place in Brazilian society after 1964 completely reorganised the cultural scene. The military coup had a double meaning. It signified first of all repression, censorship, torture and the dismantling of oppositional forces. But the military were also responsible for what several authors have called authoritarian modernisation.[21] The arrival of a 'second industrial revolution' consolidated a market for material goods and led to the creation of a national market for cultural goods.[22] As we have noted, during the 1950s there was no real national cultural market and the media still had a limited reach. After 1964 there was a major expansion in the production, distribution and consumption of cultural goods. And it is this phase that facilitated the consolidation of the great conglomerates which today control the media (TV Globo and Editora Abril). All figures indicate unmistakable growth in this sector. In the magazine market, for example, between 1960 and 1985 the number of copies sold rose from 104 million to 500 million. But it was not just quantity which characterised this emergent market: the publication sector was increasingly distinguished by specialist publications.

Editora Abril is a case in point. Founded in 1950, it began its commercial life by purchasing the rights to Donald Duck. Between 1950 and 1959 the company produced just seven titles; between 1960 and 1969 this number rose to twenty-seven; between 1970 and 1979 it reached 121 titles. In the 1950s Abril sustained itself by selling *fotonovelas* (*Capricho* [Caprice], *Ilusão* [Illusion], *Você* [You], *Noturno* [Nocturne]) and Donald Duck. In the 1960s and 1970s it appealed to a varied public: young people (*Curso Intensivo de Madureza* [Crash Course to enter Higher Edutcation]), university students (*Pensadores* [Thinkers]), the inquisitive (*Conhecer* [Knowing]). Children's titles multiplied too: *Cebolinha, Luluzinha, Disney Encyclopaedia.* Feminine tastes in the 1950s were catered for by the publication of *fotonovelas*, in particular. But from the 1960s magazines were launched on fashion (*Manequim* [Mannequin]), sewing (*Agulha de Ouro* [Golden Needle]), cooking (*Forno e Fogão* [Hearth and Home]), décor (*Cláudia*). The same occurred with the male public: cars (*Quatro Rodas* [Four Wheels]), lorry drivers (*O Carreteiro* [The Carrier]), sex (*Playboy*), motorcycles (*Moto*), sailing (*Esportes Náuticos*). Thus Editora Abril sought to exploit the potential interest of readers from diverse groups and social classes.

At this time too, the record market, which until 1970 had grown only slowly, was also given a boost. This was principally due to the ways in which it became easier to buy domestic electrical appliances (chiefly with the extension of credit to the popular classes). Between 1967 and 1980 the sale of record players grew by 813 per cent. The expansion of this market can be appreciated when one considers that between 1972 and 1979 the number of commercial records increased from 25 to 66 million. The LP, which was introduced to Brazil in 1948 but was still considered an expensive product until the sixties, was increasingly characterised as a classless consumer product.

An analysis of total advertising expenditure gives an idea of the dimensions of Brazil's cultural market. Between 1992 and 1996 it grew from US$3.9 billion to US$10 billion, making Brazil the seventh-largest advertising market in the world with a bill in 1996 of US$165 billion.

The changes that Brazil has undergone in the last few decades can be illustrated using television as an example. Until the mid 1960s the structure of television broadcasting was far from compatible with the logic of 'mass culture'. There were few channels and television production – effectively centred on the Rio–São Paulo axis – had a regional character. Technical problems were considerable and only in 1959 was the technology of videotape introduced to some programmes, permitting a limited extension of transmission to some state capital cities. Due to the low purchasing power of the majority of the population and the high price of sets (imported from the United States until 1959), the transmission of programmes was concentrated around a relatively small group of people. Fewer than a million television sets were sold in the 1950s (Brazil's population in 1960 was 70,967,000). Programmes were transmitted live, which made extensive circulation of cultural goods impossible. Figures for the advertising expenditure on different forms of media show that in 1958 the budget for television advertising was just 10 per cent, compared with 39 per cent invested in newspapers. It would be difficult in this case to apply the concept of the culture industry devised by Theodor Adorno and Max Horkheimer. Obviously, every company tried to expand its material base, but the obstacles in the way of Brazilian capitalism placed limits on its growth. Even the language used did not suit the new form. In Brazil, the model used in radio, transposed to the screen, remained the principal reference for the televisual text for more than a decade.

But this situation changed radically in the 1960s, and at this point it is worth reiterating the role of the State in promoting telecommunications policy. The ideology of National Security,[23] through the concept of national integration, created the principles behind the setting up of a Ministry of Telecommunications. A whole telecommunications system was then constructed whose reach was to be national. Television, like the telephone system, now gained great momentum. Through concessions granted by the authoritarian State, the development of communications was realised in conjunction with the exercise of political control.[24] In 1970 (significantly, during the World Cup) national transmission was begun; in 1972 colour television appeared. For the first time different parts of the country could be connected to each other, with programmes now having the capacity to integrate the public into the consumer market. The figures in relation to the expansion of television are clear-cut. In 1965 there were close to 2,200,000 TV sets in Brazil; this figure rose to 4,259,000 in 1970, meaning that television was then already reaching 56 per cent of the population. By the 1980s the television market had become consolidated. The 16 million sets reached 73 per cent of homes and the habit of watching television had spread to all social classes.[25]

It was not just television transmission that changed. In the 1950s the rationale for communications, radio, newspaper and television companies was akin to what Fernando Henrique Cardoso observed in the captains of industry in his study of the behaviour of Brazilian business-

men at the beginning of the twentieth century.[26] Family ties dominated
all undertakings while proposed objectives lacked clarity – all in all,
personal and political interests impacted upon management. Television
was no exception to this rule. Far from being ruled by the efficacy of
technological or commercial planning, it had little in common with the
modern managerial spirit. The very incipience of Brazilian capitalism,
exacerbated by technical improvisation ('making television was an
adventure'), exacerbated this state of affairs. The advent of a cultural
market transformed the companies into a culture industry, of which TV
Globo was a pioneer. Founded in 1965, it imported from the United
States a staff of administrators seeking to adjust standards of production
to meet the demands of the market.[27] The process of the industrialisation and commercialisation of Brazilian television can be traced
through the growth of advertising expenditure. In 1970 television was
already responsible for 39.6 per cent of this expenditure, compared
with 13.2 per cent for radio, 21.9 per cent for magazines and 21 per
cent for newspapers. In 1996 the distribution was as follows: television
51 per cent, radio 4 per cent, magazines 8 per cent, newspapers 38 per
cent, billboards etc. 1 per cent. Thus programming had to adjust to
commercial standards, because of the concern of companies and adver-
tisers to reach the largest possible consuming public.

It is within this context that the soap opera was to be transformed
into the lynchpin of the television industry. Up to the mid 1960s soap
operas were aired just twice a week. Filmed live, they were impossible
to circulate nationally. Generally produced by foreign companies, such
as Colgate–Palmolive and Gessy–Lever, they revamped the model which
had been a success on radio in the 1940s. From 1964 things changed.
With the use of videotape, 'soaps' became a daily event, involving
serialisations that required a high degree of industrialisation. The
success of the soap opera parallels the expansion of television sets: it
redefined television programming, eliminating the whole tradition of
theatre and television drama that had existed before. In the 1970s, with
nation-wide transmission, it became the most important product in the
Brazilian television system.[28]

The emergence and consolidation of a culture industry has important consequences in that local, regional cultures have to insert themselves into a network that is organised from above. This is not to suggest
that there exists in Brazil a process of homogenisation, or that industrialisation leads necessarily to the emergence of 'one-dimensional man'.
It is, however, necessary to make very clear the profundity of the
changes underway. Within this context the notion of the 'popular' is
redefined. First of all there is a shift from the traditional to the modern.

The 'popular' ceases to be perceived as something linked to the traditional culture of the popular classes (whether in the folkloric sense or not), and becomes something associated with goods produced and circulated by the culture industries. Secondly, this dislocation has political implications. In the 1960s there were various movements which attributed to the concept of 'popular culture' a clear political connotation. It was reformist for the intellectuals of the ISEB (Instituto Superior de Estudos Brasileiros – Higher Institute of Brazilian Studies), Marxist for the CPCs (Centros Populares de Cultura – Popular Cultural Centres), left-wing catholic for the Popular Culture Movement (Movimento de Cultura Popular).[29] The category 'popular culture' takes us therefore into something which transcends the present, driving social forces towards a utopian political project opposing the status quo. The adult literacy method developed by the pedagogue Paulo Freire is a good example of a form of popular education designed to simultaneously promote political awareness and literacy. In the same way, when dramatists and film-makers elaborated a conception of a national–popular theatre or cinema, they were embracing a perspective which recalls Sartre's *engagé* literature.[30] Through popular culture they sought to offer the popular classes a critical consciousness as a first step towards overcoming social problems. This emphasis on political issues still persists in some movements today, for example in the Comunidades Eclesiais de Base (Base Christian Communities), in which an ideology of 'option for the poor' prevails. However, the concept of hegemony has changed. The emergence of the culture industry and of a market of symbolic national goods has redefined previous meanings. 'Popular' now becomes that which is most consumed. One can even establish a hierarchy of 'popularity' among the different products offered on the market. A record, a soap opera or a play will be considered 'more' or 'less' popular because it reaches a greater or smaller consuming public.

Furthermore, the Brazilian intellectual tradition always considered the idea of national identity problematic in terms of a clear opposition between the autochthonous and the alien, the internal and the external. It is within this current of thought that an author like Roland Corbisier can write:

> Just as on an economic level the colony exports raw material and imports finished products, on the cultural level the colony is ethnographic material which lives off the importation of cultural products manufactured externally. Importing the finished product is like importing a state of being, importing the form which encapsulates and reflects the cosmic vision of those who produce it. On importing, for example, the Cadillac, Chiclets,

Coca-Cola and cinema, we do not just import objects and commodities, but also a set of values and conducts which are implied in these products.[31]

This notion can be extended to a set of cultural forms of expression which, in principle, reproduced in Brazil the phenomenon of 'foreign alienation'.[32] In the forties and fifties Brazilian cinema was a poor copy of Hollywood's, the radio soaps reproduced the standards of stories told in Cuba or Mexico, and the photo story magazines were adaptations of originals in Italian. In the sixties television was dominated by North American series.[33] A few years later things are different, and the case of television is once again paradigmatic. The comparison of American series and soap operas shows how this competition between foreign and national culture has been reformulated. In 1963 programming for the state of São Paulo included only 2 per cent soap operas and 25 per cent North American series; in 1977, when the soap opera became a 'national success' (that is, a daily, serialised industrial product), 22 per cent of audience time was filled with Brazilian soaps, as against 17 per cent of 'canned' programmes.[34] The same occurred with magazine and radio soaps – they Brazilianised themselves in content and form, articulating a more specifically Brazilian narrative to the consuming public. In diverse cultural sectors – soap operas, journalism, TV series, advertising, magazines – there is a kind of 'import substitution' (to use an economic metaphor) which parallels the expansion of Brazilian capitalism.[35] Therefore, the search for cultural Brazilianness finds itself materialised in a popular culture market which even ends up being exported to an international market (as is the case today with the soap opera, which is an integral part of the world image market).

Modernity and nation

The observations made here allow us to consider one last aspect of the problematic we have been examining: that of modernity. It is not a new idea. Modernism was perhaps one of the first movements to confront the issue in an emphatic way. When its poets spoke of the aeroplane wing, electric trams, the cinema, the jazz band or factories, they sought signs of modernity which could capture the moment of transition which Brazilian society in the 1920s was experiencing. Modernism wanted to be a break with the past, an abrupt wrench from an archaic past. Various commentators emphasise this dimension of rupture. The intellectual Tristão de Athayde commented that the movement came to fruition in São Paulo because the city's artists experienced the qualities of modern life on a daily basis: 'asphalt, the automobile, the radio, the turbulence, noise, life in the open air, the masses and cinema which informs other arts and marks them with its fragmenting aesthetic, the primacy of technology over the natural'.[36] The description is vivid if somewhat unfocused for today's reader. It is partially valid. At the beginning of the twentieth century São Paulo was the city which best represented modern Brazil. The money derived from the cultivation of coffee provided the initial capital which drove the process of industrialisation forward.[37]

But accounts from the past, mainly by artists and chroniclers of the time, tend to obscure the continued existence of a provincial, traditional São Paulo, which does not sit well with this ideal based on technology and speed. When a poet like Menotti del Picchia says, 'along the highway of the Milky Way, the automobiles dizzily speed by', suggesting with this image an approximation between the machine – a product of man – and an astral order, one question remains: How should we consider this techno-celestial relationship (certainly valid in some European countries) in a country where cars were relatively rare (they were all imported), while roads were few and often impassable? Poetic imagination should not obscure thought. Historians show that industrialisation in São Paulo was a slow process in the 1920s, and even more so in the rest of the country. Because of this the 1930 Revolution is considered an important moment in Brazilian history. It initiated a radical process of modernisation and industrialisation. In reality one can frequently forget that modernism occurred without modernisation, that there was a hiatus between the artistic intentions of the movement and the society which sustained it. Modernism is an aspiration, a project to be constructed in the future. Because of this, in Brazil as in various other places in Latin America, modernism has been identified since its emergence with the national question (in Mexico, for example, with the muralists). It is not so much about reproducing in the arts a modernity that still did not exist, but rather constructing a nation which could be distanced from its agrarian tradition.[38]

What can be said today of this search for modernity? Silviano Santiago, confronting the same question in the area of literature, wonders to what extent contemporary Brazilian writers should take the Modernist movement of the 1920s as a reference. His answer is clear:

> In our view the basic project of modernism, which was to modernise our arts through avant-garde writing and to modernise our society through an authoritarian revolutionary government, has already been realised, although we disagree with the way in which industrialisation was carried out in Brazil.[39]

A thought-provoking observation, which in my view does not apply to literature alone but has wider validity. We have seen how Brazilian society was transformed from the sixties, becoming incorporated into the process of internationalisation of the world economy. A late capitalism, it is true, but the hands of the Brazilian clock are in synch with the pace of the international order. An analysis of the cultural universe reveals this change clearly. The multiplication of the signs of modernity (computers, videocassettes, television, polluting industries, jet planes, national road networks, etc.) attests to the existence of a new reality. Unlike the past, when the Modernists were still writing their texts, it is no longer out of step with society (which does not mean that the population as a whole benefits from it). Of course, one cannot forget that in a country like Brazil the areas of underdevelopment are considerable (illiteracy, abject poverty, public health problems). There still exist gross regional inequalities. But the meaning of the industrialisation process is unambiguous: Brazil is a modern society (as its cultural life shows), although its history has been and will continue to be different from that of societies of the centre.

The idea that modernity is an imperative of our times unsettles some Brazilian and Latin American commentators. This is because modernisation was always imagined as a value in itself; it would eliminate underdevelopment, as it would injustice. This somewhat naive view of history led Brazilian intellectuals to overvalue the search for a modern identity without having a critical perspective on what the nation was seeking to construct. It was as if the idea of the modern ontologically entailed virtues such as democracy, liberty and equality. In Brazil the 'first' and 'second' industrial revolutions – that of 1930 and that of the military – were carried out by authoritarian régimes, a fact frequently ignored by those who believe that the modern is intrinsically 'good'. We know that this is not the case. Today, in addition to problems inherited from the past, we have others emerging from the new social configuration. Modernity brings with it challenges, but also other forms of domination.

When in the nineteenth century Sílvio Romero sought reasons to explain the 'backwardness' of Brazil (which he identified with racial and geographical conditions), his mind's eye was looking to the future, a history that was not yet made. The same can be said of the ISEB intellectuals in the 1950s. The motto 'There is no development without an ideology of development' confirmed the primacy of ideas over reality. The ideology had to come before it could be realised; the intellectuals showed the way by suggesting the 'correct' paths which the nation should follow. The notion of 'backwardness' therefore implied an idea of the future, or rather, the need to transcend the present. Whether in its conservative or progressive version, the Brazilian intellectual tradition therefore found itself displaced to the future tense. The changes which occurred altered the trajectory of history. Modernity is a reality, but in the context of the Brazilian tradition of modernity it becomes acritical. It is no longer a utopia, something out of step with time. To use an old designation of Karl Mannheim's, I would say that it becomes ideology, that is, a vision of the world which merely seeks adaptation to the present. In this sense acritical modernity requires the adjustment of people and political proposals to its interests. 'Backward' is that which is out of tune with the existing order. However, as this present has not materialised fully (we are not one of the countries of the 'centre'), or rather, as the present does not realise the dream of modernity, the permanence of 'tradition' (older traditions, as well as contemporary elements which do not fit into the perspective of an acritical modernity) appear inconvenient. Hence the absolute necessity for establishing clear distinctions, to adjust what 'already was' to what should be.

Modernity, modernism, modernisation are terms which are associated with the national question. The obsession with Brazilian identity was also an obsession with modernity; its absence connected the modern to the construction of a national identity. However, it will always be ironic that it was tradition which ended up furnishing the main identifying symbols of the Brazilian nation. It was not the railways (which were few and inefficient), technology, the iron and steel of which the futurists dreamed, or the Parisian boulevards (badly reproduced in the city of Rio de Janeiro during the Belle Époque) which legitimised the founding traits of Brazilianness; it was samba, carnival and football. Faced with the still insubstantial development of modern life, the social imaginary was left to seize upon traditional popular culture, transforming it into the 'national–popular'. This has changed in step with the transformations that have occurred. Samba, carnival and football are modalities which lose appeal in the new configuration of events (samba struggles to maintain legitimacy with young people against pop music; carnival, in its televised, touristic version, is a spectacle involving a minority of the population; football is one among diverse sporting specialisations). These symbols have now fallen far short of the expectations of Brazilians today. Brazil is now experiencing a period of substitution of symbols. Others, like the soap opera, advertising, Formula One, are beginning to be elaborated. The transmission of soap operas abroad, the prizes which advertisements are beginning to win at international festivals, the performance of Brazilians on international racing circuits – all of these bring with them semiological material which better suits the image of modern times. It is an identity which distances itself from the national–popular tradition.

If this text had been written a few years ago, I would have said that, in spite of its deficiencies, modernity could be seen as 'complete', in that it gives an account of a long period in which notions of popular culture, 'progress' and nation are intertwined. The issues change, however, when we consider the beginning of the twenty first century. Substantial changes have affected the problems on which we have been reflecting. I refer to the process of globalisation and the international-isation of culture. The inconclusiveness of these trends raises questions which I believe will inform the debate in Latin America in the coming decades.

Historically, the nation is the fruit of industrialism, a social formation that makes mobility one of its main conditions. It differs radically from agrarian societies of the past, in which the limits of cultures, of commercial exchange, of political loyalties are confined to particular regions.[40] The world of the *ancien régime* was constituted of disparate units. For example, there was a rural universe whose specificity was reflected in the fields of culture (particular concepts of time and space), of politics, religion and the economy. The Industrial Revolu-tion, together with political revolutions fundamentally transformed this world. Eliminating the division between estates, they advanced the circulation of citizens, goods and ideas. The nation is realised through modernity; it is a social formation whose material base corresponds to industrialism. The nation–modernity equation thus becomes prevalent, whether in countries of the 'centre' or the 'periphery'. In the former modernity becomes synonymous with civilisation, a central argument for the expansion of imperialism. Countries like France, Great Britain, Germany and the United States claimed to have a civilising mission (an ideological discourse to justify the expansion of their ambitions). But from another perspective, for countries on the 'periphery' the same equation is also valid. Of course, it is not about trying to affirm the power of an incomplete capitalism. In the 'Third World' the nation is a utopia, a search for modernity. All the nationalist movements of Latin America share this perspective. Because of this the Brazilian Modernists said that in order to be modern we must be national.

The nation–modernity relationship has in my view broken down. Historically one can say that the nation was realised through modernity and vice versa. However, from the outset, modernity contained within itself a dynamic not easily confined to national reality. With the advance of history (that is, the transformations of the capitalist system) what we are witnessing instead is a world-modernity. In this case we could say, paraphrasing the Brazilian Modernists, that it is possible to be modern without necessarily being national. This has important and often drastic consequences for Latin American societies, as traditionally the political debate has found itself intimately linked to the question of the construction of modernity. In the emerging context the very idea of a 'national project' is compromised. In fact the nation-state has lost the monopoly on conferring meaning on collective actions. This means that the debate on national identity is dislocated, whether because of internal contradictions (the emergence of 'local' identities, such as the black movement in Brazil, or the indigenous movement), or in relation to the world scene.[41] The idea of Brazilianness is criss-crossed by internal and external currents, redefining the debate. Ironically, the presence of a 'Brazilian' modernity is not totally defined. On the contrary, Brazil, like other countries, far from 'discovering its identity' finds itself, in the context of globalisation, in a state of crisis. That is, it lives in a state of confrontation between identities marked however by the objective and asymmetrical position which the country occupies in the order of nations.

Within this context the notion of popular culture will change once again. Traditional culture and the popular culture market produced by the Brazilian culture industry are no longer the only reference points. World modernity possesses its own furniture: fast food, jeans, trainers (preferably Reeboks), pop music, film stars, etc. We are 'everywhere' bombarded by these objects and images. That singularity of customs indicates the existence of an international civilising standard, in which diverse social groups actually share a common collective imaginary. They form part of an 'international–popular' culture. In contrast to the 'national–popular', its geographical origin is secondary. Produced on a global scale, this international–popular culture, closely linked to the world of consumerism, spans all nations, directly affecting their symbols of national identity. Brazil at the start of the twenty-first century is therefore experiencing a new 'crisis of identity' but, unlike those of the past, this now no longer involves the construction of modernity. The anxieties surrounding the question of identity have been transferred from a national to an international level, from the internal to the external, from that which had been 'so well defined' as being autochthonous, now challenged internally (and not from outside, as previously) by the unequal forces of the globalisation of markets and the internationalisation of culture.

Notes

1 On the problem of national identity in Brazil see Renato Ortiz, *Cultura Brasileira e Identidade Nacional*, São Paulo, Brasiliense, 1985; and Carlos Guilherme Mota, *Ideologia da Cultura Brasileira*, São Paulo, Atica, 1977.

2 Quoted in Nicolau Sevcenko, *A Literatura como Missão*, São Paulo, Brasiliense, 1984, p. 69

3 The identification of the popular classes with savages is made not just in Brazil. See Louis Chevalier, *Classes Laborieuses et Classes Dangereuses*, Paris, Hachette, 1984.

4 Nina Rodrigues, *L'Animisme Fétichiste des Nègres de Bahia*, 1890. My translation and my emphasis.

5 José de Alencar, *O Guarani*, novel published in serial form in the mid nineteenth century.

6 See Renato Ortiz, *Românticos e Folcloristas*, São Paulo, Olho d'Agua, 1992.

7 Sílvio Romero, *História da Literatura Brasileira*, vol. 1, Rio de Janeiro, José Olympio, 1986, p. 103.

8 Oscar de Souza, *O Indivíduo e o Meio do Ponto de Vista da Higiene Mental*, Rio de Janeiro, 1928.

9 Nina Rodrigues, *As Collectivadades Anormaes*, Rio Janeiro, 1939; Gonçalves Fernandes, *Sincretismo Religioso no Brasil*, Curitiba, Ed. Guaíra, n.d.; Arthur Ramos, *Loucura e Crime*, Porto Alegre, Livraria Globo, 1937.

10 Gonçalves Fernandes, *Xangôs do Nordeste*, Rio Janeiro, Civilização Brasileira, 1937.

11 Mônica P. Velloso, *As Tradições Populares na Belle Époque Carioca*, Rio Janeiro, Mec/Funarte, 1988.

12 Olga von Simson, *Os poderes públicos e a imprensa na transformação do carnaval paulistano no século XIX*, Cadernos do CERU, série 11, no. 1, (May 1985), p. 72. On carnival see also Maria Isaura Pereira de Queiroz, *Carnaval Brésilien: le vécu et le mythe*, Paris, Gallimard, 1992.

13 Olga von Simson op. cit. p. 72.

14 Quoted in Nicolau Sevcenko, op. cit. p. 69.

15 Florestan Fernandes, *Integração do Negro na Sociedade de Classes*, São Paulo, Atica, 1978, p. 168.

16 See João Batista Borges Pereira, *Cor, Profissão e Mobilidade: o negro e o rádio em São Paulo*, São Paulo, Pioneira, 1967.

17 On the theme of whitening see Roger Bastide, *Estudos Afro-Brasileiros*, São Paulo, Perspectiva, 1973.

18 Ruben Oliven *Violência e Cultura no Brasil*, Petrópolis, Vozes, 1988. See also José Ramos Tinhorão, *Música Popular: do gramophone ao rádio e tv*, São Paulo, Atica, 1981.

19 Gilberto Freyre, *Interpretação do Brasil*, Rio de Janeiro, José Olympio, 1941.

20 Quoted in Inimá Simões, *TV Tupi*, Rio de Janeiro, Funarte, s.d.p.

21 See Octávio Ianni, *Estado e planejamento no Brasil*, Rio de Janeiro, Civilização Brasileira, 1979.

22 On the emergence of cultural industries and of a market in cultural goods

in Brazil, see Renato Ortiz, *A Moderna Tradição Brasileira*, São Paulo, Brasiliense, 1988.

23 J. Comblin, *A Ideologia da Segurança Nacional*, Rio de Janeiro, Civilização Brasileira, 1980.

24 The clearest example of cooperation between the politics of the authoritarian State and the development of television in Brazil is that of TV Globo, whose consolidation is directly associated with the repressive politics of the military. See M.R. Kehl, *Reflexões para uma História da TV Globo*, Rio Janeiro, Funarte, 1982.

25 In 1997 the number of TV sets was close to 34 million, which means that in the metropolitan regions 95 per cent of the population was reached by television. Cable TV, which developed late in Brazil (1995), had 2.5 million subscribers in 1997.

26 F.H. Cardoso, *Empresário Industrial e Desenvolvimento Econômico no Brasil*, São Paulo, Difel, 1972.

27 See J.M.O. Ramos, 'Un bâtisseur d'empire: o Doutor Roberto Marinho', in G. Scheneir-Madanes, *L'Amérique Latine et ses Télévisions*, Paris, Anthropos, 1995.

28 Michele and Armand Mattelart, *Le Carnaval des Images: la fiction brésilienne*, Paris, Institut Nacional de la Communication Audiovisuelle, 1987.

29 See Caio N. Toledo, *ISEB: fábrica de ideologias*, São Paulo, Atica, 1977; Manuel Berlinck, *Projeto para a Cultura Brasileira nos Anos 60: o CPC*, (mimeo) Department of Sociology, Unicamp.

30 The text which perhaps best represents the link between Sartre, Fanon and the Brazilian intellectuals is Glauber Rocha's *An Aesthetic of Hunger – Arte em Revista*, no. 1, 1979.

31 Roland Corbisier, *Formação e problemas da Cultura Brasileira*, Rio de Janeiro, ISEB, 1958, p. 69.

32 The theme of cultural alienation linked to that of colonialism and cultural imperialism is central in the discussion of the 1950s and '60s.

33 M.R. Galvão, *Burguesia e Cinema: o caso Vera Cruz*, Rio Janeiro, Civilização Brasileira, 1981; A. Habert, *Fotonovela: forma e conteúdo*, Petrópolis, Ed. Vozes, 1975; F. P. Silva, *O Teleteatro Paulista na Década de 50 e 60*, São Paulo, IDART, 1981.

34 Figures in J. Straubhaar, 'The development of the telenovela as the preeminent form of popular culture in Brazil', Studies in Latin American Popular Culture, vol. 1 (1982), p. 144.

35 This process of 'Brazilianization' is analysed with regard to the magazine market in the thesis of M.C. Mira, *The Reader and the News-stand: the Case of Editora Abril*, Doctorate, Unicamp, 1997.

36 Quoted in Richard Morse, *Formação Histórica de São Paulo*, São Paulo, Difel, 1970, p. 348.

37 See Warren Dean, *A Industrialização de São Paulo*, São Paulo, Difel, 1971.

38 Eduardo Jardim, *A Brasilidade Modernista*, Rio de Janeiro, Graal, 1978.

39 Silviano Santiago, 'Fechado para Balanço', in *Nas Malhas da Lêtra*, São Paulo, Cia das Lêtras, 1989, p. 76.

40 E. Gellner, *Naciones y Nacionalismo*, Mexico, Alianza Editorial, 1991.
41 See Renato Ortiz 'Modernidad-Mundo y Identidad' in *Otro Territorio: ensayos sobre el mundo contemporaneo*, Buenos Aires, Universidad Nacional de Quilmes, 1996.

Translated by Lorraine Leu

6

'A Train of Shadows':[1] Early Cinema and Modernity in Latin America

Ana M. López

Faced with the challenge of analysing the impact of the media on the complex process and history of Latin American modernity over the last century, I have perversely – but, I hope, felicitously – chosen to focus on the period of Latin American media history which has been the least discussed and most difficult to document: the early years of the silent cinema, roughly 1896 to 1920. In its time, this period of cinema history was overshadowed by wars and other cataclysmic political and social events. Subsequently, for many contemporary scholars its significance has been eclipsed by the introduction and development of other media – the 'Golden Ages' of sound cinema in the 1940s and '50s, television in the 1960s and '70s – that seem to 'fit' better with the kind of narratives of Latin American modernity we want to tell, be they tales of foreign technological and ideological domination and inadequate imitation (à la Mattelart and Schiller), or contemporary chronicles of global mediations (à la Martín Barbero).[2] Yet in this early period we already find not only complex global interactions, but extensive evidence of the contradictory and ambivalent transformative processes that would mark the later reception and development of the sound cinema and other media. These early forms of mediated modernities already refract and inflect the production of self and other imagined communities; they also, I argue, lay bare the central characteristics of the processes through which subsequent media engaged with and contributed to the specificity of Latin American modernity.

The arrival

'The cinema appears in Latin America as another foreign import'[3]

This is perhaps the most salient characteristic of the experience of early Latin American cinema: rather than being developed in proto-organic synchronicity with the changes, technological inventions and 'revolutions' that produced modernity in Western Europe and the USA, the appearance and diffusion of the cinema in Latin America followed the patterns of neo-colonial dependency typical of Latin America's position in the global capitalist system, already in place at the turn of the twentieth century. As Ella Shohat and Robert Stam point out, 'the beginnings of cinema coincided with the giddy heights of the imperial project' and 'the most prolific film-producing countries . . . also "happened" to be among the leading imperialists.'[4] The cinematic apparatus – a manufactured product – appeared, fully formed, in Latin American soil a few months after its commercial introduction abroad. Subsequently, on the very same ships and railways that carried raw materials and agricultural products to Europe and the USA, Lumière and Edison cameramen returned with fascinating views of exotic lands, peoples, and their customs. Thus, in Latin America it is difficult to speak of the cinema and modernity as 'points of reflection and convergence,'[5] in the manner of US and European early cinema scholarship. We cannot argue that the development of Latin American early cinema was directly linked to previous large-scale transformations of daily experience resulting from urbanisation, industrialisation, rationality and the technological transformation of modern life, because those processes were only just beginning and/or being developed at different rates across the continent. In turn-of-the-century Latin America modernity was above all a fantasy and a profound desire.

Rather than a linear, synthetic process or rational master narrative – what Carol Breckenridge has ironically described as 'a single destination to which all lines of developmental traffic lead and all that matters is who gets there first and how high the price of their journey'[6] – modernization in Latin America (and elsewhere in 'the periphery') has been a de-centred, fragmentary and uneven process. As José Joaquin Brunner has convincingly argued, Latin American modernity (and its post-modernity) is characterised by cultural heterogeneity, by the multiple rationalities and impulses of private and public life. Unequal development has produced not only 'segmentation and segmented participation in the world market of messages and symbols' but also 'differential participation according to *local codes of reception*' which produces a de-centering of 'Western culture as it is represented by the manuals'.[7] In other words, Latin American modernity has been a global, intertextual experience, addressing impulses and models from abroad, in which every nation and/or region created – and creates – its own ways of playing with – and at – modernity. As Arjun Appadurai argues in reference to cricket in India, 'the indigenization [of a cultural practice imported by the colonizers] is often a product of collective and spectacular experiments with modernity, and not necessarily of the surface affinities of a new cultural form with existing patterns in the [new nation's] cultural repertoire.'[8]

Furthermore, one of the most crucial signs of Latin American modernity is a kind of temporal warp in which the pre-modern coexists and interacts with the modern, a differential plotting of time and space, and, subsequently, of history and time. In Aníbal Quijano's words: 'In Latin America, what is sequence in other countries is a simultaneity. It is also a sequence. But in the first place it is a simultaneity.'[9] Rather than a devastating process that ploughs over the traditional bases of a social formation – all that is solid melting into air – Latin American modernity is produced via an ambiguous symbiosis of traditional experiences/practices and modernising innovations such as the technologies visuality epitomised by the cinema. To quote Brunner again, 'not all solid things but rather all symbols melt into air.'[10] This warping effect has profound consequences for any historical project: because of temporal ambiguity and asynchronicity, teleological narratives of evolution become mired in dead ends and failed efforts and fail to do justice to the circuitous routes of Latin American modernity.

If we are to understand the 'indigenisation' of the cinema in Latin America – the 'spectacular experiments' through which it was inserted into and contributed to the specificity of the experience of Latin American modernity – our conceptual framework must link the national and continental with global practices, tracing the complex and specific negotiations between local histories and the global through different and overlapping chronologies. Any attempt to directly superimpose upon the Latin American experience the developmental grid of US and European film history is doomed to failure and frustration, for the early history of Latin American cinema already points to the intertwined chronologies and multiple branchings which would later characterise the development of subsequent media. Studying this period is made even more daunting by the paucity of available materials: most of the films produced in Latin America between 1896 and 1930 have disappeared due to the inevitable ravages of time (especially fire) and the official neglect of cultural preservation. Scholarship of this period is necessarily tenuous, limited to a few dozen existing films and for the most part based on secondary materials, especially press coverage. Nevertheless, the early history of the cinema in some countries – especially Argentina, Brazil and Mexico – has been fairly well documented; conversely, few have attempted transnational comparative studies, since so much of the available material seems bound by 'nationness'.[11]

The first step already befuddling any continental chronology is the cinema's uneven diffusion and development. As mentioned earlier, the cinematic apparatus appeared in Latin America quickly, less than six months after its commercial introduction in Europe. It followed upon the already well established routes of transatlantic commerce and pinpointed the most modern cities of the continent, which were already in the first throes of modernisation.[12]

The diffusion of the cinema throughout the interior of Latin American countries followed a similar pattern determined by, among other things, the level of development of railway and other modern infrastructures (also, of course, in the service of commerce). In Mexico, for example, where a national railway system was already well established by the turn of the century,[13] the Edison equipment enchanted Guadalajara, the nation's second largest city, in 1896; while by 1898 the Lumière apparatus had already appeared in Mérida, San Juan Bautista, Puebla and San Luis Potosí. Conversely, more inaccessible regions – that is, regions marginal to international trade – were not exposed to the new invention until significantly later. An extreme example is the remote community of Los Mulos in Cuba's Oriente province which only saw movies 'for the first time' through the auspices of the Cuban film institute's (ICAIC) cine-móvil programme in the mid 1960s, an experience documented in Octavio Cortazar's short film Por primera vez (1967).

But perhaps more significant than the speed of diffusion of the technological apparatus is an understanding of how it was used in various sites and locales – Appadurai's 'spectacular experiments' – a process of adaptation, contestation and innovation in the context of an international cinematic marketplace. The cinema experienced by Latin Americans was (and still is) predominantly foreign, a factor which is, as I shall discuss subsequently, of tremendous significance for the complex development of indigenous forms, always caught in a hybrid dialectic of invention and imitation. It was of equal significance for the development of the form of experience – mass spectatorship – necessary to sustain the medium.

Peripheral attractions

The early films that arrived in Latin America alongside the new technology were part of what Tom Gunning and other film scholars have characterised as the 'cinema of attractions' (predominant in the US until 1903–4).[14] Instead of the narrative forms that would later become hegemonic, the cinema of attractions was based on an aesthetics of astonishment: it appealed to viewers' curiosity about the new technology and fulfilled it with brief moments of images in motion. It was, above all, a cinema of thrills and surprises, assaulting viewers with stimulating sights; in Miriam Hansen's terms, 'presentational rather than representational'.[15]

But in Latin America, this aesthetics of astonishment was complicated by the ontological and epistemological status of the apparatus. In fact, the Latin American context – in which imported films have always dominated the market and usually been most popular – leads us to pose the question: An audience is clearly attracted, but to what? The cinematic attraction is 'attractive' in and of itself *and* as an import. However, beyond any purported fit with the experience of modernity in local urban life, its appeal is also – and perhaps first of all – the appeal of the Other, the shock of difference. With its vistas of sophisticated modern cities and customs (ranging from Lumière's rather sophisticated workers leaving the factory and magnificent locomotives to Edison's scandalous kiss), the imported views could produce the experience of an accessible globality among the urban citizens of Latin America – many of them less than a generation away from the 'old world'. Fashion, consumer products, other new technologies, different ways of experiencing modern life and its emotions and challenges[16] were suddenly available with tremendous immediacy: 'In its earliest days . . . the cinema was an opening to the world.'[17] But to the same degree that that experience was desired and delightful, it was also profoundly ambivalent and a source of a different type of anxiety. The cinema's complex images of distance and otherness problematised the meaning of locality and self: Where were they to be found, the spectators of the 'new world', in this brave new 'other' world of specular and spectacular thrills? On one hand, the cinema fed a nation's self-confidence that its own modernity was 'in progress': we can share and participate in the experience of modernity as developed elsewhere; we can respond to the thrill. Yet in order to do so, the national subject is also caught up in the dialectics of seeing: s/he must assume the position of spectator, becoming a voyeur of, rather than a participant in, modernity. To the degree that the cinema of attractions depended upon a highly conscious awareness of the film image *as* image and of the act of looking itself, it also produced a tremendously self-conscious form of spectatorship which in Latin America was almost immediately translated as the need to assert the self – as modern, but also, and more lastingly, as different; ultimately as a national subject.

In its form and content, early Latin American cinema clearly resonates with the technological changes and innovations generally associated with modernisation, echoing how the intersection of cinema and modernity was evidenced in Western Europe and the US and demonstrating the desire to identify local, modern 'attractions'. For example, in response to the great impact upon audiences of the Lumières' *Arrival of a Train at the Station*, one of the films included in most of the 'first' screenings in Latin America (and elsewhere), local filmmakers sought in the developed and/or developing national railway and transportation systems an equivalent symbol and the duplication of the amazement produced by the French film. One of the first national 'views' filmed in Buenos Aires, screened in November 1896, was also of the arrival of a train at a local station, described pointedly in the press as 'the arrivals of *our* trains' (emphasis mine).[18] Slightly later Eugenio Py also chronicled the *Llegada de um tramway* (Arrival of a tram) in 1901, undoubtedly seeking a similar effect. In Brazil, Vittorio de Maio filmed *Chegada de um trem a Petrópolis* (Arrival of a train in Petropolis) and *Ponto Terminal da Linha dos Bondes* (Tram line terminal) in 1897; their exhibition at the Teatro Casino Fluminense in Petropolis (a mountain resort city near Rio) in May 1897 was widely advertised.[19]

As in the rest of the world, all modern modes of transport were quickly intertwined with the emerging medium, not only as subject, but reproducing the perceptual changes they embodied. Railway travel, in particular, profoundly altered prevalent ways of seeing and produced a specifically modern perceptual paradigm marked by what Wolfgang Schivelbusch calls 'panoramic perception' – the experience of passengers looking out of a moving train window – as well as a changed temporal consciousness, an orientation to synchronicity and simultaneity.[20] Participating in the railway's modernity, the cinema in Latin America also developed a natural affinity with this mode of perception within its first decade: the railway 'view' or panoramic perception is the logical predecessor and producer of early moving camera travelling shots.[21] Sometimes the 'train effect' was pushed to its limits to produce the phenomenological experience of train travel (akin to the Hale's Tours popular in the US from 1906 to 1910): according to the Curitiba

(Brazil) newspaper *A República*, to watch the 1910 film *Viagem à Serra do Mar* (Trip from the Mountains to the Sea), spectators

> enter a simulacrum of a fully outfitted railway car, including a machine on top providing the noise and vibrations of a moving railway ... Spectators receive a total illusion of a railway trip, topped by the projection in the front end of the car of the amazing landscapes [visible from] our railways, especially our marvelous mountains . . .[22]

Mobility in general was a great attraction. In both *Carnaval em Curitiba* and *Desfile Militar* (both Brazil, 1910), for example, the degree to which the camera focuses on the presence of various means of transport overwhelms the alleged subject of the short films (carnival festivities in Curitiba and a military parade in Rio). In both we witness a veritable melée of mobility as cars, electric streetcars and horse-drawn carriages parade in front of the cameras carrying revellers in the former and behind the marching troops in the latter. These new 'visions' offer fleeting – one to three minute-long – fragments of the experience of the unheralded human mobility to be found in and around the modern metropolis.

In Latin America as elsewhere, the early cinema capitalised upon the entire panoply of modern technologies, including urban developments, media and new amusements. In Brazil, for example, Antonio Leal filmed the 1905 opening of the new urban artery, the Avenida Central (today's Rio Branco), which changed the physiognomy of the city and other urban improvements, in *Melhoramentos do Rio de Janeiro* (1908). Another thrilling modern urban development – sophisticated fire-fighting organisations – were the focus of early films in both Cuba and Chile. In Chile, *Ejército General de Bombas* (1902) was a three-minute view of the city's firefighters on parade, and the first national 'view' on record. The first film recorded on Cuban soil, *Simulacro de un incendio* (shot by Lumière cameraman Gabriel Veyre in 1897), documented a staged fire-fighting incident and featured a well-known Spanish stage actress then touring the island.[23] In the area of communication, the telephone was at the center of the proto-narrative of Eugenio Py's *Noticia Telefónica Angustiosa* (Sorrowful telephone news, Argentina, 1906), while the popularity of the phonograph suggested a series of experiments to add music and sounds to films, in particular Py's thirty-two very popular 'sonorised films' for the Casa Lepage (1907–11). Meanwhile, the developing fields of public relations and advertising were exploited early in Cuba, already following US trends. José E. Casasús' *El brujo desaparecido* (The disappearing witch-doctor, 1898), a trick film in the style of Méliès, advertised a beer company: the magician 'disappeared' to drink a beer. Somewhat later, Enrique Díaz Quesada's *El parque de Palatino* (Palatino Park, 1906) chronicled and formally reproduced the thrills of the rides in the newly-opened Palatino amusement park, a mini-Coney Island which included a movie theatre.[24] Influenced by the popularity and foreign novelty of the *bel canto* series at the newly inaugurated Teatro Municipal and other theatrical reviews in Rio, Brazilian producers created what is perhaps the 'first' Brazilian film genre: the *falados e cantantes* (spoken and sung) films. With actors speaking and singing behind the screen during each screening, these films proliferated between 1908 and 1912 and were wildly successful. They began as simple illustrated songs, but quickly progressed to complicated stagings of operas, *zarzuelas* and operettas. In short, very quickly the cinema became emblematic of modernity, and the specularity and spectacularity of its fragmentary processes the epitome of clearly local forms of a modern sensibility.[25]

The novelty of objectivity

The cinema's impulse towards display and spectacle was ambivalently linked with technology's purported affinity with science, much lauded in Latin America[26] and aligned with then-hegemonic positivist ideologies of progress. Positivism and modernity were themselves inextricably linked, the former perceived as the theoretical matrix that would permit the achievement of the latter. That through 'scientific' rational knowledge the chaos of natural forces could be controlled and social life reorganised was the intellectual rationale for the ideology of 'Order and Progress,' the motto of more than one nation, which condensed the contradictory impulses of evolving 'modern' rationalities of economics and politics within still overwhelmingly traditional societies. In fact, the new cinematic technology was rarely utilized in the service of science as such,[27] but its veneer of scientific objectivity – its ability to display the physical world – perfectly rationalized its more thrilling appeals.[28] The cinema was welcomed first and foremost as a sign of and tool for the rationalist impetus of the modern. It was thoroughly aligned with the civilizing desires of the urban modernizing elites and ignored the 'barbarism' of the national 'others'.

In Mexico, for example, it was above all the cinema's purported objectivity that first endeared it to the highly positivist intelligentsia of the Porfiriato, fully committed to its leader's 'Order and Progress' motto. Linking the cinema with the similarly new and booming illustrated press and arguing that it was against the medium's nature to lie, early commentators railed stridently against the film *Duelo a pistola en el bosque de Chapultepec* (Pistol duel in Chapultepec forest, 1896), a reconstruction by Lumière cameramen Bertrand von Bernard and Gabriel Veyre of a recent duel between two deputies, as 'the most serious of deceits, because audiences, perhaps the uninformed or foreigners . . . will not be able to tell whether it is a simulacrum of a duel or a real honorific dispute.'[29] The concern over Mexico's image abroad was explicit – after all, the film was shot by Lumière cameramen charged with collecting foreign views for international distribution – at a time when the government was already beginning to organize its pavilion for the 1900 Paris Universal Exhibition. But the paternalist reference to the 'uninformed' – the national illiterate masses contained in the above commentary – highlights the unstable relationship between the régime's much touted 'progress' and those it had bypassed. For the majority of Mexico's city inhabitants 'progress' was experienced as entertainment, not science: they had already gathered in the streets to watch the installation of electric lamp-posts and the parade of new bicycles they still could not afford; the cinema was next in line and, to the extent that it was adopted by the masses and developed its 'attractions', it was repudiated by the elites. Already the cinema functioned as a modernising force, not according to positivist scientific parameters, but by consolidating the formation of a modern mass audience. However, although abandoned by the *científicos*[30] and eventually given over to the masses as spectacle, the Mexican cinema would remain bound to the myth of objectivity, to its value as 'truth'.

If at first the vertiginous experience of the illusion of movement necessarily involved the disavowal of the frailty of our knowledge of the physical world, that thrilling anxiety was quickly sublimated into the still shocking experience of seeing 'history', both near and far, as it happened. Stimulated by the surprise of being able to see imported images – whether real or reconstructed – of the Spanish American war,[31] local filmmakers throughout the continent exploited the ostensible objectivity of the medium to record current events. It was precisely the attraction of history-in-the-making that allowed the still economically unstable medium to continue to attract audiences and develop commercially. In fact, it has been argued convincingly that the locally-financed and locally relevant actuality-newsreels constitute the only consistent and unbroken cinematic tradition of Latin American early cinema. Beginning with the chronicling of the visit to Buenos Aires by the Brazilian president (*Viaje del Doctor Campos Salles a Buenos Aires*, 1900); followed by naval operations (*Maniobras navales de Bahía Blanca*, 1901) the company of Argentine pioneer Max Glucksmann (Casa

Lepage) specialized in actuality films and produced an outstanding record of the Argentine public sphere throughout the silent and sound eras. It was joined in this endeavour by a number of other entrepreneurs, among them Julio Irigoyen (*Noticiero Buenos Aires*) and Federico Valle, who entered the field shortly after his 1911 arrival in Argentina (after working with Méliès in France) and produced, among others, the *Film Revista Valle* weekly newsreel for a decade (1920–30).

Similarly, in Brazil, actualities were also the mainstay of the early film business: Antonio Leal in Rio and regional producers (especially in Curitiba) were soon joined by Marc Ferrez and his son Julio, Francisco Serrador, the Botelho brothers, and others in the provinces. However, in Brazil the novelty of news also took on a spectacular character with meticulous restagings of sensational crimes already popularised by the illustrated press. Films like *Os Estranguladores* (Francisco Marzullo or Antonio Leal, 1908) and the two versions of *O crime da mala* (Francisco Serrador, Marc Ferrez and son, both 1908) were wildly successful: the audience's familiarity with the crimes enabled the filmmakers to tell their 'stories' efficiently without intertitles (shots with added information or dialogue). Another restaging of a news story, *O Comprador de ratos* (Antonio Leal, 1908) is of particular interest, as it unwittingly captured the idiosyncrasies of modernity in underdevelopment, serving as a particularly vivid example of the contradictions produced by 'misplaced ideas'.[32] During the Oswaldo Cruz-led campaign to eradicate yellow fever in Rio, the government announced that it would buy dead rats by the pound. The inhabitants of Rio's poor neighbourhoods found themselves in the midst of a thriving industry, breeding and fattening rats to sell to the government. In a brilliant allegory of modernity in Latin America, *O Comprador de Ratos* tells the story of a Niterói native who attempted to sell the thousands of rodents he had bred until the scam was discovered.[33]

Following the Lumière model, Mexican pioneers also quickly took to current events of national and/or local significance, perhaps with most enthusiasm after Salvador Toscano exhibited the newsreels *Guanajuato destruido por las inundaciones* and *Incendio del cajón de la Valenciana* (both 1905). In 1906, both Toscano and his principal competitor, Enrique Rosas, rushed to chronicle an official trip to Yucatán by President Díaz, whose image was still of great interest to audiences; their films exhibited a preoccupation with formal structure that pushed them beyond the simplicity of the typical documentary. Toscano's film narrated the presidential trip from beginning (Díaz's departure by train from Mexico City) to end (his farewells to Yucatán), thus substituting a chronology absolutely faithful to the *pro-filmic event* for narrative development.

Similarly, the Alva Brothers' *Entrevista Díaz-Taft* (1909), a report of the Díaz-Taft meetings in Juarez City and El Paso, also observes the chronological 'record of a trip' structure, but mediated by two additional concerns: a visible effort to record both sides of the event (some of President Taft's trip as well as Díaz's) and a willingness to disrupt the chronology of the pro-filmic event to augment the narrative impact. As Aurelio de los Reyes demonstrates in his detailed analysis, the filmmakers altered the sequence of events towards the end of the film in order to have it end, reverentially, with the image of both presidents on the steps of the customs building in Juarez.[34] This image is the visual equivalent of their interview, but is also strongly marked by an accidental pro-filmic action: as the presidents descend the steps, an observer waves a flag in front of the camera and, for an instant, the screen is filled by the flag and its large slogan, 'Viva la República,' visually affirming the national despite the alleged impartiality of its objective treatment. In fact, the cinema's 'truth value' was rather selective: the Porfirian cinema was basically escapist and did not record the more disagreeable aspects of national life such as the bloody strikes in Cananea and Río Blanco (1906 and 1907), the violence and poverty of urban ghettos, or the injustices of rural life.

Attractions of 'nationness'

Beyond the drive to identify 'local' modern thrills or to record current events, the new technology was exercised for the benefit of the imagined national community, to negotiate precisely the conflicts generated by the dilemmas of a modernity which was precariously balanced between indigenous traditions and foreign influences, between nationalist aspirations and internationalist desires. Thus the fascination with the immediate manifestations of modernity and their perceptual thrills was infected by explicit exaltations of nationhood – not just 'our' railways, but our national belonging, in a sense as 'modern' a phenomenon as the new technological forms – linked in many instances to current events.

Following the non-chronological plotting of time and history suggested earlier, this process is both sequential to and simultaneous with the fascination with modern technology and current events described above. For example, in late 1897, a notice in the Buenos Aires newspaper *El Diario* announced not only the filming of local views, but the time and location where they would be filmed: 'The views will be photographed in the morning. The first will be of bicyclists in Palermo

Park at 7:30 am. Those who would like to see their figures circulating on the screen of this theatre should take notice.'[35] Similarly, *La Nación* a few months later remarked in its column 'Vida Social':

> The views shot in Palermo, which will be projected by the marvelous machine next Monday on the stage of the Casino theater, will perhaps be of greater interest than the landscapes and exotic scenes reproduced by the 'American Biograph'. We are assured that these views are as sharp as the European and that we shall clearly recognize many of our socially-prominent citizens.[36]

Clearly invoking another kind of desire or 'attraction', these notices posit a different kind of spectatorial position, predicated on the attraction of identification and self-recognition, which was but an embryonic form of cinematic nation-forming. It is also a process which is markedly aligned with the existing power structure: the appeal is not just that of seeing ordinary Buenos Aires citizens, but seeing the socially prominent ones who metaphorically stand in for the nation itself.

In Latin America as a whole the cinema is, from its earliest moments, closely aligned with those in power, be they wealthy and socially prominent or only in government, and this alignment is a first step toward its nationalist projects. The first films photographed in Mexico, for example, were not landscapes or street scenes, but carefully orchestrated views of Porfirio Díaz (re-elected for a fourth presidential term), his family and official retinue, shot by Lumière cameramen von Bernard and Veyre in 1898. The young Frenchmen recognized the necessity of obtaining the dictator's goodwill to proceed in their commercial enterprises and had first arranged a private screening of the new technology for him and his family in Chapultepec. In the five months they remained in Mexico they filmed the president, who had quickly recognized the propagandistic value of the new medium, in all sorts of official and familiar events. As one historian has remarked, Porfirio Díaz was, by default, the first 'star' – we could say attraction – of the Mexican cinema:[37] his on-screen appearances were enthusiastically hailed with rousing 'Vivas!'[38] Similarly, the first two views filmed in Bolivia were explicit paeans to the power structure: both *Retratos de personajes históricos y de actualidad* (Portraits of historical and contemporary figures), exhibited in 1904, and the very popular *La exhibición de todos los personajes ilustres de Bolivia* (The exhibition of all the illustrious characters of Bolivia, 1909) were designed to align the new technology with those who effectively controlled and defined the nation *and* to display them for the enjoyment and recognition of new audiences.

In Mexico, however, the initial links between cinema and the urban

power elites was short-lived. In 1900 Mexico City's exhibition sites –
primarily *carpas* or tents – were closed following new city safety regulations designed to curb the 'uncivilised' behaviour of popular spectators
and to diminish the risk of fires. Production and exhibition pioneers
therefore left the city, taking the cinema with them (there were only a
handful of film exhibitions in the capital between 1901–05).[39] They
travelled throughout the national territory, showing the films in their
existing repertory but also regularly filming local views to entice the
various regional audiences. These films chronicled the activities of
small cities and towns: the crowds leaving church after Sunday mass;
workers outside their factories; local celebrations and festivities. Rather
than focusing on modern life and technology, this early cinema took a
turn toward the people, positioned in their landscape and captured in
their everyday activities. Its attraction was self-recognition: 'on premiere
nights the improvised actors would come to the shows en masse to see
themselves on film; the enthusiasm of each and every one when they
saw themselves or their friends and relatives on screen was great.'[40] But
through that self-recognition, they also began the process of producing
an image of the nation based on the traditional – the peoples and
customs of the interior rather than the modernity of the capital city –
and a more broad-based audience for the cinema.

The lynchpin of the cinema–nation symbiosis coincided with the
various centennial national celebrations around 1910. Especially in
Argentina and Mexico, filmmakers competed fiercely to record the
many patriotic celebrations and festivities and their films were quickly
exhibited to great public acclaim. But the paroxysms of patriotism
elicited by the centennials and their preparations also motivated filmmakers in a different direction, away from current events, and towards
the historical reconstruction of key patriotic moments, in an effort to
further mobilise the new medium in the service of nationhood.

National narratives

Undoubtedly, Latin American audiences were already quite familiar
with the post-1904 productions imported from the US and Europe –
dubbed 'transitional narratives'[41] by film scholars to highlight their
position between the cinema of attractions and fully fledged narrative
cinema – and had begun to experience the appeal of a different kind
of cinematic identification, one which filmmakers sought to exploit for
the national celebrations. They were influenced less by the chase films
and westerns arriving from the US than by the theatrical adaptations

filled with artistic aspirations produced by the Société Film d'Art and other European producers. Already an art form with an extensive history and of great elite and popular appeal throughout Latin America, the theatre was a natural source of inspiration for filmmakers seeking to narrativise the medium. This process is most evident in Argentina, where the appeal of films of current events waned in comparison to the enthusiasm generated by a new series of proto-narratives, beginning with Mario Gallo's *La Revolución de Mayo* (1909).

A perfect example of a transitional film, the narrative of *La Revolución* is neither self-sufficient nor internally coherent. Because the intertitles are identificatory rather than narrative, spectators *must* have extensive prior knowledge of the historical event being represented (the uprising of May 1810 which began the Argentine struggle for independence) to make sense of the film and understand the motivations linking the various tableaux. Furthermore, its style is thoroughly presentational, ranging from its direct address to its *mise en scène* (theatrical acting, theatrical drops suggesting depth and perspective rather than reproducing it, etc.). Its one purely 'cinematic' moment occurs in the last scene, where a visual device effectively supplements the film's patriotic enthusiasm: while the patriot leader Saavedra speaks from a balcony to a throng, an image of General San Martín in uniform and wrapped in the Argentine flag appears unexpectedly over the Cabildo. San Martín is the hero of Argentine independence, but, historically, he did not return to Argentina from Spain to join the rebels until 1812. Here the 1810 patriots salute him and shout 'Viva la República' (according to the titles), in a move that only an audience familiar with Argentine history can unravel. Other of Gallo's historical reconstructions developed this patriotic thematic and the theatrical style; for example, *La creación del himno* (1909), an homage to the writing and first performance of the national anthem and, later, *El fusilamiento de Dorrego, Juan Moreira, Güemes y sus gauchos* and *Camila O'Gorman* (all 1910).

Gallo's narrative–nationalist impetus was further developed by Humberto Cairo's *Nobleza gaucha* (1915), the film that most clearly exemplifies the nationalist sentiments and contradictions of this period, and perhaps the first to develop the city–countryside dialectic central to Latin America's modernity debates. Although much closer to a classical style than *La Revolución*, *Nobleza* is still a transitional narrative. Rather than depending upon the audience's prior historical knowledge, the intertitles in the film cite the great Argentine epic poem *Martín Fierro* to tell the story of a courageous gaucho who saves his beautiful girlfriend from the evil clutches of a ranch owner who had abducted her to his city mansion. The ranch owner falsely accuses the gaucho of theft, but dies when he falls off a cliff while being chased by the hero on horseback. Skilfully filmed – with well-placed close-ups, elegant lighting and many camera movements, including tracking shots from trains and streetcars – and acted naturalistically, the story line allowed Cairo to focus upon the always appealing folklore of the countryside (songs, ranchos, gauchos, barbecues, etc.) as well as the modernity of the city (shots of Constitución avenue, Avenida de Mayo, Congress, the Armenonville station and even night-time urban illuminations). *Nobleza* simultaneously exalts the traditional values of rural life – indulging in what Rey Chow calls 'primitive passions'[42] – while displaying in all its splendour the modern urbanity which must make it obsolete: the gaucho may be the hero of the narrative, but he is a figure already relegated to the status of a foundational myth like *Martín Fierro. Nobleza*'s exploration of the crisis in national identity generated by the conflict between traditional experiences and values and the internationalisation incumbent on modernity was extraordinarily well-received: the film cost only 20,000 pesos to produce but made more than 600,000 from its many national and international screenings.[43]

Thus transitional narrative styles, in all their diverse forms, were almost naturally linked to the project of modern nation building. Once the cinema had exhausted its purely specular attractions and sought new story-telling possibilities, the task of generating stories about the nation inevitably led to the problematisation of modernisation itself. The immediate modernity of urban daily life – with its railways, mobility, technology, and so on – had been exalted earlier; narratives required the exploration of the contradictions of that process at a national level. With few exceptions, the earliest successful Latin American films identified as 'narratives' were linked to patriotic themes. In Mexico, for example, Carlos Mongrand invoked well-known historical figures in *Cuauhtémoc y Benito Juarez* and *Hernán Cortés, Hidalgo y Morelos* (both 1904); later Felipe de Jesús Haro and The American Amusement Co. produced the elaborate (seven-tableaux) *Grito de Dolores* (1907), which was usually screened with live actors declaiming the dialogue behind the screen.[44] In Brazil, in addition to addressing historical events and figures (for example, *A vida do Barão do Rio Branco* (Alberto Botelho, 1910)), narrative was also aligned with comedy and sustained a thematic contrasting urban and rural lives similar to *Nobleza Gaucha*'s. *Nhô Anastacio chegou de viagem* (Julio Ferrez, 1908), recognized as the first Brazilian fiction film, presents the misadventures of a country bumpkin newly arrived in Rio, including his encounters with urban modernity (railways, monuments, etc.) within a mistaken identity love plot. It engendered a series of similar comedies, which in their attempt to produce the discursive triumph of positivism, figured the traditional and rural as nostalgically obsolete, as cultural remnants willed into history, while the modernity of the metropolis was inevitable, 'natural,' and national.

In other parts of the continent we find similar efforts. In Bolivia, for example, the conflict between indigenous/rural and urban life was explored in *La profecia del lago* (José María Velasco Maidana, 1925) and *Corazón Aymara* (Pedro Sambarino, 1925). In Colombia we find skilful adaptations of foundational fictions mediated through the conventions of European-inspired film melodrama: *María* (Alfredo del Diestro and Máximo Calvo, 1921–22) and *Aura o las violetas* (Di Doménico, 1923). Chile's version of *Nobleza Gaucha, Alma chilena* (1917), was directed by Arturo Mario, the star of the Argentine film, while *La agonía del Arauco* (Gabriella von Bussenius/Salvador Giambastiani, 1917) contrasts the indigenous Chilean landscape and people with the melodramatic foibles of its urban protagonists, and *El húsar de la muerte* (Pedro Sienna, 1925) chronicles the exploits of national hero Manuel Rodríguez.

The Chilean example highlights a curious characteristic of early Latin American cinema that perhaps explains, in part, its obsessive concern with nationhood: throughout the continent, the overwhelming majority of early filmmakers were first-generation immigrants. The evidence to support this assertion is too vast to summarise efficiently, and a few names must suffice: in Brazil, the Segreto family were newly arrived from Italy, Antonio Leal from Portugal, Francisco Serrador from Spain; in Argentina, Enrique Lepage was Belgian, Federico Figner Czech, Max Glucksmann Austrian, Eugenio Py French, and Mario Gallo and Federico Valle Italian; in Chile, Salvador Giambastiani was Italian; Pedro Sambarino, an Italian, worked in Bolivia and Peru. Originally from Italy, the Di Doménico family was instrumental in establishing the cinema in Colombia and Central America: after immigrating to Panama, they acquired filmmaking equipment from Europe and travelled through the Antilles and Venezuela, arriving in Barranquilla in 1910 and settling in La Paz in 1911, where they established a regional distribution and production company of great significance until the arrival of sound.[45] The cinema was thus not only a medium of mobility but also of great appeal to the mobile: to immigrants seeking to make their fortunes in the new world through the apparatuses of modernity yet eager to assert their new national affiliations, as well as to those who restlessly travelled throughout the continent.

A nation at war and beyond

Mexico is a case apart, not only because its cinema pioneers were almost invariably local, but because its cataclysmic Revolution determined a different, although no less nationalistic path for the cinema between 1910 and 1916–18. The films of the Revolution were the direct heirs of the earlier actualities' passion for objectivity and reportage. To the same degree that Díaz had been the 'star' of early Mexican films, Madero, the other *caudillos* and the armed struggle became the stars of the next decade. The success of the Alva brothers' *Insurrección de México* (1911), one of the first films depicting revolutionary events, demonstrated that audiences were eager for news of the Revolution and most filmmakers followed the *caudillos* and fighting troops to capture images of the complicated events taking place. Alongside the increase in production, movie theatres mushroomed in the capital to accommodate new capacity crowds, many composed of newly-arrived peasants escaping from the fighting and violence of the provinces.

In the first films of the Revolution, filmmakers continued to adapt narrative strategies to the documentation of events. *Asalto y toma de Ciudad Juárez*, for example, the third part of the Alva brothers' *Insurrección en México*, was subdivided into four parts and consisted of thirty-six scenes, the last of which was the 'apotheosis' or grand climax in which the people acclaim the victory of the hero, Orozco. Similarly, *Las conferencias de paz y toma de Ciudad Juárez* (1911, Alva brothers) ended with the military's triumphant entry into Juárez City; *Viaje del señor Madero de Ciudad Juárez hasta Ciudad de México* (1911, Alva brothers) climaxed at the intersection of two parallel narrative lines (Carranza and Madero's journeys, culminating in two scenes of triumph), and *Los últimos sucesos de Puebla y la llegada de Madero a esa ciudad* (1911, Guillermo Becerril, Jr.) ended its narrative of events with the reverential image of President Madero and his wife posing for the camera. All of these films respected the chronological sequence of events and simultaneously adopted a clearly theatrical narrative structure for their representation.

Potentially the most ambitious of all revolutionary films, *Revolución orozquista* (1912, Alva brothers) documented the battles between the Huerta and Orozco troops and was shot in extremely dangerous circumstances.[46] The filmmakers chose to present both sides of the battle with the greatest degree of objectivity and thus structured the film to tell two parallel stories without providing explanations or justifying the actions of either side. In the first part, we see the activities of the Orozquista camp, and in the second those of the Huertistas. The third part features the battle between the two camps, but we are not shown the outcome. Believing that the events were powerful enough to speak for themselves, the filmmakers attempted to assume the impartiality required of the positivist historian, and thus produced a spectacular new transitional form further developed by all the filmmakers active in this period which engaged narrative protocols while remaining wedded to documentary objectivity, and which aimed, above all, to inform.

Huerta's take-over in 1913 had a great impact upon the development of the Revolutionary documentary. Because the films had often awakened violent reactions in the already quite partisan audiences, Huerta approved legislation requiring 'moral and political' censorship prior to exhibition to curb such violence. Thus filmmakers began to give up on 'objectivity' and assumed the point of view of those in power (for example, *Sangre hermana*, 1914, which is told from a marked federalist and propagandistic perspective), or to focus on using previously shot materials to produce 'reviews' of the Revolution which were then updated regularly and shown in their entirety (*Historia completa de la Revolución de 1910–1915*, Enrique Echániz Brust and Salvador Toscano, 1915; *Documentación histórica nacional, 1915–1916*, 1916, Enrique Rosas). Eventually the Revolution disappeared from Mexican screens altogether and was replaced by a new fiction cinema:

> Before, filmmakers were pragmatists who had learned their craft by documenting people and events in order to attract audiences ... National producers had never before dealt with narrative, a term that had been used exclusively to refer to foreign fiction films. ... Now a different conception of cinema made its way. The 'views' had lost their appeal and the desire was for *films d'art* based on foreign models.[47]

An important predecessor was the Alva brothers' *El aniversario del fallecimiento de la suegra de Enhart* (1912), a short comedy about the 'daily life' of two very popular theatrical comedians (Alegría and Enhart) in the style of the French films of Max Linder. Although a 'fiction' film, it is interesting that the narrative focuses on aspects of the so-called daily life of the two comedians, including their domestic as well as professional lives. The Alvas ostensibly had not quite given up on their use of the medium to capture the real world and the camera scrutinises the very real Mexico City locations in which the fictional *mise en scène* takes place. Formally, the film is skilfully constructed, with editing that contributes to the narrative coherence by alternating between two parallel story lines (as in their previous documentaries), inserts (such as intertitles) that add to the suspense and humour, and the judicious use of special effects (like the old Méliès disappearing trick) and close-ups for comic and performative emphasis. The Alvas were perfecting their technique, but now in the service of narrative entertainment rather than information.

The turn to fictional narratives in Mexican filmmaking (from around 1916) can be attributed to a number of interrelated factors: the political restrictions imposed by the Carranza government, a desire to improve the image of the nation (which had been sullied by the Revolution itself, but also by how Hollywood films had been representing it), the popularity of Italian melodramatic films, and a widespread desire to leave the Revolution behind (especially after the 1917 Constitution and the 1919 assassination of Zapata).

Approximately seventy-five feature-length fiction films were produced in the 1917–21 period, the most prolific period in the history of the Mexican silent cinema. The most significant film, *El automóvil gris* (Enrique Rosas, 1919), highlights the complex negotiations between the almost forgotten devotion to objectivity of the Revolutionary documentary and the more modern narrative film styles from abroad. Originally a twelve-part serial with explicit documentary ambitions, the film tells the real-life story of a band of thieves who pretended to be *carrancista* troops and robbed and kidnapped wealthy families throughout 1915. The members of the band were eventually captured, tried and sentenced to death. Their execution took place on 24 December 1915, and Rosas had filmed the event for his documentary *Documentación histórica nacional 1915–1916*. Because the band had been linked to various military factions, the entire event was politically charged and Rosas' film version, combining historical facts and legends, vindicates the carrancistas. However, like Toscano's *Viaje a Yucatán* and the Alva brothers' *Revolución orozquista*, the central structuring element of Rosas' film is the historical chronology of the real events: the film presents the various house robberies and the subsequent chase by the police in strict chronological sequence. Like *Aniversario del fallecimiento de la suegra de Enhart*, *El automóvil gris* was shot on location, in the places where the robberies and chases had actually taken place (also including Rosas' previous footage of the execution of the real gang members). By comparing the two films we can see how drastically Mexico City had changed in the intervening seven years. Whereas in the earlier film we see people walking, interacting and engaging in commerce in a clean and orderly city, in *El automóvil*, the city is in ruins, dirty and almost completely empty.

El automóvil gris is the last Mexican silent film to have this kind of

documentary feel – the last gasps of the previous documentary tradition. In its combination of documentary-like realism with touches of
Italian melodrama and a sophisticated Hollywood-style cinematic
language, close-ups, the serial structure, for example, it points to the
advent of Mexican sound cinema.

Peripheral displacements

In complex negotiations between national events and traditions, and
foreign models and the demands of Westernisation, Latin America
produced a series of 'spectacular experiments' that dialectically
inscribed the cinema in national histories while recognising it as the
embodiment of dreams of modernity. National, yet also of the 'world at
large', the silent cinema was a key agent of both nationalisms and an
incipient globalisation: filmic visuality would come to define the necessarily ambivalent position of those caught in eddying whirlpools of
change, whether in the shift from rural to urban life, the displacements
of immigration, or the cataclysms of civil war. In fact, we could argue
that the cinema was one of the principal tools through which the desire
for and imitation of the foreign became paradoxically identified as a
national characteristic shared by many Latin American nations.

Throughout the continent, national producers were faced with two
significant changes in subsequent decades. First, the outbreak of World
War I redefined the international cinematic marketplace: blocked from
its usual markets and practices in Europe, US producers 'discovered'
the potential of the Latin American market and moved in aggressively.
They consolidated their presence throughout the continent and, in
most instances, effectively precluded the success of national production.
This was quite marked in Brazil, for example, where the end of the *bela
época* coincided with the arrival of subsidiaries of US firms.[48] This shift
was soon followed by a potentially far more devastating change: the
arrival of sound. Aggressively marketed, sound films from the US
quickly took over the exhibition and distribution sectors, while national
producers scrambled for capital, technology and know-how. In some
cases, the arrival of sound ended all previous cinematic activities: several
nations – Bolivia, Venezuela, Colombia and others – were not able to
resume filmmaking until nearly a decade after the introduction of
sound. Others – principally Mexico, Argentina and Brazil – by hook or
by crook, invented, adapted and experimented, producing a different
yet resonant version of the patterns of development and diffusion of
early cinema.

The centrality of the cinema as the principal interlocutor of Latin American modernity – where, as Carlos Monsiváis says, Latin Americans went not to dream, but to learn to be modern – would itself be modified by its relationship with new media: radio and the recording industry in the 1930s and '40s, and television since the 1960s. Television has, indisputably, become the locus of the experiences of nationhood in Latin America, modernity and post-modernity, in many instances constituting the only possible site where its beleaguered nations are able to imagine themselves as one.

Forty to fifty years after the arrival of cinema, the introduction and diffusion of television in Latin America embarked on a different series of 'spectacular experiments'. Once again the technology was imported, but this time its much higher costs dictated a different, centralised production base. This was not a medium for individual, local entrepreneurs (which to some extent, cinema and radio had been), but for large capital-intensive corporations that would eventually become conglomerate owners of other media as well (for example, Brazil's Globo and Mexico's Televisa). And its appeal was, at first, intensely local, since before the introduction of video-tape in the 1960s all programming was, of necessity, broadcast live. Throughout the Americas early television programming consisted either of theatrical dramas or program models borrowed from radio (musical shows featuring local talent). Thus, unlike early cinema, which brought to Latin America an aura of European and US modernity and the experience of an accessible globality, television was primarily a local experience, dedicated to the tastes of its urban and middle-class audiences and so already part of a different facet of the 'modernising' process.

Furthermore, because of its technological base, television engenders a radically different experience of modernity. The cinema provided a guarantee of authenticity (the reproduction of the real, akin to photography) combined with the universe of dreams and the imagination (narratives and unique spaces); in darkened movie theatres, spectators were offered a break from day-to-day life. In fact we could even argue that Latin American spectators may have gone to theatres to learn how to be modern, but while there they were also able to dream and especially to cry. Television, however, invades the lived-in spaces of spectators electronically with the promise of imbricated pleasure and information; it is experienced as part of everyday life. Under the cover of an implicit technological objectivity and ubiquity, the televisual rush of images is paradoxical, 'a routine', but one 'that instantly acquires the appearance of a burning bush'.[49]

Nowhere were these paradoxes more evident than in Latin America in the 1960s and '70s. With the introduction of video-tape technology, imported serials and canned programming from the US displaced the previous local focus. But as the medium became truly 'mass' in the late 1960s and '70s (when repeat transmitter links brought television even into remote rural areas) television, like early cinema, sought recourse in nationhood, and produced signs of nationhood unlike any other previously experienced. On the one hand, the transformation of television into a mass medium coincided with the consolidation of national production conglomerates. Globo, Televisa and others would adapt the models of imported programming and produce perhaps Latin America's most 'spectacular experiment' with mass-mediated modernity: the *telenovela*. As the lynchpin of the commercial development of the medium and its popularity in the region, by the mid to late late 1970s, the *telenovela* had replaced imported programming during prime-time. Thoroughly grounded in perhaps the most conservative Western dramatic form, the melodrama, the *telenovela* is also paradoxically the principal emblem of Latin American television's modernity: it is the genre that facilitated the insertion of Latin American audio-visual culture into global markets (through exports, regionally and internationally). Moreover, in an additional turn of the screw, it has consequently acquired 'national' characteristics: the Brazilian *telenovelas* are considered more realistic, using more sophisticated cinematic techniques and often addressing social issues, while the Mexican *telenovelas* are believed to be more melodramatic and conservative, and the Colombian ones are best known for their use of literary and historical themes.[50]

On the other hand, television's power to provide the nation with a common base of experiences also coincided with shifts in the nation-building strategies of Latin American states, ranging from Brazil's authoritarian military régime to Mexico's self-propagating one-party Revolutionary legacy. Despite obvious differences, the common experience provided by television – whether it be the *novela das oito* (the eight o'clock soap) seen from Sergipe to Rio Grande do Sul, the comforting authority of the nightly news program, or the weekly antics of 'Don Francisco's' variety show broadcast every weekend from coast to coast in Mexico – served as evidence of the existence and viability of the nation-state. Even when politics separate, television unifies and, ultimately, that unification boomerangs in accordance with the interests of states which, at least in theory, are committed to modernisation and internationalisation. Thus here the 'national' leads irrevocably to the global. And, in fact, despite their 'Latin-American-ness', Globo and Televisa have gone transnational, as evidenced by Sky Latin America, their joint satellite venture with Rupert Murdoch's Fox, based in the US, Globo's ownership of a station in Monte Carlo, and Televisa's interest in the US Spanish-language network Univision.

Through the nation, television has led the way towards globalisation and has been irredeemably disconnected from the nation-state. But at the turn of the twenty-first century, its experience has itself already become peripheral to the waves of new communication technologies – direct satellite transmissions, information technologies – which are becoming the site for Latin America's newest 'spectacular experiments'. As Comandante Marcos's proclamations in Chiapas are e-mailed throughout the world, street vendors in Cuzco sell *te de coca* to winded tourists on their way to Macchu Picchu; amazon.com pushes Gilberto Gil's latest CD on its 'world music' list while in Rio de Janeiro teenagers dance to the beat of 'funk' music; I watch the Mexican *telenovela La Mentira* every evening on the US Hispanic channel Univision, while my counterpart in Buenos Aires tunes in to CNN or MTVLatino. Global culure is now accessible, though still, of course, at differing levels for rich and poor. One thing is certain: at the beginning of a new century we can be sure that Latin America's encounters with modernity will always continue to be 'spectacular'.

Acknowledgements

Research for this essay was made possible, in part, by grants from the Roger Thayer Stone Centre for Latin American Studies at Tulane University. My interest in silent cinema was originally stimulated by the Getty Institute Research Centre's 'Imaging the Cities in the Americas' project, to which I contributed a report on silent cinema circa 1900–10. My thanks to Hamilton Costa Pinto, for his constant companionship, astute movie-watching and patient fact-seeking over the years.

Notes

1 Maxim Gorky's description of his first encounter with the cinema in 1896, included as an appendix in Jay Leyda's *Kino: A History of the Russian and Soviet Film*, (London: Allen & Unwin, 1960), pp. 407–9.

2 As, for example, in Armand Mattelart, *Transnationals and the Third World: The Struggle for Culture* (South Hadley, Mass: Bergin and Garvey, 1983), Herbert Schiller, *Communication and Cultural Domination* (White Plains, NY: International Arts and Sciences, 1976), and Jesús Martín Barbero, *De los medios a las mediaciones* (Barcelona: Ediciones Gili, 1987).

3 Paulo Antonio Paranaguá, *Cinéma na America Latina: Longe de Deus e perto de*

Hollywood (Porto Alegre: L&PM Editores, 1985), p. 9. Unless otherwise noted, all translations from foreign language sources are my own.

4 Ella Shohat and Robert Stam, *Unthinking Eurocentrism: Multiculturalism and the Media* (New York: Routledge, 1994), p. 100.

5 Leo Charney and Vanessa R. Schwartz 'Introduction', in *Cinema and the Invention of Modern Life* (Berkeley: University of California Press, 1995), p. 1.

6 Carol Breckenridge, 'Introduction', *Consuming Modernity: Public Culture in a South Asian World* (Minneapolis: University of Minnesota Press, 1995), p. 1.

7 José Joaquín Brunner, 'Notes on Modernity and Postmodernity', John Beverly, trans., *boundary 2*, vol 20, no 3 (Fall 1993), p. 41.

8 Arjun Appadurai, 'Playing with Modernity: The Decolonization of Indian Cricket,' in Breckenridge, ed. *Consuming Modernity*, p. 24.

9 Aníbal Quijano, 'Modernity, Identity and Utopia in Latin America', John Beverly trans., *boundary 2*, vol 20, no, 3 (Fall 1993), p. 149.

10 Brunner, 'Notes on Modernity and Postmodernity', p. 53.

11 With three exceptions: the general comparative study by Paranaguá, cited above, which begins with the silent period; Paranaguá's subsequent essay on silent cinema, 'El Cine silente latinoamericano: primeras imágenes de un centenario,' published in *La Gran Ilusión* (Universidad de Lima, Peru), no. 6 (1997), pp. 32–9; and a rather cursory and inadequately documented survey in Anne Marie Stock, 'El cine mudo en América Latina: Paisajes, espectáculos e historias,' *Historia General del Cine*, Vol. IV (Madrid: Cátedra, 1997), pp. 129–57.

12 There is journalistic evidence that British Brighton School films (using the Vivomatograph) were premiered in Buenos Aires as early as 6 July 1896 (not surprising, given the neo-colonial relationship between Argentina and Britain in this period). Confirmed screenings using the Lumière apparatus (the Cinématographe) took place shortly thereafter: in Rio de Janeiro (8 July 1896), Montevideo and Buenos Aires (18 July), Mexico City (14 August), Santiago de Chile (25 August), Guatemala City (26 September), and Havana (24 January 1897). Edison's Vitascope took only slightly longer to arrive. First it came to Buenos Aires (20 July 1896), followed by Mexico City (22 October), Lima (2 January 1897) and Rio de Janeiro (30 January). Arguably, Buenos Aires was ahead of the pack. Looking at some of the most salient indicators typically used to assess 'modernization,' Buenos Aires was the center of national industrial activity (through its ports moved the wool, beef and leather which arrived on the British-sponsored railway system linking the city to interior production centers; it housed 600,000 of the nation's four million total inhabitants); it had an efficient electric streetcar system (since 1890), a reliable electrical infrastructure already servicing business interests and two telephone companies (serving more than 10,000 subscribers in 1900). Furthermore, its population was cosmopolitan: the government-encouraged waves of immigration from Europe since 1895 had changed the physiognomy of the city, producing a fluid constituency and sumptuous public works and private palaces which coexisted alongside the *conventillos* (tenement housing) where laborers and poor recent immigrants resided. (See Gregorio Weinberg, 'La Argentina

de los viajeros,' *Nuestro Siglo* [*Historia Gráfica de la Argentina Contemporanea*], vol I [Buenos Aires, 1985].) Also quite 'modern' by continental standards, Rio de Janeiro also had electric streetcars, telegraphs, telephones and electricity, although the latter was unstable until the 1905 completion of a hydroelectric plant in nearby Ribeirão das Lajes. In contrast, a capital city like Lima was only beginning to show some evidence of modernising changes. Despite the beginnings of the urban renewal funded by the rubber boom that would eventually modernize it – especially significant was the redesign of the principal urban arteries of La Colmena and the Paseo Colón – the city still lacked a reliable source of electricity and was the center of a quasi-feudal state. The historian Jorge Basadre (*Historia de la República del Peru, 1822–1933* [Lima: Editorial Universitaria, 1968–70]) defined this state as the 'República Aristocrática', a nation in which only 5 per cent of the population had the right to vote and in which that 5 per cent governed and suppressed all peasant protests and urban popular movements. Thus it is not surprising that the 'modernity' of early cinema echoed more resoundingly – and lastingly – in Buenos Aires and Rio de Janeiro than in Lima, since even the simple films shown in these first screenings already exemplified a particularly modern form of aesthetics responding to the specificity of modern urban life. *Porteños* (Buenos Aires residents) took to the medium immediately: there is evidence that the first Argentine film – views of Buenos Aires – may have been produced as early as 1896. By the turn of the century, businessmen specializing in photography had mastered the new medium's technology and begun to produce a steady stream of 'actualities' (newsreel-like accounts of everyday and/or current events) and proto-fictional shorts, while other impresarios included imported and national films in their popular public entertainment venues (theatres, open-air festivals in the summer) and had even built dedicated movie houses as early as 1901. *Cariocas* (Rio de Janeiro residents) also became early enthusiasts. But despite a series of 'firsts' and the efforts of pioneers, the medium did not become established until reliable electricity was available after 1905. In contrast, the cinema acquired a foothold in Lima much more slowly. Although there is evidence that a national short may have been produced in 1899, the first confirmed Peruvian filmings did not take place until 1904; newsreel or actuality production was not consistent until 1909–15; dedicated movie theaters began to appear in 1909, the first fiction film was only produced in 1915, and the cinema did not develop beyond its first documentary impulses until the 1920s. See Ricardo Bedoya, *100 Años de cine en el Perú: una historia crítica* (Lima: Universidad de Lima/Instituto de Cooperación Iberoamerica, 1992) and Giancarlo Carbone, *El cine en el Perú, 1897–1950: testimonios* (Lima: Universidad de Lima, 1992).

13 William E. French, 'In the Path of Progress: Railways and Moral Reform in Porfirian Mexico', in *Railway Imperialism,* Clarence B. Davis and Kenneth E. Wilbrun, eds. (New York: Greenwood, 1991), pp. 85–102. By 1911 more than 11,000 miles of track had been laid. Mexico was so thoroughly blanketed by railways that less than 2,000 miles of track have been added to

the system since the Díaz régime. See also Jonathan Kandell, *La Capital: The Biography of Mexico City* (New York: Random House, 1988), pp. 367–70.

14 See, for example, Tom Gunning, 'The Cinema of Attractions: Early Film, Its Spectator, and the Avant Garde', *Wide Angle*, vol 8, no. 3–4 (1986), pp. 63–70, reprinted in Thomas Elsaesser and Alan Barker, eds., *Early Cinema: Space, Frame, Narrative* (London: British Film Institute, 1990), pp. 56–62.

15 Miriam Hansen, 'Early Cinema, Late Cinema: Transformations of the Public Sphere,' *Screen* vol 34, no 3 (Autumn 1993), reprinted in Linda Williams, ed., *Viewing Positions: Ways of Seeing Films* (New Brunswick: Rutgers University Press, 1997), p. 137.

16 Aurelio de los Reyes' discussion of how the practice of kissing in Mexico changed after the circulation of explicit cinematic kisses and the innovation of darkened public spaces – movie theatres – in which they could be exchanged is especially relevant here. See his 'Los besos y el cine,' in *El arte y la vida cotidiana: XVI coloquio Internacional de Historia del Arte*, Elena Estrada de Garlero, ed., (Mexico City: UNAM, 1995), pp. 267–89.

17 Guillermo Caneto, Marcela Cassineli, Héctor Gónzales Bergerot, César Maranghello, Edla Navarro, Alejandra Portela and Susana Strugo, *Historia de los primeros años del cine en la Argentina* (Buenos Aires: Fundación Cinemateca Argentina, 1996), p. 31.

18 'Visa Social,' *El Diario*, 7 Nov. 1896, cited in Caneto et al, *Historia*, p. 34.

19 Research by Paulo Henrique Ferreira and Vittorio Capellaro Jr., source unknown, cited by José Carlos Monteiro, *Cinema Brasileiro: Historia Visual* (Rio de Janeiro: FUNARTE, 1996), p. 13.

20 Wolfgang Schivelbusch, *The Railway Journey: Trains and Travel in the 19th Century*, trans. Anselm Hollo (New York: Urizen Books, 1971), pp. 57–72. See also, Lynne Kirby, *Parallel Tracks: The Railway and Silent Cinema* (Durham: Duke University Press, 1997).

21 For *Los festejos de la Caridad* (Cuba, 1909), for example, film pioneer Enrique Díaz Quesada put his camera on a streetcar to produce a travelling shot of the festivities held in Camagüey province. A similar, albeit slower effect, must have been produced by Affonso Segreto who filmed what is, if not the first, then certainly one of the earliest Brazilian 'views' as his ship pulled into the Bay of Guanabara in Rio de Janeiro in June 1898 upon his return from a trip to Europe where he had purchased equipment from the Lumières. Mexican filmmakers assiduously followed president Porfirio Díaz's many train trips, beginning with a sojourn to Puebla in 1900; during a later trip to Tehuantepec (to inaugurate a line linking the Gulf of Mexico with the Pacific), they captured 'fugitive' images of the pyramids at San Juan Teotihuacán. In Chile, Arturo Larraín filmed the funeral of President Pedro Montt in 1910 and included an extended sequence shot from the last wagon of the train carrying his remains to the capital from the port in Valparaíso (Montt died in Germany). In *Missão Militar e Diplomática Alemã* (German Military and Diplomatic Mission), an actuality about the 1913 visit of a German diplomatic mission to Rio de Janeiro shot by Alfredo Musson, what is of greatest interest are not the visiting dignitaries, but the extraordi-

nary transportation infrastructure already in place and elegantly functioning, including the electric streetcar climbing the steep Corcovado mountain and the monorail to Pão de Açúcar (Sugarloaf mountain), including magnificent vistas shot from inside both vehicles.

22 *A República* (Curitiba, Brazil, 14 Jan. 1911), cited by Jurandyr Noronha, *Pioneros do Cinema Brasileiro*, CDROM (1997), '*Viagem à Serra do Mar* (1910).

23 Raúl Rodríguez comments upon the clearly political intentions of *Simulacro de un incendio*: the firefighters were aligned with the Spanish colonial government and fought against the liberating army, the film featured a Spanish actress, and on its initial screening, was featured with three other shorts about the Spanish military. See *El cine silente en Cuba* (Havana: Letras Cubanas, 1993), p. 33.

24 See Rodríguez, *El cine silente en Cuba* and María Eulalia Douglas, *La Tienda Negra: El cine en Cuba, 1897–1990* (Havana: Cinemateca de Cuba, 1996).

25 For example, as early as 1897, the major Mexico City daily *El mundo* featured a column signed by 'Lumière' which presented what can only be described as 'fragments' or cinematic views of everyday urban life. An exemplary article from 28 Nov. 1897 is reprinted in Aurelio de los Reyes, *Los orígenes del cine en Mexico, 1896–1900* (Mexico City: Fondo de Cultura Económica, 1983), pp. 237–8.

26 All accounts of the new medium describe in excruciating detail the *technology* of the new phenomenon over and above its effects, giving precise technical information as to how the illusion of movement was produced. See, for example, the description of the Cinématographe which appeared in the Buenos Aires newspaper *La Prensa* on 3 April 1896, cited in Caneto et. al., *Historia*, p. 23, and the one published in the Mexican daily *El mundo* on 23 August 1896, reproduced in its entirety in de los Reyes, *Los orígenes*, pp. 217–22.

27 In a few instances, early films documented some scientific projects. For example, surgical pioneer Alejandro Posadas recorded two of his surgeries – a hernia operation and the removal of a pulmonary cyst – in Buenos Aires in 1900 (both films are still extant). In Brazil, the preventive work of Oswaldo Cruz was the subject of *Erradicação da Febre Amarela no Rio de Janeiro* (1909), while in Venezuela a somewhat precarious dental extraction was the subject of what may be the earliest views shot in Latin America, *Un célebre especialista sacando muelas en el Gran Hotel Europa* (Guillermo and Manuel Trujillo Durán, shown in January 1897).

28 Also linked to the ideology of scientific rationality and progress are the insistent attempts of local inventors to improve and expand the medium. In 1898 in Mexico, for example, someone 'invented' the 'ciclofotógrafo', a camera attached to a bicycle to produce travel films, while Luis Adrián Lavie announced his 'aristógrafo' which allowed spectators to see motion pictures in 3-D (de los Reyes, *Los orígenes*, pp. 174–8). In Argentina, three inventors patented a series of machines, among them the 'estereobioscopio' which also produced moving images with depth (Caneto et. al., *Historia*, pp. 47–8).

29 De los Reyes, *Los orígenes*, p. 104.

30 What Porfirio Díaz's closest advisers – the Mexican power elite – called themselves in reference to their conviction that Mexico would be transformed (ie. modernised) through science and technology.

31 Soon after the sinking of the USS Maine in Havana harbour on 15 February 1898, US Edison and Biograph cameramen began to produce views and shorts of the events unfolding in Cuba. Throughout 1898, and especially after the US entered the war, they extended the cinema's capacity as a visual newspaper (often in collaboration with the Hearst organisation) and, for the first time, used the medium to elicit patriotic sentiments from US audiences, revealing the medium's ideological and propagandistic force. The difficulties of filming in real battles also led to many 'reconstructions' of famous events, most notoriously Albert E. Smith and J. Stuart Blackton's reconstruction of *The Battle of Santiago Bay* in New York, using a tub of water, paper cut-out ships and cigar smoke. Many credit the enthusiasm generated by these films with the revitalisation of the lagging motion picture business in the US; the ongoing production of a few firms set the commercial foundation for the industry.

32 Term coined by Roberto Schwarz to explain the juxtaposition of modernising ideologies such as liberalism within traditional social structures such as the slave-owning Brazilian monarchy. Misplaced or out of place 'ideas' lead to significant discursive dislocations which critically reveal the fissures of allegedly universal concepts. See his *Misplaced Ideas: Essays on Brazilian Culture*, John Gledson, trans. (London: Verso, 1992).

33 Vicente de Paulo Araújo, *A bela época do cinema Brasileiro* (São Paulo: Perspectiva/Secretaria da Cultura, Ciência e Tecnologia, 1976), pp. 229–79 and Maria Rita Galvão, 'Le Muet', in *Le Cinéma Brésilien*, Paulo Antonio Paranaguá, ed. (Paris: Centre Georges Pompidou, 1987), pp. 51–64.

34 De los Reyes, *Cine y sociedad en México, 1896–1930: Vivir de sueños* (Mexico City: UNAM, 1983), pp. 96–8.

35 *El Diario* (29 Dec. 1897), cited in Caneto et. al., *Historia*, p. 35.

36 *La Nación* (17 Feb. 1898); cited in Caneto et. al., *Historia*, p. 35. This is also an astounding example of the speed of cinematic diffusion, not only of technology but of modes of commercialization and spectatorship. According to Charles Musser's research, the American Biograph company only began its overseas expansion in 1897, establishing a London office in March. And it was one of the characteristics of the Biograph operators to provide locally-shot scenes to theatre operators in order to enhance the programs' popularity. *The Emergence of Cinema: The American Screen to 1907* (Berkeley: University of California Press, 1990) pp. 157, 172.

37 Federico Dávalos Orozco, *Albores del cine mexicano* (Mexico City: Clio, 1996), p. 14.

38 See press reports cited by de los Reyes, *Los orígenes*, p. 153 and *Cine y sociedad*, p. 54.

39 See de los Reyes, *Cine y sociedad*, pp. 32–4, 55.

40 José María Sánchez García: 'Historia del cine mexicano', *Cinema Reporter* (30 June 1951), p. 18; cited by de los Reyes, *Cine y sociedad*, pp. 53–4.

41 According to Tom Gunning's periodisation, after the cinema of attractions'

dominance wanes (circa 1905), early narrative forms develop which begin to experiment with the specific cinematic narrative language which would become standardized as the 'classic Hollywood narrative style' around 1915–17. This 'transitional' period of over a decade is quite volatile and ambivalent; D.W.Griffith's narrative ambitions of the period were far from the norm. See Tom Gunning, 'Early American Film', *The Oxford Guide to Film Studies*, John Hill and Pamela Church Gibson, eds. (New York: Oxford University Press, 1998), pp. 262–6.

42 The modernist effort to reconceptualise origins which typically attributes to indigenous traditions the significance of a primitive past. Rey Chow, *Primitive Passions* (New York: Columbia University Press, 1995).

43 Domingo di Núbila, *Historia del cine Argentino*, vol I (Buenos Aires: Cruz de Malta, 1959), pp. 18–20.

44 De los Reyes, *Filmografía*, pp. 42–7.

45 For a family biography see Jorge Nieto and Diego Rojas, *Tiempos del Olympia* (Bogota: Fundación Patrimonio Fílmico Colombiano, 1992).

46 It is important to note that each of the principal combatants had their 'own' camera crews on hand to record their achievements. The Alva brothers followed Madero's activities; Jesús Abitia followed General Obregón – a former friend of his family – and also filmed Carranza; the Zapatistas were filmed by several cameramen; Villa and Carranza favored the US cinematographers who rushed across the border to produce news-reels and documentaries. Villa, in particular, signed an exclusive contract with the Mutual Film Co. and was known to stage battles and events such as hangings in the daytime so that they could be filmed. See, for example, Aurelio de los Reyes, *Con Villa en México: Testimonios de los camarógrafos norteamericanos en la Revolución* (Mexico City: UNAM, 1985) and Margarita de Orellana, *La mirada circular: El cine norteamericano de la Revolución mexicana* (Mexico City: Joaquín Mortiz, 1991).

47 Aurelio de los Reyes, 'The Silent Cinema', in *Mexican Cinema*, Paulo Antonio Paranaguá, ed. (London: British Film Institute, 1995), p. 72.

48 Of course, the displacement of the European by the US cinema had other ancillary effects, not only on the cinema, but on ways of life and social organization. From now on, Latin America would look to the US rather than to Europe for its modernity.

49 Carlos Monsiváis, *Mexican Postcards*, John Kraniauskas, trans. (London: Verso, 1997), p. 42.

50 Ana M. López, 'Our Welcomed Guests: *Telenovelas* in Latin America', *To Be Continued . . . Soap Operas Around the World*, Robert Allen, ed. (London: Routledge, 1995), pp. 256–75.

The Aesthetics of the Avant-Garde

Gwen Kirkpatrick

The events of the late nineteenth century – especially the war of 1898 in which Spain lost its remaining colonies in the western hemisphere and the US gained ascendancy in the Americas as well as new territories in the Caribbean and the Pacific – prompted Latin American intellectuals and artists to re-evaluate their position vis-à-vis a global culture and to search for new cultural definitions. The beginning of a new century also invited reflection on the future and the past. What Simón Bolívar had called republican Spanish America's 'originary defect', its denial of real citizenship to its indigenous survivors and descendants of slavery, and the possession of real control by the descendants of Spaniards, became even more pressing issues as Latin America saw its entrance into full modernity restricted by the effects of those exclusions (Halperin-Donghi, 1986: 747–8). This concern for the excluded, motivated not just by humanitarian ideals but also by basic questions of state and economic functions, explains some of the particular turns of modernism in Latin America.

Modernist aesthetics, difficult to define in any world area, are complicated even more by overlapping, and sometimes oppositional, aesthetic movements in Latin America. Generally referred to as the *vanguardistas* rather than modernists (*modernismo* in Spanish America refers to a turn-of-the-century literary movement associated with symbolism and post-romanticism, while in Brazil the term is equivalent to the European usage of modernism), the new wave of writers and artists found expanded public forums in the 1920s and '30s. By the 1920s surrealism and other avant-garde movements had gained a strong foothold from Paris to New York and Havana to Buenos Aires. In the US the Harlem Renaissance introduced much of the rest of the world to African American music, art, literature and spectacle. In the same year (1922) that saw the publication of Joyce's *Ulysses*, Rilke's *Sonnets to Orpheus*, Eliot's *The Waste Land*, Spengler's *The Decadence of the Occident*, Pirandello's *Henry V* and Katherine Mansfield's *The Garden Party*, Latin America witnessed the appearance of a new generation of iconoclastic artists and writers. Vicente Huidobro had already become known for his vanguard polemics, and in the early twenties César Vallejo published *Trilce*, Borges *El fervor de Buenos Aires*, Gabriela Mistral *Desolación* and Neruda *Crepusculario*, to name just a few of the best known poets. Vanguard activities were often collective efforts: the mural magazine *Prisma* of the *ultraístas* and the journal *Proa* were founded in Buenos Aires, Cuban intellectuals initated the journal *Avance*, the Mexican *estridentistas* launched their journal *Actual*, and vanguard groups emerged throughout the entire region. In Brazil, the enormously influential Semana de Arte Moderno in São Paulo infused a tradition-bound literary and artistic arena with new and defiant energies (Verani 1986: 11; also Masiello 1986; Osorio 1988; J. Schwartz 1982; Unruh 1994). As is obvious from the chronology, these artistic events took place in the context of often tumultuous political and social changes.

As the movement is generally understood, modernist (or vanguard) artists sought to liberate themselves from the obligations of realist representation in all areas. Unbound, at least in theory, from the restrictions of temporal and spatial order, they sought to disorder artistic norms and sensibilities. One cannot overestimate the impact of the emergence of the film industry, as well as technological innovation in areas such as sound and pictorial transmission in the early decades of the twentieth century. The massive audiences for film, combined with an expansion of literacy, changed the dynamics of both artistic production and reception. Some of the vanguard movements embraced the new technologies and expanded audiences, while other sectors sought to differentiate their works as much as possible from mass culture. In music, composers experimented with atonal systems as well as the incorporation of popular rhythms and themes; in the fine arts, cubists discarded spatial perspectives in favor of representation in a single plane; futurist writers and artists tried to capture the speed of modern technology; writers generally engaged in multiple experiments to recapture the multiplicity of human consciousness, including stream-of-consciousness techniques, linguistic experimentation to free language from its rules of order, and an effort to approximate the simultaneity achieved in film.

For many artists, a liberation from the strictures of Western rationalism and its accompanying aesthetics also marked an advance towards freedom in politics, society and sexuality; hence radical politics (of both right and left) frequently accompanied artistic manifestos. Latin American artists, often acutely aware of their peripheral status in relation to Western art, saw that elements of their cultures were considered 'exotic' by Western standards and capable of infusing new energies into a civilisation that saw itself as in decline. Obviously then, some of the traits that mark European vanguard movements, such as primitivism, were transformed in Latin American environments. For example, although the Parisian vogue of *négritude* may have influenced writers of the Harlem Renaissance or Caribbean writers such as the young Cuban Nicolás Guillén, this aesthetic movement could not shape or contain the social and political rebellions that informed it in contexts where there were large populations of African ancestry. Aesthetics and politics formed unusual alliances as a result of the multiple transculturations in process.

Vanguard artists identified with formal experimentation and a liberation from realistic representation. Nonetheless, a total separation of art from representation, realistic or not, is difficult to achieve for even the most radical of artists. In literature, modernism (or the vanguard moment) in culture has been described as the division between anthropocentrism and polyphony (Moretti 1996: 194–7), attributing greater independence to language itself, untied from its duties of signification. Thus any language or sign system cannot pretend to represent human experience and can only arbitrarily order sounds, images and meanings. Speech is detached from the speaker, or visual signs are freed from the burden of representation, and chance or arbitrariness are just as valid as logical systems. This has been interpreted as the moment when literature renounced its epic intent, or its realistic representation of humanity. Yet as vanguard writers searched for the 'zero degree' of language, they were inevitably confronted with the fact that language and its conventional signification are almost impossible to separate without falling into total incoherence, as exemplified in the final 'canto' of Vicente Huidobro's vanguard epic poem *Altazor* (1931). How could Latin American artists who were committed to political or social change in their societies meld modernist practice with their allegiances to specific socio-political programmes? Such artists – faced with the sudden entrance of new social actors, growing urbanisation, the presence of an increasingly powerful US, the dissolution of artistic certainties, and political revolutions – experimented in significantly different ways from their counterparts in other circumstances.

As is obvious from the proliferation of manifestos, oppositional aesthetic creeds and the increased facilities for communication between these groups and their counterparts, there could be no one reductive explanation for the upsurge in artistic ferment. Changes in social institutions, like public education, help explain some of the transformations – especially the emergence of artists from changing social sectors, like Vallejo, Mistral or Neruda. Of major importance also was the establishment in the first years of the 1920s of the Revolutionary government in Mexico and the institutionalisation, under José Vasconcelos, of a vast cultural project that included government sponsorship of mural art. In other regions, populist governments and middle-class alliances were replacing the old oligarchies in the economic and political spheres, just as new sectors were claiming a place in the aesthetic sphere. These new actors included not just the more traditional elite sectors (as was also evident in the late nineteenth century) but also: the beneficiaries of an expanded education system in many areas; an incipient urbanised middle class hungry to reap some of the benefits of cultural production; citizens educated by socialist and anarchist politics; indigenous groups pushed into action for land reform; and, last but not least, women who were entering onto at least a fringe of the public sphere. It is no wonder that the new generation would feel little affinity with the generation of leaders who had recently (around 1910) led national celebrations for the centenaries of a number of Spanish American republics.

Post-colonial citizens and modernity

Artists and intellectuals in Latin America, increasingly enmeshed in economic, social and cultural world-wide currents, sought to redefine their place in a global system. Energised by crucial events like the Mexican Revolution and the upsurge of immigration and urbanisation in the Southern Cone, and jolted by the ascendancy of the US, Latin American intellectuals seized the moment for the realization of their unique cultural capital. As post-colonial citizens they felt sharply the historic legacy of being constituted by the colonial gaze and existing in a constant state of belatedness; yet world conditions showed an opening for a reassertion of agency. As Latin Americans were well aware, historically global cultural flows are presumed to originate in the West, while other cultural flows are rendered invisible within the world system or are characterised as copies. On this view, uneven development, peripheral modernities, intellectual malaise and cultural imitation are often viewed as the inevitable results of globalising modernity, a characterisation that has been applied to the region during the last years of both the nineteenth and twentieth centuries. Thus Latin American literary production has most often been measured in these terms, with exceptions granted to primitivist aesthetic projects, politically explicit national or regional projects, or, less frequently, 'universal' writers such as Borges. Locked within this circular narrative, how could intellectuals from the periphery reassert their validity? Modernists in Brazil provided the most succinct reply – a defiant assertion of uniqueness, taking their label 'Pau-Brasil' from a wood produced only in their country, claiming their right to assimilate whatever they pleased, as in the 'Anthropophagist Manifesto'. The Brazilian group, led by Oswald de Andrade and whose greatest visual artist was Tarsila do Amaral, also held up for celebration the African and Indian roots of its culture, although largely for aesthetic display.

First, what claims for modernity could there be in such cultural mosaics throughout the continent? The narrative of modernity implies ties to an Enlightenment subjectivity – individual ability, creativity, freedom, liberty, and problem-solving through reason. Within this context of global modernity, the Latin American case can only be seen as deficient, since its particular processes of modernisation are not viewed as paradigmatic but as marginal, uneven, or even failed copies of the paradigm. Its late entrance to industrialisation; its continuing status as neo-colonial; provider of raw materials for industrialised nations; its unassimilated ethnic and linguistic communities; the failures of many of the republics to grant even minimal citizenship rights to their inhabitants – all of this seemed to mire it in a constant belatedness on every front. For centuries the solution for individual intellectuals had been to make the pilgrimage to European cultural capitals in an attempt to compensate for formative deficiencies. And the heyday of scientific racism from the mid-nineteenth century to the 1920s condemned many Latin American societies to despair about the impossibility of 'whitening' their populations at a fast enough pace to catch up with model modern areas.

Second, a narrative of subalternity or marginality is a predominant feature of twentieth-century Spanish American literatures, where increasingly heterogeneous actors became writers themselves, with the greater participation of women and the popular sectors, and confrontations between high art and popular or mass culture. How do these narratives help shape a history of Spanish American literature, especially its avant-garde movements? As suggested by Jean Franco (1969), the tension between abstract universality and American specificity, and between the transcendental and embodied, underlie much of twentieth-century production. Obviously all genres and major works cannot be included in a brief discussion, but a focus on several movements can clarify several dynamics.

An examination of Spanish American *modernismo* and avant-garde production (especially of the 1920s) reveals the tensions of the first narrative – that of globalising modernity – and its collisions with Latin American specificities. The 'universalist' emphasis (conscious or not) of major literary figures of these movements – Rubén Darío, Delmira Agustini, Vicente Huidobro, the early Neruda, Alfonso Reyes, the 'Contemporáneos' of Mexico, among many others – intersects with specific Americanist or regionalist projects by others – José Martí, Alejo Carpentier, Ricardo Güiraldes, Roberto Arlt, Magda Portal, the groups around the Peruvian journal *Amauta* or the Cuban *Avance*. Particularly complex is the strain of primitivist-infused *indigenista* or *negrista* literary projects which, in some cases, set the standards for the external reception of Latin American culture.

A singular figure in this discussion is César Vallejo, whose poetry very much embodies, linguistically as well as representationally, the paradox of modernity and its difficult translation into an American (specifically Peruvian) Spanish inflected by indigenous languages and structures. Even in his early volume *Los heraldos negros* (1918), less marked by linguistic experimentation than *Trilce* (1922), poems such as 'Nostalgias imperiales' point up the sharp contrast between the idealised visions of the Inca empire and the degradations of contemporary indigenous life, where words in Quechua accompany the brutal realities of poverty and submission. A constant in Vallejo's writings is the struggle with language as representation, and language as a stubborn, independent and resistant system which has a life and physicality of its own. The untranslatability of experience into language and the struggle to express oneself in another language serve as starting points for some of his most vivid poems. Vallejo's own story also exemplifies some of the new spatial and linguistic configurations of the modern era. With the onset of rapid technological changes in travel, commerce and communications, even the most geographically isolated artists, such as the young Vallejo, found themselves exposed to the latest artistic vanguardist experiments in the Peruvian provinces (Unruh 1984). After serving time in jail in 1922 for suspected political organising, he left Peru for exile in Paris, thus entering another circuit of international modernism. Later he, like Neruda, Nicolás Guillén and other artists of the period, found the Spanish Civil War a turning point in both ideological and aesthetic terms. Vallejo, from a social class and caste not accustomed to the cosmopolitan travel circuit, exemplifies another of the rapid social changes of the early twentieth century. His intriguing literary production, particularly his poetry, resists classification, although the influence of vanguardism and social realism is clearly evident in portions of his poetry and prose.

New narratives for post-coloniality

What historical construction could provide a different lens through which Latin Americans might shape their own valid modernities and aesthetic modernism(s)? Obviously, no single framework can account for the multiplicity of responses, but several narratives can assist in tracing significant currents in the literature of Spanish America. One is the narrative of Western 'disenchantment' and the resulting search for primitive authenticity. What Max Weber in 1917 called the 'disenchantment of the world', resulting from Western modern rationalisation and intellectualisation (quoted in Cascardi 1992: 16), was indeed a common theme in the thought of the period. Western Europe's devastation by the Great War, a widely adopted Spenglerian belief in the 'decadence' of Western culture – not to mention popular revolutions in many areas – led many to search for keys to the 'regeneration' and renewal of a disenchanted cultural organism. Anglo-American modernists reflected some of this loss of faith in reason and the intellect with their formal experimentation in fragmentation and dissonance, while surrealists had rejected the laws of reason for an exploration of subconscious depths and primeval instinct, a path in line with a rising interest in Freud's psychoanalytic work. Not surprisingly, the answers were always to be found elsewhere, not at home on the well-trodden ways of modern reason and progress. For this 'elsewhere' many looked to areas marked less by 'civilisation' and its deadening effects, searching for psychic, sexual and artistic renewal exactly where the great industrial powers had looked for primary commodities. In the spirit of Gauguin's trek to Tahiti, artists like D.H. Lawrence and Valle-Inclán sought primitive energies in Mexico, while Parisians revelled in tango, jazz and the performances of the amazing Josephine Baker, and Picasso incorporated the aesthetics of African sculpture. As Oswald de Andrade said of his and Tarsila Amaral's visit to Paris, 'Our only find in 1923 was native primitivism' (Lucie-Smith 1987: 69).

Clearly many Latin American intellectuals saw their cultures under the exoticizing gaze of Europe, and for many this served as a catalyst to take a fresh look at traditionally disparaged or heavily romanticized elements of their home cultures, like Nicolás Guillén's celebration of the African-based dance music, the *son*, in *Motivos de son* y *Sóngoro consongo* in the late twenties; or Diego Rivera's mural paintings of the grandeur of pre-Cortés Mexico; or Borges's poetic recollections of the disappearing Buenos Aires neighbourhoods of his youth in his first three volumes of poetry (*Fervor de Buenos Aires, Cuaderno San Martín, Luna de enfrente*). What does Mexican mural painting, with its obvious didactic intent, have to do with international modernism, so resistant to signification? If modernism is characterized most generally as an art of the fragment, of dissonance and escape from representation, how can the unearthing of historical experience and its links to specific political movements (such as official post-revolutionary ideologies in Mexico or socialism in Peru) form part of our understanding of Latin American vanguards?

Submerged realities and images: exoticism and abjection

The particular nature of Latin American vanguards cannot be attributed solely to a response to primitivist or nostalgic aesthetics, or even to revolutionary social movements. When Latin American artists participated in the vanguardist movements of the first decades of the twentieth century, whether they wrote or painted in Lima, Mexico City, Havana, Paris or New York, nearly all of them felt the weight of a specific American historical presence in their formulation of 'new' artistic languages. It is this awareness of a different past, and of heterogeneous cultural elements, often glaringly unassimilated in official culture, that makes the vanguardist movements in Latin America so disparate and difficult to categorise. The adoption of regional or nationalistic themes, or of pre-Columbian imagery and symbols, mixed with experimental artistic forms and revolutionary social movements in startling ways. Part of the vanguard's radical project was to bring submerged or disappearing elements of the American tradition to public consciousness – in this case not just repressed sexualities but also repressed populations, symbolic systems and languages. Perhaps the most visible traces can be found in the *indigenista* or *negritud* movements, but social and artistic radicalism is not limited to a focus on these groups. African and indigenous descendants in the Americas, no matter how much their historical representation might have been romanticized in previous centuries, were clearly marginalized and regarded as inferiors; a situation not easily solved by aesthetic movements which often did not include members of the ethnic groups that they exalted. For example, Cuzco's *indigenistas* included only one indigenous member, the photographer Martín Chambi.

Yet at the same time that vanguardism brings these submerged realities to the fore, its revolutionary aspirations call for a breaking apart of traditional means of signification. New languages or signifying codes were obviously required. In some cases these took the form of a radical break, as in the Argentinian painter Xul Solar's invention of two new artificial languages: '*neocriollo*, a pan-American language based on Latin roots and local expressions, as well as *panlengua*, one of hundreds of Esperanto-like creations typical of the period, based on simple syntax and an additive method of word-building'. These experiments influenced Borges's 'Tlon, Uqbar, Orbis Tertius' (Sarlo 1994: 35). Solar's unique paintings are evidence too of the desire to find a new 'ground zero' for making meaning, just as the poet Huidobro sought to do in the disintegrating language of *Altazor*'s descent from language (Unruh 1994), or as the painter Amelia Páez, on her return to Cuba in the 1930s after years in Paris, transformed her cubist and Léger-influenced techniques into a startling synthesis with traces of Cuban visual culture (Ades 1989: 137).

Subaltern voices

Narratives of subalternity or marginality are expressed in widely divergent ways, reflecting some of the similar trends within *indigenismo* and *negritud*. While such trends can be traced throughout all Latin American literature – from Huaman Poma to Sor Juana to gauchesque poetry and theater to José María Arguedas's incorporation of the Quechua language into Spanish texts, the twentieth century saw the entrance of other, new elements: the representation of previously hidden or romanticised ethnic groups, the emergence of women into the public sphere, the incorporation of popular culture (including film) into 'high' art, an exploration of sexualities, new representations of the body, and explorations of the malleable body of language and artistic form themselves.

Less spectacular than the *indigenista* and *negritud* movements, but critically important, was the development of a writing voice for women. There are few known examples of radical literary experimentation by women in these years, yet their rapidly growing numbers and greater readership in themselves constituted a radical change. The early part of the century had seen some celebrated writers like Delmira Agustini (Uruguay), but after 1915 an upsurge of women writers – Argentina's Alfonsina Storni, for instance – found a ready public readership, and sometimes both readership and critical recognition, as in the cases of

Chile's Gabriela Mistral, Venezuela's Teresa de la Parra, Cuba's folklorist writer Lydia Cabrera, El Salvador's Claudia Lars and Argentina's Victoria Ocampo. (Some other writers, like Nellie Campobello in Mexico, were recognised much later by feminist writers such as Elena Poniatowska.) Some of these women entered public life as schoolteachers (Storni, Mistral) or journalists, two ways open to women who were not from wealthy backgrounds.

Literary history has not always been kind to these writers, seeing them as vanguardists *manquées*, mired in the sentimentality and conventions of women's culture, and feminist revisionist scholarship has sometimes focused more on their personal struggles than on their development of new literary languages. It is clear that these writers were more resistant to the attractions of vanguard experimentation than their male counterparts, but were these conscious decisions? Did they see the vanguard groups as closed circles, indifferent to topics like maternity or feminine interiority and sexuality, and refuse to respond to the exoticising male gaze, Western or otherwise? The answers are complicated, entwined with larger questions of social class, the place of the woman in the public sphere and resulting self-censorship.

The exploration of sexualities and the body itself within this period in Latin America is not as well traced critically as are some other areas, in part because such a focus is often assumed to be in conflict with socio-political interpretations of the aims of many of these writers. The often fractured representation of the female body is well documented in surrealism, futurism and expressionism, but less so in the *indigenista* and *negritud* movements, and other avant-garde movements in Latin America. The well-known art of Frida Kahlo (primarily from the forties) incorporates Mexican popular culture in its recurring self-portraiture as a legacy of *indigenista* predecessors, but more strikingly brings into view a fractured, sexualised and suffering body. It would be trivialising her work to classify it as a compendium of elements of the previous generation, but there is no doubt that this heightening of bodily subjectivity finds resonance in earlier works such as César Vallejo's *Trilce* (1922), Oliverio Girondo's *En la masmédula*, or even Alfonsina Storni's *Mundo de siete pozos* (1937). Some writers, like Vallejo and Girondo, were more extreme in their fracturing of the body of language, as well as of the represented body itself. But as new actors entered the artistic arena from more diverse backgrounds, they brought with them their own physical and sexual histories. As Carlos Monsiváis notes in his essay on Salvador Novo and several writers of the 'Contemporáneos' group in Mexico, however, Mexican vanguardist and official circles were hostile to gay sexualities even as they exalted the breaking of bourgeois norms: 'The campaign against homosexuals is very fierce. Orozco caricaturises them, Diego Rivera mocks Antonieta Rivas Mercado . . . The cultural and literary resonances of moral lynching are vast.' (Monsiváis 1998: 53, my translation).

Popular culture began to make its way into elite art, notably in the Argentinian Roberto Arlt's novels such as *El lanzallamas*, just as forms of popular music – the samba, the *son*, jazz, tango, etc. – were becoming acceptable in elite circles. In the case of Arlt, the incorporation of the urban lower and middle class culture of Buenos Aires (sexual habits, prisons and hospitals) was influenced by 'the new ways of representing the "theatre" of the city – especially [German expressionist] films' (Sarlo 1993: 16). The representation of popular culture was not restricted to the urban sphere, however. Just as the *indigenistas* highlighted ancient elements of Aztec, Mayan or Inca cultures, musicians like Heitor Villa-Lobos in Brazil and Carlos Chávez in Mexico introduced popular motifs into symphonic music. In literature, the entrance of popular culture, especially working-class urban culture, was facilitated precisely by changes in literary form, with the important catalyst of film. The use of the fragment, juxtaposition, pastiche and the renunciation of sequential narratives allowed more easily for the interjection of popular speech or representations of the working class without incorporation into realist narratives. Although some literary historians have argued for an opposition between the vanguardists and their proletariat counterparts, as in the groupings of *Martín Fierro* and *Boedo* in Buenos Aires, in reality many of these writers shared modes of formal experimentation, although not necessarily the same ideologies.

Revolutionary energies

The Mexican Revolution (1910–20) unleashed powerful energies throughout society which spilled over across the continent. In some ways similar to the Russian Revolution of 1917, Mexico's popular uprising highlighted the fact that elements of a modern technological society existed alongside the legacies of an ancient feudal system. Efficient new railway systems, a capital city which depended largely on France for its cultural influences, increased urbanisation and a powerful foreign investment community appeared to be leading at least part of Mexico to a cosmopolitan future. Yet despite its recent celebration of the centenary of independence, Mexico could scarcely be called a unified nation. A high percentage of its people spoke little or no Spanish and claimed allegiance to indigenous tradition rather than to a Mexican one. Only the rebellion against the 'Pan y Palo' policies (providing minimal subsistence while enforcing tight social control) of the Porfiriato (1876–1911) and the temporary uniting of regional political leaders to call for agrarian reform pushed the masses toward popular revolution (Knight 1990). As Carlos Monsiváis has noted, 'The Revolution is also, and especially, social energy, the energy that foresees great deeds in symbolic battlefields. If Don Porfirio, emblem of immobility, has fallen, why not rhymed verse, academic painting, the naturalist novel, a closed and punitive society?' (Monsiváis 1998: 18, my translation).

Mexico's harnessing of the artistic energies of the Revolution found few parallels in the rest of the world. José Vasconcelos, on being named Minister of Education in the new government, called on the talents of Mexican intellectuals and artists to work for the state, bringing some, like Diego Rivera, home from Europe, and giving commissions and official positions to a new generation of artists, writers, anthropologists, archaeologists and musicians. In 1921 he appointed the young Rufino Tamayo head of Ethnographic Drawings for the Institute of Anthropology. Tamayo, unconvinced by the muralists' program, was nonetheless formed in part by the Revolution's celebration and resurrection of Mexico's pre-conquest past. Several critics have subsequently rejected the didacticism of many of the revolutionary artistic programmes – especially the social realism of many novels of the thirties and also of many aspects of mural art – yet there is no question that many of the muralists incorporated modernist techniques even in their most didactic works. Even the presentation of different historical epochs within a single space, as in Rivera's murals of the history of Mexico, attests to crosscurrents of modernist influence and its attempts to represent simultaneity. Rivera's early cubist training is also evident in the spatial configuration and flattening out of perspective of some of the allegorical sections. These examples also remind us that some modernist techniques, such as the representation of simultaneity and elimination of perspective, are in fact a return to more ancient, specifically pre-Renaissance, methods of representation.

The newness of the old

The radical energies of avant-garde movements in the region coexisted, but did not always intersect, with political radicalism. Yet even in circles more distanced from political activities, there was a heightened awareness of the need for self-definition in the face of European cultural tradition and the emerging power of the United States. Writer-activist José Martí, Cuba's hero in the wars of independence against Spain in the late nineteenth century, had proclaimed in 'Nuestra América' (1891) that Latin Americans should turn to their own pasts for models, to 'our Greece and our Rome', instead of giving slavish devotion to Western classical models, that it should keep a wary eye on the Colossus of the North, and that it should not ignore the abject conditions of culturally and socially disparaged indigenous communities and descendants of African heritage. From the vantage point of long exile, especially in the US, Martí felt the urgency of cultural redefinition. Shortly afterwards, José Enrique Rodó of Uruguay published his highly influential essay *Ariel* (1900); its publication was a sensation among intellectual youth in Latin America. His characterisation of the industrial North as barbarous Caliban, and of Latin Americans as the inheritors of the Mediterranean region's noble traditions of the spirit and the arts embodied in Ariel, had unexpected resonance. Despite Rodó's lack of acknowledgement of a pre-conquest American past or of its multi-ethnic and linguistic heterogeneity, his message found exponents even in the intellectual elite of the Mexican Revolution, as well as in various indigenist circles, and helped to create a new space for the humanities and arts in a positivist and pragmatic *fin de siglo*. Even Rubén Darío in 1896 had stated in his preface to *Prosas profanas*, a high point of *modernista* poetic production in Latin America: 'If there is poetry in our America, it is in old things, in Palenque and Utatlán, in the legendary Indian, in the sensual and fine Inca, and in the great Moctezuma in his golden throne. The rest is yours, democrat Walt Whitman.' (1968: 546, my translation). Despite this assertion, Darío, often considered Latin America's finest poet, rarely evoked this indigenous American world in his poetry, but drew his mythological images more from classical tradition, or from medieval Spanish and later French writings. Nonetheless, his statement was somewhat prophetic of a subsequent resurgence of artistic interest in the specificities of Latin America's heterogeneous cultural traditions.

In the context of international modernism, with radical experimentation in all the arts, Latin American artists found possibilities for expressive change in their oldest possessions – the legacies of its non-European cultures and the archipelago created by its transculturations with a variety of cultural layers. Artists seized on the fact that Latin American societies, over four centuries after the conquest, had not become completely *mestizo* societies; that despite centuries of coexistence there was not a melting pot of cultures and peoples, but disparate groups of very different cultural origins not always in communication –

what Antonio Cornejo-Polar has theorised as cultural heterogeneity (1983). At the same time that several national policies, especially in Mexico, were built on the foundation of an assumed *mestizaje*, artistic and literary production often signalled the fissures in these comprehensive nationalist conceptions. To be sure, interest in Latin America's autochthonous aspects was not ubiquitous. The assertion of universalist intent by writers such as the vanguard Mexican group 'Los Contemporáneos', or Borges's suspicions of the potential uses of indigenist and nationalist formulations at the service of political propaganda, were clear proof of the impossibility of categorising modernism in Latin America solely according to its nativist facets. Yet the stamp of the return to the past or the search for 'origins' is, nonetheless, an important distinguishing factor in evaluating modernisms in Latin America (R. González-Echevarría 1985).

The year 1910 had marked the beginning of a series of centenary celebrations in Latin America, as states celebrated the consolidation of their national cultures after a century of independence. The same date also marked the beginning of the Mexican Revolution and stirrings of populist revolt in many other countries. Celebrations to mark political and social stability were punctuated with warning signs of a dissolution, not just of political institutions, but of cultural legacies as well. Cities such as Buenos Aires and São Paulo, rapidly expanding with European immigrants into industrial centres, saw workers organize into socialist and anarchist movements, while an expanding middle class in other areas chafed against the old oligarchic order. What Angel Rama has called the *ciudad letrada* ('lettered city') – the traditional union of power with writing in Latin America – was starting to unravel (A. Rama 1984); the democratic aspirations of the newly-lettered and the unlettered threatened its enforcement in traditional institutions and literary forms. As critics such as Antonio Cornejo-Polar, Julio Ramos and Martín Lienhard have argued, the ongoing dialogue and frequent clashes of lettered culture and oral traditions symbolised centuries-old cultural struggles not present in the same way in European tradition. The radical heterogeneity of cultural experience – and even of languages in many regions – had formed a matrix with which 'international' modernism, identified as it was with the literature of Joyce, T.S. Eliot, Virginia Woolf, European dadaists, surrealists and futurists, had not been forced to deal.

The re-evaluation of the American cultural legacies was tied to Latin America's increased participation in a global system, but also, importantly, to a specialised discourse within that system: the growing importance of anthropology and its exploration of 'primitive' cultures, and the accompanying primitivist aesthetic movements, so critical to the very foundations of modern art (Clifford 1988; Torgovnick 1990). Writers and artists such as Alejo Carpentier, Miguel Angel Asturias and Wilfredo Lam found inspiration in Europe's ethnographic obsession for their pioneering work in reformulating the Latin American aesthetic through their explorations of, respectively, Afro-Cuban music and religion, the survivals of Mayan culture and the representation of indigenous elements as an integral part of the new post-revolutionary Mexican nationalism. Anthropologists like Mexico's Manuel Gamio, Cuba's Fernando Ortiz and Brazil's Gilberto Freyre, who wrote foundational stories of their nations' cultures, also participated in the international circuits of the social sciences (Luis-Brown 1998). The term 'transculturation', developed by Ortiz in his *Contrapunteo de tabaco y azúcar* to describe the Caribbean's particular cultural heterogeneity (and as an alternative to the assimilative connotations of 'acculturation'), can also be applied to the history of the resignification of anthropological discourse into specific nationalist or regionalist traditions in Latin America. For example, the Guatemalan Miguel Angel Asturias published *Las leyendas de Guatemala* in 1930, a reworking of Mayan legends transmitted orally across the centuries, inspired in part by Asturias's exposure in Paris to anthropologists studying the Mayan heritage.

In part these movements of historical revival included strategies of social redemption, as in Mariátegui's idealisation of the Inca past in Peru, or in *negritud* movements in the Caribbean which sought to reassert the value of the stigmatised African heritage. In part they also helped to obscure the actual conditions of many of the mythologised groups, such as indigenous peasants in Mexico; their state-sponsored celebrations of indigenous culture, as in mural painting or the intensification of recovery of pre-Columbian objects and folklore, did not correspond to attempts to preserve living cultures (Rowe and Schelling 1991). In Mexico, later works such as Juan Rulfo's *Pedro Páramo* (1955) or Rosario Castellanos's novels *Balún Canán* (1957) and *Oficio de tinieblas* (1962) subsequently unmasked the earlier exalted claims of artistic and political *indigenismo*. In a similar vein, although less scathingly, the hero of Carpentier's *Los pasos perdidos* (1953) shows the impossibility of the return to origins, the impasse of a utopia built on an Edenic vision of pre-conquest America. Despite its failures, however, the specific aims of the movement did combine to a striking degree the vanguardist ideals of revolutionary politics and radical art as united practice.

Another variant of indigenism can be found in an extensive novelistic production that tends more to social realism, often with doses of local colour, that marks the end of a kind of romantic Indianism prevalent in the nineteenth century. Some of the best known representatives of the Andean region are: Jorge Icaza's *Huasipungo* (Ecuador), Carlos Medinaceli's *La Chascañawi* (Bolivia), Alcides Arguedas's *Raza de bronce* (Bolivia) and Ciro Alegría's *El mundo es ancho y ajeno* (Peru). A number of the Mexican *indigenista* novels, many written by women, focused on *mestizaje* and the incorporation of the Indian into mestizo society (López). Meanwhile, visual artists like José Sabogal (Peru) and Camilo Egas (Ecuador) connected indigenous pasts to current social realities. The circuit of printmakers throughout Latin America, particularly in Mexico, Brazil, Ecuador and Uruguay, made a traditional art form unique through their attention to local particularities and popular traditions (Ades 1989: 188–93).

Worthy of special attention is the influence in Peru of José Mariátegui, whose programme and influence were important in both aesthetic and political circles. Founder of the Peruvian socialist party and the journal *Amauta* in the twenties, Mariátegui's *Siete ensayos de interpretación de la realidad peruana* (1927) was influential for decades to come. Ingeniously, he re-imagined the real conditions for popular revolution in the Andean region through his interpretation of pre-conquest history. He found in Inca societies a utopian template for a future socialist society, focusing on the *ayllu*, an ancient communal social form, as a historical foundation for Peru's future. Mariátegui was an astute critic of the arts and literature; his essays on contemporary literature and film (especially Charlie Chaplin) are some of the most farsighted of the period.

Global vanguardist itineraries

The tension between a revival of the autochthonous as a tool of radical rupture and an exaltation of the local as a form of nostalgic conservatism traverses the aesthetic history of the twentieth century in Latin America. Is Pablo Neruda more 'authentic' in his early (1920s and '30s) *Residencias* poetry written in Chile, Asia and Spain, influenced by surrealist and modernist dissonances, or in his later *Canto General* (1950), a vast poetic historical epic of the Americas? Should we read *One Hundred Years of Solitude* (1968) as a reclaiming of the specific 'magic' of Latin American tradition or as modernism's finally coming full circle, in a restoration of 'the link that Joyce's generation had severed: technique – and anthropocentrism' (Moretti 1996: 235). Could the *Ficciones* (1944) of Borges have been produced anywhere, or only within the specific heritage of Buenos Aires, where remnants of gaucho culture are celebrated in this metropolis modelled on Paris? How did his youth in Zurich and Madrid inflect the trajectory of his later works? This type of question recurs in almost all discussions of Latin American literature, especially of its vanguardist groupings, in which Borges participated as a leader of *ultraísmo* in Argentina and Spain.

Global circuits

In 1934 the visual artist Joaquín Torres-García returned to Uruguay after nearly forty years abroad, in Barcelona, New York and Paris. Re-established in Montevideo, he founded the *Asociación de arte constructiva* which led to the formation of the important artistic workshop 'Taller Torres-García', which influenced Latin American art for decades to come. In the following year he published a manifesto for 'The Southern School':

> There should be a great Art School in our country . . . I have said Southern School because in fact *our north is the South*. We shouldn't have a north, except to contrast with our South.
> So let us turn the map upside down, and voilà, that is our real position, not how the rest of the world sees it. The tip of America, from here on, extending upwards, insistently indicates the South, our north . . . Because the north is now down there. And facing our South, the east is on our left.
> That correction was necessary. So, now we know where we are. (quoted in Ades, 1989: 320)

Torres-García was not the first to issue a manifesto concerning the particularity of Latin American aesthetic possibilities. For more than a decade writers and artists from all parts of Latin America had issued manifestos, new magazines and non-traditional art exhibitions in order to make clear their break with a past considered too stifling and repressive because of its allegiances to European academicism and insularity. Paradoxically, almost all the declarations highlight their openness to multiple outside influences while proclaiming their American distinctiveness. As Torres-García states optimistically:

> And I add:
> *we can do everything* (now I'm talking about essence, what we could call telluric, what gives everything its own particular character) so we must *not exchange what is ours for what is foreign* (that is unforgivable *snobbishness*), we should *assimilate foreign things* instead. I believe the age of colonialism and imports is over (now I'm talking primarily about what we call culture), so away with anyone who speaks, in literary terms, a language other than our own *natural*

language (I don't say *criollo*), be they writers, painters, or composers! If they didn't learn the lesson of Europe when they should have, too bad for them, because the moment has passed. But if they think typical music is better, they're wrong; it is worse, even more unbearable. And anyway, that is *passé* too. Didn't they realize? (Torres-García, 1989 [1935]: 321)

Torres-García might seem an unlikely spokesman for the artistic currents sweeping Latin America. His long residence abroad, his leadership in constructivist art groups in Paris, association with artists like Piet Mondrian, and his resistance to realist or mimetic representation were not apparently good building blocks for turning upside down the north–south axis. Part of Torres-García's vision was rooted in his fascination with pre-Columbian indigenous iconography, especially that from the Andean world, which he saw as a possible foundation for new American artistic cosmologies and as a link with his work in abstract art. His reversals of the global map, shifting the south to the north and vice versa, are powerful symbolic representations of a will to shift centres of cultural power.

His articulation of a specific artistic programme, as well as his leadership of an artistic movement, makes Torres-García a revealing case study for a discussion of modernist aesthetics in Latin America. New levels of mobility in travel and immigration allowed new class sectors to partake of several cultures, most notably in Europe. Torres-García's trajectory in Europe contains similarities with the routes of other visual artists, writers and musicians, such as Wilfredo Lam of Cuba. Lam first studied in Madrid, where he met his compatriot Alejo Carpentier, who was then composing his Afro-Cuban opera, *Ecué-Yamba-O* (1933); then in Paris, where he was strongly influenced by Pablo Picasso's appropriations of African sculpture; next he went to Marseilles, meeting artists and writers such as André Breton and Claude Lévi-Strauss; and then to Martinique with Breton and Lévi-Strauss, where the poet Aimé Césaire revolutionized his thinking by exposing him to the political as well as artistic realities of *négritude*. (Lucie-Smith 1987: 86). After a few years in his native Cuba, Lam returned to Europe where he firmly established himself as Latin America's foremost visual interpreter of the Afro-Caribbean experience. The careers of both Torres-García and Lam, through their combinations of abstract art with specific American motifs, reflect the paradox of the incorporative, but simultaneously resistant and transformative, strategies of modernity in Latin American.

The multiple moves by painters such as Torres-García or Lam and their adoptions of aesthetics and politics in different parts of the world do not undercut their own claims to Americanness or make them derivative artists. They were simply artists of their times, living in a world of increased communications, mobility, neo-colonial allegiances and the readier translatability of visual forms across cultures.

Postmodernities

In recent decades literature has claimed new genres for inclusion – *testimonio*, popular song movements and oral narratives, among others – and the visual arts have emphasised even more the constructed nature of their work. It could be said that the modernist aesthetic crisis was in part a challenge to the arts' ability to encompass the new cultural manifestations produced by subaltern actors, as well as by the discursive practices of other media, particularly the rapidly expanding genres of film, photography and radio. Writers especially were forced to face the limits of representation itself; but, as is clear from even a cursory summary of vanguardism in Latin America, intellectuals were often in practice assertive in reclaiming representation, particularly of sub-merged or repressed traditions, and even within their most dissonant or fragmented productions. Who are the contemporary inheritors of the vanguards in Latin America? For the visual arts, nearly everyone, especially with the acceleration of electronic reproduction which makes art accessible to a wider public. This refers not just to the specific works of these artists which have been transmitted to a larger public, for their visual experimentation has also been incorporated into popular domains. The very ways that vanguardists challenged the field of representation have been absorbed so completely into the larger cultural matrix that many of their contributions (radical juxtapositions of different elements, stream-of-consciousness techniques, abstraction or deformation of natural objects) have become naturalized in the visual fields of popular culture, such as advertising and television. In specific cases, as in Brazil and Mexico, certain elements celebrated by vanguardist culture became foundational blocks in creating new national identities, such as a commonly understood *mexicanidad* or Brazilian *tropicalismo*.

What were vanguardism's failures? Critical opinion is divided, especially along political lines, but most critics have agreed that the revolutionary zeal of experimental art was rarely accompanied by or translated into effective social action, despite claims to the contrary by its practitioners. While the vanguardists may have brought into public view images usually sealed off from artistic practice, they were less successful in bringing into their circles of practice the human bearers and makers of these images. Their pronouncements of immediate social and artistic change were indeed inflated, yet there is no doubt that their work contributed to the reshaping of social imaginaries in ways different from nationalist or social movements.

Just as Latin America engaged in economic trade with the rest of the world, so its early twentieth-century literary and cultural life was a constant journeying and transformation. Critics have long debated the authenticity or originality of Latin American vanguards. The very nature of entwined and journeying economies, peoples and cultures – not to mention the dispersion of printed materials away from their original contexts – makes the topic of imitation and originality a constant preoccupation of literary histories in Latin America. Literary theories of dependency, neo-colonialism, transculturation, *mestizaje*, hybridity, heterogeneity, or Brazilian modernism's *antropofagia* – among many others – show a constant preoccupation with the question of models or 'original' forms and their imitation, transformation or refusal. This dialectic of 'inside' and 'outside' forces gives shape to many histories of Latin American literature. It is an essential component of any recounting of Latin America's literacy legacy, but it is worth remembering that many of these approaches are derived from the imperative which sees cultural life as an organic totality, with specific origins and subsequent growth and transformation. Acting on a world stage where economic and commercial movements made exchanges inevitable, Latin Americans of the modernist period were inextricably bound up in a number of cultural and artistic systems, making complete autonomy or total originality an impossibility. Indigenous American cultures, among others, had served as raw material for European primitivism and dreams of cultural regeneration. Vanguard intellectuals, in the impossible task of being 'original' in a global cultural economy, found themselves freed to some extent from always answering back to a dominant culture. With their actual independence mediated by a vast range of national and individual situations, Latin American modernists seized the moment of artistic ferment in the rest of the world to look closer to home (itself not a mediated space) for their materials.

Bibliography

Aching, Gerard (1997), *The Politics of Spanish American Modernismo: By Exquisite Design*, Cambridge: Cambridge University Press.

Ades, Dawn (1989), *Art in Latin America*, New Haven & London: Yale University Press.

Balderston, Daniel & D. Guy, eds. (1997), *Sex and Sexuality in Latin America*, New York: New York University Press.

Benítez-Rojo, Antonio (1989), *La isla que se repite: el Caribe y la experiencia postmoderna*, Hanover, NH: Ediciones del Norte. (In English (1996), *The Repeating Island: The Caribbean and the Postmodern Experience*, 2nd ed., tr. James E. Maraniss, Durham and London: Duke University Press.

Cascardi, Anthony (1992), *The Subject of Modernity*, Cambridge: Cambridge University Press.

Clifford, James (1988), *The Predicament of Culture*, Cambridge, MA: Harvard University Press.

Cornejo-Polar, Antonio (1983), 'La literatura peruana: totalidad contradictoria', in *Revista de Crítica Literaria Latinoamericana* 18 (1983), 37–50.

Cornejo-Polar, Antonio (1994), *Escribir en el aire*, Lima: Editorial Horizonte.

Darío, Rubén (1968), *Obras completas*, Madrid: Aguilar.

Day, Holliday T. & Hollister Sturges, et al, eds. (1987), *Art of the Fantastic: Latin America 1920–1987*, Indianapolis, IN: Indianapolis Museum of Art.

Foster, Hal (1996), *The Return of the Real: The Avant-Garde at the End of the Century*, Cambridge MA: The MIT Press, October Books.

Franco, Jean (1969), *An Introduction to Spanish American Literature*, Cambridge: Cambridge University Press.

Franco, Jean (1989), *Plotting Women: Gender and Representation in Mexico*, New York: Columbia University Press.

Garciá-Canclini, Néstor (1997), *Imaginarios urbanos*, Buenos Aires: Editorial Universitaria de Buenos Aires.

González-Echevarría, Roberto (1985), *The Voice of the Masters: Writing and Authority in Modern Latin American Literature*, Austin, TX: University of Texas Press.

Graham, Richard, ed. (1990), *The Idea of Race in Latin America, 1870–1940*, Austin: University of Texas Press.

Halperín-Donghi, Tulio (1986), *Historia contemporánea de América Latina*, Madrid: Alianza.

Kirkpatrick, Gwen (1989), *The Dissonant Legacy of Modernismo*, Berkeley and Los Angeles: University of California Press.

Knight, Alan (1990), 'Racism, Revolution, and Indigenismo in Mexico, 1910–1940', in R. Graham (1990), op. cit., 71–113.

Lasarte, Javier (1995), *Juego y nación: (Posmodernismo y vanguardia en Venezuela)*, Caracas: Fundarte.

López, Miguel (1998), *(De)generando heterogeneidades: Relecturas femeninas del mestizaje en la novela indigenista mexicana*, Diss., University of California, Berkeley.

Lucie-Smith, Edward (1987), 'A Background to Latin American Art', in *Art of the Fantastic: Latin America, 1920–1987*, ed. Holliday T. Day & Hollister Sturges, Indianapolis, IN: Indianapolis Museum of Art, 15–35.

Luis-Brown, David (1998), *Waves of Decolonization: Towards an Inter-Americas Cultural Studies*, Diss., University of California, Santa Cruz.

Masiello, Francine (1986), *Lenguaje e ideología: las escuelas argentinas de vanguardia*, Buenos Aires: Hachette.

Miller, Francesca (1991), *Latin American Women and the Search for Social Justice*, Hanover and London: University Press of New England.

Monsiváis, Carlos (1998), 'Prólogo', *Salvador Novo. La estatua de sal*, Mexico: Consejo Nacional para la Cultura y las Artes, 11–41.

Moretti, Franco (1996), *Modern Epic: The World System from Goethe to García Márquez*, tr. Quintin Hoare, London & New York: Verso.

Ortiz, Fernando (1987), *Contrapunteo cubano del tabaco y el azcar*, Caracas: Bibleoteca Ayacucho.

Osorio, Nelson, ed. (1988), *Manifiestos, proclamas y polémicas de la vanguardia literaria hispanoamericana*, Caracas: Biblioteca Ayacucho.

Rama, Angel (1984), *La ciudad letrada*, Montevideo: Fundación Internacional Angel Rama. (English translation (1996), *The Lettered City*, tr. J.C. Chasteen, Durham, NC, & London: Duke University Press.)

Ramos, Julio (1989), *Desencuentros de la modernidad en América Latina: literatura y política en el siglo XIX*, México: Fondo de Cultura Económica.

Rowe, William & Vivian Schelling (1991), *Memory and Modernity in Latin America*, New York: Verso.

Sarlo, Beatriz (1993), *Jorge Luis Borges. A Writer on the Edge*, London & New York: Verso.

Sarlo, Beatriz (1994), 'The Case of Xul Solar', *Art from Argentina; Argentina 1920–1994*, ed. David Elliott, Oxford: The Museum of Modern Art, Oxford, 34–9.

Schwarz, Jorge (1991), *Las Vanguardias Latinoamericanes: Textos programáticos y críticos*, Madrid: Cátedra.

Schwarz, Roberto (1982), *Misplaced Ideas: Essays on Brazilian culture*, ed. John Gledson, London and New York: Verso.

Seminar on Women and Culture in Latin America (1990), 'Toward a History of Women's Periodicals in Latin America: An Introduction', *Women, Culture and Politics in Latin America*, Berkeley and Los Angeles: University of California Press, 163–171.

Subirats, Eduardo (1997), *Laterna mágica: vanguardia, media y cultura tardomoderna*, Madrid: Ediciones Siruela.

Sussekind, Flora (1994), 'Cenas de fundção,' *Moderndidaèe e modernismo no Brasil*, ed. Annateresa Fabris, Campinas: Mercado de Letras, 67–87.

Torgovnick, Marianna (1990), *Gone Primitive: Savage Intellects, Modern Lives*, Chicago: University of Chicago Press.

Unruh, Vicky (1984), *Latin American Vanguards: The Art of Contentious Encounters*, Berkeley, Los Angeles and London: University of California Press.

Verani, Hugo (1986), *Las vanguardias literarias en Hispanoamérica (Manifiestos, proclamas y otros escritos*, Rome: Bulzoni Editore.

8

Brazilian Modernism:
The Canonised Revolution

Beatriz Resende

Modernism was, without doubt, the most influential and enduring movement of Brazilian culture in the last century. Opinion is still divided on whether it has in fact concluded or been replaced by the polemical notion of post-modernism, which has become almost impossible to ignore.

At the risk of crossing swords with defenders of modernism, it is no longer possible to discuss the modernist movement without proposing a revision of values and a questioning of dogmas and, above all, without acknowledging plurality.

Consequently, this consideration of modernism seeks to be a critical revision which examines the contours of the movement in Brazil south of the Equator,[1] evaluating its significance in terms of the key issues facing those involved in the study of literature and culture today. First is the identification of a Brazilian cultural identity which turns out to be multiple, plural and hybrid, rather than singular and stable as it was thought to be in modernist times. Second is the questioning of an official canon which has not only absorbed modernist rebellion, but has enthroned modernism as an exclusive way of producing art, identifying the modern with *high* culture as opposed to any expression of *low* culture, concerned with satisfying the public. Third is the re-negotiation of memory, of patrimony, of cultural heritage, understanding 'the discourse of memory as a great cultural symptom of Western societies', as Andreas Huyssen puts it.[2] These three concerns inevitably enter into any critical study which seeks to investigate modern cultural manifestations in Brazil, establishing articulations and negotiations between

modernism and post-modernism. I shall begin with a chronological
overview of the development of modernism in Brazil.

The course of modernism

The Modernist Movement was responsible for decisive formal innovations and the introduction of new themes, which liberated Brazilian
literature definitively from a conservative model of writing which persisted up to the beginning of the twentieth century. It also provided,
mainly during the early 'heroic years' from 1922 to 1928, an opportunity to rethink questions of cultural identity, contributing to the
construction of an idea of modern Brazil.

The predominance of the Movement minimised the importance of
all the literary manifestations which had already broken with the
traditional Parnassian aesthetic, and which had preceded Modernism.
Literary History has classified this output as Pre-Modernism, important
only as a prelude to what became consecrated as Modernism, despite
the emergence during this period – the first twenty years of the century
– of works by writers such as Euclides da Cunha (*Os sertões*) and Lima
Barreto (*Triste fim de Policarpo Quaresma* and other novels, short stories
and chronicles).

The vanguardist cry which marked the historical moment of the
emergence of the Modernist Movement in Brazil was uttered by the
Week of Modern Art, which took place in the São Paulo Municipal
Theatre in February 1922. The proposal for the event emerged out of
conversations at the house of Paulo Prado, the intellectual (author of
the classic *Retrato do Brasil* [Portrait of Brazil]) and São Paulo businessman who would give financial support to the event, with active participation from the Rio de Janeiro painter Di Cavalcanti. In Rio de
Janeiro, Manuel Bandeira, Ribeiro Couto and the young Sérgio
Buarque de Hollanda – studying law in the capital – assisted with the
preparations.

Many leading figures participated in the controversial and exciting
artistic events of the Week of Modern Art. Among them were: the
composer Heitor Villa-Lobos; the sculptor Brecheret, whose work had
won prizes in Paris; the painters Anita Malfatti, Rego Moteiro, John
Graz and Di Cavalcanti, who exhibited their work in the foyer of the
theatre. Contemporary poets who read some of their work included
Mário de Andrade, Oswald de Andrade, Luís Aranha, Sérgio Millet and
Ribeiro Couto.

It was the painter Anita Malfatti and the poet Manuel Bandeira who were the real pioneers of avowedly modernist innovation. Malfatti's first exhibition of paintings in 1917 had already revealed a modernist aesthetic, acquired while studying in Europe, but the harsh criticism levelled at her caused her to return to Europe, reconsider her proposals and restrain her own modern impulses. As for Bandeira, he had already published *Cinzas das horas* (1917) and *Carnaval* (1919), which includes the poem *Os sapos*, read by Ronald de Carvalho during the Week, where the rigorous rhyme and meter of his Parnassian contemporaries are satirised:

> . . . The frogs clamour
> Their sceptical criticisms
> Poetry is no more
> But there are poetic arts . . .[3]

More than for its vanguardist irreverence, *Carnaval* is important for its affirmation of free composition and the sensuality of everyday life, for its rupture with the idea of the sublime. At one point during his lengthy correspondence with Bandeira, Mário de Andrade dubbed him the 'St. John the Baptist' of modernism.

The creation of the journal *Klaxon*, the 'modern art monthly' launched three weeks after the Week of Modern Art by the participants, initiated and consolidated the project of disseminating the new aesthetic – always in a defiant tone. *Klaxon* ran until 1923, during which time nine numbers appeared. Then, in 1924, the most celebrated living poet of the French language arrived in Brazil, one of the creators of Cubism in literature: the Swiss Blaise Cendrars. The critic Nicolau Sevcenko says of him, 'Blaise Cendrars had an obsession: modernity. He was irresistibly attracted to all the most extreme manifestations of the modern phenomenon.'[4] Cendrars would fan the fire of the young intellectuals involved in the Movement. In Rio de Janeiro, visiting everything, including jails and *favelas*, he would awaken them to the effervescent modernity of the cosmopolitan city and with his travels across the country, visiting the historic cities of Minas or admiring the Atlantic tropical forest (Mata Atlântica), he would contribute to the impetus to reassess Brazil from its colonial origins onwards.

The year 1924 represents a significant year for Modernism in Brazil, for both here and in other countries the manifesto was confirmed as a literary genre. Among the first to appear was the *Manifesto da Poesia Pau-Brasil (Brazil-Wood Poetry Manifesto)*, by Oswald de Andrade, published in March 1924, in which he defined the new poetics: 'Poetry exists in facts. The saffron and ochre shacks in the green of the *favela*, under the Cabralian-blue sky,[5] are aesthetic facts'; and further on, 'No more formulae for the contemporary expression of the world. *See with unfettered eyes.*' At the end of the *Manifesto*, de Andrade anticipated two tendencies which would characterise modernism after 1930. The first was the concern with regionalism. De Andrade proposed that 'the task of the Futurist generation was a Cyclopean one. To adjust the imperial clock of national literature. Now that this has been done, there is another challenge. To be regional and true to our time'.[6] Second, at the end of the text, de Andrade emphasizes the importance of preserving the national patrimony, constituted of heterogeneous elements – nature and culture, tradition and modernity: 'Barbarians, candid, picturesque and tender. Newspaper readers. Brazil-wood. The forest and the school. The National Museum. Cooking, iron ore and dance. Vegetation. Brazil-wood.'[7] As we will see, this task would fall to Mário de Andrade, one of the ideologues of the policy of preserving the historical patrimony established by the Modernists.

In 1925 it was Mário de Andrade's turn to launch an important essay which also took the form of a manifesto: *A escrava que não é Isaura: Discurso sobre algumas tendências da poesia modernista* ('The Slave Who Isn't Isaura: Discourse on some Tendencies of Modernist poetry'). The main concern of this manifesto was to define the new lyricism. According to the author, two factors determined the 'modernising concept of Poetry':

> 1st – respect for the freedom of the subconscious. As a consequence: the destruction of poetic themes.
> 2nd – the poet reintegrated into the life of his times. Because of this: the revival of sacred inspiration.[8]

The importance of this manifesto lies, above all, in its proposal of a new possibility for literary criticism, that of theorising artistic activity.

In May 1928, however, the manifesto which was to hold the greatest importance for an understanding of Brazilian cultural identity appeared: the Cannibalist Manifesto, published by Oswald de Andrade in the *Revista de Antropofagia*, year 1, no. 1, in the '374th year of the Devouring of Bishop Sardinha'. The manifesto presented the premises of a group of intellectuals including the poet Raul Bopp and the painter Tarsila do Amaral; thus the Cannibalist Movement was founded. (Two master works of Brazilian culture were also produced in this year, Mário de Andrade's narrative, *Macunaíma*, and Tarsila do Amaral's painting, *Abaporu*. Since the painting *A negra* (1923), do Amaral had been devouring the ideas of the French Concretists with whom she had studied, such as Fernand Léger, and rearticulating them with Brazilian colours and themes. This influence was to be even more apparent in her 1929 painting *Antropofagia*.)

On the eve of the Revolution of 1930, which sought to modernise the Brazilian state, Modernism had already spread significantly across Brazil, frequently organised around art, literature and cultural journals. In Cataguases, in the interior of Minas Gerais, the *Verde* (Green) group appeared; in the capital of the state, Belo Horizonte, *Revista*'s collaborators included a figure who would be one of Brazil's greatest poets, Carlos Drummond de Andrade, who was based in Rio de Janeiro after 1934; in the south Augusto Meyer belonged to *Madrugada* (Dawn).

But attention soon came to be focused on the north-east of the country. In Recife, to where he returned after five years of study in Europe, the sociologist Gilberto Freyre, initiator of Anthropological Studies in Brazil, established the Regionalist Centre of the North East in 1924 and two years later promoted the first Regionalist Congress of the North East. Regionalist ideas would influence the poetry of Jorge de Lima and Ascenço Ferreira, as well as the novels of José Américo de Almeida and José Lins do Rego. In 1930, north-eastern regionalist fiction was consolidated with the publication of Rachel de Queiroz's novel *O quinze*. Gilberto Freyre would be responsible for the formulation of the theory of 'miscegenation', according to which racial mixture in Brazil is the product of the cultural peculiarities and modes of behaviour characteristic of the country. The presence of mulattos was seen as the result not of the subjugation of blacks, but of a certain *tolerance* which resulted in 'so many little *crias*,[9] the master's illegitimate offspring . . . who ascended, socially and economically, by taking full advantage of their upbringing', as the author stated in the 1933 classic *Casa grande e senzala: Formação da Família Brasileira sob o Regime de Economia Patriarcal, (The Masters and the Slaves)*.

Two novels by Graciliano Ramos published in the same decade – *Caetés* (1933) and *Vidas Secas* (Barren Lives, 1938) – illustrate the emergence of a 'raw' prose with strong social preoccupations which became a feature of fiction from the north-east.

By the 1950s not only was Modernism still flourishing, it was producing great moments in Brazilian literature. During the period of 'High Modernity', from the 1950s to 1964, an astonishing group of writers was producing their most important works. The novelist Clarice Lispector reinvented the urban novel, while João Guimarães Rosa magically re-created regionalist prose. Murilo Mendes and Carlos Drummond de Andrade continued to produce excellent works. From the so-called 'Generation of 45', who were concerned with a return to objectivism, the geometric poet João Cabral de Melo Neto would emerge, a writer of extraordinary poetry completely devoid of superfluity.

In 1964 a military regime was imposed on the country and the suppression of democratic freedoms began. Until 1968 cultural expression was still possible and the Tropicalist Movement, popularised by music and the theatre, turned to the heroic years of Modernism for inspiration, in particular to the still little-known theatrical works of Oswald de Andrade. But by the end of this year political repression was to prevent the multiple possibilities of artistic expression from manifesting themselves.

By the end of the 1970s, with the gradual return to democracy and of the exiles who had left the country, literature began to free itself from the self-censorship which had led to a formalist, coded writing. For a while literature assumed the role which the press was unable to fulfil, and testimonial literature revealed the extent of the suffering caused by political oppression.

By the return to democracy in 1984, the culture industry (including the publishing industry) had already become a reality and television had become the strongest vehicle of mass communication in Brazilian society. But, above all, the world order had already been transformed.

Critiques of modernism

The first critical evaluation of Modernism was made by Mário de Andrade in his famous lecture of 1942, 'The Modernist Movement', still one of the most valuable analyses of the movement today. In discussing the movement, de Andrade, still close to the events of 1922, recognised its heroic, innovative spirit, but, with characteristic foresight, was also able to highlight questions which would only surface much later, such as the elitism of a movement which concerned itself solely with what today we call 'high' culture. He began: 'Manifested mainly through art, but also violently destabilising social and political customs, the Modernist Movement was the precursor, the preparer and, to a large extent, the creator of a national state of mind.' Further on he declared:

> This was the Modernist Movement, whose most significant collective cry turned out to be the Week of Modern Art. There is undeniable merit in this, although for us early Modernists . . . from the caves, grouped around the painter Anita Malfatti and the sculptor Brecheret, it is as though we were loudspeakers for a universal and national force much more complex than we ourselves were.[10]

In that same lecture de Andrade recognised that the Modernist Movement was strongly marked by its birth in the drawing rooms of São Paulo. It was innovative but inaccessible, capable of opening up new creative possibilities in the country, yet co-existing uneasily with anything which did not comply with its own standards of aesthetic value: 'The Modernist Movement was clearly aristocratic. Because it had the character of a risky game, because of its modernist internationalism, its fierce nationalism, its anti-popular gratuitousness, its powerful dogmatism, it was aristocratic in spirit.' He concluded: 'Practise or refuse to practise the arts, science, trades. But don't be confined to this, to being spectators of life, disguised as experts on life, watching life pass by. March with the multitudes.'[11]

In spite of such restrictions, Modernism would continue to be dominant in Brazil until the end of the 1970s. In 1979 the critic José Guilherme Merquior, in the book *O fantasma romântico*, introduced a topic then unknown in this region – post-modernism. It was then that the debate on Modernism emerged: was it an unfinished project or an exhausted possibility?

As a result of this debate, a new theoretical framework has emerged which is of vital importance for an understanding of Latin American culture. Its emergence has gone hand in hand with the questioning of 'master narratives' and paradigms which deal inadequately with our contemporary situation, particularly with regard to the new relations between the local and the global, mass and elite culture, centre and periphery, and with the ascendancy of post-colonial theory and the rejection of Eurocentric discourses. Above all, it is a warning against the effects of different kinds of totalitarianism, thus allowing – with the kind of critical revision of Modernism possible today – for the creation of links between the Modernist Movement and contemporary themes.

The Anthropophagist Manifesto and the configuration of a national identity

In her seminal book on Futurism[12] Marjorie Perloff talks about the manifesto as a form of art, specifying 1913, the eve of the first World War, as the peak of the manifesto fever which swept across Europe. It would not be long before the 'new literary sport' was practised by Brazil's Modernists.

One day, after having enjoyed a lunch which consisted of frogs, Tarsila do Amaral and Oswald de Andrade began, half-jokingly, to elaborate the theory of anthropophagy. A few days later they baptised

do Amaral's latest painting *Abaporu* or 'cannibalist' (aba = man; poru =
eater). Today *Abaporu* is one of the most famous and valuable paintings
of Brazilian modern art, although unfortunately no longer in the
country, having been acquired by an Argentinian collector. The art
critic Carlos Zílio points out that do Amaral's work demonstrates that it
was clearly

> the intention of the movement to create a national modern art, which was
> 'our own work', but could also be exported. Even her relationship with the
> post-cubism she had absorbed, would be intimately linked to perceptions of
> Brazil. Tarsila's painting therefore constituted a demarcating exploration of
> the Brazilian landscape, which she re-elaborated in pictorial terms, merging
> post-cubist style with popular elements.[13]

In the Cannibalist Manifesto Oswald de Andrade states:

> Only Anthropophagy unites us. Socially. Economically. Philosophically . . . I
> am only interested in what is not mine. The law of man. The law of the
> cannibal . . . We were never catechised. What we made was Carnival. The
> Indian dressed as a senator of the Empire . . . But it wasn't crusaders who
> came here. They were fugitives from a civilisation which we are devouring,
> because we are strong and vengeful like the Jabuti.

And finally,

> The struggle between what you might call the Uncreated and the Created –
> illustrated by the permanent contradiction between man and his taboo.
> Daily love and the capitalist way of life. Cannibalism. Absorption of the
> sacred enemy. To transform him into a totem.[14]

Perloff also argues that talking about art is the same as producing
art, that theory is practice. The proposition, the will, the project,
precede the work, which may never even come into existence. Even
though it may not actually exist, in a sense it already does in the form
of a manifesto. The language of the manifesto is close to that of
advertising, closing the gap between 'high' and 'low' art, as seen in the
Concretist-inspired ways in which titles are used and graphics intrude
in the manifesto designs. In 1922 these were already features of the
journal *Klaxon*, whose arresting cover featured a gigantic 'A' in the title,
dominating the graphic design of the page. The first issue also assumed
the manifesto format, and the proximity to advertising language could
be seen in its taste for improvisation, the unfinished, the experimental.
This aspect of Brazil's artists, which we would today describe as 'performative', reflects above all the precept that art equals life. For many
years, almost tirelessly performative behaviour would be one of Oswald
de Andrade's characteristics, with his constant desire to *épater les bour-*

geois. But it was Oswald himself who recognised the distance between his work and the public he wished to reach politically, when he said that one day the masses too would eat of the 'finery' that he produced. In other words, the artist is well aware that, in spite of the pamphleteering tone, the manifesto is designed less for the 'people' than for his fellow artists.

Since the *Brazil-Wood Manifesto,* the vanguardists had sought to create a modern art and literature in Brazil without simply imitating the European avant-garde movements, in search of an 'authentically national' modern art. But how were they to innovate, to be modern, without copying the envied European models, which were also concerned with promoting forms of primitive art, such as African art? Cannibalism seemed, therefore, a way of reconciling the desire for Brazilianisation, for constructing a native cultural identity through art, while still admiring the European vanguards.

In cannibalism, enemies deserve to be eaten only if they demonstrate special qualities. In order to be devoured and not just killed, the victim has to reveal attributes such as courage in battle and in defeat. The cultural critic Heloísa Buarque de Hollanda, who has systematically studied cannibalism as a way of understanding cultural production in Brazil, calls these qualities 'enviable difference'. She states: 'Cannibalism was caused by extreme fascination with otherness and "difference", while Anthropophagy showed the extent to which the national interpretation of Brazil reflected a drive towards the Other.'[15] Thus, only what was admirable in the Other was consumed and through this 'consumption' the uniqueness of the Other was destroyed. In spite of everything the Brazilian Modernist presented himself as particularly hospitable, always prepared to receive (and absorb) the Other. It is evident then, that Sérgio Buarque de Hollanda's notion of the 'cordial man', developed in his book *Raízes do Brasil* (Roots of Brazil) in 1936, does not appear out of thin air. This expression, borrowed from Ribeiro Couto, which refers to cordiality as a presumed national characteristic, is not synonymous with courtesy; it has nothing to do with the cordiality evident in elaborate formal rituals, which do not have a marked presence in Brazilian everyday life. For Sérgio Buarque de Hollanda, this cordiality involves a rejection of formalism and social convention and it 'does not only include positive feelings and harmony'. Enmity can be as cordial as friendship. And he concludes his reflection by stating that the Brazilian 'is free, therefore, to give himself to the whole repertoire of ideas, gestures and forms which he may encounter in his path, assimilating them frequently without great difficulties'.[16]

What is interesting about the re-reading which Heloísa Buarque makes of the cannibalist theory is the fact that it points to the Brazilian preference for absorbing difference, rather than confronting or challenging it – a notion which has recently become polemical, with studies of race and gender that question the idea of peaceful intermarriage as a characteristic of social relations in Brazil. Using this debate to focus on socio-cultural relationships in contemporary Brazil (and herein lies the value of the paper from which I quote) she states: 'In order to understand the current structure of discursive formations on race and gender in Brazil, it is important to bear in mind this idea of how the discourse on Brazil's identity reflects this constant but partial assimilation of difference.'[17] The critic ends by pointing out that the belief in the 'subversive' power of the Law of the Cannibal is beginning to be questioned. It is precisely contemporary theoretical reflection arising out of studies of gender and race in Brazilian society which has allowed for a more definitively questioning position on the *dangerous relationships* between hegemonic and peripheral cultures – the struggle between the uncreated and the created suggested by Oswald de Andrade. Today cannibalism is a category to be re-read, emphasising the need to seek common objectives, interests which unite (or should unite) classes, races, sexual choices, professional categories and cultural manifestations.

The Modernist canon and the rejection of its fellow travellers

In literature, the contemporary question of the crossing of boundaries occurred as a result of several decisive critical attitudes, among them the questioning of the canon and its legitimation by established academics, critics and official institutions. Paradoxically, considering the desires and attitudes in certain of the artists who marked the early period – the futurists and vanguardists – Modernism in Brazil became absolutely canonical. It is in this sense that Paolo Portoghesi's statement on the hegemony of Modernism is important. He observes: 'The history of architecture and modern taste was written and re-written with diverse methods and criteria, but always from the perspective of the Modernist Movement, from within a tendency which disdainfully refused to recognise the part played by its fellow travellers.'[18]

The power acquired by Modernist literature led to the exclusion from literary studies of any contemporary works not considered a legitimate expression of Modernism, even if they bore similarities to Modernist expression. Similarly, the almost militant taste for an art dedicated to noble causes, to the creativity expressed by the indisputably new, to the search for art which was incomprehensible and inaccessible to the majority of the public, was identified with great modern art, distinguishing itself from all art which approached popular or 'mass' taste. A significant proportion of the literature written by 'fellow travellers' of the more illustrious Modernist writers was produced in Rio de Janeiro, a city concerned at that time with urban expansion and with its role as capital of the country. This literary production incorporated the taste for, even the fascination with, the conquests of the modern world – the speed of the coupé, industrialisation and the innovations it introduced in the domestic sphere; it was also drawn to the world of consumption and an aesthetic position that did not deride the so-called superfluous and decorative, which was gradually becoming part of the everyday life of a city that prided itself, above all, on its cosmopolitanism.

One could define this literature, with reference to American architectural tastes and influence, as 'art-deco' literature; produced from the 1920s onwards, it was subsequently (from the 1930s) vigorously excluded, even though it continued growing until almost 1935. In 1930, it was no longer a priority to follow the taste of the vanguards. Cosmopolitanism, as Rio de Janeiro's dominant taste and mode of conduct, began to be questioned, to be seen as a denial of the reality of the rest of the country. One of the pretexts used to precipitate the revolution of 1930 was that the federal capital of the frenetic 1920s was excessively aligned with the European spirit and had turned its back on the agrarian interior of the country.

Three writers, born or based in Rio de Janeiro, represent this art-deco literature in a special way: Théo Filho (1895–1973), Cecília Bandeira de Melo, known as Mme. Crysanthème (1870–1948), and the one who attained the highest prominence – Benjamin Costallat (1897–1961). What do these authors have in common? They were all popular with the public. In a country with few readers where, even today, publishing runs rarely surpass 3,000 copies, these writers managed – to take Costallat's case – to sell 70,000 copies of a novel. They were authors in tune with the public's taste for 'modernity', who published feuilletons or wrote chronicles, a genre between the short story and journalism, intrinsically linked to the life of the city. However, no trace of this literature is left. Considered 'second class', in spite of gracing the bookshelves of a large sector of the population, it is now impossible to find even in the largest libraries, including the National Library in central Rio de Janeiro. That is to say, they were swept out of collections or archives that were meant to house works considered to be 'literature'. Rejected by the canon for not being modern enough or for being excessively popular, they were not thought to merit a place in cultural institutions.

The works of these three authors deal with the personalities and the spaces in which they circulated in the city of Rio de Janeiro: seductive women in low-cut dresses, Bohemian male figures, variations on the dandy with his androgynous appearance. Among the characters of Mme. Crysanthème's major novel, *Enervadas*, are Lúcia, a wealthy, spoilt young woman, and her friends. Madalena Fragoso is

> beautiful, with the beauty of a fading flower. She began to inject morphine, which soon gave way to cocaine. Now she considers morphine child's play, devoting herself entirely to the formidable white powder, which transforms her into a creature outside of the world of reason and equilibrium.[19]

Then there is Maria Helena, who loves other women and who 'had started sporting a kind of masculine clothing which gave her the appearance of an asexual adolescent, with her cropped dark hair which curled around her delicate, white neck'. Another is Laura, who 'recounted her love affairs to me one after the other, like the list of dishes on one of those long menus at a cheap restaurant'. Finally, Margarida, happily married (her husband dances the shimmy) and always pregnant, the most faithful friend, sums up the others well, 'But then, you all talk only of love affairs, cocaine, tangos, maladies . . .' In the course of the novel there are no condemnations, nor is there any real final repentance. The important thing was to present these bold young women, created in the image and likeness of women of the Parisian Rive Gauche.

Théo Filho was an immensely popular novelist, and the titles of his novels are very revealing: *365 dias de boulevard* (*365 Days on the Boulevard*), *Praia de Ipanema* (*Ipanema Beach*), *Romance tropical* (*Tropical Romance*) and *A grande felicidade* (*Great Joy*). A successful feuilletonist, he ended up best known as a journalist. A victim of his own success, he anticipated the problems which the seductions of the best-seller would bring to writers after him. His most important and most political novel is *Ídolos de Barro* (*Clay Idols*). At certain moments of the novel the beautiful view of Rio de Janeiro from the hillsides interrupts and punctuates the narrative. It is the *leit-motif* of the novel. There are invaluable descriptions of the city, its bars and restaurants, their clearly differentiated clientele co-existing in a proximity of apparent intimacy between the inhabitants of the city from the poorer and wealthier areas.

Benjamin Costallat was the most popular of these writers, and his works were often chronicles of Rio de Janeiro. Their titles suggest their main characteristics: cosmopolitan taste, an interest in the American influence which emerged through the architecture of sky-scrapers and film, an interest in the conquest of the reading public. Apart from the literary aspect, two unusual characteristics of Costallat's work are notable. The first is the way the book is treated as an object which should awaken the reader's interest initially because of its visual aspects. In the introduction to *Mutt, Jeff and Co*, he makes mention of 'brilliant covers by brilliant artists'. Among these are the illustrators Álvarus and J. Carlos and the Modernist painter di Cavalcanti. Second, in keeping with the idea of the professionalisation of the writer, who should be able to earn a living and support a family through his efforts, Costallat was given to writing advertisements and announcements for newspapers, magazines and trams, to which he brought not just his style, but also elements from the characters in his novels.

Among his works, *Melle. Cinema*, 'a novel of customs', written in 1922 and published in 1923, was the biggest publishing success of the Old Republic: 75,000 copies were sold in five years, and according to the latest figures I was able to obtain, sales totalled 140,000 copies. Paris, cigars, love affairs, cocaine and a smattering of prostitution run through almost all of the novel. Everything which belongs to the best tradition of the French feuilleton is present in the story of *Melle. Cinema* – the American 'garçonne', the little flapper from the age of the shimmy, a creature of 1923, brought up to the sound of jazz.

In architecture, the term 'Copacabana Style' was used to refer to the style which emerged in the late 1920s and the beginning of the 1930s. The decorative elements of the area which had become fashionable, adopting the Americanism of art deco, were incorporated into buildings and entrance halls. It was to Copacabana that the elegant set went when they left the centre of the city, or 'Cinelândia', as the area where the cinemas were grouped was dubbed. Its buildings were designed in the daring art deco style, in chrome, decorative themes suggesting modern machinery, the symbols of speed, human gymnastics and energy. The Cinelândia and Copacabana of this literature go in and out of style, but do not enter the Modernist libraries, even as documents of their time and of the taste of contemporary readers.

Today the validity of the decorative style is recognised in architecture, and its importance as the initiator of original design in furniture, objects and clothing is indisputable. But because of the influence which the literature of the Modernist Movement has had on the formation of the literary canon, works created according to different standards, emphasising the moment when the boundaries began to crumble between high culture and mass culture, between erudite and popular, unfortunately remained sidelined. It is up to contemporary literary

studies to rescue them so that the chorus of voices of our modernity
can be complete.

Construction of memory, construction of identity

Modernism's great contribution to an understanding of Brazilian cultural identity and to the relationship between art and popular culture
was discussed in great detail by Mário de Andrade. One of the country's
most productive intellectuals, he united his originality as a writer (story-
teller and poet) with his talent as a musician and the qualities of an
exceptional researcher and scholar of popular art and folklore. Unlike
other São Paulo Modernists, de Andrade was not afraid to become
involved in matters of state, in jobs usually filled – in the eyes of the
young Modernist intellectuals – by the most lowly kind of petty bourgeois, the civil servant with a fixed position and guaranteed salary at
the end of the month (as opposed to the generous monthly allowances
from capitalist, land-owning parents or patrons in a São Paulo which
coffee had rapidly made wealthy). De Andrade was one of the main
people responsible for the creation of the *Serviço do Patrimonio Historico
e Artístico Nacional* (National Service of Artistic and Historical Patrimony) in the 1930s, an organisation charged with listing buildings and
works which represented the most important moments of national
history – that is to say, an organisation responsible for constituting the
memory of the nation. Although not always successful in the proposals
he put forward to the government, his work with the Service provided
a vital opportunity for the formulation of what de Andrade understood
as the formation of an identity as plural as his own.

In a detailed analysis of Mário de Andrade's contribution to this
public organisation during 1937, Annateresa Fabris identifies in official
documents dictated by him, and in his correspondence, the basic
guidelines of the conservation policy he proposed and, furthermore,
his understanding of what constituted the cultural patrimony of the
country.[20] What interested de Andrade was not the traditional value
judgements which sought only to recognise beauty. This can be seen in
a creative account of his public service, in which he maintained his
modernist style:

> The church is extremely important as a building, but ugly as sin . . . I didn't
> take a snap of it, but I've already regretted it. Ugly or beautiful, I think one
> should snap any church façade which for whatever reason is to be listed . . .
> I snapped the awful door because of its style, a rather grubby pulpit and
> interior frontispiece, dismal as a month of wet Sundays.[21]

Mário de Andrade looked for specific Brazilian elements in the listing of buildings to be conserved, even those dating from the colonial period. He wrote in another account:

I think that the Carmo roof departs greatly from the canons of European decoration. However, rather than seeing this as a deficiency, would it not be more logical to view such a work through a gaze which has not been refined by Europe?[22]

Evidently, the question of canonical limitations was already informing his research.

The most interesting of all his documents, however, is the account that de Andrade gave in November 1937 of two paintings in a church in São Paulo, where tropical fruits form part of the image of the Last Supper:

The detailed engraving of a watermelon opposite Christ, in the Last Supper, is a raw touch of delicious ingenuousness. One cannot help smiling when faced with this cornucopian national table. The copier must have been Brazilian, or perhaps Portuguese with an intimate acquaintance with our national exuberance . . . He could not restrain himself, he failed to understand the mystical frugality of Da Vinci's table, he filled empty plates with engravings of watermelons . . . It is perhaps more on account of the abundance of the laden table, than because of the engravings of a possibly native watermelon, that these paintings reveal Brazil.[23]

In these details of de Andrade's conservationist project, Annateresa Fabris draws out the concerns of the São Paulo artist: equal attention to the erudite and the popular, to pure art and craft; interest in the landscape transformed by human labour; the inclusion in the notion of national patrimony of 'immaterial' elements derived from folklore, resisting the state's tendency to create a unitary idea of national culture identified with the taste of the traditionalist, retrograde elite. If more notice had been paid to de Andrade, Brazilians might not be experiencing the deleterious effects of living in a country where, despite the strong cultural influence of African religion in both the past and present, there are thousands of listed catholic churches, while only recently was a *candomblé terreiro* recognised as part of the country's historic patrimony. In the positive evaluation of cultural manifestations meriting conservation, de Andrade recognised the spatial and temporal imaginary in which the local intervenes in the *reading* of the religious image inherited from the colonisers.

Unfortunately, Mário de Andrade's permanent questioning of a monolithic, static notion of cultural identity didn't do him much good. The certainty that differences should co-exist in the composition of

identities led to his demotion from the directorship of the Culture
Department in São Paulo, where he was the representative of the
Service. He moved to Rio, protected by a minister of education in
Getúlio Vargas's 'New State', Gustavo Capanema, whose office was
managed by the poet Carlos Drummond de Andrade. When he eventu-
ally returned to São Paulo his life was nearly at its end.

The enlightened minister Capanema was largely responsible for the
victory of Modernism in Rio de Janeiro, as the driving force behind
one of the most important expressions of Brazilian Modernism –
architecture. In 1935 Capanema initiated a competition inviting architectural proposals for the construction of a headquarters for the
Ministry of Education and Public Health. The winner was an art deco
design. Capanema awarded the prize but never had the building
constructed. He consulted his Modernist advisers, Manuel Bandeira,
Carlos Drummond de Andrade and Rodrigo Melo Franco de Andrade,
and ended up turning responsibility for the building over to Lúcio
Costa. Costa brought the French Modernist architect Le Corbusier to
Rio de Janeiro, and the final building bears his original stamp. In its
construction the building brought together Lúcio Costa and Oscar
Niemeyer (the duo who in the 1960s would raise the country's most
radical urban Modernist monument – the new capital of Brasília).
Cândido Portinari was responsible for painting the frescoes and murals.
The building was inaugurated in 1945, and the question of national
identity surfaced once again. The minister wished to erect a twelve-
metre tall statue on the patio of the building, representing the figure
of the 'archetypal Brazilian'. In an effort to define the image of an
authentic national type, sociologists, anthropologists and biologists were
all given a hearing. The debate covered everything from the theme of
the '*mestiço* and creole sub-race' to the 'eclectic type modelled by our
cosmic environment'. Mário de Andrade was invited to mediate and
attempted to convince the best sculptors, including Victor Brecheret,
to collaborate. The most important sculptors of Brazilian Modernism
contributed significantly to the collection of sculptures which the
building still houses, but the image which was to have represented the
synthesis of the 'archetypal Brazilian' was never realised.[24]

Conclusion

Stating that the present can no longer be seen either as a rupture or as
a link with the past, but as a consciousness of discontinuities, the
cultural critic Homi Bhabha emphasises that the use of 'post' in

contemporary jargon does not indicate sequentiality or polarity, which would mean that post-modernism signifies merely anti-modernism. According to Bhabha: 'These terms that insistently gesture to the beyond, only embody its restless and revisionary energy if they transform the present into an expanded and ex-centric site of experience and empowerment.'[25]

It is in this sense that Mário de Andrade, concerned with the building of our national patrimony, became a figure of articulation between modernity and post-modernity. He brought to the debate on the present images of the past which had not become history because they did not match the 'official', univocal understanding of Brazilian culture, even during the most enlightened moments of its Modernism. By rejecting a dichotomous approach, we are free to see in the critical analyses and surveys of Brazil's patrimony carried out by the writer the possibility of renegotiating its cultural legacy.

Let us end with a last reference to this plural artist and intellectual par excellence. It was Mário de Andrade's visionary foresight, concerned with the culture of the most diverse popular groups and ethnicities, that made possible the creation of the novel which did indeed present the plurality of Brazils which forms our imagined community. The novel *Macunaíma: o herói sem nenhum caráter* ('Macunaíma: the hero without any character') was written in 1927 and is the story of the Indian Macunaíma, black as the night, who becomes white, abandons the virgin forest for São Paulo and ends up becoming a star. A modern novel, *Macunaíma* represents the vital connection between Modernism and the contemporary period, in the shared desire of the two moments to disrupt the hegemony of Western culture produced in the northern hemisphere, in order to seek an understanding of our own condition. Mário de Andrade had already arrived at an understanding of the importance of hybridity in the constitution of culture. Only this realisation could have enabled the creation of a character like Macunaíma, hero of our people.

Notes

1 Translator's note: A description of Brazil which refers to the notion that there is no concept of sin south of the Equator, originally a condemnation of Brazil's presumed tropical immorality which has been traced back to the seventeenth-century writings of the Dutch historian Gaspar von Barleus.

2 Huyssen, Andreas, *Memórias do Modernismo*, Rio de Janeiro, Editora UFRJ, 1997, p. 12.

3 Bandeira, Manuel, *Carnaval*, Rio de Janeiro, Edição Crítica, Nova Fronteira/Fundação Casa de Rui Barbosa, 1986, p. 28, my translation.

4 Sevcenko, Nicolau, *Orfeu extático na Metrópole: São Paulo, sociedade e cultura nos frementes anos 20*, São Paulo, Companhia das Letras, 1992.

5 Pedro Álvarez Cabral was the Portuguese explorer who discovered Brazil in 1500.

6 De Andrade, Oswald, 'Manifesto da Poesia Pau-Brazil' in G. Mendonça Teles (ed.), *Vanguarda Européia e Modernismo Brasileiro*, Ed. Vozes, 1977: 270.

7 Ibid.

8 De Andrade, Mário, 'A escrava que não é Isaura' in L. E. Cabral Schutel (ed.), *Ensaios e textos comentados sobre autores contemporáneos brasileiros*, Educom, 1976.

9 Translator's note: *Crias* were black and mulatto children who enjoyed the privilege of being brought up in the master's Great House.

10 De Andrade, Mário, 'O Movimento Modernista', in *Aspectos da Literatura Brasileira*, São Paulo, Martins, 1967, p. 220 (my translation).

11 Ibid.

12 Perloff, Marjorie, *O movimento futurista: Avant-garde, avant-guerre, e a linguagem da ruptura*, São Paulo, Edusp, 1993.

13 Zílio, Carlos, *A Querela do Brasil: A questão da identidade da arte brasileira*, 2nd ed., Rio de Janeiro, Relume/Dumará, 1997, p. 51.

14 De Andrade, Oswald, 'Manifesto antropófago' in G. Mendonça Teles (ed.), *Vanguarda Européia e Modernismo Brasileiro*, Ed. Vozes, 1976. Translator's note: The Jabuti is a trickster turtle prominent in indigenous and black mythology.

15 De Hollanda, Heloísa Buarque, 'The Law of the Cannibal or How to Deal with the Idea of "Difference" in Brazil', unpublished conference paper presented at New York University, April 1998.

16 De Hollanda, Sérgio Buarque, *Raízes do Brasil*, Rio de Janeiro, José Olympio, 9th ed., 1976.

17 De Hollanda (April 1998), op. cit.

18 Portoghesi, Paolo, *Album degli anni venti*, Editori Laterza, Rome, 1976, p. 7.

19 Crysanthàme, *Enervadas*, Rio de Janeiro, Leite Ribeiro, 1922, p. 5.

20 Fabris, Anna Teresa, 'Modernidade e vanguarda: o caso brasileiro', in Fabris, A. (ed.), *Modernidade e modernismo no Brasil*, São Paulo, Mercado das Letras, 1994, p. 9–25.

21 De Andrade, Mário, *Cartas de trabalho*, Brasília, Secretaria do Patrimônio Histórico e Artístico Nacional/Fundação Pró-Memória, 1981, p. 82.

22 Ibid., p. 125–6.

23 Ibid., p. 117.

24 See Lissovsky, M. and Sá, Paulo Sérgio Moraes, *Colunas de educação: A construção do Ministério da Educação e Saúde*, Rio de Janeiro, MINC/IPHAN, 1996.

25 Bhabha, Homi K., *The Location of Culture*, London, Routledge, 1994.

Translated by Lorraine Leu

Part IV

Modernity in Politics, Ideology and Religion

9

Modernity and Alternative Development in the Andes

Nelson Manrique

An ethnocidal modernisation

Modernity, as it unfolded in Europe in the late nineteenth century, has seduced the educated sectors of Latin American society throughout the twentieth century. The ruling elites of the Andean region have not been immune to its enchantments. However, the ideals proclaimed by European modernity openly contradicted the prevalent social order on which the authority of the elites rested, as the extension of citizenship implied the eradication of a still unresolved colonial legacy. The impossibility of reconciling both expectations gave rise to what Fernando de Trazegnies, following Barrington Moore, has called 'traditionalist modernisation'.[1]

At present there is a heated debate in the Anglo-Saxon academic world on the pertinence of the term 'colonial legacy'. The use of a new concept, the 'post-colonial', originating in the rousing national histories of the former British colonies, especially India, is becoming increasingly widespread. The term 'post-colonial' has also suffered a peculiar fate in the area of cultural studies. Authors of recent works on Andean social history, like Florencia Mallon and Deborah Poole, as well as Paul Gootenberg, make use of this term.[2] Mark Thurner proposes the use of the term 'post-colonial legacy' to define the problems of the Latin American societies which emerged after the break with Spain.[3] According to Thurner, the term 'colonial legacy' is obsessively repeated by scholars of Latin America like a mantra and should be eradicated once and for all from the lexicon of history and the social sciences.[4] However, it is of course not a question of exchanging one mantra for another, but of arriving at a term which sheds more light on the problems we seek to understand. This discussion does not deal with categories which define a self-assumed identity, in the sense that the inhabitants of the Andes do not consider themselves either 'colonial' or 'post-colonial'. These are terms used by scholars and the choice of one over the other should take their explanatory power into account.

The term 'post-colonial' refers to the condition of national societies that emerged from the process of decolonisation following the end of the Second World War. Indian intellectuals, when they reflect on the nature of their societies, are faced with the problem of defining the place from which to construct their discourse, given that they belong to a nation with a colonial past, which has had a profound effect on their culture.[5] The same problem arose in Latin America a century before. In that sense, except for the chronology of decolonisation, there should not be vast differences between the problems faced by Indian intellectuals and those faced by the intellectuals of the young nations formed out of former Spanish colonies. If the 'post-colonial' alluded simply to 'what follows the colonial', it would have no specific content (it says nothing about the *nature* of the societies to which it refers) and there would be no reason to propose it as a replacement for the category 'colonial legacy'. But in the use of the term 'post-colonial' in certain studies – especially in Mark Thurner's book referred to above – a difference of degree is presented. While the category 'colonial legacy' emphasises continuities rather than the change in political régime imposed by Latin American independence, the term 'post-colonial' emphasises the ruptures and discontinuities that this represented.

I believe that the term 'post-colonial' would be useful here if socio-historic realities in India and Latin America were sufficiently similar to make the use of one term valid for expressing both accurately. If this were so, the new category would only have to shed light on phenomena which the previous one ('colonial legacy') was incapable of explaining. However, in my view there are substantial differences between the nations which emerged from decolonisation after the Second World War on one hand, and the Latin American nations on the other, which became independent at the beginning of the nineteenth century. This is particularly true in those areas where there was a significant indigenous population at the time of independence, such as Mexico, Meso-America and the Andean region. This difference stems from the very nature of the colonial order which was being dismantled and makes the use of the term 'post-colonial' problematic for considering the specificities of the national societies of the Andean region.

In order to elucidate this question, it is useful to reflect on the nature of the persistence of the colonial in the Andes. It is customary to underline the importance of the maintenance of the structures of colonial domination,[6] evident in a number of practices: the restoration of the tributes paid by indigenous people to the state after independence (re-established in Peru under the term 'personal contribution'), the retention of free labour services for the state (the old colonial *mita* transformed into 'labour for the Republic', public works for the state and the municipal councils, and, between 1920 and 1930, the 'road conscription'); and the different legal status of indigenous peoples, enshrined in the legislation of the 1920s that treated Indians as minors, placing them outside of the nation, into which they had to be 'integrated'.[7] Indeed, indigenism played a significant role in this infantilisation of indigenous peoples.

But it is not just that these structures remained in force until the beginning of the twentieth century, for there is a further continuity: *that of a social subject who embodied*[8] *the continuity of colonial domination and who had led the thrust for Latin American independence – the Spanish American*. It is worth noting that the term 'Spanish American' referred to a self-assumed identity; the term *criollo* (creole) was originally considered pejorative. Benedict Anderson has repeatedly emphasised the identification of this sector with that of the peninsular Spaniards with whom they were to break. The original creoles were sons and daughters of Spaniards, spoke Castilian Spanish, dressed, ate, thought and lived according to Spanish custom, and their aesthetic tastes and ethical preferences were the same as those of peninsular Spaniards. Furthermore, a significant number of young Spanish Americans (including Bolívar and San Martín) made the pilgrimage to Madrid, seeking to be recognised at court, and San Martín even fought under the flag of the Spanish King before taking up arms against the Empire.

An abyss separated this social stratum of the population from the indigenous majorities of their countries, with whom they sought to construct new nations. An Indian from the *sierra* (mountain range) or the forest, who spoke different variations of Quechua, Aymara, or any of the dozens of languages of the Amazon region, had another vision of the cosmos, another material and spiritual culture, and ate, dressed and dreamt in a different way. These Indians were much more distant from the new Republican elites than the latter were from the colonial power from whom they had proposed to break.[9] Perhaps the full tragic dimension of this abyss was revealed to the Peruvian creole population in 1880, when around 10,000 Indians from the interior were mobilised and sent to the city of Lima, to defend the Peruvian capital from an attack by the Chilean army. As officially recounted by the Peruvian military, half of the Indians enrolled did not speak a word of Spanish, and, as the military officials were ignorant of indigenous languages, thousands of Indians were dispatched to frontline combat without even being instructed on how to use their rifles.[10]

Thus, in the midst of the great political upheaval which brought independence, the existence of an element of society which did not propose social revolution, but whose members believed themselves to be the inheritors of a position of power which had remained vacant since the invasion of Spain by Napoleonic forces and the imprisonment of the King, persisted as a decisive continuity.[11] This mentality, which dominated the struggle for independence, was outlined in Simón Bolívar's famous *Letter from Jamaica*:

> We [creoles] are neither Indian nor European, but a species in-between the legitimate owners of the country and the Spanish usurpers: in short, *because we are Americans by birth and have inherited the rights of Europe*, we have to dispute these with the country's original inhabitants, while standing against the invasion of the usurpers; thus we find ourselves in a most extraordinary and complicated situation. (my emphasis)

For the creoles it was not a question of dismantling the mechanisms of power used previously by the colonial bureaucracy and the Spanish Crown, but of appropriating them and using them for their own benefit. If the necessities of war against Spain initially required the support of the indigenous population, gained by abolishing the demands for tribute and free labour for the state – in addition to eliminating the term 'Indian', which would later be replaced by 'Peruvian' – these reforms were dismantled a few years after independence. We are dealing with a transfer of power which did not modify existing colonial structures; a political revolution without social revolution.

In these circumstances, is it possible to maintain that the ruptures were greater than the continuities? Although the situation of the indigenous people evolved and changed throughout Republican history, the differences between the condition of the Indians before and after independence seem less pronounced than, for example, their situation during the early colonial period – with exploitation centred around the *mita* and the tribute – and later in the colonial period, when the fundamental mechanism of exploitation revolved around the compulsion to buy imported goods. A similar situation can be observed if one compares their condition before and after the agrarian reform of recent decades.

Are there similarities between this historical process and what happened in India? For an exact parallel, there would have to have existed in India a social category of 'English Indians', sons and daughters of the elite and culturally English officials of the colonising power, who settled in India, identifying themselves as inheritors of state control, as racially and ethnically English, and feeling alienated from and incompatible with the majority of the population of their country due to the racial, linguistic, cultural and religious differences; but this was not the case in India. Although there are numerous differences of class, ethnicity and caste among Indians from India, they do not prevent the existence of major elements of community, on which to build a more inclusive national project than any derived from their links with the old colonial power.[12]

Colonial racism

The existence of ethnic cleavages in Andean countries, which separate their inhabitants and pit them against each other, has been frequently suggested as the major impediment in the way of national integration. Without denying the importance of this factor, I believe that one has to focus attention on another dimension of the problem, namely the existence of a profound racism, in both theory and practice, which has constituted the main obstacle to the extension of citizenship – a prerequisite without which no form of modernity is conceivable.

This view is strongly contested by a significant group of intellectuals, who maintain that the widespread biological and cultural *mestizaje*, or mixing, that was produced during the last two centuries has eliminated the bases on which the racist discourses, so widespread during the first half of the twentieth century, were founded. I believe that posing the problem of racism as a question of classifying races and of considering their relative numbers, in order to say that racial discrimination has been overcome, is to forget that we are talking about a phenomenon that essentially lives and reproduces itself in socially constructed subjectivities, through which the objective facts are 'refracted'. The objective and the subjective do not share the same temporality and it is not unusual for them to evolve asynchronically. To invoke biological *mestizaje* as 'evidence' that racial discrimination does not exist is to forget that, in sexual unions, relations of imposition, marginalisation, discrimination and violence also intervene. Biological reproduction does not require equal relationships between those who are involved in the sexual act: with the right biological conditions, sex can be as procreative if there is love between the two parties as if there is none. Those who maintain opposing views are apparently oblivious to the unilateral and asymmetrical character of *mestizaje* from the beginning of the European presence in America. It was invariably founded on the copulation of *male* Conquistadors with Indian *women*. *Mestizaje* between Indian males and Spanish women existed as an exception in the frontier territories, inhabited by nomadic, unconquered indigenous groups, who eventually made military raids on the camps of the invaders (for example, the *malones* from the Araucanía) and carried off Spanish women as war booty – the 'Christian captives'. It is therefore impossible to understand the nature of racial discrimination if the link with gender discrimination is severed. And the exception cited allows for an understanding of the profound nature of the phenomenon: the direction of *mestizaje*, seen from a gender perspective, is dictated by the naked truth of force (in this case, military force).[13]

While ethnic discrimination is recognised and has prompted significant consideration in our society, there is strong resistance to acknowledging the existence of racism, which is not surprising given that those who deny it are those who discriminate. But there must be a very profound reason for those who suffer racism to also deny its existence. I propose the following explanation: racism generates very deep wounds in the self-image of those discriminated against – what the psychoanalysts call 'narcissistic wounds' – as it is aimed at the nature of one's very being. In the face of this, the most primary and efficient defence is denial: 'If racism does not exist then I have not been discriminated against.' Ethnic discrimination leaves the way open, theoretically at least, for overcoming it by human agency. That is, it is possible to resist it on an individual level, by changing one's social, economic or cultural conditions, religious and political beliefs (in an adaptive strategy), or on a social level, from a revolutionary perspective, by transforming society from below in order to modify its system of values. Racial discrimination, however, is seen as based on nature, on firm and immutable biological facts. The ways in which it can be overcome therefore depend on the disappearance of those discriminated against, whether through breeding with members of 'superior races' (an alternative fervently promoted by Andean Republican elites), or by the physical extermination either of those discriminated against or of the discriminators. This represents the most terrifying alternative, examples of which have been provided by history: the ending of differences by the elimination of different groups. Racism is a double-edged sword. One the one hand it creates and justifies contempt, domination and abuse; on the other, it generates a profound resentment, continually fed by the experience of daily humiliation. One of its possible consequences is usually the explosion of violence.[14]

Republics without citizens

There is a consensus that in the Andean nations anti-indigenous racism has been one of the basic components of the social domination imposed by the national oligarchies which govern in alliance with the vigorous local powers of the interior. Racism fulfils a decisive function in the legitimation of exclusion, by 'naturalising' social inequalities, consecrating an order in which each person has an immutable position, which does not appear to have a social origin, but seems rooted in a changeless nature. Like all human products, racism has a history which can be reconstructed. In the social dynamic, racism is an ideology above all else, and as such it serves to maintain a given status quo, so that it changes as socio-economic structures and the established relations of power change. Thus, there is not just *one* racism; like all historical constructs, it assumes diverse forms according to the social context in which it is generated. Its history cannot be separated from social history.[15]

In the construction of colonial American racism, two factors are in open conflict: that which affirms the superiority of the conquering race and exalts 'purity of blood' as the supreme value on which social co-existence should be organised, and the objective and undeniable fact of widespread *mestizaje* between conquistadors and indigenous women in the colonial domain. The question becomes even more complicated with regard to the African slave population. An attempt was made to overcome this contradiction by emphasising the separation between the 'Republic of the Spaniards' and the 'Republic of the Indians', a project destined to failure owing to the continuation of widespread *mestizaje*.

In its origin colonial racism is a phenomenon that belongs to the terrain of *mentalities*, 'that confused magma of inherited assumptions', to use Georges Duby's expression, which is constructed over a long period of time and which forms that common subconscious of unreasoned images and certainties from which our ways of representing the world and our most elemental reactions emerge. At the same time, racism fulfilled a very important function as an *ideology* that legitimised the colonial order, actively intervening in its preservation and reproduction. Like all dominant ideologies, colonial racism was not just propagated by the colonisers, but was internalised and accepted as a 'truth' by the colonised. This contributed greatly to the stability of the colonial order.[16]

The elimination of the indigenous aristocracies represented a very significant historical moment in this process. On paper at least, they had enjoyed a set of privileges granted to the nobility in accordance with the Law of the Indies. Until the end of the eighteenth century the condition of the Indians was much more heterogeneous, as, together with the 'commoners' (*indios del común*), there were 'noble chiefs' (*curacas de sangre*), who enjoyed certain prerogatives, as well as relative social esteem. The defeat of the rebellion of Tupac Amaru II paved the way for the disappearance of this whole sector of society and for the decline of the overall condition of Peru's indigenous population. By the middle of the nineteenth century the noble stratum of Indian society had disappeared and the condition of 'Indian' ended up being equated with 'peasant' and 'poor' (without all peasants and all of the poor necessarily being Indians). This widespread socio-economic marginalisation contributed to reinforcing the stereotype of the 'natural inferiority' of the Indian. From then on, the path to progress would depend on the de-indigenisation of the country.[17]

Racism constructs the object of racial exclusion. The 'Indian' is the product of a long and contradictory process of the generation of ideas on the nature of the nation to be constructed and the images which would express it.[18] The prosperity afforded the country by guano offered the economic bases for the consolidation of this project, while Gobineau's convoluted reflections on race, enthusiastically appropriated by Latin American elites, gave racism the legitimacy of scientific fact.

Traditionalist modernity

The situation did not change substantially with the rupture of the colonial ties which linked us to Spain. Because the colonial character of the internal structure of domination did not undergo any essential transformations, colonial racism ended up playing a supporting role in the domination of society by the creole elite, who assumed power after independence.[19] It is because of this that social conflicts in republican Peru have perennially been intertwined with the racial–ethnic question. The racist component permeated the diverse projects of nation-building elaborated throughout the nineteenth century, from those which saw the extermination of the Indian population as a necessary condition for national development[20] to those which proposed different alternatives for 'integrating the Indian into the nation'. They saw Peru essentially as an 'empty country' – since the native population was not considered Peruvian – and believed it necessary to promote European immigration,[21] as much to facilitate the exploitation of natural resources as to 'raise the quality' of the Peruvian population through biological mixing with 'superior races', as well as simply to repopulate the country, replacing the native population.

Social domination in Peru was reinforced by the ethnic racial solidarity established between the dominant elite and the imperial powers that replaced Spain – first Britain, then the United States – in the neo-colonial subjugation of the country. This in turn contributed to creating an abyss between these elites and the great majority of the population, from whom they felt distant, alienated and superior. The predominant power bloc during the Aristocratic Republic (1895–1930), whose composition remained virtually unchanged until the late 1960s, was established through an alliance between the Lima plutocracy, the agro-exporting bourgeoisie and the traditional landowners of the interior. This alliance was opposed to the transformations designed to modernise the country, because it could not conceive of doing away with the colonial matrix on which the republic had been founded and on which its members' privileges were based. To explain the contradictions of this political elite, the legal historian Fernando de Trazegnies, as already mentioned, coined an expression which aptly summarises their paradoxical nature: 'traditionalist modernization'. This refers to an attempt by reformist oligarchical intellectuals to introduce changes into the material base of their societies, with the aim of assuring the continuation of the privileges they enjoy – making tactical concessions to avoid real change.[22]

It is not that the Andean elites were averse to the changes occurring in the world. After the legacy of the Pacific War (1879–1884) – which involved Chile, Bolivia and Peru – was forgotten, there was a naive confidence that the country had entered a stage of uninterrupted development, in which internal peace would consolidate development. The elites shared the illusions of the European Belle Époque, fed by the unusual peace enjoyed by Europe between the Franco-Prussian War of 1870 and the beginning of the First World War. Paris was the Mecca towards which the gaze of Latin America's elites was turned, and Peru was no exception. The most lucid ideologue of the civil intellectual aristocracy, the young Francisco García Calderón, wrote the text which best formulates the political project of his class, *Le Pérou Contemporain*, and published it in French in 1907. The book was translated into

Spanish only in 1981, four decades after the death of its author. It is
clear that the readers whom the brilliant essayist addressed were not
the popular masses, whom he held in contempt, but that intellectual
aristocracy for whom he considered himself a spokesperson and which,
as he saw it, embodied the nation. In his view the educated classes
should exercise a benevolent dictatorship, occupying the place
accorded them by right because of their intelligence, while the people
should limit themselves to enjoying and being grateful for the benefits
of such guidance. Meanwhile, his brother Ventura García Calderón
wrote a book called *La Venganza del Condor*, whose protagonists were
mysterious Indians with exotic customs, and which was translated into
several languages. Ventura and his brother Francisco were nominated
for the Nobel Prize for Literature.

In their own way, the intellectuals of the Aristocratic Republic had
discovered the Indian[23] – or, rather, they had constructed one, who
had very little to do with reality. The writers of the civilising oligarchy
had discovered an exotic world, which could serve well as a literary
source for romantic works, previously set in the mysterious Orient,
Persia, Damascus, Baghdad or India. This was nothing more than the
continuation of a tradition of profound ignorance and lack of interest
in the interior of the country, in relation to which the elites felt foreign
and distant and which they only considered as a potential source of
wealth to be exploited. The Indian could be included in the inventory
of natural wealth – that marvellous, coca-chewing creature who in the
mines of the *sierra* could work continuously for thirty-six hours, with
only a twelve-hour break, during the two or three months for which he
was contracted, as Alejandro Garland noted with obvious enthusiasm.[24]
The traveller Squier said that for every inhabitant of Lima who was
acquainted with Cuzco, there were thirty who had been to London.
Even in 1901 Manuel Candamo, the president of the Senate, who in
1903 would become President of the Republic, stated that the problems
of the country resided not in its laws but in its people, and that this
would be solved in time with '*the crossing of races*' and the change in
character of the Peruvian people (my emphasis).[25]

The civilising perspective

Unfortunately, the radical thinkers did not have a truly inclusive project
either. The critique formulated by José Antonio Encinas in the early
1920s maintained that the indigenous problem was essentially socio-
economic and could not be solved without dealing with the problem of

land.[26] But the debate on the 'Indian question' opened by Encinas and
the indigenists between the 1920s and '30s did not offer proposals
which really considered the integration of the Indians as protagonists
of national history, as Deborah Poole has rightly emphasised:

> The majority of texts and discussions which followed manifestations of
> indigenism – and the rebellions and land invasions of the Indians themselves
> which preceded them – was not so much a testimony to the success of the
> political polemic raised by the former, as to the struggle to define, know of
> and normalise the presence of these 'new' and silent members of the
> national community.[27]

Was it possible to consider different alternatives to the mental
universe existing at the time? Reviewing those contemporary positions
on race and the 'problem of the Indian', one can conclude that the
margin for the production of egalitarian alternatives was very narrow.
To ignore this would run the risk of projecting a politically correct
critique retrospectively, and anachronistically, on to the past.

This is clear when one analyses the positions of the Peruvian José
Carlos Mariátegui, founder of Marxism in Latin America and one of
the most original thinkers of the continent. His essays on the artistic
vanguards of the 1920s represent one of various testimonies to his
enthusiasm for modernity. But when Mariátegui reflects on the 'problem of the Indian' (he incorporated the phrase as the title of one of
his famous *7 ensayos de interpretación de la realidad peruana*) he cannot
resist that vision which considers the disappearance of the Indian (in
this case the cultural disappearance) a condition for integration into
the nation. This is less an expression of Mariátegui's personal limitations than of the limitations of the world-view he shared with his
contemporaries – a mentality established with European modernity and
which marked social thought in Latin America until the recent crisis of
Marxism. Marxism has always assumed that one of the natural consequences of the process of unification of the world, which impels the
growing internationalisation of capital, will be a progressive cultural
homogenisation that will dissolve individual identities into a common,
universal one, shared by all people.[28] With the question posed in this
way, the integration–assimilation of some cultures by others is inevitable, and Western culture (of which, it must never be forgotten,
Marxism is an offshoot) is the one which has the greatest chance of
imposing itself. The consciousness of the *historical necessity* of this
evolution seems evident to Mariátegui: 'What is important . . . in the
sociological study of the Indian and *mestizo* strata, is not the extent to
which the *mestizo* inherits the qualities or defects of the progenitor

races, but his ability to evolve, more easily than the Indian, towards the social state, or the level of civilisation, of the white population.'[29]

Here a problem is posed which had already been clearly perceived and posed by Max Weber. Modernity is inseparable from the development of capitalism and the latter is linked to the history of a concrete social space: Europe from the sixteenth to the twentieth centuries. Capitalism gave birth to it, but was, in another sense, a product of it. Marx's great eulogy on the bourgeoisie in the *Communist Manifesto* is a recognition of its transcendental historical role, demonstrating all that human activity can produce when freed from the ties of tradition. But the conditions which made modernity possible in Europe do not of course apply generally to the whole world. Thus for Weber the possibility of *another modernity* which was different to that of Europe was not conceivable. Nor was this conceivable to the intellectuals of the dependent countries who thought of modernity as a desirable prospect for the development of their own societies. The European cultural world was the mirror into which their societies should look.

Similar subjects are found in the early anthropological work of one of the writers least open to the suspicion of harbouring anti-indigenous prejudice: José María Arguedas. In the fifties Arguedas dedicated several key anthropological essays to the communities of Valle del Mantarin, in which the solution to the problems of the Indians depends on their disappearance as such, through *mestizaje*, understood as a process of *de-indigenisation*. The Indians should assimilate to the dominant culture in order to enjoy full citizenship.[30]

The notion that the solution to the 'problem of the Indian' lay in the disappearance of the Indian was therefore a form of common sense generally ingrained in Peruvian society. The anti-indigenous racism that served as an ideological support for the oligarchical order had deep roots. Although, like any ideological construct, the category 'Indian' was shot through with contradictions, nevertheless this didn't undermine its efficacy as an instrument in the construction of excluding social orders. Several recent studies have called attention to the way the term 'Indian', considered in univocal terms to define a segment of society in opposition to the rest (Indians/non-Indians), fragments within local and regional communities into a set of meanings of which the only thing that is certain is the complete relativity of such terms.[31]

Return to the future

With this kind of mentality, it is possible to understand the limits of the developmentalist projects put forward from the 1950s onwards in the Andean region, based on evolutionist views of history, as in the work of W.W. Rostow,[32] in cultural anthropology and agricultural development work, and vigorously promoted in the countryside through the Interamerican Service of Agricultural Co-operation (SCIPA). Not even the most radical manifestations of populism, such as the eruption of the agrarian revolution in Bolivia, were capable of overcoming this mentality. The need for cultural ethnocide to integrate the indigenous population, as a necessary condition for successfully realising the modernisation of Andean societies, was seen as a given. The reforms proposed during the following decade, within the ambit of the Alliance for Progress, and with which the Kennedy administration proposed to neutralise the pernicious influence of the Cuban Revolution, merely represented a more sophisticated form of the same ideological repertoire. Neither the proposed state reform nor the 'green revolution' could overcome this mentality, which saw European civilisation as the 'natural' culmination of the evolution of the human species. Towards the end of the 1960s in Bolivia, a decade after the manifestation of peasant radicalism, the 'military–peasant pact' would oppose Che Guevara's attempt to begin a continental revolution from the Bolivian jungle.

Latin American populisms failed in their attempt to modernise the region. They brought about significant changes, generally resisted by the conservative elite, but the results they obtained were far from the objectives they had proposed. In order to stimulate industrialisation in Peru, a policy was pursued which favoured the development of the cities to the detriment of the countryside, and of the coast to the detriment of the *sierra*. This aggravated an agricultural crisis, and one result of this was the disruption of the balance in the relationship between human beings and the land. The impact of this situation can be measured in the evolution of the population: between 1940 and 1961 the urban Peruvian population grew three times more quickly than the rural and between 1961 and 1972 the speed of its growth was ten times greater than that of the peasant population, which entered a state of virtual stagnation.

In addition to this, a substantial change in the nature of the international division of labour took place. The imperialist powers, which up until the Second World War were importers of agricultural goods, after the war became net exporters of food, thanks to the technological revolution achieved in their agricultural systems, but also owing to an aggressive state policy of subsidising agriculture. On the other hand, the policies of the Andean states sought to favour industrial growth, reducing the cost of the labour force, using as a fundamental strategy a programme of lowering food prices, removing price restrictions, eliminating subsidies and carrying out massive importation of cheap foodstuffs from the metropolitan countries. The traditional agriculture of the Andean *sierra* – impoverished, with a rudimentary level of technology, and vulnerable to the whims of nature – had to compete with imported, subsidised products, while at the same time facing a continual rise in the price of production materials. Far from being spurred on to modernisation, agriculture was pushed into a state of general stagnation and chronic crisis. This was expressed in the decline of the *sierra*, the region where the majority of the Andean peasantry is based. The figures speak eloquently in this regard: between 1954 and 1959 per capita income on the coast grew by 4 per cent, while in the *sierra* it fell by 7 per cent; between 1960 and 1969 national revenues increased by 350 per cent in current values, but the participation of those involved in independent agriculture fell from 14 per cent to 11 per cent.[33] Millions of peasants were therefore obliged to migrate to the cities, in a process recalling the demographic transition experienced by Europe a century or more before, with the difference that in this case there was no process of industrialisation able to incorporate the migrant peasants into modern capitalist production.

The agricultural crisis provoked a progressive reactivation of the peasant movements, which from 1956 to 1964 acquired a mass character, and for the first time in Peruvian history gained an effectively national dimension, involving millions of peasants in the largest mobilisations since the late eighteenth century. The synchronisation of the movement in the north, centre and south, on the coast, in the *sierra* and jungle – a phenomenon which had not occurred in any previous historical period – contributed decisively to precipitating the crisis of the rural traditional order, creating the conditions which would culminate in the disappearance of the land-owning class. The latter was left so weakened that it was unable to defend itself when the Agrarian Reform of 1969 was declared.

These dramatic transformations have been the backdrop for certain radical changes in racial perceptions, which do not signal the disappearance of racism but pose it in new terms. The most significant expression of this is the continued reduction in the numbers of the sector of the population defined as 'Indian' in Peru. At the beginning of the twentieth century the anarchist ideologue Manuel González Prada estimated that Indians constituted nine-tenths of the Peruvian population. José Carlos Mariátegui and Víctor Raúl Haya de la Torre stated that indigenous people represented four-fifths. In 1940 – when the first national census of the twentieth century was conducted, and the last in which 'race' figured as a census criterion – it was concluded that 'whites' and 'mestizos' represented 52.89 per cent of the population,[34] 45.86 per cent were 'Indians', 0.47 per cent blacks, 0.68 per cent 'yellow', while 0.10 per cent were defined as 'undeclared race'.[35] Today, on an exceedingly impressionistic basis (owing to the difficulty of defining what constitutes an 'Indian'), it is believed that the indigenous population represents 25 per cent of the total.

There has not been a substantial change in the composition of the population; what has changed are the criteria for racial classification. An important element in explaining this is the decline in the country's rural population. In Peru the condition of 'Indian' has been associated with that of peasant: not all peasants are considered Indians, but all Indians are considered peasants.[36] Migration changed the nature of Peruvian society radically. While in 1940 35.5 per cent of the population was urban and 64.5 per cent rural, in 1993 the percentages were 70.4 per cent and 29.6 per cent respectively. We are therefore now dealing with a predominantly urban country. The demographic decline of the *sierra* has also had an effect, given that the condition of 'indigenous' is associated with that of *serrano* (inhabitant of the *sierra*). As in the previous case, however, not all *serranos* are considered Indians. Between 1940 and 1993 the population of the coast, as a fraction of the total population, increased from 24 per cent to 52.2 per cent; that of the *sierra* was reduced from 63 per cent to 35.8 per cent; while that of the forest remained almost static, decreasing only from 13 per cent to 12 per cent. If formerly the *sierra* represented almost two-thirds of the population, today it represents barely one third, while the coast, previously home to less than a quarter of the total population, today contains more than half. The Peruvian population is now predominantly coastal and is strongly concentrated in the capital. The population of Lima has grown from 600,000 inhabitants in 1940 (a tenth of the country's total) to approximately 6.4 million in 1993. Today one in three Peruvians lives in the capital.[37] The decline in the indigenous population is the result not so much of an accelerated increase of biological *mestizaje*, but more of the demographic increase on the coast at the expense of the *sierra*, and of the cities at the expense of the countryside.

The great changes experienced in the last fifty years could be summarised as follows: Peru has ceased to be rural, indigenous and agrarian, and has become predominantly urban and *mestizo*, with an agriculture in crisis and a high degree of centralisation.

The end of racism?

These changes have led to claims that the bases on which racial and anti-indigenous discrimination were built have disappeared. Moreover, the colonial institutions whose function it was to perpetuate racial segregation – such as the indigenous tribute and the almost feudal servitude to which Indians were subjected on traditional *haciendas* – no longer exist. External cultural differences – such as the use of native languages and typical clothing – have been eroded, as widespread education has increased the number of Spanish speakers and cheaper Western-style clothing has prevailed. The relative geographical isolation of the indigenous populations (previously confined to the *sierra* and the jungle), the small degree of national integration, and the weakness of the central state (on which *caciquism* grew), have disappeared, or soon will. The disappearance of racism is therefore only a matter of time.

In fact, as suggested earlier, these changes have modified the ways in which the racial question is posed, but they have not eliminated racism. Alongside persistent anti-indigenous racism, racial discrimination within the *mestizo* class itself is becoming increasingly significant, and favours the maintenance and reproduction of an authoritarian and excluding social order. Any proposal for the democratisation of Peruvian society that fails to take this dimension into account is doomed to failure.

Racism is a fundamentally intersubjective phenomenon. Objective social changes do not occur at the same pace as subjective ones, and when there is a significant gap between the two, a powerful potential source of violence can develop. If certain conditions are added, generated out of the current widespread social crisis, the result can be the emergence of a political project like *Sendero Luminoso* (Shining Path).[38]

The characteristics of Peruvian racism (and this should be applicable to the situation of other countries in Latin America) make it a phenomenon which cannot be understood with the analytical categories developed in other social contexts. For example, the racism of 'whites' against 'blacks' in the Anglo-Saxon countries implies an 'objectivisation' of the person who is being discriminated against. As biological mixing is more of an exception in these areas, the discriminating 'white' considers the 'black' victim of discrimination as something alien and external – an *object* which does not involve her/him and onto which s/he can project discrimination, hatred and contempt. In today's predominantly *mestizo* Peru, such an 'objectification' of the target of discrimination is not possible, since on the whole the discriminating subject cannot separate her/himself from the 'object' against which s/he discriminates. To use the term 'Indian' to insult another person, while having Indian blood in your veins, implies a denial of part of your own identity – and discrimination, hatred and contempt for elements of which you are comprised. This is a form of radical alienation, a self-mutilation the price of which is the impossibility of recognising your own face in the mirror.[39] Thus a kind of racism which is profoundly complicated and difficult to confront is produced.

The ideology of *mestizaje* affirms that as biological and cultural mixing increases, it will bring about the racial homogenisation of the Peruvian population, eliminating the causes of racism. This has not occurred. With the great migrations from the *sierra* to the coast and from the country to the city, there is a greater interrelation between the diverse cultural matrices of the country, as well as the creation of new matrices of meaning which emerge from this contact, but racism continues to wield enormous power. In a survey recently conducted in the ten major cities among adolescents between the ages of eleven and seventeen, 65.3 per cent of those surveyed believed that racism existed in Peru, as against 28 per cent who did not. Of these, 45.1 per cent thought that those most affected by racism were the *cholos*, 38.7 per cent singling out blacks, 12 per cent indigenous people and 0.4 per cent Japanese and Chinese. Moreover, 90.9 per cent believed that the most racist group was the whites, followed by the Japanese (3.1 per cent) and blacks (2.2 per cent). The decline in the importance conceded to anti-indigenous racism and the rise of anti-*mestizo* racism constitutes a general revolution in mentalities. On the other hand, the force of the overwhelmingly majority opinion, which attributes the most pronounced racism to the white sector, reflects a worrying social polarisation.[40] Racism has not disappeared, but having previously been predominantly anti-indigenous, it has now become a racism fundamentally exercised against *mestizo* sectors of the population, and within this sector itself.

In Peru the racial question cannot be severed from the social question, as a change in the condition of the group most discriminated against (the Indians) relies on overcoming poverty. The problem therefore has a firm socio-economic base and cannot be solved simply by denouncing racism. The change in mentalities must be accompanied by radical changes in socio-economic structures and by the dismantling of the internal structures of colonial domination, which find expression in anti-indigenous racism.

The return of the Indian

The above term is taken from an essay published by Xavier Albó in 1991, in which he calls attention to the widespread phenomenon of indigenous re-ethnicisation which has been growing in Latin America since the 1960s and which reached a considerable scale in the late 1980s. This process advanced according to different rhythms in different Andean countries, owing in part to the political restrictions imposed by the military régimes which were installed in the region throughout the 1970s. To the 'traditional' demands of indigenist movements – like land, credit, basic services and fixed prices for agricultural goods – others were added, including the recognition of their own cultural identity and rights to autonomy for their organisations, the administration of justice, education in their own language and the support of their ancestral religions:

> That more globalising vision explains why increasingly, across the length and breadth of Andean countries, concepts such as 'class' and 'trade union', which were used almost exclusively not so long ago, are now considered inadequate, and why there is a return to notions such as 'community', 'indigenous', 'originary' and even, increasingly, those of 'nationality' and 'nation'. But in contrast to the European nationalist movements, these nations do not propose their transformations in terms of independent states, except in the excessively theoretical discussion of a few intellectuals.[41]

For Albó, this process constitutes a reaction and counterpoint in the face of the homogenising tendencies of the dominant model of development:

> In summary, therefore, we are faced with a dialectical situation which, on the one hand, is part of the homogenising tendency of society whereby the Indian should cease to be Indian in order to insert himself into society. But on the other hand, this Indian is not willing to lose his particular way of life and the very contradictions of the system confirm the validity of his own vision.[42]

An indirect consequence of the commemoration of 500 years since the colonisation of America (in 1992) was the meeting of diverse indigenous groups from within the continent which, by putting leaders of the Indian movements of several countries into contact, gave a

significant boost to their demands. Throughout the 1990s this crystalli-
sed into a set of changes expressed, among other ways, in the incorporation of indigenous demands into the constitutions of eleven countries
of the region. Several organisations emerged articulating indigenous
demands, especially in Bolivia and Ecuador where Indian leaders
succeeded in gaining a significant presence in the state apparatus.

One of the great achievements in this process was the election in
1993 of Víctor Hugo Cárdenas, a prominent Aymara leader and member of the Bolivian Katarist movement, to the vice-presidency of the
Republic as a member of the presidential platform of the MNR (Nationalist Revolutionary Movement). This case also reveals the limits faced
by the most advanced Indianist projects. The Katarist movement consi-
tutes the most highly developed expression of Indianism. Since its
inception Katarismo was a plural movement, cut across by doctrinal
conflicts around the definition of the path that Bolivian society should
take in order to bring about the changes needed to satisfy indigenous
demands. The election of Cárdenas was the result of the electoral needs
of the presidential candidate of the MNR, Gonzalo Sánchez de Lozada.
For the general elections of 1993 Sanchez de Lozada, a political leader
close to the United States politics and ideology, requested the services
of a North American electoral marketing company. It reached the
conclusion that in order to win elections in the city of La Paz, which
has traditionally eluded the MNR and was key to winning the elections,
it was necessary for the presidential platform to incorporate a political
figure who would compensate for the inadequacies of the presidential
candidate, who was too closely identified with North America and
culturally very distant from his potential electors. They focused then on
Víctor Hugo Cárdenas, who had a radical rhetorical style and a reputation as a notable parliamentary speaker. From the point of view of the
MNR this strategy paid off, as it succeeded in winning La Paz, and with
it the general election.

The situation was different for the Katarist movement which, faced
with imminent elections, proposed to participate as an autonomous
political movement, putting Cárdenas forward as its presidential candidate, with no expectation of winning the elections but with the intention of gaining strength for the following presidential election.
Cárdenas, meanwhile, had privately conducted negotiations with the
MNR and decided to join the presidential platform, with only the
support of the political activists immediately around him. This decision
profoundly divided the Katarist leaders and ideologues, some of whom
were radically opposed to Cárdenas's decision, while others supported
him enthusiastically.

Those who questioned Cárdenas's participation in the presidential platform of the MNR pointed to the evident contradiction of participating in an election as a candidate of the most conspicuous political force of the Bolivian right – the organic representative of the neo-liberal project, whose main victims, the poorest sectors of Bolivian society, were precisely the Indians whom Katarism sought to represent. For those who supported Cárdenas's decision there was enormous symbolic weight attached to the fact that an Indian might occupy the vice-presidency of the Republic, and also that the presence of Cárdenas in this position would open up a space for gaining important positions in the struggle to meet indigenous demands. Furthermore, several laws were promulgated granting significant rights to indigenous sectors. Some redistribution of resources was also achieved, through a reform according to which a certain quantity of resources was assigned to municipal authorities, relating to the size of its population. The claim for indigenous territories has been equally significant.

For their detractors, these achievements are primarily symbolic and have not facilitated the effective strengthening of the Indianist movement. In fact, Cárdenas's election and the circumstances which surrounded it precipitated a crisis in Katarism, leading to its virtual dissolution as an organic political movement. At present Katarism, rather than a real political force, is an ideological ferment expressing itself through the discourse of Indianist leaders who make policies from within the different parties on the Bolivian political scene. The widening of its audience, claimed as a success by supporters of this option, was achieved at the cost of the dissolution of Indianism as an autonomous political current.[43]

It is too early to tell what will happen in Ecuador, but there are clear similiarities to the Bolivian process. The pragmatism which the directors of the most important Indianist organisation, the Confederation of Indigenous Nationalities of Ecuador (CONAIE), have adopted (in order to gain positions in the state apparatus by allying themselves with political organisations which openly preach a neo-liberal doctrine) resembles the Bolivian situation. Like the Katarists, CONAIE has succeeded in placing representatives in the national parliament, with the result that important indigenous demands have been included in Ecuador's legislation, in spite of the fact that these representatives operate with equal 'pragmatism', to the detriment of the unity of the movement.

Víctor Hugo Cárdenas and his followers' assessment of their alliance with the Bolivian MNR is optimistic, underlining the importance of what has been achieved and, it would seem, ignoring the trap into which the Indian movement has fallen immediately after the end of the MNR period of government and the rise to power of General Hugo Banzer in 1997. An obvious result of this process – over and above the conclusions one may draw regarding this period of development of Indianism in Bolivia – is that the appeal to Indianism as an ideology is insufficient as the doctrinal base for the forging of an alternative, autonomous politics. The achievements of Katarism in power were made by renouncing the political autonomy of the movement, and the cost of this option was to question the very viability of Indianism as an autonomous political alternative. It is important to point out that the most radical ideologues presented Indianism as an excluding alternative, messianic in character. In the face of Western decadence, Andean Indians and their culture were put forward as the new alternative for the regeneration of humanity. It is not hard to find in these discourses, rightly criticised for their essentialism, echoes of the inflamed sermons of the Peruvian indigenists of the 1920s.

I do not deny the justice of Indian demands, nor the political importance of the Indianist movement, from the perspective of building an effectively democratic order in the Andean region. What is in question is the attempt to present ethnic identity as an excluding option, to which other oppressed and exploited social sectors should be subordinate. It is necessary to recognise the validity of these claims and their political expression as an important – but not exclusive – part of a broader movement for the affirmation of democracy. This is a prerequisite for the construction of a political order which can be considered truly modern.

The Peruvian exception

The question remains: Why has the process of re-ethnicisation which has enveloped the continent not been echoed in Peru, a country whose social composition and historical tradition would seem to make it a 'natural' scene of Indianist discourse? I believe I can identify at least three reasons for this. In the first place there is the weakness of Andean power structures. As we have already seen, the defeat of the Túpac Amaru II movement at the end of the eighteenth century opened the way for the destruction of the indigenous elites; the indigenous world never recovered from this loss. Second, the absence of *urban Indians*, a social category which has been central in Bolivia and Ecuador for the emergence of intellectuals capable of theorising indigenism as a political alternative. And third, the impact of political violence throughout the 1980s. The dirty war between Sendero Luminoso and the Peruvian State did not allow spaces for the emergence of new political alternatives.

One organisation which has been relatively successful in putting ethnic identities forward as a cohesive element is that of the indigenous members of the Peruvian Amazonian ethnicities, grouped around the Inter-ethnic Association of the Development of the Peruvian Rainforest (AIDESEP) – itself a member of the Indigenous Co-ordination of the Amazon Basin (COICA), which represents the indigenous forest feder-ations of the Amazonian countries.[44] However, the indigenous people of Amazonia constitute less than 1 per cent of the Peruvian population. As long as it continues to be an organisation which does not represent the Indians of the Peruvian *sierra*, Indianism will continue to be a marginal movement in Peruvian politics, in spite of the evident import-ance of the project for the indigenous population of the Amazon region.

By way of conclusion

The theme of modernity in the Andes already has a long history, the fundamental characteristic of which is the inadequacy of ideas imported from Europe and the United States, both by local elites and by the left (mainly Marxists). This is due to the radical inability to insert them into existing Andean historical traditions: an inability for which I have attempted to offer an explanation.

The developmentalist project which was imposed in Latin America after the last world war (which was common to the left and the right) reduced the problem to the existence of a 'gap' which separated Latin American countries from the developed countries – the model they sought to imitate. This was to be closed through an aggressive process of industrialisation. Although the most complete formulation of this project, in the form of 'import substitution industrialisation', was elaborated by the Economic Commission for Latin America (ECLA), the thinking underlying this project was in fact shared by the majority of political organisations and intellectuals. For those concerned only with the modernisation of the region, such as the technocratic elites who supported the dictatorships imposed in the region, (and in the Southern Cone), throughout the 1970s, the role of the countryside was to furnish the necessary capital and labour to bring about the process of industrial take-off. The primary means designed to achieve this goal in the economic sphere was agrarian reform, and in the cultural sphere, *mestizaje* – conceived, since the Indianist Congress of Patzcuaro (1940), as the *de-indigenisation* of the Indians. The indigenous peasantry was seen more as an object of the policies aimed at incorporating them into the modern world than as their subject.

Behind this concept of development there were three firmly rooted convictions. In the first place, cultural homogenisation was regarded as a fundamental requisite for modernisation. The possibility of integrating the indigenous population into the modernising project was not denied, but the condition for including them was that they ceased to be Indian. Indigenism presented a fundamental obstacle to the development of a viable modernity insofar as this project was rejected by the indigenous population. Second, the assumption was that there was *one* model of development – that offered by the West – and everything that did not fit it should be seen as an obstacle ('tradition') which had to be removed – whether this might be community-based peasant life, the political institutions of indigenous populations, or their traditions of mutual assistance. These policies were vigorously implemented from the 1950s, under the influence of North American culturalism and structural functionalism. Third, it was assumed that city and countryside were irreconcilable domains, and while the first embodied modernity (as in Europe), the second was the redoubt of tradition. The cities provided the civilising model under whose guidance the backward countryside would be redeemed.

Today this model is unsustainable. The crisis of developmentalism revealed its limitations, with millions of Andean migrants occupying the cities which, far from transforming them into proletarians, have integrated them into this vast and plural society, including them in that immense conceptual grab-bag called the 'informal sector', and Andeanising the old Hispanic city of colonial origin. The bigger problem for the social integration of migrant sectors into the political order of the Andean republics revolves around the persistence of an unresolved colonial legacy, whose main manifestation today is racism.

Although the defenders of the colonial order are still powerful, the situation is changing. There is a growing contradiction between a modern, egalitarian and democratic discourse (which has deeply penetrated the consciousness of the popular strata, who were previously at the margins of political activity but are now becoming increasingly incorporated into it) and the persistence of forms of ethnic and racial discrimination. The growing awareness of being systematically robbed of one's rights feeds social conflict, which has found one form of expression, among others, in political violence.

Moreover, the speed of the changes in objective reality does not correspond with people's perceptions of those changes, which tend to fall behind, particularly in periods of profound social crisis such as the present. This gap tends to deepen the crisis, since the hegemonic ideological discourse – which should guarantee the stability of the system without the need to resort to coercion – is questioned because of its increasing divergence from immediate social reality.

The political power achieved by Indianist movements in the majority of countries since the 1980s demands a revision of developmentalist assumptions and the recognition of the existence of elements of tradition and modernity in both the city and the country; the supposed economic and social stagnation of the countryside, however, has been vigorously challenged by recent studies and by the emergence of new social movements.

The Indianist movements that grew in strength in the region throughout the 1990s have succeeded in gaining significant positions within the state apparatus, brought about significant political reforms and incorporated Indian demands into the constitutions of eleven of the continent's countries. However, they have shown the limitations of Indianist ideologies as a doctrinal base for constructing autonomous policies. Indian demands have gained political space at the expense of the political autonomy of the Indian movement.

The recognition of what is 'Indian', and the legitimacy it has gained at a political level, seem to be logical correlates of the tendencies which on a global level have transformed the demand for the *right to difference* into an accepted element of the new prevailing common sense. This global change of sensibilities in the period of late capitalism can help in understanding the relative ease with which Indianist demands have been received. The possibility of constructing social and political orders which do not have cultural homogenisation as a necessary prerequisite (as occurred during the period of mass industrial society), has affected the revolutionary strain contained in the resurgence of ethnic identities. The reclaiming of the 'Indian' is a step forward in the affirmation of more democratic orders, but only as long as the exclusivity proposed by those who see in the condition of 'Indian' an immutable historic essence, charged with messianic possibilities, is rejected.

Notes

1 Fernando de Trazegnies, *La idea de derecho en el Peru republicano del siglo XIX*, PUCP Fondo Editorial, Lima, 1980.
2 Florencia Mallon, *Peasant and Nation: The Making of Postcolonial Mexico and*

Peru, University of California Press, Berkeley/Los Angeles/London, 1983; Deborah Poole (ed.), *Unruly Order: Violence, Power and Cultural Identity in the High Provinces of Southern Peru*, Westview Press, Boulder/San Francisco/ Oxford, 1994; Paul Gootenberg *Imagining Development: Economic Ideas in Peru's 'Ficticious Prosperity' of Guano, 1840–1880*, Berkeley 1993.

3 Mark Thurner, *From Two Republics to One Divided: Contradictions of Postcolonial Nationmaking in Andean Peru*, Duke University Press, Durham/London, 1997.

4 Ibid., p. 149.

5 See especially Partha Chatterjee, *Nationalist Thought and the Colonial World: A Derivative Discourse?*, Tokyo, 1986; Homi K. Bhabha, *Nation and Narration*, London/New York, 1990; Ranajit Guha, *Elementary Aspects of Peasant Insurgency in Colonial India*, Delhi, 1983.

6 Stanley and Barbara Stein, *The Colonial Heritage of Latin America*, Oxford University Press, New York, 1970.

7 As I go on to demonstrate, this integrationist perspective is not limited to conservative intellectuals. It also appears in the discourse of radical theorists.

8 See Peter Gose, *Embodied Violence: Racial Identity and the Semiotics of Property in Huaquirca, Antabamba, (Apurímac)*, Boulder/San Francisco/Oxford, 1994.

9 Benedict Anderson, *Imagined Communities: Reflections on the Origin and Spread of Nationalism*, Verso, London, 1983.

10 Nelson Manrique, *Campesinado y nación: Las guerrillas indígenas en la guerra contemporánea Chile*, Lima, 1981, pp. 55–71.

11 Tulio Halperín Donghi writes: 'The rebels did not see themselves as rebels, but inheritors of a power which had collapsed, perhaps forever: There is no reason whatsoever to see dissidence in that administrative political patrimony which they then considered theirs and which they understood that they must use to serve their own ends.' *Historia contemporánea de América Latina*, Alianza Editorial, Madrid, 1970, p. 90. Explaining the way in which Peru's second president, José de la Torre Tagle ended up imprisoned in the castle of King Felipe, together with what were the last royalist forces, who restored his rank of Brigadier General of the armies of the King, Jorge Basadre observes: 'A tenacious idea was also cultivated . . . that the Spanish were not irreconcilable adversaries in an implacable international war, but one of the parties in a civil war, in which one could take either side'. *Historia de la República del Perú, 1822–1933*, T.I., Lima, 1983, pp. 52–3.

12 A negative manifestation of this nationalism was in evidence when all of India's social sectors closed ranks around their government in the face of international condemnation of nuclear testing in 1997. In Peru in the 1920s José Carlos Mariátegui clearly pinpointed the nature of the problem of the separation between elites and the people in his polemic with Haya de la Torre, provoked by the idea of organising Apra (Alianza Popular Revolucionaria Americana) like a 'Latin American Kuo Min Tang':

> The collaboration with the bourgeoisie, even by many feudal elements of society, in the Chinese anti-imperialist struggle, is explained by reasons of race and of a national civilisation which do not exist among us. The noble or bourgeois Chinese feels Chinese to the core of his being. The contempt

for the white man and for his stratified, decrepit culture corresponds with pride in their millenarian tradition. Chinese anti-imperialism can therefore rely on this feeling and the nationalist factor. In Indo-America the circumstances are different. The aristocracy and the bourgeoisie do not feel any solidarity with the people, based on the tie of a common culture and history. *In Peru, the aristocracy and the white bourgeoisie have contempt for the popular, the national. Above all, they consider themselves to be white.* The *mestizo* petty bourgeoisie follows this example. (Emphasis mine)

José Carlos Mariátegui, 'El antiimperialismo y el Apra', (1928), in *Ideología y política*, Lima, 1973, p. 86.

13 We can add in passing that the Peruvian imagination surrounding *mestizaje* remains imprisoned within the first primary scene of the rape of the Indian woman by the white conqueror. Apparently, it is unthinkable that the spread of biological *mestizaje* might be produced, from a determined historical moment, fundamentally by means of *mestizo* unions.

14 I have traced the significance of this in the emergence of Sendero Luminoso, in Nelson Manrique, 'Political Violence, Ethnicity and Racism in Peru in the Time of War', *Journal of Latin American Studies*, Vol. 4, No. 1 (1995), London.

15 I have attempted to return to the historical genesis of Hispanic colonial racism. It was constructed out of the mind-set of the conquistadors, which reflected the conflicts faced by the Christians with Muslims and Jews in Spain in the crucial period of the establishment of the nation. The foundation of Spanish identity ended up being that of the 'old Christian', the possessor of 'pure [uncontaminated] blood', distinct and racially superior to the 'new Christians', contaminated by their 'impure' or 'infected' blood. An intolerant and excluding Christianity therefore emerged, which evolved from religious and cultural persecution to the point of open racial persecution of Jews and an obsession with racial purity that culminated in the introduction of the 'statutes of purity of blood'. These became widespread from the mid fifteenth century and throughout the sixteenth century: the same period in which America was conquered and colonised. This would have had a profound impact on the construction of the colonial order. Nelson Manrique, *Vinieron los sarracenos. El horizonte mental de la conquista de América*, Lima, 1993.

16 Its persistence has been proved during the fieldwork of more than one Caucasian anthropologist requested by Indians to procreate with their daughters, so they may 'have a gringo grand-child', or, more openly, 'to improve the race'. Not only has the conviction of their own racial inferiority been interiorised, but also that the only solution is biological mixing with the 'superior races'.

17 This process is key to an understanding of the historical weakness of Indianist ideas in Peru, compared to Bolivia and Ecuador. The disappearance of the Indian nobility deprived Peru of the social sector from which intellectuals could have emerged with the ability to produce ideologies capable of strategically projecting their demands. Add to this the fact that, in contrast to Bolivia and Ecuador, urban Indians were virtually non-existent in Peru and one can understand why in Peru the Indian problem would become a subject for consideration by the *indigenists* – creoles and *mestizos*, distant from the indigenous movement, but on whose behalf they claimed to speak.

18 Deborah Poole offers an excellent analysis of the process by which the use of technologies of mechanical image reproduction were used to this end. Deborah Poole, *Vision, Race and Modernity: A Visual Economy of the Andean Image World,* Princeton, 1997.

19 I will analyse the Peruvian case, with which I am most familiar and because it is different from that of Bolivia and Ecuador, countries where the location of the capitals in the *sierras,* densely populated by indigenous peoples, has important symbolic connotations. Peru, with its capital situated on the coast, with its back to the interior, demonstrates more clearly the process which I describe.

20 We are dealing with an ideological concept so powerful that it was even upheld by social sectors whose existence depended directly on indigenous labour for extracting economic surplus. Apparently its defenders failed to realise that the disappearance of the Indians would also signal their own disappearance as a distinct social group.

21 Even the Colonisation Law of 1893 defined immigrants as '*foreigners belonging to the white race*', N. Manrique, *Mercado interno y region: La sierra central 1820–1930,* DESCO, Lima, 1987 p. 240, PUCP Fondo Editorial, Lima, 1992.

22 Fernando de Trazegnies, *La idea de derecho en el Peru republicano del siglo XIX,* PUCP Fondo Editorial, Lima, 1992.

23 Perhaps this was an echo of the war with Chile, as the arrival in 1880 of approximately 10,000 Indians in Lima, rounded up to defend the capital from attack by the Chilean army, represented a wholly extraordinary experience for the inhabitants of the city, as the wife of Manuel González Prada, Doña Adriana Verneuill, recounted in her memoirs (1947).

24 He expressed these opinions in a booklet published in English in 1906, designed to attract foreign capital, pointing to the great advantages the country offered to investors. Nelson Manrique, *Mercado interno y región,* op. cit., pp. 252–3.

25 Jorge Basadre, *Historia de la Republica del Perú,* T. VIII, Lima 1983, p. 102.

26 José Antonio Encinas, *Contribución a una legislación tutelar indígena,* Lima, 1920, p. 9.

27 Deborah Poole, 'Ciencia, peligrosidad y represión en la criminología indigenista peruana', in C. Aguirre and C. Walker: *Bandoleros, abigeos y montoneros: Criminalidad y violencia en el Peru, siglos XVIII–XX,* Lima, 1990. The author uses 'normalise' in the Foucauldian meaning of the term – that is, the imposition of disciplinary régimes and the elaboration of disciplines of knowledge for the individuals in a society. See Michel Foucault, *Vigilar y castigar,* Mexico, 1976. Poole has contributed an important analysis of the hidden correspondences between the notion of what was an 'Indian' for the indigenists, who, like José Antonio Encinas, advocated laws of defence and redemption of the Indians, and the ideas of Positivist racists. Both shared a criminalised view of the Indian, strongly influenced by the ideas of the Italian Enrico Ferri.

28 This problem was considered to some extent in the debates on the construction of socialism and 'proletarian culture' of the last half century.

29 José Carlos Mariátegui, *7 ensayos de interpretación de la realidad peruana,* Lima, 1968, p. 273.

30 It must be pointed out that Arguedas's anthropological writing from this

period was strongly influenced by the North American culturalism dissemi-nated by Luís E. Valcárcel. See Nelson Manrique, 'José María Arguedas y el problema del mestizaje', Lima, 1996.

31 Nathan Wachtel, *Le retour des ancêtres: Les Indiens Urus de Bolivie XXe-XVIe siècle. Essai d'histoire régressive*, Éditions Gallimard, Paris 1990; Marisol de la Cadena, 'Las mujeres son más indias: etnicidad y género en una comunidad del Cusco', (*Revista Andine*, No. 17, 1991; 'La decencia y el respeto. Raza y etnicidad entre los intelectuales y las mestizas cuzqueñas', Lima, 1997. See also W. Stein's reflection on the deconstruction of the terms 'indigenous' and 'Indian', and the essentialisation of identities, constructing the 'Indian' or the 'indigenous person' as an 'other'. William Stein, 'The Fate of 'El proceso del gamonalismo': Some Vicissitudes or the Other', (ms.), Buffalo, 1997.

32 Walt Whitman Rostow, *The Stages of Economic Growth: A Non-Communist Manifesto*, Cambridge, 1960.

33 J. Cótler, *Clase, Estado y Nación en el Peru*, Instituto de Estudios Peruanos, Lima, 1978, pp. 284–6.

34 One might suspect that these two categories were grouped so as not to show the white population as a clear minority.

35 Ministry of Agriculture and Commerce, General Statistics Office, Censo Nacional de Población 1940, 9 vols., Lima, 1944, I:267.

36 The cases of Bolivia and Ecuador are significantly different, due to the fact that the capital cities are located in the *sierra*, in the middle of predominantly indigenous populations. This has allowed for the existence of a virtually non-existent category in Peru and one which has played a crucial role in the emergence of Indianist movements: that of *urban Indians*.

37 National Institute of Statistics and Information Science, Peru, 1993.

38 I have developed these ideas in the essay 'Political Violence, Ethnicity and Racism in Peru in the Time of the War', *Journal of Latin American Studies*, Vol. 4, No.1, London, 1995.

39 When advertising executives are criticised for presenting Caucasian aesthetic models (different to the phenotype of the majority of the population) as the ideal to be imitated, it is generally obvious that this is because consumers themselves are prepared to identify with these archetypes.

40 Rädda Barnen, 'Voces con futuro: Sondeo Nacional opinión de niños e adolescentes' ('Voices with a Future: National Opinion Poll of Children and Adolescents'), No.15, Lima, July, 1995.

41 Xavier Albó, 'El retorno del indio', *Revista Andina*, 9, No. 18 (1991), Cuzco, p. 302.

42 Ibid., p. 331.

43 Xavier Albó co-wrote an essay with Víctor Hugo Cárdenas in which they evaluated the historical significance of the emergence of Katarism as a politi-cal alternative: 'From MNR istas to Kataristas to Katari', in Steve J. Stern (ed.), *Resistance, Rebellion, and Consciousness in the Andean World: 18th to 20th century*, Madison, University of Wisconsin Press, 1987. After the alliance of Cárdenas with the MNR Albó wrote another essay entitled 'Del Katarismo ¿al MNR?' A reading of both texts offers an interesting view of this political process.

44 The presence of non-governmental development organisations has played an
important role in this process, accompanying the organisation of indigenous
groups. Furthermore, this phenomenon is common to the development of
Indianism throughout the region.

Translated by Lorraine Leu

10

The Hesitations of the Modern and the Contradictions of Modernity in Brazil

José de Souza Martins

I

The theme of modernity is closely bound up with the idea of progress. For that reason, it is a theme of wealthy societies and, above all, it is a European theme.[1] In Latin America it is still confused, by some, with the theme of the modern in opposition to the traditional, in a curious revival of the dualist concepts of the 1950s and '60s. This interpretation, of positivist origin, reinforces a conception of history as following determined stages and relegates to the past that which supposedly does not belong to the period of modernity, such as the traditionalism of poor rural migrants, popular culture and poverty itself. These are regarded as anomalous and obsolete manifestations of a social formation which, with the growing and inevitable diffusion of modernity arising out of economic development and globalisation, has become extinct.

As I see it, however – and I hope to demonstrate this here – the study of modernity in Latin America does indeed involve acknowledging its anomalous and inconclusive nature, despite the fact that in this underdeveloped region, modernity has become almost an obsession in this era of globalisation: more than a reality, modernity is a topic of discussion. Unemployment and underemployment, and the values and the mentalities produced by dependent development are integral parts of modernity, although from a theoretical and typological perspective they do not form part of it.

Modernity is only present when it can be both the modern and the critical consciousness of the modern – the situated modern, an object of consciousness and reflection.[2] Modernity, in this sense, is not to be confused with the objects and signs of modernity, because it is not restricted to them, nor can it be separated from the rationality which created the ethic of the multiplication of capital – an ethic which introduced calculation, through which social action becomes a means to an end, into the social life and morality of the average person in the street.[3] I am referring to the ethic which transforms the subject into an object, including an object of an individual person, the subject as a stranger to the self.[4]

As a trend and a moment modernity is also the permanence of the transitory and the uncertain, in the face of linear and supposedly infinite progress: finite life confronting social reality, the future, supposedly without end.[5] Modernity resides not only, or even principally, in the collection of signs of the modern which traverse all our lives in different ways; modernity is the social and cultural reality produced by the consciousness of the transience of the new and the present.

Modernity, moreover, is not constructed through the homogenising union of humanity's diversity, as the concept of globalisation suggests. It consists of unequal rhythms of economic and social development, in turn produced by accelerated technological advances and disproportional capital accumulation, by the immense and increasingly globalised misery of those who hunger and thirst not just for what is essential to sustain human life, but also for justice, work, dreams, happiness.[6] This hunger and thirst are for the democratic realisation of the promises of modernity – for what is in reality accessible only to some but which, simultaneously and paradoxically, appears to be for all.

Modernity thus announces the possible, but fails to realise it.[7] Modernity is a kind of demystifying mystification of the immense possibilities of human and social transformation which capitalism was able to create, but is not able to realise. It mystifies as it demystifies because it places before the consciousness of each human being, and in the daily life of everyone, the whole immense catalogue of concepts and alternative ways of life which are available on the global market. You need only the resources to have it all. It mystifies as it demystifies because it announces that there are things which are possible in a possible world, but there is no item in this immense market which can tell you how to obtain such resources, which performs the simple miracle of transforming the possible into the real. This each of us has to discover alone; this the collectivity of victims, those included but in an excluding way, have to discover for themselves.

In contrast to what happened in the period of classical capitalism, the capitalism connected to the theoretical and interpretative models which emerged between the second half of the nineteenth century and the Second World War, is no longer enclosed in a functional cycle of effective deceptions and mystifications. It is no longer possible to effectively conceal the contradictions by means of ideologies which cover them over with their coherent and logical deceptions. Modernity is precisely that moment in contemporary history in which the concern is not to conceal the injustices, exploitation and human degradation suffered by those condemned to carry the weight of history on their shoulders. Modernity is, in a certain sense, the kingdom of cynicism: it is constituted by a denunciation of the inequality and the rifts which characterise it. In it, capitalism anticipates the radical criticism of its chief victims.

It is, in this sense, also the critical consciousness of the modern – that is, the rejection of transience and the impotence that it implies. Modernity exists only in the perspective of history and the historicity of humanity – in the certainty, rather than the uncertainty, that life and praxis lead to the constitution of the human, the humanisation of man, and not simply and permanently to objectification.[8] But this can be realised only where the rationality of capital is fully and openly proposed; in the Third World it is proposed only in an unfinished, uncertain and disguised way.

Modernity proposes itself much more as a strategy for understanding and administering the irrationalities and contradictions of capitalist society than as the limitless dissemination of Western and capitalist rationality. What it proposes as an everyday experience is not limitless rationality, but its problems, its inconclusiveness, its difficulties. The average individual has to discover and invent ways to overcome them. Modernity is installed when conflict becomes a daily experience – in particular, cultural conflict, disputes over social values, the permanent need to choose between one thing and another, between the new and the fleeting on the one hand, and custom and tradition on the other. However, it is a choice exhausted right from the start, because it is an impossible choice: the world, including the world of daily life, is no longer one thing or the other, it is various and diverse. Modernity is not just the modern, and modernism even less so.[9] In Latin America, it is a modernity constituted simultaneously of diverse historical times, of temporalities which are not its own, incorporating vestiges of other structures and situations which still, however, represent living, vital realities and relationships,[10] and which announce the historicity of humanity in these collages – these mismatches of times, rhythms and possibilities.

In different societies these difficulties present themselves in different ways. It is necessary therefore that we also understand and handle them in different ways. If modernity is the permanently provisional – and the transitory as a way of life, a fashion – our concern is to find out what form it assumes in societies such as those of Latin America and Brazil in particular, in many ways so different from the rest of Latin America. If, ultimately, modernity is the transitory, and the consciousness of the transitory, how do the singular social conditions of this society propose a singular and unique consciousness, a critical consciousness of the modern, which is part of the modern but which is not, at the same time, an expression of a conservative consciousness – and – therefore a rejection of the modern?

In Britain, E.P. Thompson drew attention to the importance of tradition in placing social limits on the imposition of capitalist rationality and the dominance of the profit motive at all levels of social life.[11] He demonstrated that modern social rights lay in this resistance rather than in the universalisation and unilateral imposition of the interests of capital. This imposition signified the transformation of the human subject into an object, into a victim of the modernising rationality which, despite being modified by social interests and resistance to it, created a way of viewing oneself in society in an objective and impersonal way.

According to Erich Fromm's premise, logic imposes a state of wakefulness as a way of life while the nocturnal and dream consciousness, the irrational in other words, remains as a counterpoint which humanises the growing rationalisation of society.[12] It is this anguish to which Weber refers when he speaks of the movement which defines civilisation, and in the contemporary period defines the modern and modernity: infinity, an absence of rhythms, the anguish of inevitable death and the consciousness of the finite in the face of an imaginary of infinite progress and the eternal.[13]

In the Latin American and, in particular, the Brazilian case, the critical element within modernity is generated by cultural 'hybridity', by the conjunction of past and present, the finished and the unfinished. It arises out of the recourse to traditionalism and conservatism, which questions modern social reality and the concepts which are part of it and mediate it; the oppression and the absurdity of the modern, of rationality, quantity, the transitory and fleeting as a permanent way of living and being.

It is in Brazilian literature more than in the social sciences that this fundamental sociological dimension of its reality appears in a clear fashion. Macunaíma, Mário de Andrade's character, is the hero without character, the indefinite, the hybrid. But it is in Guimarães Rosa's work that the founding characteristic of the country's social history and of Brazilian culture – the crossing – is posed in the most beautiful and coherent way. It is in the crossing, the passage without arrival, in the unfinished and inconclusive, in the permanently incomplete, that our way of being is present – in the dangers of the indefinite and of liminality, which render living itself dangerous. And above all, it is in this idea of a literary consciousness of doubles, of the different expressions of the false,[14] of the detachment of form from content, that our understandable fear of crossings, our condition as victims rather than beneficiaries of modernity is located.[15]

But it is also in literature that our difficulties in making the crossing are posed in a clear way. In *O Coronel e o Lobishomem* (The Colonel and the Werewolf), by José Cândido de Carvalho, the character does not distinguish between the world of the living and the world of the dead; he does not distinguish between the real and the fantastic. This is a very Latin American theme: it is present in *Cien Años de Soledad* (*One Hundred Years of Solitude*), by Gabriel García Márquez, where life is diluted in the uneven rhythm of a time which has slowed down and in the consciousness of that slowness; in *Redoble por Rancas* (Drums for Rancas), by Manuel Scorza, in the fence which advances by itself, as if endowed with a life of its own, enclosing, obstructing and defeating the man between late afternoon one day and dawn of the following day; it is present in the lack of distinction between the mythical and the real in *Pedro Páramo* and in *El Llano en Llamas* (The Burning Plane), by Juan Rulfo; it is in Carlos Fuentes' beautiful television series, *El Espejo Enterrado* (*The Buried Mirror*).[16]

This difficulty is also articulated in Rulfo's extraordinary photography, in the depth of perspective which reveals the impotent smallness of humans in the New World, or their residual character with respect to ruined monuments and scenes, the world of the margin, of the most remote places in society, of human labour lost on the horizon.[17] It is apparent in Sebastião Salgado's photography, which portrays members of the human race in the Third World confronted with objects and situations which defeat them, swallowed up by the immense works of capital, marked and weighed down by the burden of work where accumulation is still primitive accumulation. This is clear in the photographic series on the Serra Pelada gold mine in Brazil: faces covered with coal dust; bodies covered in petroleum, in mud; people physically converted into extensions of objects.[18] Even through Lévi-Strauss's foreign gaze, in his beautiful series of photographs on Brazil, the signs of modernity in the city and the countryside appear distant or invasive, or like diffuse difficulties of the crossing into modernity.[19] Incidentally, it is in the engravings and drawings of European travellers of the nineteenth century that the strangeness of modernity comes to Brazil: it comes as a startled gaze which highlights the anti-modern, the exotic and the tropical in people and scenes. Modernity comes to us, therefore, in reverse and through its foreignness, as an expression of seeing and not of being, living and happening. It comes to us as an immediate and uncomfortable modernity, in the guise of the burden borne on the back of the black slave, himself a denial of capital and capitalism, but nonetheless a human and dehumanised representation of wealth at that historical moment. It comes to us in the form of the daily invigilation in the hidden panopticon of a whole São Paulo Railway workers' town, Vila de Paranapiacaba (built in the nineteenth century, in Alto da Serra, São Paulo).[20] More than a hundred years later the streets are still haunted by the phantasmal disciplining gaze and the power of capital over labour, in the order of the street layout and the position and shape of the houses.

What parameters does modernity set in order to 'see itself', situate itself, understand itself (deny itself) in these situations? It turns to the (un)modern, to the not modern, to the rustic world, to the backlands, where our roots supposedly lie; in that which remained as a residue at the margin of the limited rationality of the profit motive in the colonial world, and during the process of constituting the internal market in the post-colonial world; in that which seems external to the new order, which does not seem to be part of it.

The point of reference for a critical understanding (both Brazilian and Latin American) of modernity, in art, literature and the social sciences, has been this confrontation between the new – with its logical, rational and secularised norms – on the one hand, and what tradition has left us – the works of the past, which are also the left-overs, irrelevant, invulnerable to the mechanisms of domination and exploitation – on the other. That is the way in which what is false, alien and 'foreign' about the modern in relation to ourselves has been made apparent; by focusing on the clash between historical times which marks and delineates Brazilian and Latin American reality, social relations, mentalities and utopias. Our social inequalities are also an expression of the historical chasm between ourselves and what is already real elsewhere, which comes to us fragmentarily, incompletely. The vigour of our social, economic and stylistic forms is what makes us agents of an apparent modernity, divested of profound links with social processes, and is thus a declaration of our deprivation.

It is in the consciousness of these clashes and confrontations that the interpretative method present in literature, in art and the social sciences, takes shape. It can appear as positivism here and dialectics there, or it can be the hybridised confusion of both epistemological frameworks. In the formal differences between these distinct canons of production of knowledge and social consciousness, there is an underlying procedure which is revealing: both positivism and dialectics, although in radically different ways, refer to the incongruous co-existence of historical periods, to the inequalities they express, to the historical obstacles in Latin America to the complete fulfilment of promises and possibilities fulfilled more easily and naturally in the metropolitan and hegemonic countries.[21]

Our criticism, the criticism which pervades our social consciousness in the documents which express it – literature, art, the social sciences – is not a humanist criticism, where resistance is engaged in the production of the new and constituting a part of it, as in Thompson's analyses to which I referred earlier. Nor is it a criticism which arises from the social interests of the victims of dependent and distorted development, already a basis for understanding the shifts and social transformations centred on profit and accumulation, and the social problems which they generate (the basis, therefore, for an active antagonism). Our criticism consists rather in resistance to the new, which highlights the irrationalities and the dehumanisation which it contains and disseminates. But it is passive resistance, dissimulated, not echoed in doctrines, parties or organised cultural and political action.

Even the nationalist consciousness which feeds off popular tradition represents a political recognition of the irrationalities of the modern. It is an incongruous combination, because the nationist ideology underpinning the developmentalist policies of recent decades upholds the modern without promoting modernity. It champions the rationality of profit, the rational organisation of labour, the colourful spectacle of the mass media – but it is at the same time conservative, resistant to the way of life associated with modernity – that is to say, it resists the social instability arising out of political and cultural plurality and difference. Politically, we have a liberal bent, but it is a liberalism based on the traditions of personal power and political clientelism. The contradiction flutters on the national flag: 'Order and Progress'. With us, progress has been subordinated to the primacy of order, even when we appear to be convincingly modern.

Consequently, in Brazil the traditional only slowly became a vantage point for criticism of the irrationalities of the modern, while modernity was greeted by us with fits of laughter, theatrical, literary and musical irony, and even with street anecdotes – as if it didn't really bring with it profound social transformations, as if it were only an error of history.[22] *Sertaneja* music (an urban musical genre rooted in rural, *caipira* traditions) emerged in São Paulo at the end of the 1920s, on the eve of the modernising Revolution of 1930. It was from the beginning a biting critique of the most representative elements of modernity in the city, as well as a means of comprehending it – a musical genre which combined elements from the old travelling circus and the new possibilities offered by records and the radio.[23] It was a genre which emerged on the point of the decisive emergence of the contours of modernity in Brazil, in contrast with the rural and traditional world that was crumbling away.

The best expression of our critical consciousness of modernity is mockery, rather than social demands or social criticism which could lead to some control over the paths of modernisation, in the interests of those damaged by it. This is the origin of our distorted form of criticism. The period following the Revolution of 1930 – characterised by an intense diffusion of the modern and a transformation of the stabilities and certainties of the traditional, agricultural society into the instabilities and uncertainties of an urban–industrial society – was also marked by the conscious recovery of the traditional as a counterpoint and as the basis of this ironical perspective.

In contrast to what occurred in England, as described by Thompson, the criticism of modernity in Brazil did not involve opposing customary rights to the voracity and exploitation of capital, to modernisation and developmentalism. Laughter is a clear indication of this. There was a simple reason for this: the world of tradition was and had been much more associated with faith and festivity than the world of rules relating to labour relations, customary rights and privileges linked to craft associations. Brazilian society, based on slavery and institutionalised ethnic and social inequality, in which craft associations were extremely weak – more instruments of the King's control over the people than a means of affirming the rights of the people in the face of an absolute monarchy – never drew on a code of social rights. It was more a society of punishment and deprivation than a society of privilege. A polity stratified on the basis of estates, Portugal regulated social relations in Brazil only where it was necessary to guarantee the privileges of the white, catholic elite and maintain the social differences on which they were based. And even independent and republican Brazil has been slow to affirm the social equality of all, blacks and whites, women and men, poor and wealthy.

In Brazil traditionalism acted as a point of reference for a national rather than a social consciousness. Even as nationalism declines in this era of globalisation, popular culture, the most lively expression of traditionalism, has apparently experienced no difficulties in adjusting to modernity. In contrast to what other commentators may think, I believe that there is a contradiction here to be explained. Popular culture carries its historical time with it, which is only slowly diluted to give way to uprooted cultural forms deprived of the ties of authenticity which gave them meaning in other times and other situations. Undoubtedly modernity can process the traditional and customary, which it needs as pure forms, into disposable realities. Even then, the recovery of popular culture and the traditionalism it expresses and contains can be integrated into modernity only as an anomaly and a problem – especially since this traditionalism encapsulates the past (even if brought up to date) while modernity is dominated by the transitory.

In this context, the constitution of the national doesn't *necessarily* express a moment of modernity, but rather the difficulties of the modern. In the Brazilian case, the modernisation brought about by the Revolution of 1930, with its political centralisation and its economically developmentalist politics, sought its legitimacy in popular culture and tradition, which formed the cultural roots of nationalism. In that sense the constitution of the national expresses not the non-viability of the modern and of modernisation, but the hesitations of modernity.

However, in my view, the situation is more complex. In the above-mentioned references, it appears as if artistic and literary thought incorporates the popular in order to create authentic, local forms not based on mere imitation. But, in fact, what is made evident here is that we are inauthentic. As I see it, that combination suggests the search for specificity and uniqueness in order to achieve distance from cultural imitation – a search for authenticity. What is made evident here is that we are inauthentic. Macunaíma is not authentic; he has no character.[24] *Umbanda* is an inauthentic form of *candomblé* distorted by police repression.[25] Aren't contemporary Pentecostal sects an inauthentic protestant-ism brought forth by the present day conditions of capitalist development? They are an emotional version of protestantism – an affirmation and negation of historical protestantism. And popular catholicism is fundamentally an inauthentic form of Roman Catholicism. Our authenticity resides in the inauthentic.

II

From this perspective, I think that it is methodologically necessary to conduct research into Brazilian modernity through a different route from the thesis that argues that the popular is incorporated by modernity in order to lend it a character and identity of its own. I propose that a more fruitful approach to the question of modernity in Brazil lies in investigating the way that the modern and the signs of the modern are incorporated by the popular. It is in this mediation that the difficulties and dilemmas of modernity can be observed.

The numerous observations I have made in the peripheries of the big cities, in the countryside and at the expanding frontier of Brazilian society[26] reveal the modern transformed into simulation, mask, an expression of inauthenticity. In these instances, the modern is captured and drawn into a web of social relations which have not been modernised beyond a certain point, hindered by the condition of dependency in the peripheral regions generated by capitalism. Traditional, peasant society itself constitutes the basis of the critique of the modern, the indistinct criticism which expresses itself much more in laughter than in organised thought. Even so, it is still criticism and it undoubtedly illuminates the incongruities, failures and irrationalities of modernity. This critical laugh is contained precisely in, and born out of, the disjointed and grotesque juncture between what is actually modern and what is not; in the forced co-existence of mismatched relationships, cultures juxtaposed and thereby disfigured. The modern, in that case, is not substantively itself. Because of this we are all ambiguous, imprisoned in the uncertainties of an inconclusive and aimless crossing.

These difficulties are present not only in the sphere of culture but in real social relationships. The extensive spread in the last few years of peonage or debt slavery, in the new ranches along the frontier which have opened up with the new wave of occupation of Amazônia (to give one example) reveals a structural difficulty in the expansion of the capitalist mode of capital reproduction and hence at the very heart of modernity. Here things are combined in strange ways. The ranches where the greatest numbers of enslaved workers have been found actually belong to large economic conglomerates, frequently to multinationals. Slavery here is not a legacy from a past of large estates and hardened landowners clinging to traditions of personal dominance. On the contrary, these are ranches organised according to the most advanced ideas and possibilities of large scale capital.

When it still belonged to the German Volkswagen group, the Vale do Rio Cristalino ranch, which reared cattle for slaughter and export to Germany, used the most sophisticated technology: chips were implanted in the animals as a means of monitoring their health and determining the optimum moment for slaughter. The information obtained in this way, in the pastures of the south of Pará, in Amazônia, was processed by computer and transmitted daily to the headquarters of the company in São Paulo, where the crucial decisions were made. The slaughtered cattle were immediately loaded onto Boeing aircraft and unloaded the following day in Germany. However, the basis of all these notable expressions of modernity was the work of 500 slaves employed in deforestation and the creation of pasture.

That is just one case among many revealed and denounced by humanitarian organisations, and even government authorities, in the last thirty years or so. Eighty thousand such captives were recorded in that period, taking into account only cases which came to light and were verified. Large financial corporations and multinational companies use slavery to extend modernisation to the new frontier territories. It is possible to demonstrate, as I have already done, that such socially irrational and non-capitalist labour relations insert themselves rationally into the process of the increased reproduction of capital, because they are more lucrative than salaried labour. The so-called primitive accumulation of capital, on the periphery of the capitalist world, is not a moment which pre-dates capitalism, but is contemporary with actual capitalist accumulation.[27] Undoubtedly this is a contradiction, which renders an understanding of social dynamics more complex.

If at one extreme of capitalist development we are confronted with difficulties such as these, at the opposite pole we also find situations which make modernity into an artifice. The colonial economy was based on the combination of the direct production of subsistence goods and the production of goods for sale to the metropolitan countries: sugar and coffee.[28] The workers generally produced items for their own subsistence, but also dedicated themselves to the production of an exportable commodity, generally on land which was not their own. In the sphere of subsistence production each worker created (and still does) a world of non-capitalist social relations: not only are the techniques primitive (agriculture is still based on the hoe), but social relations are family- and community-based.

Obviously this world suffers various contaminations from the market economy, due not only to the commercialisation of surplus subsistence products, but also to the purchase of articles which are complementary to subsistence (cloth, kerosene for lighting, some foodstuffs, medicine), and possibly, also, to the monetary return, albeit low, earned by tending the products specifically destined for the market. Although the direct production of subsistence goods has had and still has the function of reducing the labour costs associated with commercial or export goods, it did give rise to a way of life which is characteristic of the rural areas. Commodities arrive at the worker's house as a luxury or as something which is alien to that way of life, and it is not by chance that these goods end up acquiring an almost fetishistic value.

Tins and plastic bottles are reused for many more purposes than they were originally intended to serve: disposable plastic cups are washed and re-employed for domestic use; empty tins of condensed milk are still transformed into mugs for water or coffee; empty kerosene containers become water pitchers or watering cans; even containers of lethal agricultural pesticides are recycled into domestic utensils. What Oscar Lewis defined as a culture of poverty,[29] characterised by this accumulation of the refuse of the wealthy, reveals itself to be an increasingly integral part of modernity, in contradiction to what anthropologists previously believed.

Evidence of the cultural need to distinguish what is new from what is used and reused is not difficult to find. In a journey I made between Marabá, in Pará, and Imperatriz, in the Amazonian region of Maranhão, the bus stopped repeatedly along the route to pick up and drop off passengers, as buses do in the north-east. During the long journey, my companion was a relatively young man who night and day wore Ray-Ban-type sunglasses, like the ones associated with photos of General MacArthur. To my surprise, I saw that one of the lenses still bore the golden sticker of the manufacturer's trademark. The heat and the dust were terrible. Every so often, the passenger carefully took off his sunglasses and, with a handkerchief already dirty with sweat and dust, he 'cleaned' the lenses carefully, taking care not to remove the sticker.

That is undoubtedly one indication of a certain consciousness of the transience of the modern, of the possibility of the symbolic deterioration of the object; but it is also an indication that in that periphery of the modern world artifice is used to prolong the state of the new, according to the traditional, peasant logic of use-value – the logic of the user rather than the consumer. Rather than preserving a state of newness in the object, this action operated to preserve a *signal* of newness. However, the symbol of the new, the dark glasses, is swallowed up by an anti-modern logic, although it continues to appear modern. That is the point: to look modern, more than actually to be modern. Modernity appears, therefore, as a mask on show. It is situated more in the sphere of what is seen than what is lived. Now, even if the time of masking belongs to the past, the mask is the superficial and phenomenal identity characteristic of modernity. The temporalities contained in things and in their relationships in a way become false, articulated by a contemporary force which values appearance above all else.

At another cultural level, I recall something I observed when I was conducting some research into traditional, *caipira* music in a quite typical area of subsistence agriculture, a little more than 100 kilometres from the city of São Paulo. I was interviewing an elderly and famous *caipira viola* player of the rural district, a well-known master of the São Gonçalo dance.[30] At one point his son, still quite young, turned up. I asked him if he played the *viola* too. He said no, that the viola was a hick thing, for yokels, although he also lived and worked on the land. I wanted to know if he played any other instrument. He answered that he played the guitar. As we know, in Brazil the *viola* is a sign of the rural and the guitar a sign of the urban. He showed me his guitar. In order to erase all doubt that his musical taste could not be confused with his father's 'backward' and 'uncultured' tastes, he had placed a sticker of a vision of *Nossa Senhora Aparecida* (Our Lady the Appeared) on the front and next to it he had had engraved: 'Ai love iú bêbi' (I love you baby)!

Everywhere, in rural areas or in the poor periphery of big cities, one can see phrases and words in English which come with globalisation as signs of modernity. The word arrives, but the language – even the meaning – does not. It is not unusual to attend mass in churches in the poor suburbs, with an illiterate or superficially literate population, and see people wearing tee-shirts with some obscenity or erotic phrase written on the back.[31] Basically, what attracts the user is the form and colour of the letters, even though he or she may be completely unaware of the meaning of the words.

Even objects capable of defining their own use, like the car and the bus, end up being used according to a logic opposed to that of the modernity which they supposedly represent. I remember a journey I made between Porto Alegre do Norte and São Félix do Araguaia, in Mato Grosso, on a bus which made the trip three times a week. It left at dawn, and was always full. Once it set off, the bus quickly reached the last streets of the little village. A passenger got up and timidly asked if the driver would pass by the house of Compadre So-and-So, as he needed to pick up some sacks of rice to sell, which was the reason he was making the journey. The angry driver told him that it was a bus, that it had a timetable and an itinerary. The passenger said nothing, waited a while, returned to his seat and then went back to the driver: 'Ah! Then I'd better not go.' He was left at the side of the road, in the darkness of early morning, already some distance from the village.

Throughout the journey similar kinds of thing happened: passengers waited for the bus to come to a complete stop before beginning their lengthy farewells to fellow travellers right at the back of the vehicle, as if they were taking leave of friends at one of those typical rural get-togethers; others, waiting for the bus at the roadside, waited until it came to a standstill before they began to bid farewell to those who had accompanied them as far as the bus stop, imparting innumerable pieces of advice on the care of their domestic animals and asking to be remembered to people they had said goodbye to only moments before.

This obvious clash between the body educated in the principles of decorum and tradition, and therefore in the principles of the precedence of the person over the object, and the vehicle conceived and used according to the contrary logics of time and money, brings both into contact and into tension the rhythms and conceptions of contrasting worlds. The social world is old and antiquated, but the bus of modernity has arrived.

The big cities in Brazil are replete with signs of the anomalies of modernity. Daily life is progressively dominated by behaviour, gestures and mentalities where cultural hybridity makes itself present: in styles of dress, in food, as well as in the use of the private car among the middle classes and the wealthy. It is not unusual for modern automobiles to be driven as if the drivers were riding a wild horse, without the least consideration for what is undoubtedly one of the components of modernity: traffic rules and regulations. It is as if each person's 'animal' made its own rules.

The situation of the so-called excluded, in big cities like São Paulo, leads to a complicated combination of modernity and extremes of poverty and destitution (or might destitution be one of the components of modernity?). In the São Remo *favela*, which grew following an invasion of public and private lands near the University of São Paulo as well as on land belonging to the university itself, there is a chaotic group of unfinished, disorderly houses, whose inhabitants form a small part of the services staff of the university.[32] However, a surprising number of satellite dishes indicate that many of these incomplete and precarious houses are no strangers to sophisticated satellite technology and the luxurious and manipulable imaginary of television. It is as if people lived inside the image and survived on images. In the imaginary of modernity, the image has become a nutrient as fundamental as bread, water and the book – or even more so. It justifies all sacrifices, deprivations and transgressions.

As I see it, this arises out of an occurrence of what Henri Lefebvre has defined as the power of forms, referring to a situation in which, with the development of capitalism, different social and ideological forms acquire a life of their own. The theory of capitalist development has for a long time tended to insist on a necessary connection between

economic development, social development and the formation of ideologies and institutions. Time has shown, however, that these distinct
spheres develop differently, and the more capitalism grows globally and
extends spatially, the more autonomous social forms seem to become.
At the same time, these forms grow in their capacity to capture the real
and the imaginary.

This apparent autonomy is responsible for the intermingling of
dissimilar and non-contemporaneous elements, which is precisely one
of the basic characteristics of modernity as a way of thinking and a way
of life. It seems as if everything can be combined. Strangers no longer
appear strange. It is not surprising, therefore, that where there is a lack
of food there is a glut of images. In this specific world, which is the
world of modernity, the fissures which divide and separate what should
not be together, are cemented together by the imaginary. Essentially,
as Lefebvre posits, modernity has stimulated the imaginary (the capacity
for fabrication) and restricted the imagination (the social capacity to
develop innovative solutions to problems). With this, the social capacity
for rationalising and justifying the unjustifiable has increased. Imaginative competence has become a strategy for life and even for survival.

I can illustrate the dramatic force of this situation with a recent event
which I learnt of quite by chance. As no doubt occurs all over the
world, the President of the Republic receives a large number of letters
from the country's citizens on a daily basis, containing the most diverse
appeals and requests. A team of letter-readers are in charge of directing
them to the appropriate departments, from where they will receive an
answer. One of these letters was written by a teenage girl and read: 'I
am black and ugly. But my life's dream is to be one of Xuxa's *paquitas*'.

False modernity is documented in that moving letter. The writer
believes that the President of the Republic is capable of resolving one
of the most serious of the country's social problems – racial prejudice –
which she herself involuntarily propagates. Xuxa is a famous children's
presenter on Brazilian television; white, blonde and light-eyed, she is a
descendant of migrants from the north of Italy. She appears on
television surrounded by a court of teenage girls, the *paquitas*, her
assistants, who are also white. In the letter and the incident several
traces of our problematic society are evident: racism, a naive conception
of how power operates, and the power of television to disseminate an
imaginary which makes a black teenage girl see herself as ugly because
she is not blonde and blue-eyed, and does not conform to the most
revered image. In the end, this is a simulacrum of citizenship and
democracy: all citizens can now address the President of the Republic
freely; but the request of the black teenager is not a request that

democracy can entertain. She is the victim of a double misunderstanding: on the one hand, the confusion between citizen and mendicant; on the other, the confusion between the real and the imaginary. Defenceless, she is ensnared by the imaginary and ends up negating herself.

Another expression of anomalous modernity is the way in which public and private buildings in the city of São Paulo, the icon of urban modernity in Brazil, are completely defaced by spray-paint graffiti. It is rarely possible to discern a single word that makes sense. Generally, they are signs of a hermetic knowledge accessible only to youth gangs. This graffiti is the inscription of nothingness. Writing in this case is a scrawl, a sign of the sign, document of the hybrid, but, above all, of the inconclusive and of the superficiality of the modern represented by the can of paint and the possibilities of its domestic or artistic use. It is only a symbolic demarcation of territory, possession and command. Without a doubt, in evidence here is an expression of a desire for power and, at the same time, an acknowledgement of one's own impotence in the face of the modernity which excludes and deprecates those who do not have access to it and are not included in it.

This kind of graffiti indicates a wish to possess the city, not through its use, as a citizen or as a socially integrated individual would, but by the predatory consumption of those whose relationship with the city in which they live is one of alienation and disaffection. It is not about creating meanings and forms, but destroying them, of disfiguring the scenario and the references of the everyday and of everyone. It is the portrait of a lack of social consciousness, of the discontinuity between the functional illiteracy of those who deface property and the culture of the monument (and the civilisation which it represents and signifies). It is the attempt to impose the visual language of the illiterate on the visual and artistic language of the building. It is a war of symbols. It is a denunciation of the gap between the included and the excluded (and of the fact that the exclusion is also cultural and much more extensive than economic exclusion). It is a denunciation, moreover, of the lack of consciousness of the discrepancy between the scrawl and the word; a document, in fact, of easy access to the modern instrument, the spray-can, and the lack of access to the best modernity has to offer: graphite, the art of graffiti, words and images with meaning.

The most vigorous social movement in Brazil at present is also an expression of the clashes of this alien and uprooted modernity. The Rural Workers Landless Movement,[33] a powerful organisation of peasants expelled from or deprived of land which they need in order to work, rally to socialism in their struggle. The organisation's political radicalism goes as far as its members refusing to participate in the political process, even to nominate candidates to the National Congress through the Workers' Party, which they support and which supports them. I heard from a national director of the Movement, at a public conference in Rio de Janeiro, that when an anxious worker asked him if the participants of the Movement were revolutionaries and if they were preparing the revolution, he replied that yes, they were revolutionaries and that because of this they did not intend to nominate any candidate to the country's 'bourgeois parliament'.

Curiously, however, in the peasant settlements organised and directed by the Movement, the most important ingredient is technological and economic modernisation, accompanied by extraordinary social creativity – a real reinvention of society, representing an explicit reaction to the perverse effects of an excluding development and of modernity itself. In general, there is a large number of young people, especially young couples, in the land occupation camps, in the settlements and on land officially distributed by the government. This is explained by the fact that the Movement is above all a movement of young rural workers for whom continuous work on the land is no longer viable due to the lack of land on small-holdings capable of permanently sustaining more than one family, in general the paternal family.

The members of these settlements are young workers who come from very conservative families, with a family-orientated vision of the world, who remain aloof in the company of people they do not know. In the camps, because of the struggle for the land and as a result of living and engaging in collective confrontations with strangers, they are re-socialised. In the settlements, with their horizons broadened by the unstable social condition of the camps, they become receptive to the outside world. However, at the same time, they return to the fundamental familial structures of the rural neighbourhood. In the modernising re-socialisation of the camps, in fact, traditional ideas with respect to kinship and other relationships are reinforced, acquiring a new dynamism. Thus, in the camps society is literally being reinvented, opening up to broader conceptions of social relations, while at the same time strengthening the organising concepts of social life derived from the legacy of familialism.

With the new practices on the settlements, participants learn to reorder the productive structures characteristic of family-based forms of agriculture. Following the same traditions of intense utilisation of the labour-time of all members of the family, inherited from their parents and grandparents, the young workers diversify their economic activities, combining handicraft industry and agriculture, and incorporating modern techniques and equipment as well as modern practices of commercialisation. The experience of the camps has already taught them extra-familial and extra-neighbourly forms of co-operation, which have more to do with a new and more modern division of labour than with strictly older forms of mutual assistance. Thus it is precisely modern technology and the modern economy which end up making traditional forms of organisation, production and social life viable and profitable, as is also happening in Asian countries.

A similar phenomenon occurred with the Parakatêjê Indians in the south of Pará. Almost extinct, having been virtually enslaved, gathering Brazil nuts for FUNAI, the National Foundation for the Indian, they revived their traditions and institutions when they discovered, with the help of an anthropologist, how to earn money from the gathering activities in which they were engaged. They then began to administer their own resources and commercialise the Brazil nuts directly. Very soon the tribe had a sizeable bank account.

In order to motivate the tribe and to avoid the divisive effects of money, the indigenous chief now invoked tribal traditions on the use of communal goods – in relation to hunting, for example. He strengthened his own authority as chief, sharing the goods out to others first, waiting until last himself. Televisions, a calculator, a computer, and brick houses were distributed in accordance with the traditions of the tribe, and a men's house in the centre of the village, also made of brick and containing a television, became the designated site for the evening ceremonies. Thus modern materials and tools were entirely absorbed by the old institutions, concepts and forms of tribal tradition.

This is the form that modernity assumes for those populations less likely to integrate into the modern world. It is in fact making capitalism viable for populations that even the left has always thought to be condemned to historical non-viability and eventual disappearance. In essence, these populations are significantly extending the terrain of modernity and of the capitalism which sustains and justifies it.

In the case of the landless, their socialist ideology, as I see it, seems to fulfil the same function of creating a civilised modernity which the privileges of the craft associations and the customs of a moral economy once had in the constitution of social rights, as Thompson observed in the English case.

This collage of disparate social realities points to a further characteristic of Latin American modernity which is not limited to Brazil: the precariousness and fragmented quality of everyday life, the continuous interactions between dream, play, fantasy, carnival, religion (or rather religions, given the prevalent syncretism in the daily life of each person) and the struggle for survival.[34]

Here historical times are mixed and confused in everyday life, while similarly the cognitive styles of the different worlds which define our social life are confused and inverted. It is as if we were already post-modern before modernity arrived; or, as suggested by Canclini, it is as if we were post-modern centuries ago.[35] Unfortunately, our social scientists have not been sufficiently interested in the wealth of anthropological detail contained in the expression of social alienation arising out of the historical peculiarities of capitalist development in Latin America. Rather, as mentioned above, it is Latin American literature that has captured the imperceptible continuity between reality and fantasy – between real, social relations and the imaginary.

III

What we are faced with is a deeply ingrained culture, marked by an assimilationist, integrationist logic, capable of uniting the diverse and, above all, of conciliating antagonisms as a means of resisting innovation and transformation. What remains clear are the colonial roots of this cultural logic, invented by the missionaries to civilise the Indians, and assimilated in inverted form by them in order to preserve themselves culturally and resist the irresistible zeal of the missionaries. This is the logic of the double, of being and appearing to be, of what is practised and what is revealed – the logic of the soul divided between two contrasting postures, that of the colonised and that of the coloniser.

There is more to this than the cultural hybridity of which Canclini speaks.[36] A culture can be defined as hybrid if it is sterile and merely juxtaposes alien, fragmented cultural elements. However, the most common situation is that of a hybrid cultural multiplicity being experienced by the same subjects, thus tending to constant ambiguity. On the contrary, however, this particular cultural hybridity produces a peculiar historical reality – that of slowness, and of slow decision-making[37] – and an equally peculiar social strategy and basic characteristic – that of dissimulation.[38] This hybridisation is not passive or mechanical. It nurtures the possible creativity and inventiveness of this society, in which the double – the transformation of the authentic into the inauthentic through concealment, becomes a fundamental characteristic of its culture.

In addition to concealment, the diffusion of an anomalous modernity stimulated the development of an imitative culture, whose most significant feature is the importance of being seen. With us, the counterpart to the theatricality of the processes of social interaction[39] characteristic of the modern way of life is imitation. Thus we have something that is not really modernity, and yet at the same time it is. There is no attempt at imitation as part of a rational strategy to produce a calculated impression; the reward is greater self-esteem and the assertion of one's own identity. Here, this theatre ends with the very act of imitation, as if simulation were in fact the content of what is being imitated.

Dissimulation, the counterpart of inefficient, complacent repression and social control, indicates that Brazilian society doesn't completely deny or erase traditional, irrational and incongruous behaviour. It merely points to the ways in which the modern and rational, and above all the dominant, is transformed into theatre. Responding to pressures from Britain, the 1824 Constitution laid down that protestant churches would be allowed in the country. But it maintained the restriction that they could not have *the exterior form of a church*,[40] because those who had been only superficially indoctrinated by colonial catholicism might confuse protestant with catholic churches. Religious truth lay in the façade of the church and not in the faith of its people – an anomaly produced by the arrogant certainty of having a monopoly of people's souls. The exterior is what is important, what can be seen. In spite of being an indication of religious tolerance and modernisation, there is evidence here of a baroque mentality, an over-valuing of forms and exteriors. That was the way our baroque was – it was about poverty and not an exuberance of ornaments flaunting a superfluous, colonial wealth, since most of the wealth generated by gold was sent to the metropolis. Our baroque is residual and, in a way, almost sober; and our culture continues to be baroque.

This exaggeration of the external form probably has to do with the need to give meaning to an empty historical and artistic reality. Colonial wealth was not sufficient to revolutionise social relations and affect the content of society; it did not allow, for example, for the invention of unique styles or the substantial re-creation of styles and concepts. The most that was allowed was the adaptation of the ornamental. Creativity was exercised in the superfluous. Even today this is the case. It is apparent in the exaggerated concern with personal appearance visible on the streets of the big cities, in which people exhibit an extraordinary carnivalesque combination of styles and references. The success of fakes in Brazil is a good indication of this mentality. Adopting signs of prosperity, cleanliness and beauty while throwing rubbish and refuse in the streets is another indication of an absolute disregard for the social action and for life. Individuals empty their own lives of meaning: they like perfumes and new, beautiful clothes, but pollute the space around them with cigarette packets and butts, used matches, plastic cups, empty cans of soft drink or beer. The not always obvious rules of personal appearance do not extend to the surrounding space and collective responsibility for what is actually public. Thus everything appears trivialised.

That is why the private sphere is so precarious for us. It doesn't establish a modern and impersonal social consciousness. Personalised relations, rather than the formal rights and obligations of individuals characteristic of modernity, continue to be central to the way our society operates. However, the world of modernity is the world of the individual. More than the person, the desire to be a person dominates situations, and this desire is in our ornaments, our signs. Even the citizen, in a large number of cases, is a mere imitation, as political and electoral behaviour is frequently servile, subject to debts of loyalty arising out of personal dominance, clientelism and populism. S/he is a citizen who votes out of obligation and not out of duty, and who does not consider her/himself invested with rights with respect to the conduct of those elected, to the law or to institutions. Precisely because of this, while s/he is not a true citizen, neither is s/he the human agent of a conservative way of thinking, agent of the transformation of tradition into a set of ideas, principles and practices which establish the basis of a life choice and a consistent social critique.

It is not the modern which simply incorporates the traditional and the popular. Rather, it is tradition which adapts fragments of the modern without, however, adopting a modern consciousness (as is evident in the works of Thompson that I have mentioned).

In its lack of authenticity, Latin American modernity borrows from the conservative consciousness implicit in our traditionalism. It lives in symbiosis with that which denies it. Herein lies the proof that the modern consciousness is incomplete; social relations, gestures and customs have this *additional alienation,* quite different from the alienation represented by the complete submission to modern rationality in developed countries. This is why forms retain the exaggerated function that they still have in Brazilian society. The anomaly lies in the fact that we are dealing with a modernity without criticsim – without awareness of its transience, of the fact that everything is subject to the fluctuations of fashion. It is modernity, but its constitution and diffusion are caught up in references to a traditionalism that is not necessarily, or exclusively, conservative. Here, too, we are faced with the inconclusive, the insufficient and the false.

Notes

1 Schelling rightly suggests that 'in order to understand the process of formation of a specifically Latin American modernity, it is necessary to examine how aspects of metropolitan modernity are appropriated in this context of uneven development and re-articulated with the local dynamic of cultural production and of economic and political structures, as well as relations of class, gender and race.' Vivian Schelling, 'Latin America and other Models of Modernity' in *The Legacy of the Disinherited*, T. Salman (ed.), CEDLA, Amsterdam, 1996.

2 See Henri Lefebvre, *Introduction à la Modernité*, Les Éditions de Minuit, Paris, 1962, p. 10.

3 See Benjamin Franklin, *Autobiografia*, trans. by Aydano Arruda, Ibrasa, São Paulo, 1963, pp. 77–86, in which Franklin establishes a set of criteria to order his daily life. This text was used by Max Weber as a document of almost classic purity on the spirit of capitalism. See Max Weber, *The Protestant Ethic and the Spirit of Capitalism*, trans. Talcott Parsons, Charles Scribner's Sons, New York, 1958, pp. 48–50.

4 It is necessary to distinguish between *stating* and *defining* modernity philosophically and *explaining* it sociologically. In this sense, although modernity appears in social consciousness in the eighteenth century (see Jürgen Habermas, *Il Discorso Filosofico della Modernità*, Editora Laterza, Bari, 1991, p. VII), it is in the nineteenth century that it finds its first sociological explanation. Marx does it in several of his works. See Karl Marx, *Economic and Philosophic Manuscripts of 1844*, Foreign Languages Publishing House, Moscow, 1961, pp. 67–83 ['Estranged Labour']; Karl Marx, *Capital – A Critical Analysis of Capitalist Production*, Volume I, Lawrence & Wishart, London, 1974, pp. 76–87.

5 See Max Weber, *Ciência e Política – Duas Vocações*, trans. Leonidas Hegenberg and Octany Silveira da Mota, Editora Cultrix, São Paulo, 1970, p. 31:

> The civilised man . . . places himself in the middle of the path of a civilisation which enriches itself continually with thoughts, experiences and problems, he can feel 'tired' of life, but not 'full' of it. As a result, he can never possess but an infinitesimal part of that which the life of the spirit incessantly produces, he can only capture the provisional and never the definitive.

6 I incorporate here the concepts of Heller on *radical needs*, a notion originally developed by Henri Lefebvre. See Agnes Heller, *La Théorie des Besoins chez Marx*, Union Générale d'Éditions, 1978, especially pp. 107–35.

7 See Henri Lefebvre, op. cit., p. 174.

8 This conception of modernity is contained in different works by Henri Lefebvre: *Critique de la Vie Quotidienne*, I, L'Arche Éditeur, Paris, 1958; II, L'Arche Éditeur, Paris, 1961; III, L'Arche Éditeur, Paris, 1981; *La Vida Cotidiana en el Mundo Moderno*, Alianza Editorial, Madrid, 1972; *La Présence et l'Absence*, Casterman, Paris, 1980; and also, Norbert Guterman and Henri Lefebvre, *La Conscience Mystifiée*, Le Sycomore, Paris, 1979.

9 See Henri Lefebvre, *Introduction à la Modernité*, op. cit., pp. 9–10.

10 In this chapter, I engage in constant dialogue with ideas such as those developed by Néstor García Canclini in *Cultural Híbridas. Estrategias para entrar y salir de la modernidad*, Grijalbo, Mexico, 1990. It is a pity that Canclini did not incorporate into his thinking Henri Lefebvre's concepts of the dialectical totality and the multiplicity of historical times in the present, as it would have broadened and enriched his theoretical framework. However, it must be said that he expressly points to the epistemological importance of totality in the study of Latin American modernity (p. 25). On this aspect of the work of Lefebvre, see José de Souza Martins 'As temporalidades da Historia na dialética de Lefebvre' in José de Souza Martins (ed.), *Henri Lefebvre e o Retorno à Dialética*, Editora Hucitec, São Paulo, 1996, pp. 13–23.

11 On the socially creative function of tradition, see E.P. Thompson, 'The Moral Economy of the English Crowd in the Eighteenth Century' in *Past and Present*, no. 50, Past and Present Society, February 1950, pp. 76–136.

> The traditions of the trades were usually associated with some vestiges of notions of 'adequate' price and 'fair' salary. The moral and social criteria – subsistence, self-confidence, pride (in certain levels of qualification), the customary rewards for the different grades of ability – stand out as much as the strictly 'economic' arguments in the first trade union disputes.

See E.P. Thompson, *The Making of the English Working Class*, Penguin Books, Harmondsworth, 1968, p. 261. This theme was also developed by T.H. Marshall, *Cidadania, Classe Social e Status*, trans. Meton Porto Gadelha, Zahar Editores, Rio de Janeiro, 1967, esp. pp. 57–114.

12 See Erich Fromm 'Conciencia y sociedad industrial' in Erich Fromm et al., *La Sociedad Industrial Contemporanea*, trans. Margarita Suzan Prieto and Julieta Campos, Siglo Veintyuno S.A., Mexico, 1967, pp. 1–15; Roger Bastide, 'Sociologia do sonho' in Roger Callois and G.E. von Gruenbaum (eds.), *O Sonho e as Sociedades Humanas*, Livraria Francisco Alves Editora S.A., Rio de Janeiro, 1978, pp. 137–48; José de Souza Martins (ed.), *Desfiguraçoes – a Vida Cotidiana no Imaginário Onírico da Metropole*, Editora Hucitec, São Paulo, 1996, passim.

13 From the perspective of a bitterly pessimistic sociologist, this Weberian theme reappears in Michel Maffesoli, *La Conquista del Presente*, Editrice Ianua, Rome, 1983. In addition this observation of Lyon's is also pertinent: 'A significant series of Western ideas begins with 'providence', which is transposed to 'progress' and from there moves to 'nihilism'. See David Lyon, *La Conquista del Presente*, Open University Press, Buckingham, 1995, p 5.

14 See Walnice Nogueira Galvão *As Formas do Falso (um estudo sobre a ambiguidade no Grande Sertão: Veredas)*, Editora Perspectiva, São Paulo, 1972. In this excellent work, the author studies what she appropriately defines as a founding ambiguity.

15 I examine this theme in a case study on the appearance of the devil among female factory workers at one of the largest and most modern factories in the suburbs of São Paulo, immediately following the doubling of the company's installations and extensive technological modernisation. See José de Souza Martins, 'A aparição do demonio na fábrica, no meio da produção', in *Tempo Social* (Revista de Sociologia da USP), Vol 5, Nos. 1–2, November 1994,

pp. 1–29. Lefebvre noted and examined the relation between the devil and modernity.

16 Apart from other sources, Schelling also points out the persistence of the magical and the mythical as expressions of an incomplete secularisation of popular memory, an indication of the hybrid and the inconclusive. See Vivian Schelling, op. cit., p. 257.

17 For Rulfo's photographs see Juan José Bremer et al, *Juan Rulfo (Homenaje Nacional)*, Instituto Nacional de Bellas Artes/SEP, México, September 1980.

18 An anthology of the photographs of Sebastião Salgado can be found in Jean Lacoutoure, *Fotografie di Sebastião Salgado*, Edizioni Gruppo Abele, Turin, 1996.

19 See Claude Lévi-Strauss, *Saudades do Brasil*, trans. Paulo Neves, Companhia das Letras, São Paulo, 1994.

20 It was the architect Marcos Antônio Perrone Santos who discovered and studied, based on Foucauldian analyses, the panoptic structure of Vila de Paranapiacaba, in the municipality of Santo André, (SP), conceived according to the prison model developed by Jeremy Bentham in the eighteenth century. This structure afforded and affords probing and concealed views of the dwellings, the rail station and the marshalling yard. See Marcos Antônio Perrone Santos, 'Análise das relações panópticas das distribuições espaciais', in João Ferreira, Silvia Helena Passareli and Marcos Antônio Perrone Santos, *Paranapiacaba – Estudos e Memória*, Prefeitura Municipal de Santo André (SP), Santo André, 1991, pp. 1–43. On this theme see Michel Foucault, *Discipline and Punish (The Birth of Prisons)*, Penguin, Harmondsworth, 1979. In the case of Paranapiacaba, contributing to the panoptic character of the town is the constant mist on the edge of the mountain range, which can suddenly cut off visibility and just as suddenly disappear. Far from disrupting the efficacy of this structure of surveillance, it intensifies the element of surprise and the unexpected.

21 Florestan Fernandes, one of Brazil's best known sociologists, had a Positivist background and the influence of Positivism can be traced in almost all of his works. He was, however, among the intellectuals considered subversive by the military dictatorship (1964–85), who were kept under surveillance, repressed, imprisoned and finally expelled from the university. An acute observer of Brazilian reality, long before he was victimised in the first incidents of repression, he wrote: 'From this perspective, commitment is not fundamental, the condition of the 'responsible' intellectual is 'action'. If the researcher manages to be objective, as observation, description and scientific explanation demand, their analyses and interpretations can become something much more *radical* or *revolutionary* than the existence of conflicting ideologies might suggest.' See Florestan Fernandes, *Sociedade de Classes e Subdesenvolvimento*, Zahar Editores, Rio de Janeiro, 1968, p. 14.

22 In an inspired article in his book on modernity, Lefebvre underlines the historical importance of irony and says: 'The theoretical and practical methods which investigate the differences – all the differences, those of individuals, groups, peoples, cultures – in order to highlight them in their life-styles and thought, need irony and the negative.' See Henri Lefebvre, *Introduction à la Modernité*, op. cit., p. 24.

23 'Moda do bonde camarão', by Marinao da Silva e Cornélio Pires, is one of the songs which places a *caipira* (whose concepts, rhythms and spatial references are peasant and rural) in one of the most modern forms of urban transport of the time in the city of São Paulo. The narrative of the clashes between the body and the interpretation of the caipira and the movement of the tram ridicules the modern. But above all, it denounces the transformation of the body of the passenger into an unadapted extension of the transport machine. Here laughter is the expression of a criticism of modernity and also a part of it. This precursory musical work contains many of the ingredients of Chaplin's *Modern Times*. On this aspect of *sertaneja* music see José de Souza Martins, 'Música sertaneja: a dissimulação da linguagem dos humilhados', *Capitalismo e Tradicionalismo*, Livraria Pioneira Editora, São Paulo, 1975, pp. 103–61.

24 On the relationship between Macunaíma and modernity, see Vivian Schelling, op. cit., p. 17.

25 Lapassade and Luz pointed to this duality in the macumba *terreiros* of Rio de Janeiro. Up to a certain point during the night the rituals are *umbanda*. From late in the night Exu takes over the *terreiro* (temple) and reveals with his presence the hidden and the secret contained in the earlier toned-down rites tolerated by the police. See Georges Lapassade and Marco Aurélio Luz, *O Segredo da Macumba*, Paz e Terra, Rio de Janeiro, 1972.

26 Brazil is a vast country and one of the last regions of the world with a living, disputed frontier in a process of occupation. It is a country marked by a long history of slow territorial occupation, which still continues today, and which was and has been the history of the subjugation of indigenous peoples, whether through their submission to slavery or through their extermination. Since the 1930 revolution this process has acquired a new orientation. The occupation of territory for the national State became part of a programme aimed specifically at guaranteeing national sovereignty and promoting the country's economic development. It is possible here to distinguish three great, distinctive historical moments: the first, the Getúlio Vargas dictatorship in the 1930s and '40s, the so-called March for the West, with the contact and acculturation of dispersed and unknown indigenous groups and the establishment of landing strips and radio stations for the monitoring of flights in and over Brazilian territory; the second in the 1950s, during the Juscelino Kubitschek government, the opening of the Belém-Brasília highway, the founding of Brasília and the consequent occupation of new lands, and the founding of cities all along the highway in Goiás and Pará; the third, with the military dictatorship installed in 1964, an extensive programme of road-building and fiscal benefits to companies interested in the occupation of virgin land in Amazônia, including the north of Goiás and the state of Maranhão. I refer particularly to this last period.

27 See José de Souza Martins, *Fronteira – A degradação do Outro nos confins do humano*, Editora Hucitec, São Paulo, 1997, especially pp. 79–112.

28 See Maria Sylvia de Carvalho Franco, *Homens Livres na Ordem Escravocrata*, Instituto de Estudos Brasileiros da Universidade de São Paulo, São Paulo, 1969, passim.

29 See especially, Oscar Lewis, *Five Families (Mexican Case Studies in the Culture of*

Poverty), The New American Library, New York, 1965; Oscar Lewis, *The Children of Sánchez (Autobiography of a Mexican Family)*, Penguin Books, Harmondsworth, 1972.

30 The dance of São Gonçalo is an ancient ritual and religious dance, which is Catholic and Portuguese in origin. It is practised as a form of votive offering. In Brazil the requests are from women who are growing old and have not yet found a husband, as São Gonçalo is a matchmaker for older women. He is also the patron saint of men who wish to become 'violists' and are having difficulty learning to play the instrument, as São Gonçalo was a *viola* player himself. There are also people who have pains in their legs and hope for a cure by dancing all night for the Saint. Up until the nineteenth century, the dance of São Gonçalo was actually practised inside the churches. See Maria Isaura Pereira de Queiroz, *Sociologia e Folclore – A Dança de São Gonçalo num Povoado Bahiano*, Livraria Progresso Editora, Salvador, 1958.

31 In the Brazilian case, the English language is turning into the symbolic language of inauthentic modernity. In 1954, the American evangelical churches, particularly the Pentecostalists, held a World Congress of Evangelicalism in Brazil. There were hundreds of missionaries, preachers and musicians in São Paulo holding huge proselytising and healing rallies, including a group in the Pacaembu gymnasium. Months afterwards, the sects and small temples directed by lay preachers were already proliferating, having recruited from among the mass of the population. I remember a north-easterner who preached to the faithful in a strong English accent, imitating the American campaign preachers, who spoke through translators. I even witnessed situations, in Pentecostalist groups, in which people who could speak in foreign languages were accompanied by an interpreter who translated into Portuguese. A clear fetishisation of foreign speech and mediations – a theatrical concept of modernity.

32 In 1979, there were 463 shacks in the *favela*, 24 of them inhabited by families of workers employed directly by USP and 55 employed indirectly. Almost two thirds of the *favela* dwellers stated that they lived there because they were unable to pay rent on a house. See Eva Alterman and Heloisa H. De Souza Martins, 'A favelização dos funcionários da USP', in *Ciência e Cultura*, Volume 32 (4), Sociedade Brasileira para o Progresso da Ciência, São Paulo, April 1980, pp. 418–20.

33 The MST (Movimento dos Trabalhadores Rurais Sem Terra) emerged formally in 1984, as an organisation of small farmers and rural workers expelled from land or threatened with losing land as a result of the expansion of cattle raising and large agricultural companies, like those involved in soya production, and more specifically as a consequence of ongoing land appropriation for the building of the dam and lake for the huge Itaipu hydroelectric power station, on the frontier between Brazil and Paraguay. The MST initially arose out of the efforts of pastors of the Lutheran Church and Catholic pastoral workers of the Pastoral Land Commission, organ of the National Conference of Bishops in Brazil. In April 1998 the MST had more than 60,000 landless workers in its camps.

34 I am using here Schutz's theory of multiple realities. See Alfred Schutz, *On*

Phenomenology and Social Relations, The Unversity of Chicago Press, Chicago and London, 1973, especially, pp. 245–62.

35 See Néstor García Canclini, op. cit., p. 19.

36 Ibid., passim.

37 See José de Souza Martins, *O Poder do Atraso (Ensaios de Sociologia da História Lenta)*, Editora Hucitec, São Paulo, 1994.

38 See José de Souza Martins, *Capitalismo e Tradicionalismo*, op. cit. pp. 103–61 ('Música sertaneja: a dissimulação na linguagem dos humilhados'); José de Souza Martins, *A Militarização da Questão Agrária no Brasil*, 2nd edition, Vozes, Petrópolis, 1985, pp. 113–27 ('O boiadeiro Galdinho – do Tribunal Militar ao Manicômio Judiciário'); José de Souza Martins, *A Chegada do Estranho*, Editora Hucitec, São Paulo, 1993.

39 See Erving Goffman, *The Presentation of Self in Everyday Life*, Doubleday & Company, Inc., New York, 1959.

40 The still widely used and highly significant popular expression in Brazil, 'Isso é para inglês ver' (that is put on for the English), used for circumstances when one is compelled to do something involuntarily or to act in a certain way to comply with the wishes of those in charge – when it is necessary to dissimulate – probably dates from this time.

Translated by Lorraine Leu

11

An Enchanted Public Space:
Religious Plurality and Modernity in Brazil

José Jorge de Carvalho

Dispute of the spirits

Let me begin by stating that in Brazil truly vast transformations in the sphere of religion have occurred, set in motion from that inconclusive moment in Western history which we call modernity. These transformations range from the more traditional catholicism and protestantism to the kind of Christian cults modelled on the culture industry and the simulacrum of television. There are the more orthodox Afro-Brazilian religious traditions, like *candomblé, xangô, batuque* and *tambor de mina,* as well as the more syncretic, hybrid or imaginative variants, like *umbanda, jurema* and *umbanda esotérica.*[1] There are also ethnically exclusive and impermeable religions, such as those practised by many indigenous nations, and new international or cosmopolitan movements, like the New Age movements. Extremely innovative and radical theological discourses, such as Liberation Theology, exist alongside several conservative and even fundamentalist Christian values, catholic as well as protestant. In addition to all of this, there are rich oral and mythical traditions, for example frequent outbreaks of messianism and shamanic practices which extend beyond their original indigenous context. As many recent studies show, the interfaces, superimpositions, oppositions, continuities and singularities within this field are increasingly numerous; finding a logical or structuring nexus which would allow us to apprehend them as a totality is a huge task, which still remains to be done. From a heuristic point of view, it would perhaps be more productive to postpone totalising definitions and to treat this religious universe simply as one which is composed of distinct, yet intercommunicating elements. To be more specific, this variety of religious movements, churches, sects, cults and groups represents different degrees of inclusion in national society, as a result of varying historical and social conditions.

The most common way of defining this articulation is based on the idea that, fundamentally, all of these religious movements are in dialogue with catholicism, the hegemonic religion in Brazil up until now, with which greater or lesser degrees of compatibility are possible. However, I propose here to radically invert this theoretical construction and attempt to understand this rich articulation of contemporary Brazilian religiosity from the point of view of the so-called peripheral or marginal religions. It is these religions, generally known as Spiritist, that permeate the space of a specifically religious dialogue characteristic of the country.

As the majority of scholars of the so-called religious dimension of alternative culture maintain, we are dealing here with a phenomenon of religious plurality.[2] This plurality is clearly visible in Brasília, a city where the religious universe is particularly open to invention. To give an example, the average inhabitant of the Plano Piloto (the centre of the modernist project of the Federal District), whether or not he or she practises a Christian religion, occasionally goes to mystical fairs, attends lectures at New Age esoteric centres and experiments with a range of methods for meditation and manipulation of spiritual forces and energies. The moment they experience a more serious crisis in their state of health or their inter-personal relationships – whether at work or in their love life – they can go to one of these centres in search of spiritual support. The word 'centre' (a key term on the contemporary Brazilian religious scene) is used to define different kinds of networks which connect to the supernatural. There are *umbanda* centres, *candomblé terreiros* (temples), Kardecist centres, a mixture of these three, and occasionally places which deal with a kind of Spiritism unknown to established religions (see below). Finally, there are mystical or esoteric communities like the Vale do Amanhecer (Valley of the Dawn), the Cidade Eclética (Eclectic City), the Fraternidade da Cruz (Fraternity of the Cross) and the Fraternidade do Lótus (Fraternity of the Lotus).[3] Although differences in status and class position may make for a diverse clientele, there is always a point of contact and a process of superimposition which facilitate the dissemination of an identifiable religious ethos.

The example of Brasília alone raises innumerable questions about the constitution of such a diverse field. On the one hand, one has to consider what kind of structures are esoteric communities such as *umbanda terreiros*, or the Valley of the Dawn – whether they form autonomous or integrated symbolic universes, and whether there is a fundamental common ground between them. On the other hand, it is interesting to discover what kind of synthesis an individual constructs out of these different religious elements – whether they are transformed into a whole or kept separate. It is here, where external pluralities are confronted with internal ones, that I believe the issue of contemporary religion should be situated. That is to say, where religious movements, which may or may not revolve around a symbolic centre, meet individual experience, which may or may not achieve an internal synthesis.[4]

In Spiritism, we are dealing with a movement whose role in the constitution of Brazilian religiosity has not yet been sufficiently emphasised. It was enthusiastically received in Brazil from the first years of its development in France by Alan Kardec in the 1860s, and its influence in the formulation of a religious code of practice with Brazilian characteristics is still growing. The practice of crossing Kardecism with Afro-Brazilian religious traditions, as well as with various esoteric traditions, began in earnest as early as the second half of the nineteenth century. Although an offshoot of a paradoxically positivist vision of the world, Spiritism is also Christian (or 'neo-Christian'), in the sense that it reintroduces, or re-emphasises, Christian notions such as charity. It does not simply redefine aspects of Christianity, it also introduces the world of the spirits in a much wider form, complementing equivalent doctrines practised within the esoteric traditions and the Afro-Brazilian religions (which emerged in a climate of symbolic and political negotiation known as syncretism).[5] Thus a fairly decisive change in the characteristics of religion in Brazil from the 1930s onwards – a result of the growing interrelation between *umbanda*, Kardecist Spiritism and the various esoteric traditions – was the re-stating of the differences between the psychic (or emotional) level and the actual spiritual level of religious experience, an important question which had been practically abandoned by Christianity.

In the case of Spiritism, the Kardecist doctrine itself offers a possibility of dialogue with the so-called esoteric traditions by postulating a hierarchy of spirits, developed to varying degrees, which in a theosophical tradition could be equated with the hierarchy of mental planes, ranging from the inferior to the superior.[6] Therefore, what for a particular esoteric school would be the various stages of encounter with the pure spirit (also called the atmanic I) can in Spiritism be interpreted as an open fan which spreads from the spirits of darkness to the spirits of light. And *umbanda* also conducts another reading of this same spiritual continuum, with so-called spirits 'of the left' (malign, violent, obscene), as opposed to 'refined' spirits (benign, peaceful, gentle), resulting in another possible version of this same hierarchy.[7] The word 'spirit' here is not necessarily the same as that used by Christians; and the difference between the spiritual and the psychic, systematically formulated in many esoteric movements, may seem strange to a Kardecist or practitioner of *umbanda*. However, what is important is that spiritual hierarchies are widely discussed and that this discussion forms a part of the belief system of these groups.

Because of all this, we can propose a kind of complex 'ideology' of spiritual evolution as central to an understanding of current manifestations of religion in Brazil. This ideology, which is thoroughly articulated in the religious discourse of *umbanda*, Spiritism and the esoteric schools, is also present in *candomblé* (with its various entities and forms of trance) and even in the Pentecostal sects. The latter, as we will see, reflect back to *umbanda* its own relationship with its spirits, re-evaluating them, albeit in a negative way.

In other words, Pentecostalists 'exorcise' the spirits worshipped in *umbanda*, for they see them as spiritual impurities which need to be eliminated rather than worshipped. Finally, add to this universe the spiritual world view of the new Japanese religions (the Messianic Church, Seicho-no-Iê, Perfect Liberty and Mahikari), which are spreading fast throughout the country and already have a following of millions. These Japanese religions also entertain the notion of spirit possession, which is handled in a manner similar to the exorcism practised in *umbanda*. Obviously, all the resulting metaphors of spatiality, luminosity and polarity comment on social and political hierarchies, depending on the social and religious spectrum out of which they arise.

There is, then, intense activity on the part of practitioners, in the attempt to map these spirit worlds and understand how they are articulated, giving rise to what I call a *querela dos espiritos* ('dispute of the spirits'). After all, there are millions of Brazilians who enter into trance regularly, receive entities or establish personalised relationships (either disturbing or supportive) with the most varied range of spirits. This should encourage us to formulate a general theory of this world, in which rationalist, psychologising, materialist, esoteric, Thomist, Calvinist, Lutheran, and various African and indigenous positions should confront each other. As Gilberto Velho rightly points out, the experience of possession is one of the keys to understanding Brazilian social experience (Velho 1992). It is also important to point out that, as far as I know, up until now this whole discussion has been mainly developed by the Afro-Brazilian cults, Spiritism and esoteric sects – that is, essentially at the margins of established Christianity.

This 'dispute of the spirits' is also theoretically challenging because it provides us with the opportunity to introduce methods of evaluation necessary to situate comparatively the various religious doctrines which make up this pluralist scenario.[8] In confronting this dispute, we have to be willing to enquire to what extent the meeting of religious traditions in Brazil is something more than a mere translation into symbolic discourse of hierarchical relationships between groups, movements and social classes who share the political dialogic space of the nation. And there is no way to escape this uncomfortable theoretical challenge, unless we renounce the inquiry into what is specifically religious in the social and cultural phenomenon we are examining. This 'dispute of the spirits' therefore presents what, in my view, is the greatest challenge for the social scientist interested in understanding the religious phenomenon: the impossibility of separating studies of the mystical from studies of the political.[9]

In this area of spiritual practices we encounter yet another theoretical question: the difficulty of reconciling, without running the risk of being reductive, the modern, Western view of the cosmos with different or traditional world views. The former is a rationalist and scientistic outlook, characterised by the disenchantment of nature; while the latter, developing parallel to the modernising project, are sustained by metaphysical and supra-natural precepts, which form an integral part of ritual beliefs and practices. The current paradigm, therefore, which is fundamentally based on instrumental reason, separates any given physical action (for example, the act of breathing) from the particular branch of metaphysics to which it belongs from the point of view of the teacher who has introduced it to the West. The result, at best, is a cultural misunderstanding. But more frequently it is a spiritual misunderstanding, or occasionally even an ethical one.

Directly related to the instrumental use of spiritual practices is a new historical process of massification within these religions. The diversification of religious choice occurred in tandem with other transformations in the sphere of culture, giving rise to religious forms which manifest themselves as spectacle. Thus a religious counterpart to Ortega y Gasset's 'mass culture man' emerges, a being who does not wish to tread the path to individual perfection, who is not self-critical and who is immediately satisfied with whatever novelty is presented to her/him. Not all contemporary religions advocate self-questioning, or expect it from their followers; that is to say, not all forms of religion aim to reveal a path to the true self. Paraphrasing Walter Benjamin, it is possible to speak of a 'religious barbarism', similar to the 'artistic barbarism' outlined by him in his critique of turn-of-the-century art and culture, characterised by the loss of tradition, of the narrator, and the experience of depth. As a result, religion now also exists as experience (*Erfahrung*: tradition, recreated by the individual and lived in the bosom of the religious community as part of the very process of keeping it alive), side by side with the religious as mere sensation or shock-experience (*Erlebnis*: religion seen as an instantaneous and often fleeting connection to a ritual technique or a set of beliefs whose symbolic implications, cosmological articulations, myths, transcendental inner meanings, are unknown, or considered irrelevant).[10] In short, I venture that today it is not just art, sport and politics, but also religion, which is being transformed into spectacle.

A large number of contemporary religious movements, both oral and lettered, are concerned with finding a form of expression which simplifies the act of interpretation and hence can establish a much more direct means of influencing the new adherent. I refer to a religious style which is the exact opposite of those discussed previously, which seek to restore an esoteric dimension to religion. Instead of advocating a period of initiation or a preparatory stage, it tries to eliminate any conceptual, philosophical or spiritual resistance in the faithful so that they may immerse themselves in that particular sacred universe. In other words, the kind of religion which is perhaps growing the fastest in terms of number of adherents is that which relies unequivocally on the exoteric; that is, a religion which positions itself closer to objectification. In short, instead of emphasising the process, it emphasises the product.

Tradition and imagination in religious movements

I would like to illustrate now, in greater detail, these significant innovations in the area of religion in Brazil, by describing the main characteristics of two very well-known religious movements in Brasília which exemplify the ever expanding character of the constant meetings, fusions, syncretisms and hybridisations that occur in this field. The first of these is the Vale do Amanhecer (Valley of the Dawn), a religious community with a Spiritist base, which was founded in 1959 by a woman, Tia Neiva (Aunt Neiva). The community has thousands of followers and has already expanded to various states throughout the country. Aunt Neiva, endowed with an extraordinary religious imagination, experienced revelations which were derived in the main from the vast Afro-Brazilian imaginary, from Spiritism and also from popular catholicism. In this way, she widened the spiritual world vision much more than could have been imagined by Alan Kardec, founder of the doctrine, or even Francisco Xavier, its greatest exponent in Brazil. Fully exercising her mythological and ritualistic creative powers, she carried out a Spiritist reading of a number of other religious traditions, within a basic context which could be considered *umbandista*, or Afro-Brazilian. For example, the principal entity worshipped in the Valley of the Dawn is Seta Branca (White Arrow), a *caboclo* or spirit linked to the forests which represents indigenous and *mestiço* spiritual power and, by extension, that of all Brazilians.[11] This entity could easily belong to the pantheon of traditional Afro-Brazilian cults, like the *jurema, pajelança, macumba*, as well as *umbanda*.[12] On the other hand it can equally be interpreted as a Christian figure, in the sense that Seta Branca is also seen as an incarnation of Saint Francis of Assisi.

One of the basic concepts of the Valley of the Dawn's belief system is that of the Seventh Ray, a term used in the cosmological schemes of Theosophy. Aunt Neiva is the seventh ray of the *caboclo* Seta Branca, the latter is the seventh ray of Saint Francis, who is the seventh ray of Christ, the seventh ray of God. Therefore, Seta Branca must be an actualisation of Jesus Christ in the context of the particular reality of this cult in Brazil. Thus the Valley of the Dawn, whose plurality of signs and rituals forms the most complex religious universe that I know of, attempts to position itself, fundamentally, within this classically Brazilian Spiritist ethos. It can be seen as one of many recombinations of this traditional ethos based on the visions of a single leader. Yet, without breaking with the dominant religion, it challenges it head-on, by proposing a syncretism or parallelism with the divinity, Jesus Christ, who is seen as one and indivisible in the eyes of the catholic and protestant faithful.

What is most fascinating in the Valley of the Dawn is the symbolic imagination at work. It has a number of legions with more entities than exist in any *umbanda* or Kardecist centre: Aztec, Maya, Inca, Egyptian, Tibetan, Chinese, Christian. The women who belong to the Hellenic legion dress like Greeks; those who belong to the oriental phalanx dress like Indians; others dress as Egyptians; still others as medieval fairies or princesses – all with beautiful ornaments, coloured robes, decorations and veils. Thus a kind of court or sacralised aristocracy is evoked, created from the socio-historical imaginaries of diverse civilisations. The Valley as a whole has a typically 'orientalist' climate. The male followers, called jaguars, wear long, brown capes evocing at the same time the garments of the European aristocracy, chief priests of esoteric sects like Freemasonry and the Rosicrucian Order, musical maestros and the so-called malign spirits (the violent Exus) of *macumba* and *umbanda.*

Aunt Neiva left a door open to accommodate all kinds of spirits, within a great imaginary paradigm she called the Indian Current of Space, and which is derived from a concept of the cosmos which would make any Alexandrine theological–philosophical system appear simple, and would probably delight great interpreters of the Islamic and Judaic esoteric traditions, like Henry Corbin and Gershom Scholem. In the sense that it is a total invention, without known precedent, the Valley of the Dawn is a religion which challenges current concepts of authenticity and kitsch, in addition to questioning the parameters used to define sacred art. And it is not just the clothing and the ritual objects which are original and exclusive – architecturally, the religious complex as a whole is very inventive. It has an artificial lake surrounded by statues of feminine figures, such as sirens, water nymphs and *iemanjás,*[13] who probably allude to the image of Aunt Neiva herself. The fundamental symbol of this complex of temples is an ellipse, whose image in sculptures and paintings can be considered a female fertility symbol. In fact, the Valley of the Dawn is perhaps the first *yoni*[14] cult in Brazil. And the temple itself reflects the extraordinary complexity of the ritual system. Various kinds of healing are practised here, inter-linked with a Spiritist-type rhetoric. The few metaphors from Newtonian physics found in Alan Kardec's texts more than 100 years ago are merged here into a sacred language which fuses and juxtaposes terms originating in the most diverse areas of human experience, from religion and history to electromagnetism and astrophysics.

We can say that the Valley of the Dawn is a religion in a process of constant transformation. The Aunt Neiva period meant continuous expansion of the belief system, the creation of guidelines, phalanxes, concepts, methods of prayer and healing, which continued to be expanded after her death, according to the models she had laid down. However, although this fascinating belief system may in future still lay down its central tenets more precisely, it could nevertheless be argued that it has established a greater variety of links and connections between Spiritism, Christianity, *umbanda* and esotericism in Brazil than has hitherto been the case. At any rate, it is still faithful to a certain style of popular Brazilian religiosity of a traditional nature, and does not maintain connections with the styles of the New Age.[15] It is also worth pointing out that the majority of the Valley of the Dawn's followers come from the popular classes, although the complex also attracts people who belong to the more privileged sectors of society.

Another religious movement which illustrates this same tendency to Spiritist hybridisation (albeit with more modern packaging) is that which is currently developing in a temple constructed by the Legião da Boa Vontade (Legion of Good Will) in Brasília. This 'Temple of Unrestricted Ecumenicalism', as the faithful call it, takes the shape of a large pyramid of white marble which is already one of the principal icons of modernist architecture in Brasília today. The history of its construction is emblematic of this mythical–religious porousness we have been discussing. A Rosicrucian architect, who sought to pay homage to ancient religions by designing an esoteric pyramid somewhat similar to the pyramid of an existing Rosicrucian temple in Brasília, was commissioned for the project. Thus, it can be seen as the realisation of the dream of various new religious groups which are linked to traditional doctrines. There is a vague reference in the architecture as a whole to a transcultural God, represented as a kind of pantheist entity, with Christ referred to as the Universal Statesman. It is worth briefly considering some of the pyramid's more prominent characteristics.

The temple has a nave and two basements. In the pyramid's peak, which projects over the nave, a huge crystal has been placed which the legionaries claim is the largest in the world. In the centre of the nave there is a circle, out of which emerges a white spiral inter-linked with a black one. On entering, visitors head for the outer extreme of the black spiral and walk barefoot along it, in meditation and prayer, with their arms open and hands raised, until they reach the centre of the nave, beneath the peak of the pyramid. Here they stop and receive the energy of the crystal suspended from the roof. Once sufficiently energised they return, this time along the white spiral, until finally they leave by the opposite side from which they entered. The path of the black spiral signifies the material, earthly, inferior side which, according to the legionaries, is the place from which all should depart in their search for the divine. After reaching the centre and receiving the pure energy of the crystal, they follow the path of the white spiral, which represents the superior, celestial, spiritual side of every human being. This takes them physically to a point called the throne and altar of God, made up of a small staircase with seven landings, which supports an altar where there is a holographic work of art representing the four elements of nature. After passing through this area, the visitor can then withdraw from the nave and move towards other sectors of the architectural complex.

The architect of the building has revealed the most intriguing aspect of this great work of the imagination that is the Legion of Good Will temple: he had never planned that this ritual of walking should take place. He researched the construction of temples in various texts on the religions of the ancient world, and conceived the spiral design of the floor only in order to avoid the monotony of a single colour. Initially the visitor could walk around the interior of the nave in any direction, linear, circular, or diagonal. However, once the temple was inaugurated, it was soon apparent that people were intent on following the spiral circuit. As a result the building – which, at the outset, was meant to be divested of ritual and serve only as a place for meditation and recollection – immediately came to generate its own style of spiritual practices. In short, in less than a year it became the base for a movement of religious invention or re-discovery.

In the first basement there is a stone fountain, created by a Japanese artist, from which twice-filtered water gushes. The water passes underground and under the crystal three times, and is considered to be highly energising and beneficial. For several years now it has been usual to see visitors entering the temple with bottles, descending to the Japanese fountain, filling them with water, placing their names on the bottles and leaving them on a table on the nave above. At six o'clock there is a ritual of fluidification, after which they retrieve their bottles and take them home. This custom of fluidification of water is common to Kardecist Spiritism, to the Valley of the Dawn, to *umbanda branca* and sectors of popular catholicism. As well as this practice of fluidification, time has recently been set aside each week for the *toma de passes* (laying on hands) conducted by various *sensitivos* in the city who lend their services to the Legion of Good Will.[16]

The Legion of Good Will temple can be considered a work of art in itself and, in a way, it functions as a permanent gallery. There are crystals, paintings, floral arrangements, internal gardens, *bonsais*, mosaics, fountains, sculptures, murals, mausoleums – and everything is in a state of constant expansion and change, as in a museum of contemporary art. And here we can observe another extremely modern characteristic of its conceptualisation, namely the aestheticisation of religion, which contrasts radically with the archaic, traditional side of this esoteric pyramid, with its subtleties, secrets and Rosicrucian connection. There is also a shop in one of the corridors of the pyramid selling sacred and energising objects, books and souvenirs.

In light of the foregoing discussion, we can imagine that visitors to this pyramid possess a kind of diffuse spirituality and that the temple offers a potentially neutral structure for the expression of this spirituality. The temple is rare in that it dispenses with the presence of a leader which brings us to a very important theoretical point. Of all the contemporary religious systems discussed here, the Legion of Good

Will pyramid is perhaps the first religious tradition created in Brazil which does not rely on a living spiritual leader, and does not appear to need such a presence. Its founder is dead and his successor appears to be a more political or administrative leader of the institution; it remains unclear to what extent he represents a continuation of the founder's divine power. In fact, the only thing which seems to convey the founder's charisma is his recorded voice, which is reproduced daily in the temple. Spiritual transmission from the master perhaps occurs through the magnetism of his voice, albeit recorded, at the moment of collective prayer. In any case we are faced with a thought-provoking scenario – that of a greatly expanding religious tradition which seems to have found an original symbolic way of avoiding the question of the incarnation of the leader.

These two examples of religious creations in Brasília seem to capture the complexities and contradictions of a great deal of creative and diffuse contemporary Brazilian religious practice. As is the case with many historical leaders, Aunt Neiva's ignorance of theology did not prevent her from developing her spiritual quest to the point of experiencing a revelation and moulding it into an extraordinary cult. Clearly following the line of thinking already introduced by practitioners of *umbanda*, the Valley of the Dawn takes Spiritist doctrines, rooted in the Brazilian population for more than a century, almost to the limit of semiotic complexity and rational intelligibility. In this way, it epitomises the view of those scholars like me who believe that the predominant religious feeling in Brazil is in fact Spiritism.

With regard to the temple of the Legion of Good Will, we are faced with a more difficult and more important question. What degree of intensity and development can one attain, intuitively or collectively, by 'discovering' a spiral path which leads to 'the centre', but without direct contact with a leader to whom this form has been revealed as a result of a spiritual experience? This extreme case (of the absence of a religious leader) also touches on another predicament, as I see it, of the current Brazilian religious scene. That is, that while there are many expanding religious movements, there are few leaders who impose themselves with spiritual force within the religious sphere as a whole.

Another very important issue, directly linked to the undermining of experience as continuity with the past, is raised by the invention of religious signs. That is to say, instead of an immersion in tradition, there is a progressive construction of increasingly syncretic systems, always changing and increasingly kaleidoscopic, and based on a religious culture in a process of constant expansion. In other words, due to the mass media, a kind of universal religious culture has already become much more accessible to anyone who might be interested. This culture is constructed out of standard agglomerations of the religions of the world – including those of the Aztecs, Incas, Chinese, Japanese, Indians and Greeks. All of this informs the character of a kind of religious common-sense which is beginning to present itself now as 'pan-traditional', or cosmopolitan, in the strictest sense of the term. As discussed earlier, one of the results of this process of invention is the emergence of religious discourses with very distinct levels of internal and external articulation, some of them without even a cohesive nucleus, or any form of integrated vision of the world.

Inter-religious confrontations and enchanted public space

This radical change in the composition of religious universes leads to a significant change in the way in which they co-exist to form an overall picture of contemporary religious plurality. We no longer live according to that old model of religious coexistence (rather than peace) in which identities were mutually acknowledged (Jews, Christians, Muslims, etc.). Nowadays the authenticity of group identities is questioned on all sides. A religion may be closed in on itself, presenting itself as ethnically exclusive and so outside of the intercommunicating, cosmopolitan, external circuit. The Hellenic Church in Brasília is an example of this: mass is conducted in Greek, no concessions are made to proselytising and no special overtures are considered necessary to non-Orthodox Greeks. Or, alternatively, a religion may select options from a wide spectrum of possible interactions. Such choices can provoke any response, from the most civil and open to debate (as in the oriental and esoteric critique of Christianity, which proposes various fronts of 'inter-religious dialogue'), to aggressive rejection and open violence (exemplified in the attitude of the Pentecostal religious movement of the Universal Church of the Kingdom of God towards Afro-Brazilian cults – see below). In any case, what is important is that these interfaces are increasingly frequent, and because of this the language of fraud, deceit, the false and the inauthentic becomes the shadow of contemporary religious cosmopolitanism. Inter-religious suspicion is the price paid for this very cosmopolitanism, which succeeded in abolishing, at least in the majority of cases, the repressive and silencing religious intolerance of previous periods. Where my interpretation differs from that of many of my colleagues analysing the contemporary religious scene in Brazil is that, far from pointing to a process of rationalisation and secularisation, I see this suspicion as a symptom of the plurality of an increasingly demanding and challenging spiritual quest.[17] In short, I am convinced that the crisis of religious authority does not necessarily indicate a weakening of the enchantment created by religion.

At present, when religious choice frees itself from the ties of structured identity, all religions are susceptible to accusations of falsity. Many evangelical Pentecostal sects, such as the Cathedral of the Blessing of Taguatinga, openly collect large quantities of cash from their followers, thereby demonstrating to outsiders the limitations of an experience which does not seem able to transcend immediate emotion. By demonstrating this so clearly, the sect therefore instantly reframes the question of how to define the spiritual experience, as it is only by understanding this that we can comprehend the religious dimension. There is thus a certain phantasmagoric quality appearing now in the spiritual field. This element of phantasmagoria – which previously expressed itself in the first industrial objects, in art held to be inferior, in the kitsch – is now appearing in the area of religion too. It is the spirit, spiritual power, the *samadhi*, illumination, the *satori*, the Christ-like state, which has also taken on a fetishistic quality now, as if on commercial display as an image of power, as a commodity.[18] The possibility of a trance, a transfer of energy, an embrace of divine love, etc. can appear as desirable in the present social context, as the acquisition of a new car, an electrical appliance, or travel to an exotic destination. Self-consciously or not, religious advertising, like any advertising in a consumer society, has already incorporated the mimetic desire for possession.

There are claims that Mahikari, Seicho-No-Iê, *umbanda*, the Rosicrucian Order, the Cathedral of Blessing, and the Catholic Church all represent false paths to the spiritual. Similarly, the oriental gurus who now come to the West are all viewed with suspicion: Maharishi Maheshi, Swami Bhaktivedanta Prabhupada, Guru Mahara-Ji, Shri Bhagwan Rajneesh, and Satya Sai Baba, among others. The same applies to Afro-Brazilian priests, protestant pastors, catholic priests and other leaders. Few contemporary spiritual leaders exemplify so clearly the difficult ground on which spiritual authority rests as does Shri Bagwan Rajneesh, a figure who provokes the most extreme opinions. Some consider him (and others like him) the consummate charlatan, while others see in him the most divine state attainable by the human being. The same has been said for years about Bishop Edir Macedo, who founded the Universal Church of the Kingdom of God with a level of rhetorical aggression not seen in Brazil since the Inquisition in the seventeenth century. And the same is now said about Father

Marcelo Rossi, veritable media star of the Catholic Charismatic movement.[19]

Today, it seems, we are living in a climate of religious confrontation, freedom and mobility, which presupposes constant criticism and doubt. The most visible form of this confrontation is the so-called 'holy war' unleashed by the Universal Church of the Kingdom of God against Afro-Brazilian cults. Through intensive use of radio, TV and mass rallies in stadia and public squares, Bishop Macedo developed exorcism rituals in which the entities worshipped in Afro-Brazilian temples are directly identified with the devil and exorcised from the bodies of the faithful by means of dramatic forms of trance. Furthermore, groups of followers of the Universal Church have antagonised members of *candomblé* and *umbanda* temples by positioning themselves nearby and hurling insults over loud-speakers, and occasionally singling out worshippers for insult. As if this were not enough, Afro-Brazilian entities are verbally attacked daily on the Church's television and radio programmes.

We are therefore faced with a complex system of interaction and symbolic contamination, in the sense that the same supernatural entities migrate from one religious system to another. Divinities like the *Exus, Pretos Velhos* and *caboclos*, widely worshipped in the Afro-Brazilian cults, are made diabolical in the rituals of the Universal Church of the Kingdom of God. This 'holy war' has provoked many contrasting interpretations from Brazilian scholars. Luís Eduardo Soares (1993) views it positively, considering it evidence of the expansion of democratic space in Brazil. Whereas not long ago religious interaction was portrayed in terms of the vertical hierarchy of the Catholic Church, such interaction is now horizontal, and the dispute has reached the public arena. Already Mariza de Carvalho Soares (1990) has been concerned with uncovering the specific methods (similar to those of an advertising campaign, or political propaganda of the kind used by authoritarian regimes) by which the pastors of the Universal Church seek to intimidate the practitioners of Afro-Brazilian religions.[20]

Due to their prolonged experience of social marginality, Afro-Brazilian religions have produced a sacred body of texts which comment not only on syncretism and symbolic hybridisation, but also on the confrontation of beliefs and inter-religious dialogue transferred to the public arena. There are the *macumba* and *umbanda* cults, for example, which ritualise and mythologise spaces of urban traffic (such as the street and the crossroads) and supernatural interaction (which represent allegories of social interaction). Similarly, there is a sacred text in praise of *Pomba Girá*[21] sung in the *jurema teruples* of Recife, which speaks of a ritual sacrifice placed at an urban crossroad. It begins:

Quando você passar
pela encruzilhada
ver uma moça bonita
com uma rosa na mão
peça licenca e passe
só não apanhe o que estiver no chão

(When you pass / by a cross-road / and see a pretty girl / with a rose in her hand / ask permission and go / but don't pick up what's on the ground)

Like any poetic text (particularly sacred lyrical texts, which transfer meanings from the domain of social experience to the spiritual sphere), this is a polysemic text.[22] On first reading it seems simple: the poetic subject advises that it is in your best interest to respect the offering to the gods left at a crossroad, or you could suffer the effects of a curse meant for someone else. Yet, this text is also a prescription for inter-religious co-existence in an enchanted public space. You may not be a practitioner of *umbanda*, but you must respect its sacred (or magic) objects and not disturb its ritual intervention in the crossroads of urban space. *Pomba Gira* requests this cosmopolitan, pluralist and respectful behaviour and at the same time warns – or threatens – the potential transgressor that she will take revenge for any profanation of her cult (the abrupt descending melodic leap of the words of the last verse, 'don't pick up what's on the ground', is ironically threatening).

Two opposing dimensions of metropolitan co-existence are integrated here. The citizen's respect for the beliefs of others diminishes the danger of fundamentalism (evident in some variants of Pentecostalism) and guarantees a secular attitude. At the same time, it reminds everyone of the possibility of supernatural sanction, independent of individual belief. Secularity and enchantment threaten each other, and pushed to their limits would destroy each other. The best recipe therefore for uncensored, modern social harmony is the acceptance of incommensurable difference.

It is in terms of this dualistic character, benign to those who respect it and merciless to those who defy it, that *Pomba Gira* defines herself, in the third person, in another song, also from the *jurema* cult in Recife:

Não mexa com ela não
Que ela não mexe com ninguém
Ela é ponta de agulha, Senhores Mestres
Quando ela mexe, mexe bem.

(Don't mess with her, no / for she messes with no one / she's razor sharp, my good men / and when she moves, she really touches you.)[23]

The Afro-Brazilian religions have also met with opposition in various Brazilian cities on the matter of where the *despachos*, or offerings to the gods, are left. In the name of environmental protection and ecological awareness, the places traditionally used for the offering of sacrifices – lakes, rivers, waterfalls, forests – have been protected, or at least their use has to be negotiated with other bodies of the state and civil society. At any rate, some progress has been made here, in that thirty years ago leaving offerings on the road, on street corners, or even on wasteland was considered a symbolic act of pollution by catholics, who felt they had a monopoly on representing religion in Brazil as a whole. It was also a 'symbol of backwardness' in terms of the advance of modernity and a source of shame to those who viewed secularity as a sign of 'evolution' and 'social development'. Today discussion can overcome prejudice and become negotiation between equals over a common interest – the public sphere. Despite its authoritarianism, the Christian view of the world, historically more adapted to a reality of self-conscious co-existence, is beginning to influence politically the practitioners of Afro-Brazilian cults in their traditional vision of nature, while respecting its place in the public sphere. This does not, however, signify the immersion in a process of secularisation already so familiar to followers of Christianity.

In summary, what we see in contemporary Brazil is an open and intense confrontation between the movements working in favour of the secularisation of the public sphere and those with a pluralist approach, attempting to enlarge or renew the religious dimension of this sphere. What we have here, in fact, is an experience of reflexivity, but one which is the opposite of that understood by sociologists who theorise on reflexive modernity; the latter are usually quite sceptical with regard to spirituality and understand reflexivity as a movement completely distanced from and opposed to the mystical dimension of life. The interpretations of Anthony Giddens, Pierre Bourdieu and Marcel Gauchet on the decline of religion in modernity, for example, could not be less apt to the contemporary religious scene in Brazil.[24]

Here we can return to Benjamin's famous argument on the opposition between *Erfahrung* and *Erlebnis*, mentioned earlier. The passing, or loss, of *Erfahrung* is never total. For many religious individuals (especially those who practise religions which are marginal to those advocated by monotheist systems), the very loss of this consciousness is not just present on a rational level. It is transmuted so that it manifests itself as a new type of spiritual consciousness, whose living myths are adapted, thus developing a new religious experience in a clear reaction to the move towards secularisation.

Here is one more example (taken from the *catimbó* cult in Pernambuco and Paraíba) of this reflexive enchantment, capable of co-existing with the discourse of the modern without departing from its traditional religious base:

> Dei um balanço no mundo
> E o bom Jesus nasceu.
> Assim tremeu a terra,
> Tremeu o céu,
> Mas o Caboclo não tremeu.

(I gave the world a shake / And good Jesus was born. / So the earth trembled, / as did the sky, / but the *Caboclo* didn't shy.)[25]

In this example, the Afro-Brazilian cults intervene in a traditionally catholic space to propose a syncretic equivalence in which Jesus Christ is absorbed within *jurema* or *umbanda*. Jesus is born out of a typically hierophantic event, the trembling of the earth and the sky, apparently in a cosmic time subsequent to the appearance of the *caboclo*. Additionally, the text offers us a highly unusual image in the poetic subject's claim, in the first person, to have created the conditions which led to the birth of Jesus. Despite this apparent heresy of heresies, attributing the status of demiurge to the poetic subject, nevertheless the adherents of *jurema* are able to negotiate a peaceful co-existence with the Catholic Church, while clearly contradicting Vatican doctrine.

On the other hand, the Universal Church of the Kingdom of God has been demonstrating an increasing intolerance towards catholicism, and this antipathy was epitomised in the attack on the image of Nossa Senhora Aparecida (Our Lady the Appeared) launched by one of its pastors during a television programme in 1995. The manifest 'theological' intention of the pastor was to prove that the figure of the Virgin was merely a clay image, incapable of bringing money and prosperity to the faithful devoted to her. This aggression towards the image of the patron saint of Brazil generated great polemic (still ongoing) about the limits of religious tolerance in the country. In a further twist, due to various financial scandals, Bishop Macedo has also been likened to much-criticised figures of North American TV evangelism, such as Oral Roberts and Jimmy Swaggart. The aggressive methods employed by leaders of the Universal Church to extract money from their followers, so widespread in the country today and theologically rationalised as the moral correlate of the struggle against idolatry – the so-called Theology of Prosperity – were recently satirised in *Guerra Santa* (Holy War), a popular song by Gilberto Gil:

> Ele diz que tem como abrir o portão do céu
> Ele promete a salvação
> Ele chuta a imagem da santa, fica louco-pinel
> Mas não rasga dinheiro, não . . .
> Não lembra de nada, é louco
> Mas não rasga dinheiro.

(He says he has the means to open the gates of heaven / He promises salvation / He kicks the image of the saint, he goes mad / But he doesn't tear up money, no way . . . / He doesn't remember a thing, he's crazy / But he never tears up money, no way.[26]

As far as I know, this is the first time that a political–religious conflict between variants of Christianity has reached the universe of Brazilian popular music. Gilberto Gil offers a sociologising and sceptical interpretation of the pastor's behaviour. He is not crazy, because he doesn't destroy the money he collects from the faithful; therefore his apparently irrational behaviour must be seen as a rhetorical ritual of persuasion which polarises the religious beliefs of his group and those of the catholics. The incident is thus inscribed as an allegory of recent proposals for the modernisation of the country, which include the Theology of Prosperity, a movement which links Brazil to the mercantilist ethos that characterises, and indeed caricatures, North American evangelism.

Finally, in spite of the fact that religious plurality initially brings to mind de-centring, superficiality and inconsistency, there is a religious dimension which seems to me to be very much alive in our society and which suggests a path that has not become disenchanted, as Max Weber supposed. This is the symbolism of the quest, which confers meaning on this constantly expanding labyrinth. For many people today, if not for the majority, religion is no longer simply handed down (and therefore easily dispensed with), but something to be sought, to be attained. The 'dispute of the spirits' appears to be the privileged language in which to talk about this quest in a pluralist, syncretic society, subject to profound social, political and economic transformations, as is the case with contemporary Brazil. And it is this movement of spiritual quest – alive, intense, imaginative, always surprising and disturbing – which we must follow with interest.

Notes

1 See the glossary at the end of the book.
2 As a basic ethnographic reference for situating this diversity, see the three

volumes of the series *Sinais dos Tempos* (Landim 1989a, 1989b and 1990), which include discussions of recent transformations in catholicism, protestantism, Afro-Brazilian religions and Spiritism and of the so-called new religious movements.

3 On these groups see Carvalho (1992).

4 Rubem César Fernandes has already called attention to this 'polycentric' character of Brazilian catholicism, on contrasting it with Polish catholicism, which possesses a definite centre, such as the sanctuary of Czestochowa: 'Polish catholicism is an integrator of multiple symbolic levels while Brazilian catholicism segments itself into multiple levels' (1992: 75). Also see Sanchis (1997) for this opening up to the syncretism which he considered constitutive of the Brazilian religious ethos. On the centrality of the concept of syncretism in the context of Brazil, see also Carvalho (1994a).

5 It is worth emphasising that 'the spirit world' of Afro-Brazilian and indigenous religions, together with catholicism, Judaism and protestantism, forms the bedrock of religion in Brazil, with its origin in the colonial period.

6 I am mixing two highly influential doctrines here, that of Alan Kardec (1984) and H. P. Blavatsky (1991).

7 This is exactly the kind of fusion practised in *umbanda esotérica*. On this spiritual ethic of violence and obscenity, see Carvalho (1994b).

8 I am interested here merely in indicating the centrality of this question. In another essay, to an extent complementary to this one, I have sought to develop a conceptual model which facilitates a comparison between different experiences of spirituality (see Carvalho 1994c).

9 Peter Winn, in a chapter dedicated to religion in Latin America in his volume *Americas*, synthesises the dilemma I described to him in an interview: 'the question that this poses . . . is how to pass from the world of the spirits – to the world of the Spirit'. (Winn 1992: 393).

10 For a formulation of the concepts of *Erfahrung* and *Erlebnis*, I draw directly from Walter Benjamin's classic essays (1969 and 1985). See also Howard Caygill's excellent exegesis (1998), which shows how Benjamin connected the loss of experience with the return to New Age styles of religion, in particular the section entitled 'The Experience of Modernity' (Ibid: 29–33). I will return to this discussion in the final part of this essay.

11 For an analysis of the symbolism of the *caboclo*, see Jim Wafer (1991).

12 See glossary.

13 See glossary.

14 *Yoni*: a term from classical Indian religious tradition which means 'sacred vagina' (hence the symbolic pair lingam (penis) – yoni (vagina)). *Yonis* are found in the form of sculptures in many Indian temples, particularly those dedicated to the god Shiva. Clearly, images of female genitalia would never acquire symbolic sacred status in Christianity. The ellipse in the Valley of the Dawn is similar in form to some representations of the *yoni* in India.

15 For a discussion of the New Age movement in Brazil, see Leila Amaral (1994).

16 The *toma de passe* is a common practice in various religious traditions, known in Christianity as the laying on of hands. It is used to transmit

spiritual and physical energy through the hands. In Brasília *sensitivos* are people with visionary or healing powers, generally linked to Spiritism or *umbanda*.

* fluidification – The act of turning water 'fluidified' (full of spiritual fluids). This is a widespread practice of Brazilian Kardecism which entails transmitting spiritual energy to fresh water, so that it can be used as a healing element and a form of protection against evil influences. Glasses or bottles are fluidified by being placed on the table where the spiritualist ritual takes place; through prayer and singing the spiritual 'fluids' enter into the water.

17 Flávio Pierucci (1997a and 1997b) and Reginaldo Prandi (1997) have vehemently argued the Weberian concept of secularisation, particularly in the contemporary version elaborated by Bourdieu. Two different interpretations, which reinforce my own, are those of Otávio Velho (1995 and 1997) and Rita Segato (1997).

18 For an exegesis of Walter Benjamin's analysis of the fetichism of commodities, see Jean Lacoste (1982), Susan Buck-Morss (1989) and Rainer Rochlitz (1996).

19 The Catholic Charismatic movement emerged in the United States and shares striking similarities with the pentecostal movement. Widespread in Brazil, it seeks to recuperate the liturgical exuberance and the emotional dimension of the catholic religious experience, as an obvious response to the social doctrine of the church developed by Liberation Theology.

20 There is much discussion of the strategies of intolerance and self-legitimation practised by the Universal Church and the consequent effects on the co-existence of religions in Brazil. See, among others, Ari Oro (1996 and 1997), Cecília Mariz (1997) and Patrícia Birman (1997).

21 See glossary.

22 In another essay I present an annotated body of Afro-Brazilian (*umbanda* and *jurema*) mystical texts in Portuguese and propose a reading of them, comparing them to other sacred texts of universal mysticism (Carvalho 1997).

23 My thanks to Maria Lúcia Felipe da Costa, from Recife, for teaching me these two *Pomba Gira* songs.

24 Giddens (1991) supposes, in a mixture of evolutionist and functionalist arguments, that religion has been supplanted by technology. Equally unsatisfactory is the functionalist explanation offered by Bourdieu (1990) when he describes the field of specialists who have cultural capital of 'psychosomatic healing', capable of competing with the priests; while Gauchet (1997) already points to the sensibilities of survival of religious culture in a disenchanted world – that is, once the religious period of humanity has come to an end. In another work (Carvalho 1998a) I offer a more systematic argument against this scepticism in the social sciences.

25 Traditional *jurema* and *catimbó* song, this version was taken from the work of Octaviano da Silva Lopes (n.d.: 72).

26 Gilberto Gil, *Quanta*, double album, Warner Music Brazil, 1997.

Bibliography

Amaral, Leila Nova Era (1994), 'Um movimento de caminhos cruzados', in *A igreja Católica diante do Pluralismo Religioso no Brasil* (III). São Paulo: Paulus.

Benjamin, Walter (1969), 'On some motifs in Baudelaire', in *Illuminations. Essays and Reflections*, 155–200. New York: Schocken Books.

—— (1985), *Experiência e pobreza*, in *Obras Escolhidas*. Vol. *1*, 114–19. São Paulo: Brasiliense.

Birman, Patrícia (1997), 'Males e maleficios no discurso pentecostal', in Patrícia Birman, Regina Novaes & Samira Crespo (eds.), *O Mal à Brasileira*, 62–80. Rio de Janeiro: Ed.UERJ.

Blavatsky, H. P. (1991), *A Chave para a Teosofia*. Brasília: Editora Teosófica.

Bourdieu, Pierre (1990), 'A Dissolução do religioso', in *Coisas Ditas*. São Paulo: Brasiliense.

Buck-Morss, Susan (1989), *The Dialectics of Seeing*. Cambridge, Mass: MIT Press.

Carvalho, José Jorge (1992), 'Características do Fenômeno Religioso na Sociedade contemporânea', in Maria Clara Bingemer (ed.), *O Impacto da Modernidade sobre a Religião*, 133–195. São Paulo: Edições Loyola.

—— (1994a), 'Idéias e imagens no mundo clássico e na tradição afro-brasileira. Para uma nova compreensão dos processos de sincretismo religioso', in *Humanidades*, Vol. 10, No. 1, 82–102.

—— (1994b), 'Violência e Caos na Experiência Religiosa. A Dimensão Dionisíaca dos Cultos Afro-Brasileiros', in Carlos Eugênio Marcondes de Moura (ed.), *As Senhoras do Pássaro da Noite*, 85–120. Sõ Paulo: Axis Mundi/EDUSP.

—— (1994c), 'O Encontro de Velhas e novas Religiões. Esboço de uma Teoria dos Estilos de Espiritualidade', in Alberto Moreira e Renée Zicman (eds.), *Misticismo e Novas Religiões*, 67–98. Petrópolis: Vozes/USF-IFAN.

—— (1994d), 'Tendências Religiosas no Brasil Contemporâneo', in *A Igreja Católica Diante do Pluyralismo Religioso no Brasil-III*, 21–36. Col. Estudos da CNBB, Vol. 71. São Paulo: Paulus.

—— (1997), 'A Tradição Mística Afro-Brasileira', in *Religião e Sociedade*, Vol. 18, No. 2, 93–122.

—— (1998a), 'Antropologia e Esoterismo: Dois Contradiscursos da Modernidata', in *Horizontes Antropológicos*, Ano 4, No. 8, 53–71.

—— (1998b), 'Religião, Mídia e os Predicamentos da convivência Pluralista', in Alberto Moreira (ed.), *Cultura e Religião na Sociedade Global*. Petrópolis/ Bragança Paulista: Vozes/IFAN.

Caygill, Howard (1998), *Walter Benjamin. The Color of Experience*. London: Routledge.

Fernandes, Rubem César (1992), 'Imagens da Paixão: A Igreja no Brasil e na Polônia', in Pierre Sanchis (ed.), *Catolicismo: Modernidade e Tradição*, 66–89 Saõ Paulo: Edições Loyola.

Gauchet, Marcel (1997), *The Disenchantment of the World. A Political History of Religion*. Princeton: Princeton University Press.

Giddens, Anthony (1991), *As Consequências da Modernidade*. São Paulo: Editora da UNESP.

Kardec, Alan (1984), *O Livro dos Espíritos*. Brasília: Federação Espírita Brasileira.

Lacoste, Jean (1982), 'Notes du Traducteur', in Walter Benjamin, *Charles Baudelaire, Un poète lyrique à l'apogée du capitalisme.* Paris: Petite Bibliothèque Payot.

Landim, Leilah (ed.) (1989a), *Sinais dos Tempos. Igrejas e Seitas no Brasil.* Rio de Janeiro: ISER.

—— (1989b) *Sinais dos Tempos. Tradições Religiosas no Brasil.* Rio de Janeiro: ISER.

—— (1990) *Sinais dos Tempos. Diversidade Religiosa no Brasil.* Rio de Janeiro: ISER.

Lévi-Strauss, Claude (1972), *Antropologia Estrutural.* Rio de Janeiro: Tempo Brasileiro.

Lopes, Octaviano da Silva, *Catimbó no Brasil.* Rio de Janeiro: Editora Espiritualista.

Mariz, Cecília (1997), 'O Demônio e os Pentecostais no Brasil', in Patrícia Birman, Regina Novaes & Samira Crespo (eds.), *O Mal à Brasileira* (1997), 45–61. Rio de Janeiro: EdUERJ.

Oro, Ari Pedro (1996), *Avanço Pentecostal e Reação Católica.* Petrópolis: Vozes.

—— (1997), 'Neopentecostais e Afro-Brasileiros: quem ganhará esta guerra?' in *Guerra Santa,* Debates do NER, Ano 1, No. 1, 10–36.

Prandi, Reginaldo (1997), A religião do planeta global, in Ari Pedro Oro & Carlos Alberto Steil (eds.), *Globalização e Religião,* 63–70. Petrópolis: Vozes.

Pierucci, Flávio (1997a), 'Reencantamento e Dessecularização', in *Novos Estudos Cebrap,* Vol. 49, 99–117.

—— (1997b), 'Interesses religiosos dos sociólogos da religião', in Ari Pedro Oro & Carlos Alberto Steil (eds.), *Globalização e Religião,* 249–61. Petrópolis: Vozes.

Rochlitz, Rainer (1996), *The Disenchantment of Art,* London: Guildford Press.

Sanchis, Pierre (1997), 'O campo religioso contemporâneo no Brasil', in Ari Pedro Oro & Carlos Alberto Steil (eds.) (1997), *Globalização e Religião,* 103–15. Petrópolis: Vozes.

Segato, Rita (1997), 'Formaçoes de diversidade: Nação e opções religiosas no contexto da globalização', in Ari Pedro Oro & Carlos Alberto Steil (eds.), *Globalização e Religião,* 219–48. Petrópolis: Vozes.

Soares, Luís Eduardo (1993), 'A guerra dos pentecostais contra o afro-brasileiro: Dimensões democrficas do conflito religioso no Brasil', in *Comunicacções do ISER,* No 44, Ano 12, 43–50.

Soares, Mariza de Carvalho (1990), 'Guerra Santa no País do Sincretismo', in Leilah Landim (ed.), *Sinais dos Tempos. Diversidade Religiosa no Brasil,* 75–104. Rio de Janeiro: ISER.

Velho, Gilberto (1992), 'Unidade e fragmentação em sociedades complexas', in Gilberto Velho & Otávio Velho, *Duas Conferências,* 13–46. Rio de Janeiro: Forum de Ciência e cultura/Editora da UFRJ.

Velho, Otávio (1995), 'Religião e modernidade: roteiro para uma discussão', in *Besta-Fera. Recriação do Mundo.* Rio de Janeiro: Relume Dumará.

—— (1997), 'Globalização: Antropologia e Religião', in Ari Pedro Oro & Carlos Alberto Steil (eds.), *Globalização e Religião,* 43–61. Petrópolis: Vozes.

Wafer, Jim (1991), *The Taste of Blood. Spirit Possession in Brazilian Candomblé.* Philadelphia: University of Pennsylvania Press.

Winn, Peter (1992), 'The Power and the Glory', in *Americas. The Changing Face of Latin America and the Caribbean.* New York: Pantheon Books.

Translated by Lorraine Leu

Glossary

batuque – name used in Porto Alegre for traditional Afro-Brazilian cults. It has clear similarities to the *candomblés* Kêtu and Ijesha of Bahia and the *xangô* of Recife. More generally it is used to refer to dance and percussion music of African origin.

bloco – a group of carnival revellers

bumba-meu-boi – is a form of dance-drama bringing together Amerindian, African and Iberian traditions. It is practised mainly by the popular classes of Brazil during specific days of the calendar of catholic festivities, depending on the particular region in Brazil. The central plot revolves around the death and resurrection of an ox who is impersonated by a figure carrying around his waist or across his back a wooden frame covered with an elaboratedly decorated cotton cloth, to which a mask with horns is attached. In several cities of the north of Brazil, each neighbourhood has its own ox and band of musicians.

caboclo – an intensely revered divinity in *jurema* and *umbanda*. *Caboclos* and *caboclas* represent the spirits of the Indians who lived (and live) in the jungles and forests of Brazil.

caciquism – derivative of *cacique,* any strong local leader who maintains himself in power through nepotism, clientelism and the use of force.

caipira – of or relating to the Brazilian backwoods; a term often used pejoratively to mean boorish or rustic.

candomblé – name given in Bahia to various traditional cults of possession of African origin. The principal religious styles (or 'nations' as they are called) are: Kêtu and Ijesha, of Yoruba origin; Gegê, of Fon and Ewe origin; and Angola, of Bantu origin, especially kimbundu and kicongo.

capoeira – an Afro-Brazilian martial art which is simultaneously a form of dance and play accompanied in its performance by singing and the playing of specific instruments such as the tambourine and a string instrument called the *berimbau*. It is thought to have originated primarily in the slave quarters and poor areas of Rio de Janeiro ca.1800.

catimbó – cult similar to *jurema*, widespread in the north-east of Brazil, which consists of a syncretism between African religious traditions and the traditions of Indians from the north-eastern region.

caudillo – originally a term used to describe leaders after the Wars of Independence in Latin America in the 1820s and 1830s, who organised private armies among the rural population to maintain a local power base. Since then it has been used more broadly to describe personalist and authoritarian rule at a regional or national level.

cordão – term used to refer to groups of disguised carnival revellers from the popular classes during the street festivities of carnival in Rio de Janeiro. What originally characterised these at the beginning of the twentieth century, when the music and dance of the Afro-Brazilian population began to define carnival, was their use of themes related to nature or religion. They were known by such names as 'Lovers of Saint Teresa' and 'Club for the Recreation of Angels'.

cholo – colloquial term used for people of mixed race in Peru.

corrido – a musical form or ballad in popular music in Mexico. It can be epic, lyrical or narrative; it is similar in many ways to medieval romances.

ex–votos – offerings given to a virgin or saint for help obtained. These include images of parts of the body healed by divine intervention, a sheep in thanks for a good harvest, money or lighted candle.

import substitution industrialisation – a term used in the field of development studies as a description of an industrialisation strategy used by many Latin American countries in the twentieth century. Essentially, it involved protecting national industries in order to produce locally the manufactured goods formerly imported from abroad; one of the primary aims of this strategy was to diminish Latin America's dependence on the export of primary commodities.

entrudo – a form of carnival revelry inherited from Portugal in the seventeenth century in which, during the street festivities, people bombarded each other with flour while from the surrounding houses revellers threw oranges and lemons made of wax containing water on the people below.

estridentismo – vanguard artistic and literary movement in Mexico (1922–1927), primarily led by Manuel Maples Arce, whose goal was to reflect the extreme changes of technological and social change.

Strongly influenced by Italian futurism, the group's literary wing experimented with visual poetry, favoured mechanical images, and celebrated the masses and the daily life of city streets and factories. They founded the magazine *Actual* which included their manifestoes. In addition to Maples Arce, other members included Luis Quintanilla, Germn List Arzubinde, Arqueles Vela and Salvador Gallardo.

Exu – divinity from the Yoruba pantheon, who plays the role of messenger to the other gods. Dangerous, Exu can do good as well as evil; he is thus considered a trickster god.

favela – Brazilian term for poor districts in the cities of Brazil; shanty town.

jurema – Name given in the north-east of Brazil to a syncretic cult of possession, centred around the relationship to entities called Mestres (Masters) but which also includes other spirits cultivated in *umbanda* temples, with which it has similarities.

malandro – a rogue or trickster. In the field of Brazilian cultural and literary studies it refers more broadly to an attitude to life apparent in the practice and lyrics of popular music and in certain literary characters. It involves using the institutions, representatives and upholders of the established order in order to pursue illicit interests, frequently in connivance with that same order rendering the opposition between order and disorder ambiguous. This has been referred to as the 'dialectic of *malandragem*'.

marchinha – a musical genre played during carnival inherited from Portugal.

maxixe – a form of dance among the popular classes of Rio de Janeiro in the 1870s consisting of a fusion of rhythms of African origin, (the *batuque*) and polkas and mazurkas of European origin.

mestiço/mestiçagem or *mestizo/mestizaje* – race mixture. Beyond this literal meaning the term is central to broader debates about the identity of Latin America as culturally and racially mixed.

metropolis – a term associated with neo-Marxist theories of development according to which the relative economic backwardness and poverty of 'developing' countries is due to their economically and politically subordinate position within capitalism seen as a world system. The whole system has a hierarchical structure in which the developed world, defined as the 'centre' or 'metropolis', gains economic advantage at the expense of the 'developing' world defined as the 'periphery'.

musica sertaneja – a genre of music of peasant origin dealing with the joys and difficulties of rural life in Brazil. In the 1930s it was gradually transformed by the mass media into a successful commercial genre of music sung by duos dealing with themes of love and life in the city.

négritude – a cultural movement that argued that people of African descent throughout the world shared a cultural heritage. Its founders were Aimé Césaire (Martinique), Leon Damas (French Guyana) and Leopold Senghor (Senegal). The term was first used in Paris in the early 1930s as an act of defiance against the view that black was inferior and as a challenge to blacks who rejected their African heritage. In Spanish America the literary movement of *negrismo* predates the *négritude* movement. Thematically, *negrista* poetry incorporated rhythms and language inherited from Africa and the sounds of African musical instruments and rituals.

pajelança – an Afro-Brazilian syncretic cult of possession, centred on the worship of spirits of nature, practised in all states in the north of Brazil.

Pomba Gira – feminine divinity cultivated in the cults of *umbanda* and *jurema* in Brazil. Linked to the subterranean world, she has great sexual and magical power and is a kind of female equivalent to Exu. Many *Pomba Giras* are represented as prostitutes and 'women of the night', seductive and dangerous.

Preto Velho – very important divinity in the *umbanda* pantheon, both in masculine and feminine form (*Preta Velha*). He represents the Brazilian black, in his condition as slave and free person confronted with the hardships of post-abolition Brazil.

rancho – a term used to describe a procession of dancers, primarily in the north of Brazil, representing shepherds on their way to Bethlehem during the days of the Nativity in December. These 'ranchos' also contributed to shaping the popular street carnival of Rio de Janeiro in the 1920s in that they joined the street festivities singing the repertory of songs of the traditional December festivities.

Tambor de Mina – name used in São Luis and Belem do Pará for traditional Afro-Brazilian cults. The principal religious influence here is the religious tradition of Togo and Benin.

telenovela – soap operas serialised on television.

terreiro – name given to the temple in which *candomblé* and *umbanda* are practised.

ultraismo – a literary movement founded by Jorge Luis Borges in the early 1920s in Argentina. Its aim was to create a poetry made up of patterns of images without logical or syntactic connections.

umbanda – syncretic nation-wide Afro-Brazilian cult of possession, whose pantheon includes not just African divinities, but other kinds of supernatural entities, such as *caboclos* (indian spirits), black slaves (*Preto Velho*), spirits of the forest, rivers etc.

umbanda esotérica – type of fusion between *umbanda* and esoteric sects, especially prominent in Brasília and São Paulo.

viola – a traditional guitar-like instrument used in Brazil.

xangô – name used in Recife for traditional Afro-Brazilian cults, similar to the candomblé cults Kêtu and Ijesha of Bahia. It is also the name given to a deity in the pantheon of candomblé divinities. He is associated with lightning and thunder.

Zé pereira – according to historians of the carnival festivities of Rio de Janeiro 'zé pereira' was the name of a character in the 1920s who initiated a new form of carnival revelry which involved walking down the streets with a group of friends and neighbours, loudly banging on a variety of drums and percussion instruments. Since then, this form of carnival merriment is referred to as 'zé pereira'.

Notes on Contributors

Néstor García Canclini is Professor of Anthropology at the Metropolitan University in Mexico City. His recent works include *Hybrid Cultures: Strategies for Entering and Leaving Modernity* and *La Globalización Imaginada*.

José Jorge de Carvalho is Professor of Anthropology at the University of Brasília. He is the author of *Shango Cults in Recife, Brazil* (with Rita Segato), *Cantos Sagrados do Xangô do Recife* and *Mutus Liber: O Livro Mudo da Alquimia* and *Rumi – Poemas Místicos*, and the editor of *O Quilombo do Rio das Rãs*.

Gwen Kirkpatrick is Professor of Spanish at the University of California, Berkeley. She has published *The Dissonant Legacy of Modernismo*, is co-author of *Women, Culture and Politics in Latin America*, and has edited and co-edited volumes on Güiraldes and Sarmiento. Currently she is serving as Director of the University of California Study Center in Santiago, Chile.

Ana M. López is Associate Professor of Communication and Latin American Studies at Tulane University, where she is the director of the Cuban Studies Institute. She is co-editor of the *Encyclopedia of Latin American Culture*, *The Ethnic Eye*, *Mediating Two Worlds* and *Third and Imperfect: The New Latin American Cinema*.

Nelson Manrique is Professor of Sociology at the Catholic University of Peru. His recent works include *Vinieron los sarracenos. El universo mental de la conquista de America* and *Amor y fuego, José Maria Arguedas, 24 años despues*.

José de Souza Martins is Professor of Sociology at the University of São Paulo and a Fellow at Trinity Hall, Cambridge University. His recent works include *O Poder do Atraso* and *Fonteira: A degradação do Outro nos confins do humano*.

Ruben George Oliven is Professor of Anthropology at the Federal University of Rio Grande do Sul (Porto Alegre, Brazil). He is the author of *Tradition Matters: Modern Gaúcho Identity in Brazil*.

Renato Ortiz is Professor of Sociology at the University of Campinas. His recent publications include *Mundialização e Cultura* and *Um Outro Território: ensaios sobre o mundo contemporâneo*.

Beatriz Resende is Associate Professor of Comparative Literature and Literary Theory at the Federal University of Rio de Janeiro. She is author of *Cronistas do Rio* and *Lima Barreto e o Rio de Janeiro em fragmentos*, and has written essays on modernism and Art-Deco literature in Rio de Janeiro and urban culture.

Beatriz Sarlo is Professor of Literature and Cultural Studies at the University of Buenos Aires. She is the editor of the independent journal *Punto de Vista*. She has written many books on Argentine culture and literature, among them *Jorge Luis Borges: A Writer on the Edge* and *The Technical Imagination*.

Vivian Schelling is Senior Lecturer in Third World and Development Studies at the University of East London. She is author of *A Presença do Povo na Cultura Brasileira* and co-author (with William Rowe) of *Memory and Modernity: Popular Culture in Latin America*.

Nicolau Sevcenko is Professor of Contemporary History at the University of São Paulo. He is the editor and one of the authors of *História da Vida Privada uo Brasil*, vol. 3, and co-editor of the *Journal of Latin American and Cultural Studies*.

Index